CREATIVE CAPITAL

CREATIVE CAPITAL

MANAGING PRIVATE WEALTH IN A COMPLEX WORLD

Gregory Curtis
Chairman, Greycourt & Co., Inc.

iUniverse, Inc.
New York Lincoln Shanghai

CREATIVE CAPITAL
MANAGING PRIVATE WEALTH
IN A COMPLEX WORLD

All Rights Reserved © 2004 by Gregory Curtis

No part of this book may be reproduced or transmitted in any form or by any means, graphic, electronic, or mechanical, including photocopying, recording, taping, or by any information storage retrieval system, without the written permission of the publisher.

iUniverse, Inc.

For information address:
iUniverse, Inc.
2021 Pine Lake Road, Suite 100
Lincoln, NE 68512
www.iuniverse.com

ISBN: 0-595-33200-5

Printed in the United States of America

*Lege feliciter!**

* "Read happily!" From the epigraph to *An Ecclesiastical History of the English People*, by The Venerable Bede, completed in 732. The book recorded events in Britain from the raids by Julius Caesar (55 BC) to the arrival in Kent of St. Augustine (597). Bede's practice of dating events from the time of Christ's birth (i.e., anno Domini or AD) caused that convention to come into general use. Unfortunately, since the concept of zero was unknown at the time (Christ would have been age zero at birth, not age one), Bede's dating system initially caused a great deal of mischief.

CONTENTS

Preface

Private Wealth in a Complex World

Nothing corrupts a man so deeply
as writing a book.
—Nero Wolfe[1]

Live by the pen, die by the pen.
—Mark Laskow (*inter alia*)[2]

Over the years, thousands of investment books have been written. A precious few have become classics in the field, but the rest are long, and probably best, forgotten. Given this ponderous history, even the author himself must wonder whether he may be trying the patience of the reading public with yet another book on investing.

I plead this: I am approaching the investment challenge from a different perspective than most—indeed, than virtually all—of my predecessors. In the first place, I am addressing a very special audience—wealthy investors. In the second place, the purpose of most investment books is to make us better investors. But this book has an importantly different objective—to help significant investors to become better stewards of their assets, whether or not they ever become good investors in the professional sense of the word. Finally, this book, and especially Part One, constitutes a *cri de coeur* for the importance of private capital in the American free market economy—something too many people, including too many wealthy people, fail to understand.

As noted later in this Preface, good stewardship involves much more than investing capital soundly. It involves the ongoing growth and nourishment of a family's human capital in the broadest sense. And it involves the recognition

1 Rex Stout, *The Mother Hunt* (1963).
2 CEO, Greycourt & Co., Inc.

that the responsible management and creative use of private wealth is crucial to the continued vitality of the American free market democracy. But good stewardship begins with the sound investment management of a family's capital.

Being Wealthy

What is a wealthy investor? Who qualifies? Probably the best definition of a wealthy person is someone who *feels* wealthy. The actual amount of money required to make one person feel wealthy may differ very substantially from the amount required to make someone else feel wealthy. Consider Bill and Laura Klaas,[3] who have liquid assets of almost $40 million. Laura's father was an affluent physician who invested in an overnight package delivery startup, then promptly died. Bill and Laura inherited the stock, whose value subsequently skyrocketed. Their primary residence is in La Jolla, California, but they also have a summer home near Woodstock, Vermont and a lovely condo on the beach in Naples, Florida. Every other year they spend three months in Tuscany, where they rent a small villa and where Laura spends her time photographing the ancient villages that grace that part of Italy. She even published a book of her photographs.

By almost anyone's standards, Bill and Laura are a wealthy family. But you wouldn't know it by talking with them. It isn't just that they have the common touch or try to disguise their wealth—they simply do not think of themselves as wealthy. Being wealthy, to the Klaases, is being someone like Bill Gates, who has billions of dollars. Bill and Laura keep their liquid assets with an old-line trust company in New York and rarely pay any attention to how the firm is performing. The fact that the Klaas's spending is alarmingly high by long-term sustainability standards doesn't bother them, in part because they aren't aware of it and in part because no matter how much they spend, it is highly unlikely that they can blow through the whole $40 million in one lifetime. The Klaases have helped out their two daughters financially from time to time, but have become convinced that "bailing the girls out" of their problems has caused more harm than good.

For a family like the Klaases, the concept of stewardship means little because they aren't, at least in her own minds, rich. The question of what might happen to their fortune once it passes into the hands of daughters wholly unprepared to manage it doesn't bother them at all. The issue of philanthropy doesn't resonate with them, not because they are congenitally ungenerous but simply because philanthropy is, to the Klaases, something rich people worry about. They have

---

[3] Like most families in this book, this is not their real name.

made many donations here and there, of course, but have no idea whether their money is doing any good. Finally, the Klaases have no sense that they should be thinking about a family legacy. Although there are no particular rifts in the family, the elder daughter is in Seattle, the younger daughter is in Atlanta, and Bill and Laura are all over the place. The family rarely gets together and doesn't particularly think of itself as a family unit.

In a very real sense, then, being wealthy is a state of mind. A family can't be wealthy in the sense used in this book unless it has a great deal of money—$10 million, anyway, more likely considerably more—but a family can have a great deal of money and not be wealthy in any useful sense of the word. A truly wealthy family comes out on the opposite sides of all the issues we have just discussed about the Klaases. They care deeply about the preservation and growth of their wealth. If they give money away they give it thoughtfully and purposefully, trying hard to make a difference in the world. They understand the important role private capital plays in the American economic system, and they take their obligations as owners of capital seriously. They believe strongly that their wealth cannot persist or do good for very long unless everyone in the family is educated in the importance of stewardship.

Stewardship

What is the difference between being a good investor and being a good steward of wealth? In the first place, stewardship is a much broader issue. It has to do with all the things that will bear on the long-term success of the family.[4] Investing has to do with one particular issue—the management of private capital. While that issue is central to the question of stewardship, and is the main subject of this book, investing is only a part of the broader issue. And because investing capital successfully is only part of the challenge associated with being wealthy, it isn't necessary for every member of a wealthy family—or any members, for that matter—to become professional investors.

What *is* necessary is that members of the family—preferably all of them—gain enough of an understanding of the investment process and the capital markets to enable the family to be an astute consumer of investment services. This requires a certain amount of hard work (see Chapters 3 through 17), but it doesn't require that family members become investment professionals themselves. It also requires that the family develop ways of working together, ways

4 There are many useful books that bear on the issue of stewardship, but James E. Hughes, Jr.'s *Family Wealth: Keeping It in the Family* (Bloomberg Press, 2004) is especially helpful. This, incidentally, is the revised and expanded edition of Hughes original classic, published in 1997.

of sharing information, ways to make cohesive and intelligent decisions about assets that may be widely scattered in many family "pockets."

It's possible—indeed, likely—that Bill and Laura Klaas will live a perfectly happy life, despite their belief that they aren't wealthy and that stewardship is a non-issue for them. It's even possible, though less likely, that their daughters and their daughters' families won't have their lives and their happiness disrupted when they suddenly inherit large sums of money they are ill-prepared to deal with. The great probability, however, is that instead of contributing to the happiness of Bill and Laura's family and to the betterment of the world they live in, the Klaas family money is probably headed for a train wreck.

The whole point of stewardship is to avoid this train wreck. Having wealth brings with it serious responsibilities, for two reasons. The first is that money, at least in large dollops, has the power to destroy lives. We don't behave irresponsibly around dynamite or loaded pistols, and we should never behave irresponsibly around millions of dollars. The second reason is that private capital plays a crucial role in the way America has chosen to organize its society and its economy. Failure of stewardship by a wealthy family is a very large failure, an act of irresponsibility by the very people who have been most favored by the American economic system.

Most of this book is an attempt to help wealthy families discharge their stewardship obligations more effectively. But it is also important for the wealthy—and for the non-wealthy—to understand just how crucial a matter it is that private capital be properly managed. That important point is the subject of Part One of this book.

Best Investment Practices

Anna Karenina famously begins with Tolstoy's remark that, "All happy families are alike; every unhappy family is unhappy in its own way." Whether or not Tolstoy was right about families and happiness in general, his idea certainly applies to families as investors. All "happy" families—that is, those who are able to preserve and grow their wealth across the generations—are very much alike in the sense that they follow what I refer to in this book as "best investment practices." These are practices that have demonstrated their worth in the portfolios of the world's largest and most sophisticated investors over many decades. It is a principal purpose of this book to identify best practices for taxable investors, to explain why they are important, and to show family investors how best to employ them in their own investment portfolios.

It is also the case that "unhappy" families—those whose wealth disappears—tend to be unhappy in their own ways. While there is only one certain way to preserve wealth (namely, to follow best practices ruthlessly throughout the entire investment process), there are many, many ways to destroy wealth. Some of these tend to occur slowly over time: poor strategies and managers and unnecessary investment costs and taxes act like portfolio cancers, slowly destroying wealth over the years. Other bad practices destroy wealth quickly, as the result of one spectacularly bad decision (holding all our wealth in one stock in a company we no longer control, for example).

Complex Markets

My subtitle refers to the challenge of managing private wealth "in a complex world." The world that private investors occupy is complex in many ways. The first complexity investors face is, of course, the capital markets themselves.

Most of us will never be forced to deal with a system more complex than the capital markets. No one completely understands how markets work or why they behave the way they do. No one can anticipate when markets will go up or down or how much they will move. Markets encompass all the complexity of the human beings who deal in and with them, as well as all the complexity of any system that is made up of millions of moving parts, some of which are related to each other and some of which aren't. And ultimately, of course, all this complexity is at the mercy of technically unrelated matters, such as the stability and vigor of the societies that provide the structures and mores through which capital markets must operate.

Thus, attempts to understand how markets work must inquire into Modern Portfolio Theory (which builds models that, at least over long periods of time, tend to describe the operation of markets); behavioral finance (which attempts to describe how human beings respond in the face of investment decisions and market events); law (which governs the legal properties and enforceability of financial instruments); economics (which attempts to explain how economies function); chaos theory (which attempts to describe the behavior of incredibly complex systems); and so on.

On top of this complexity is the issue of the costs associated with managing private capital. No one in the financial industry works for free, and most charge not what is fair in relation to the value they bring, but rather what the market will bear. Consider that as investors we face high money management fees, the roundtrip costs of brokerage commissions, the spread between bid and ask prices, the cost of market impact, and opportunity costs (price movement that occurs between the time we decide to act and the time our transaction is executed). Our wealth will be further diminished by inflation, taxes and spending. Finally, given the complexity of the capital markets, our wealth will also be diminished by the impact of the inevitable investment mistakes we make.

A Complex Industry

No one who takes an honest look at the modern financial services industry can reach any conclusion other than that it is operated in ways that are mainly hostile to the interests of investors. Most firms, for example, are organized in a manner that presents serious and ongoing conflicts of interest with their own clients. And many firms, especially those dealing with smaller investors—but even many tonier firms—cheerfully hire large numbers of inexperienced professionals who are superb at selling investment products but who understand virtually nothing about the successful management of capital—a good working definition of hostility to the clients' interests. Finally, like any industry, the financial services business has its fair share of crooks, swindlers, con men (and women) and others for whom the term "venal" fits quite nicely.

I am as critical of the industry as anyone—indeed, I have devoted a long chapter to criticisms of the industry (see Chapter 7). But let's be realistic. All firms—not just financial firms—are in business to make money. The main reason the industry gets away with its deplorable practices is that *we are lousy clients*. Alongside the rotten firms and callous individuals there are also many superb advisory firms and many, many honest, hard-working financial professionals. Good clients easily gravitate to these people. Moreover, even imperfect advisors can be managed by well-informed clients to minimize damage to their portfolios and maximize the value the advisor is bringing to the relationship.

Yes, the financial industry badly needs to be reformed, and the fact that most of the regulators have long been asleep at the switch is discouraging, indeed. (Remember that it was a state attorney general—New York's Eliot Spitzer—reaching far beyond his traditional authority, who tackled the worst abuses by Wall Street investment analysts and mutual funds.) But investors needn't wait for the regulators to wake up. By educating ourselves about the industry and the investment process, we can go a long way toward avoiding the worst the financial services industry has to offer and to create, instead, fertile partnerships with the many honest, competent advisors available to us.

Complex Societies

Wealthy investors everywhere live in societies that are often hostile, and that are always indifferent, to our attempts to preserve and grow our wealth. In a way, this seems an odd circumstance.

Consider that few would deny the importance not just to the investors themselves, but to society generally, of the sound management of the portfolios of middle income investors, pension plans, charitable endowments, foundations. If middle income investors mismanage their money (especially, but not exclusively, their 401(k) plans), they face an impoverished old age, an outcome that has profound social, political and economic consequences. If corporate and public pension plans mismanage their portfolios, either taxpayers will have to bail them out (via the Pension Benefit Guaranty Corporation or new laws that allow pension plans to remain under-funded), or higher contributions to the plans will reduce available spending for new jobs and capital equipment, with the consequent impact on economic growth. If endowments and foundations mismanage their portfolios, a society that relies heavily on private philanthropy, rather than government funding, will find services, amenities and creative new ideas slashed.

Even with wealthy families, when the capital takes the form of control of an important corporate enterprise no one would argue that mismanagement of the enterprise—the family's capital in corporate form—is a matter of no consequence. Most businesses in America are privately held, and some of them are spectacularly large—privately held Cargill is a $50 billion (revenues) company. Mismanagement of this form of private capital would have momentous consequences, indeed.

Yet, when it comes to the management of the passive investment portfolios of the wealthy, hostility and indifference set in. Some of this is, to be sure, nothing more than envy, or, when private capital blows up, Schadenfreude. But it is more than that—it signifies a profound ignorance of the importance of private capital to American society.

Private Capital and Free Market Democracies

The serious opportunity to get seriously rich is what distinguishes America from other free market democracies, and it has made America the most dominant civilization in the history of the world. If simply having an essentially free market were all that was required for economic domination, France and Sweden would be powerhouses. But France and Sweden, healthy economies, to be sure, are a pale version of the American free market for the simple reason that getting rich is discouraged in those countries, and being rich is despised.

In America, entrepreneurs are heroes, but in much of Europe and Scandinavia entrepreneurs are viewed more like dangerous cranks who are simply trying to make everyone else look bad.

Indeed, even cases that appear at first glance to represent the very worst aspects of American-style capitalism appear quite different under more thoughtful analysis. During the Internet boom of the late 1990s, for example, a number of young entrepreneurs became quite wealthy even though it later turned out that their business models were highly flawed (or even outright worthless). But let's consider exactly such an example to see what it actually says about American economic vitality.

Jerry Slait and His Internet Startup. In 1996, Jerry Slait was a 26-year old software engineer slotted into an entry-level position with a commercial insurance brokerage firm in Baltimore. But Jerry had an idea for an Internet firm: an online grocery ordering and delivery service to be called Food2You.com. Backed by his own meager life savings, a reluctant uncle and an even more reluctant father-in-law (the proverbial "friends and family" equity round), Jerry quit his job, job, moved to San Jose and completed preliminary work on his software package. He also put together a rudimentary business plan and, somewhat to his own surprise, managed to raise several million dollars from eager venture capital firms.

Jerry staffed up his small company, served free Starbucks coffee to his employees, and a year later, even though he had yet to sign up his first customer, Food2You was taken public. The stock experienced a good "pop" on the day it came out and the price continued to rise, buoyed by the euphoria surrounding anything that ended in ".com." Six months after that—it is now mid-1997—Food2You was acquired by another online grocery company for the sum of $300 million in stock. The acquiring firm was doing a "rollup" in the online grocery business, convinced that by eliminating the many "mom and pop" startups it could achieve "scale" and "acquire pricing power" in the marketplace. For a brief instant in time, Jerry, now all of 28, was a centi-millionaire.

The stock Jerry received in the acquisition was subject to a six-month lockup (in other words, Jerry couldn't legally sell it for six months), but as soon as possible Jerry began to sell it. The public announcement of these sales emphasized that Jerry continued to have every confidence in the company (of which he was now an executive vice president), but that, like every other investor, it was appropriate for him to achieve diversification in his portfolio.

By the spring of 2000, Jerry had achieved diversification to the tune of some $65 million, and a damn good thing it was, too, because at that point both Internet stocks in general and online grocery business stocks in particular went into a sickening swoon. By July of 2000, in fact, and notwithstanding the continued rosy projections being issued by the investment banking firm that took Food2You public, the firm that had acquired Food2You declared bankruptcy and its assets were sold at auction for less than $1 million.

In the cold light of day it was now clear that the two key components of Jerry's brilliant idea—that people would rush to order their groceries online and that such a business could be conducted profitably—were deeply flawed. People, it turned out, weren't much interested in ordering groceries online, and the grocery business, already operating on the thinnest of profit margins, simply could not support the additional costs required to deliver groceries nationwide on time.[5]

Yet, there was Jerry with $65 million in the bank. Jerry Slait would appear to be a poster child for ill-gotten wealth made possible only by an American version of capitalism gone nuts.

But let's think about this for a moment. It's true that Jerry's idea turned out to be a bad one—as many ideas do, including, even, some of my own. Maybe it was even the case that any sober-minded person would have known back in 1996 that the online grocery business was a bad idea. But if so, where were those people? The ideas about new businesses held by people who would never leave their comfortable jobs and endanger their comfortable lives are simply not worth listening to. *Every* new business idea will seem idiotic to such people.

What matters is the opinion of people who are willing to put their money and their reputations where their mouth is, and those people rather liked Jerry's idea. Sure, it didn't work out, but if starting new businesses was a risk-free proposition everyone would be rich. There was nothing special about the Internet boom, after all. Think back to the days when the invention of the internal combustion engine made the automobile possible. Hundreds, maybe thousands, of people started car companies, and other people backed them with hard cash. Most of those cars turned out to be white elephants—seen a Hupmobile lately? And, of course, most of those early entrepreneurs went down in flames and took their investors with them. A few went down in flames but their investors made millions.[6] And a few, the forerunners of the Jerry

5 Interestingly, several *regional* online grocery businesses seem to have prospered, including FreshDirect in New York City.

6 William (Billy) Crapo Durant founded General Motors but went bankrupt during the Great Depression, mainly because his enthusiasm for GM shares caused him to buy them on margin. But most investors in the company, which became the largest firm in the world, did just fine.

Slaits of the world, saw their investors go down in flames but made millions themselves.[7]

In other words, what is important is that Jerry Slait lives in an economic world where it is possible to dream large dreams, take large chances, and at least occasionally succeed in becoming rich. It's not that the economy needs to reward only good ideas with wealth—that would be a far-seeing economy, indeed! It is the *phenomenon* of people like Jerry that we celebrate and that has made the American experiment so successful. Though it may sound odd, that phenomenon cannot persist if we start making silly rules like "only people with really good ideas get to become rich." No, what matters is that the US economy views the Jerry Slaits of the world as heroes, as men and women without whom we would be a vastly poorer, less efficient, less productive and less just society.

So let's not begrudge the wealthy their millions. They took their chances while the rest of us were punching the time clock and staying out of the rain. And while most of the budding entrepreneurs took their lumps, a few vastly enriched our world. And the capital they assembled, now in its liquid form, represents the most creative capital available to people and companies with good ideas anywhere in the world. That is why private capital is precious and why it deserves our respect and our serious attention.

A Note to Smaller Investors

This book is addressed to families with very substantial capital to invest. But the truth of the matter is that, just as "a rose is a rose is a rose," a best investment practice is a best investment practice, whether we are investing $100,000 or $100 million. For middle income investors who are serious about the stewardship of their capital, this book may be worth looking into. Many "best investment practices" favored by large investors, after all, have been repackaged and made available to smaller investors.[8] Thus, while some of the recommendations I make can be implemented only by investors with serious capital,

---

7 During the Internet boom, far more people got wiped out than got rich. There are thousands of technical professionals in San Francisco who have been unemployed (or under-employed) for years. In one case morbidly detailed by the New York Times, a 50-year-old tech whiz earning $300,000 a year at the peak ended up selling khakis at Gap. Jonathan Mahler, "Commute to Nowhere," New York *Times Magazine*, (April 13, 2003), p. 44.

8 I am thinking of such developments as money market funds, mutual funds, registered hedge funds, and so on.

most can be implemented by anyone who wishes to take the trouble to distinguish between good and bad investment practices.

A Note to Institutional Investors

This is a book about the challenges of taxable investing, and hence many of the techniques I discuss are appropriate for family investors but may not be appropriate for non-taxable, institutional portfolios such as foundations, endowments, and pension plans. On the other hand, it will always be obvious when I am discussing a strategy that should be followed only by taxable investors. Hence the managers of institutional portfolios, and the members of endowment investment committees, may find much of interest in this book. That said, it is only fair to point out that the best book ever written on the management of non-taxable portfolios was published just a few years ago: David Swensen's *Pioneering Portfolio Management*,[9] which should be required reading for all investors.

Organization of the Book

Part One

You will quickly notice that I have organized this book in an odd way—odd, anyway, for an investment book. The book is divided into three parts, plus an Afterword. But Part One—*The Importance of Private Capital*, doesn't discuss investment issues at all, at least as they are generally understood. Instead, Part One provides the context for and emphasizes the importance of the enterprise we are launched upon: the sound management of private capital.

Part One discusses the importance of private capital to the peculiar American version of free market democracy. Investment capital isn't something that exists in isolation from the broader society, nor is it a marginal factor in that society. If it were, the sound stewardship of capital would still be important to the families who have it, but it would be a matter of little consequence to the society at large.

In fact, however, private capital—both the lure of accumulating it and its disposition thereafter—is utterly essential to the way economic America works. It is the widespread and widely encouraged ability to become rich, and to be free to employ those riches in creative ways, that distinguishes American capitalism from its many cousins. After all, all free market democracies have

[9] The Free Press, 2000.

strong middle classes, relatively free markets and democratic forms of government. One might imagine that, as a result, all free market democracies would have roughly equivalent outcomes. We might assume that these economies would grow at about the same rates, with smaller economies naturally growing faster than larger economies (just as small companies grow faster than large companies), that innovation rates would be about the same across societies, that citizens of every country would work equally hard, that military strength would be roughly evenly distributed, that each nation would export its pro rata share of the world's culture.

But, as we know, that has not been the case at all. While it is true that most free market democracies operate on a roughly competitive plane, one of them—the United States—has so vastly outperformed the others that it has become the most dominant nation that ever existed. This has been, if we reflect on it, an astonishing outcome. In a post-industrial world of free societies, ideas migrate at the speed of light and innovation is no sooner made in one place than it is copied (or even improved) someplace else. In such a world, of all possible worlds, we would never have expected extraordinary dominance to arise.

I argue in Part One that American distinctiveness, American vitality, arises quite simply from the ongoing encouragement of American citizens to be productive by offering them the lure of great wealth, and by the resulting profusion of independently managed private capital—the most creative and least constrained source of capital in the world. I also speculate about why it is that America, far more than any of the older free market democracies, has managed to preserve its vigor. In other words, there are crucially important reasons why private capital needs to be managed properly, and those reasons go far beyond the narrow interests of the possessors of that capital. That is the message of Part One, and it provides the context for the rest of the book.

Parts Two, Three and the Afterword

Parts Two and Three of the book are more traditionally investment-related. Part Two, *The Stewardship of Wealth*, consists of seven chapters (Chapters 3 through 9), each discussing a broad issue that investors of private capital face. Chapter 3, for example, is entitled "Hard Slogging: The Challenge of Long-Term Investment Success." It illustrates just how difficult it is to compound private capital over any significant period of time. Chapter 4, "Understanding and Managing Risk," discusses risk in its many dimensions. Chapter 5, "Investment Theory and Investment Success," considers how useful the field of modern portfolio theory really is for real-world portfolios.

Chapter 6, "Financial Crooks and Investor Trust," addresses an issue that is on the minds of many investors early in the 21st century, namely, whether we can actually trust the capital markets to operate honestly. It discusses the corporate scandals (Enron, etc.) as well as scandals inside the financial world (the mutual fund trading scandals that exploded in 2003). Chapter 7, "Facing Off Against the Financial Industry: Conflicts of Interest and the Destruction of Wealth," takes on the crucial issue of conflicts of interest in the financial services industry and what investors and the industry can do about it. Chapter 8, "Finding the Right Advisor," outlines the steps we should take to ensure we match ourselves with an appropriate financial advisor. Finally, Chapter 9, "Making Family Investment Decisions," discusses the importance of creating sound governance and investment decisionmaking processes, especially in families where, as is often the case, more than one individual will be involved in the decisionmaking process.

Part Three, *The Nuts and Bolts of Successful Investing*, is just that: a description of best investment practices in every important aspect of the investment process for private investors. Part Three consists of eight chapters and is organized in the order in which most families will take up investment issues. It is thus designed to be read straight through, from Chapter 10, "Designing Taxable Investment Portfolios" (which discusses the asset allocation issue), to Chapter 16, "Monitoring and Rebalancing Taxable Portfolios" (discussing how to properly monitor and rebalance portfolios in a taxable environment). A final chapter in Part Three discusses a variety of investment challenges that either do not seem to justify full chapter treatment or that, while they may be of great importance to some investors, are not commonly enough encountered to justify a full chapter of their own.

On the other hand, Part Three can also be used as a refresher course when the time comes to grapple with a specific issue. For example, when a family is grappling with the asset allocation process they may find it useful to re-read Chapter 10, "Designing Taxable Investment Portfolios." When the family is ready to select money managers, they may wish to re-read Chapter 13, "Working with Money Managers."

The Afterword to this book attempts to make the important point that, after all, it is not wealth that matters in life, but happiness. I argue that there is little about the struggle for happiness that is any different for wealthy families than for other families—"All happy families are alike"—but that the specific form those challenges take does differ. I also point out that the one sure way for a wealthy family to become unhappy is for the family to fail in its stewardship obligations.

*   *   *

Writing this book has been a great pleasure for me, and I hope that reading it will bring at least a modest pleasure to my readers. For a small handful of them, perhaps, it will make a difference in the quality of their stewardship—and, therefore, in their personal happiness, the happiness of their children and grandchildren, and the continued success of the society that has nurtured them. It would be a rare writer who could ask for more.

Acknowledgements

Acknowledgements often leave me
with the impression that I've been lied to.
—Ben Cheever

For anyone interested in a close observation of the more basic human emotions on amusing display, it is hard to beat the acknowledgements section of most books. Here we find inadvertently laid out for inspection such passions (more usually closely guarded) as jealousy, ambition, insecurity, unctuousness, feckless gratitude, insincerity, lack of judgment, and, as Mr. Cheever points out in the epigraph, good old fashioned deceit. In bygone days, the "acknowledgements" section of a book was really nothing more than a dedication, typically addressed to a nonentity who happened to have deep pockets and whose favor the author was trying to curry. Insincere, to be sure, but at least with a healthy pecuniary motive.

Today, however, a really good acknowledgement, firing on all cylinders, will list several times as many contributors to the book as there are ideas in it. An even modestly energetic author will not omit to thank his neighbors, pets, sisters-in-law, fourth grade homeroom teacher, and even (in the case of Alice Walker) assorted flowers, trees and "most especially, the [non-pet] animals."[10] We are left to wonder if it might not be a useful improvement to the copyright laws to deny authorship (and royalties!) to anyone who claims that more than, say, two dozen people contributed importantly to the book.

Well, far be it from me to spit into this self-absorbed headwind. I therefore cheerfully admit that everyone I have ever known or read or read about or heard about, to say nothing of the millions of people I have never heard of,

---

[10] Preface," *Living by the Word: Selected Writings 1973–1987* (New York: Harvest Books, 1989).

have all contributed importantly to this book, and I thank them all. To paraphrase Ben Schott, if there are errors in this book, it's probably their fault.[11]

On the other hand, there actually are a small handful of people whose contributions were more direct and critical, essential in the sense that parts of the book would have been quite different, and quite worse, had these people not existed. These persons fall into the following categories:

- My clients. While it is true that few clients are deeply knowledgeable about investment matters—they made their money being brilliant at other things altogether—every conversation we have with our clients tells us whether we are meeting their needs or not, whether we are explaining the investment world in words that can be understood.
- My partners at Greycourt. This book was built in an unorthodox way. I would write a chapter of the book, then convert many of those chapters into "white papers" designed to be distributed to Greycourt's clients and friends. Before being distributed, those white papers had to pass through an internal peer review process in which they were circulated to each Greycourt Managing Director for comment. I did not keep detailed track of which comments were useful or non-useful, which were incorporated intact and which simply informed a revision, or even of the many that corrected glaring errors. But many of the chapters that follow were decidedly and thoroughly improved by my partners' comments. And far beyond that peer review process, my ongoing conversations with the senior professionals at Greycourt have vastly enriched my own understanding of the investment process and how its essential attributes can and cannot be communicated. Finally, a portion of the chapter on money managers (originally published elsewhere) was co-authored by my partner Gregory R. Friedman, Greycourt's Chief Investment Officer.
- Other writers in the field. I have read dozens and dozens of investment books over the years, and even the worst of them has probably taught me something—if only about what not to do. But it has been the best of these writings that have educated and inspired me. By "the best" I refer, in alphabetical order, to Warren Buffett's Annual Reports on Berkshire Hathaway,[12] Charles Ellis's *Winning the Loser's Game*,[13] Benjamin

---

11 "Acknowledgements," *Schott's Original Miscellany* (New York: Bloomsbury, 2003).

12 The reports are available on the Berkshire Hathaway Web site, www.berkshirehathaway.com.

13 McGraw-Hill Trade, 4th ed., 2002.

Graham's *The Intelligent Investor*[14] (and its in-depth original, *Security Analysis,* written with David L. Dodd),[15] David Salem's multitudinous-but-trenchant essays published by The Investment Fund for Foundations,[16] and David Swensen's *Pioneering Portfolio Management.*[17] Anyone who reads those writings carefully will no doubt wonder why I bothered to write this book.

I want to say a word of thanks to Greycourt's shareholders. This accomplished group of men and women had faith in the quixotic idea of Greycourt way back when its chances of success seemed laughably small. They remained loyal to her while she wandered in the wilderness that is the natural terrain of startup companies everywhere. Without them the idea of open architecture—to say nothing of Greycourt itself—would not exist.

Finally, it is customary to thank one's spouse. A writer worth his salt should be wary of what is customary, but in this case the shoe fits. My wife, Simin, who leads a busy professional and public service life of her own, put up with my many absences from our large and complicated family, as I stole every possible opportunity to work on this book. In addition, she read the entire manuscript (except this paragraph) and was generous with her praise and careful with her blame (the perfect critic!) Her own education and career were put on hold while she helped me launch Greycourt into the world. If this book were to become a classic in its field, worthy of being mentioned in the same breath with the writings listed above, it could not possibly compensate her for her contributions, her kindnesses, her patience, or her love.

* * *

Almost all the material in this book was written for it, but much of that material was published elsewhere before the book appeared. In particular, many of the chapters, or parts of chapters, first saw the light of day as white papers published by Greycourt & Co., Inc., the financial advisory firm where I serve as Chairman. Although I appear as sole author on most of those papers, my partners at Greycourt often supplied many helpful comments. All material has been reprinted with the permission of the original publisher.

The original references for material first published elsewhere are Gregory Curtis, "Investment Considerations Associated with Complex Estate Planning

---

14 HarperBusiness, rev. ed., 2003.

15 McGraw-Hill Trade, 2nd ed., 2002.

16 Available on the TIFF Web site at www.tiff.org.

17 Free Press, 1st ed., 2000.

Strategies," *Greycourt White Paper No. 6* (August, 2001); Gregory Curtis, "Corporate Crooks and Investor Trust," *Greycourt White Paper No. 22* (July, 2002); Gregory Curtis, "Modern Portfolio Theory and Quantum Mechanics," *Greycourt White Paper No. 20* (August, 2002), subsequently published as Gregory Curtis, "Modern Portfolio Theory and Quantum Mechanics," *The Journal of Wealth Management,* Winter 2002, pp. 7-13; Gregory Curtis, "Hedge Fund Investing: The End of the Beginning," *Greycourt White Paper No. 25* (October, 2002); Gregory Curtis, "A Modest Proposal: Let's End Conflicts of Interest in the Wealth Advisory Business," *Greycourt White Paper No. 24* (February, 2003); Gregory Curtis, "Numeracy, Innumeracy and Hard Slogging," *Greycourt White Paper No. 29* (April, 2003); Gregory Curtis, "Reinvigorating the Investment Committee: Introducing the Investment Committee Operating Manual," *Greycourt White Paper No. 31* (September, 2003); Gregory Curtis, "The Mutual Fund Scandals," *Open Letter to Clients and Friends of Greycourt & Co., Inc.* (November 13, 2003); Gregory Curtis and Gregory R. Friedman, "The Challenge of Identifying Managers Who Will Outperform in the Future," *Greycourt White Paper No. 32* (February, 2004); Gregory Curtis, "The SEC Inquiry Into Pension Consultants," *Open Letter to Clients and Friends of Greycourt & Co., Inc.* (March 31, 2004); Gregory Curtis, "Portable Alpha: What's All the Buzz About?" *Greycourt White Paper No. 34* (May, 2004); Gregory Curtis, "Modern Portfolio Theory and Behavioral Finance," *The Journal of Wealth Management*, Fall 2004, pp. 16-22.

Pittsburgh
September 2004

PART ONE

The Importance of Private Capital

Introduction to Part One

The role of private capital is poorly understood, both by Americans in general and also by the wealthy Americans who own that capital. Most wealthy families take the stewardship of their capital seriously, to be sure, seeing that stewardship as the discharge of an important duty to their families. But beyond the importance of wealth to its owners, substantial families can legitimately wonder if private wealth is a positive or negative feature of American life. Families who work hard to maintain and grow their wealth often see their work as an intensely private activity existing outside of, unrelated to, and largely irrelevant to the major thrusts of US society—a kind of fringe element in the American democracy. Nothing, however, could be further from the truth.

The building of wealth, the management of wealth, and the deployment of wealth are activities that lie at the very soul of what has made America great. Abundant private wealth is what distinguishes America from other free market democracies. It is the lure of wealth that encourages Americans (and would-be Americans) to develop and implement the ideas that drive contemporary civilization, whether those ideas are in business, science, the arts, education, entertainment or almost any other activity that we value as human beings. And it is the creative deployment of wealth that enriches American society far beyond the dreams of other civilizations—including other modern, post-industrial democracies. These two characteristics of wealth—its ability to bring out the competitive best in citizens and its enriching qualities that permeate society—are at the center of the special American version of free market democracy, and they are largely responsible for America's preeminence. Lying between these two aspects of wealth, and the lynchpin that holds them together, is the management of private wealth. If wealth were simply created and then dissipated, it would be of little use to its owners. Far more important, it would be of little use to society.

Parts Two and Three of this book are focused intensely on the management of wealth—on the lynchpin. But in Part One, I focus on the first two characteristics of wealth. Thus, Chapter 1 emphasizes how America differs from its free market cousins in the continuing encouragement of its citizens to pursue wealth. As a result, American competitiveness is the wonder of the world. In

Chapter 2, I turn to the deployment of wealth—the creative use of private capital that gives this book its title. The ultimate point of Part One is to demonstrate that wealthy families lie at the very center of the American experiment. Private capital is an essential, even a definitive aspect of the American version of democratic capitalism. Without private capital on a grand scale—the lure of accumulating it and the creative use of it—it would be impossible to imagine America.

Wealthy families need to be both proud of what their families have accomplished and proud of what their capital can and will continue to accomplish for America and for the world. Private capital has made America the most vigorous, the most creative, the most diverse—in short, the most powerful society ever organized. And given the increasingly feeble state of other liberal societies around the world, it is the vigor of America, and only the vigor of America, that offers hope for freedom and democracy anywhere on the globe. If America declines, freedom and democracy will have no champion worthy of the name. And the best way to ensure the decline of America is to reduce the role that private capital plays in our remarkable success.

One

Chapter 1

Wealth in America

Every man thinks God is on his side.
The rich and powerful know he is.
—Jean Anouihl

Kill the Rich.
—Title of a song by the punk rock band, Anti-Flag (sic)

Few Americans—including few wealthy Americans—have given much thought to the role that wealth plays in the American polity. We tend to take it for granted that America always has and always will consist of wealthy families, middle income families and poor families. And when we do think about it, most Americans—including most wealthy Americans—tend to imagine that wealth constitutes, at best, a necessary flaw in the way the American democracy should work. Perhaps, we concede, the lure of wealth is necessary to encourage people to work hard, to come up with and commercialize new ideas, to build the companies that provide employment. But still and all, in a society where we are all created equal, there is something incongruous about the fact that some people have so much more money than others.

If the wealthy constitute a "flaw" in the way American society should work, why should we tolerate it? If we really put our minds to the problem, couldn't we come up with a system that offered similar incentives but that didn't produce wealthy families in such profusion?

What is it, then, that accounts for the persistence of wealthy families in the American democratic republic? Why do we tolerate the rich, with their God-like influence over people and affairs, when it is abundantly clear that the wealthy, like everyone else, are not endowed with God-like wisdom in deciding how to wield that influence? Certainly it is apparent that the rich, whether they are dealing with their own companies, with politics and the affairs of state, with social and cultural issues, with charitable organizations, or even with their own families, have far more impact than other citizens, for good or ill. The rich are a bit like the gods of the Greeks or Romans: not one omnipotent, all-seeing sage, but powerful, fascinating, mischievous creatures we don't completely understand but which we find riveting, annoying, alarming and, like it or not, essential.

Indeed, the wealthy, *virtually alone in a democratic society*, constitute a natural, unelected aristocracy. I say "natural" not because there is anything fundamentally natural about wealthy aristocracies, but because the development of wealthy families is an organic byproduct of the way we have chosen to organize our economic affairs in the United States. The American market economy is designed to pit individuals against each other in a free economic competition, the incentive to compete being the possibility of becoming rich. We believe that this sort of competition is most likely to lead to improved conditions for the broader society, including those who "lose" in the competition to create wealth (the poor), and including those who refuse to compete at all: individuals who select professions that rarely lead to wealth, such as academics, social workers, nurses, artists, and so on. (Even these people compete for power and recognition in their chosen fields.) We can easily imagine societies in which wealth-creation activities would not be valued so highly—communist, socialist and many primitive societies, for example—and in those societies different individuals would perhaps[18] constitute the "natural" aristocracy.

I say "unelected" because the wealthy are not selected by any representative body. They simply happen as the result of economic competition and opportunity, much the way great athletes simply happen when athletic competition and opportunities are made available. That's not to say that people who create wealth don't work enormously hard at it, just as great athletes work enormously hard at it. But no group of people sits down and conducts a vote to determine who the best athletes are going to be, and no one sits down to vote on who the wealthy are going to be. The same is true of great artists, musicians, writers, and so on. Rules that define excellence are established through complex cultural mechanisms, but thereafter individuals compete with each other and there will be winners, losers, and a great body of people in the middle who

---

[18] I say "perhaps" because, whether the incentive is to create wealth, as in a market economy, or power, as in a non-market economy, the same kinds of people are likely to win the competition: the most competent, the hardest-working and, perhaps, the most ruthless.

develop competence but not greatness (as well, of course, as people who chose not to compete at all).

Most individuals in American society who possess influence on a scale equivalent to that of the rich actually *have* been elected in one way or the other. Politicians are the most obvious example, but union chiefs, university presidents, heads of large non-profit organizations, corporate bigwigs and even capos of crime families have all been elected by some body that is considered reasonably representative in those worlds. The Governor of California, an elected official, is undoubtedly the most powerful individual in that state. But I could name eight or ten wealthy men (and two or three women) who would share Top Twenty billing for power-wielding in that biggest of American states, alongside a few elected officials and a few corporate CEOs. No one elected those men and women, but they made their fortunes and have used those fortunes in part to influence California affairs. Appalling as this might be to some, it is and always has been a fact of life in America.

I say "aristocracy" because, as noted in the California example, the wealthy have power and influence far beyond that of other unelected centers of excellence: they represent an aristocracy in the precise meaning of the term.[19] The difference between the wealthy and great athletes (or great artists, musicians, writers, etc.) is that the former end up, through the power of their wealth, with the ability to influence much of what we hold dear in our world, while the latter, except in rare instances, exercise little influence beyond their area of specialization. It is so natural to expect the rich to wield influence over important matters that we hardly stop to think about how unusual it is that one social sub-group should have been vouchsafed this influence. Why should wealth-creating skills be entitled to far greater influence than, say, the skills required to score consistently from the three-point line or the skills required to compose a piano concerto?

The Indispensable Rich

America didn't decide to organize a society that would produce wealthy families—far from it. America organized a society that produces wealthy families as a byproduct of an economic competition that is considered desirable. That byproduct may have been anticipated, but it is not universally welcomed. Indeed, in a land where "all men are created equal" it may easily be considered

---

19 "Government by a privileged minority," *Webster's New World Dictionary* (Simon & Schuster, Inc., 1996). The term "aristocracy" originally referred to a government by the best citizens in the state.

an unhappy byproduct. Because the wealthy have *unelected* power and influence, must it not be the case that the wealthy have *illegitimate* power and influence? Do not the rich constitute a serious flaw in the way a democratic society should operate? Is it not, indeed, an important task of the democratic process to eliminate or minimize the disproportionate influence of any one group? And since there are ways to operate democratic republics without producing so many wealthy families—the Scandinavian and most Western European societies are organized in this way—might not Americans be tempted to adopt those models as well? Certainly the persistence of the rich in a democratic society is at the very least incongruous.[20]

In this introductory chapter, I will argue that private wealth persists—indeed, grows luxuriantly—in the United States for reasons that are not only sound, but which go to the very heart of America's success in its competition with other civilizations. Wealthy families are not simply a minor pothole on the grand highway leading to uniform middle-classness in America. On the contrary, the production of private wealth is a crucial aspect of the singular success of the American experiment. Private wealth, as distinct from and as a counterweight to government wealth, is both central to and the principal symbol of America. Moreover, given America's special role among nations, America's wealthy families also play a central role in the evolution of other nations and of the prospects for billions of people worldwide.

Democracy and Capitalism

The apparent contradiction of private wealth in a democratic republic is best examined by viewing democracy in the only economic context in which it can flourish: a free market system. Largely capitalist economies can exist outside the context of democratic political systems (Singapore and, increasingly, China, are examples), but democratic political systems cannot exist outside the context of free market economies. We cannot be free politically but enslaved economically. The institutions of civil society that liberal democracies establish and protect—especially private property and the rule of law—enable extremely diverse populations to coexist and work together productively; they enable, in short, civilization to exist.[21] Since this is the case, there will be consequences flowing

---

20 Many observers consider the persistence of the rich in America to be both unacceptable and a symptom of incipient decline. See, for example, Kevin Phillips, *Wealth and Democracy: A Political History of the American Rich* (Broadway Books, 2002).

21 In John Gray's words, "[C]ivil society is the matrix of the market economy." John Gray, *Post-Liberalism: Studies in Political Thought* (Routledge, 1993), p. 246.

from the economic system that would not necessarily be welcomed if the political system could somehow exist independent of its economic context: the production of wealth that is not evenly distributed being a principal consequence.

American democracy is, far more than elsewhere, intertwined with a capitalist attitude. The opportunity to pursue one's economic aspirations—the opportunity to become rich—is inextricably a part of the American dream, a dream that captures the imaginations of the poor worldwide, as well as immigrants to America, our working poor, the lower middle classes, and aspiring middle class families. Reinventing America to establish a society that prevented people from getting rich wouldn't hurt those who are already wealthy, but it would seriously damage the aspirations of the poor. An America that was no longer perceived as the land of opportunity would be an America essentially unrecognizable to most Americans, as well as to most non-Americans and most would-be-Americans.

We are so used to the vigorous spirit animating America that it is difficult to keep firmly in mind how rare this spirit is, especially among our peer group—the largely Western[22] post-industrial liberal democracies. It is worth our time to examine in some detail the nature of these societies, if only as an example of what America would look like without private capital to fuel its competitive spirit and to irrigate its exotic garden of ideas.

Capitalism and Its Contradictions

Karl Marx famously maintained that capitalism contained the seeds of its own destruction, that the exploitation of labor would ultimately cause the emerging, alienated working classes to rise up and crush bourgeois society, replacing capitalist systems with socialist "dictatorships of the proletariat." While many of Marx's criticisms of capitalism were alarmingly accurate, he was notoriously wrong in his prediction of its demise. Indeed, free market democracies have proven to be the most resilient of all forms of sociopolitical organization.

---

[22] Japan straddles this world, as an advanced post-industrial society with the trappings of liberal democracy but the soul of a civil society that is quite different from, and that developed largely independently of, Western-style democracy. Japan's distinctiveness would be far more clear if it were not for the Western-style constitution and government imposed on Japan by the US after World War II.

In terms of social peace and economic productivity, the determinative question turns out to be not so much whether labor is or is not "exploited"[23] or how big the gap may be between rich and poor.[24] Instead, what seems to matter is whether or not citizens—especially including the poor—have a real opportunity to improve their condition on an absolute basis. If so, the relative size and stability of the resulting middle classes (the hated bourgeoisie of Marxist theory) will increase rapidly. This is, of course, exactly what has happened in all advanced industrial and post-industrial free market democracies.

In America, as elsewhere among free market democracies, the native[25] poor have come to represent an ever-smaller percentage of the population, as poor families have tended to move into the middle classes—or even to become rich—in one or two generations. This phenomenon has occurred because the vigor of free market economic activity has been so great that massive opportunities were made available to virtually anyone who wished to seize them. As a result, poor families have cared less about whether they were being "exploited" and more about seizing opportunities to improve their circumstances. Certainly, of course, the poor (along with blacks, women, the handicapped, gays, etc.) have historically faced more obstacles than others along the road to economic success, and it is an important part of the job of America, and of America's rich, to demolish those obstacles. But the effort to pull down obstacles to economic success is powerfully assisted by the need of free market societies for the talents of the disenfranchised.

---

23 All labor is, in a literal sense, "exploited" if we accept John Roemer's Marxist definition: "[A] person is exploited if the labor that he expends in production is greater than the labor embodied in the goods he can purchase with the revenues from production." John E. Roemer, *Free to Lose: An Introduction to Marxist Economic Philosophy* (Century Hutchison, 1989), p. 161. But such a society would be a static one, indeed. Given that labor is also "exploited" under any other conceivable economic system (especially socialism and Communism), we ought to prefer the system that maximizes the economic wellbeing of the worker.

24 The wealth gap between Bill Gates and America's poorest families is very nearly as large as was the wealth gap between the Sun Kings of Egypt and their slaves. The difference is not in the size of the gap but in the fact that Egyptian slaves would always be slaves, as would their children, while poor citizens in America can, and do, aspire to be the next Bill Gates.

25 Poverty in America is more closely associated with immigration—no sooner does one immigrant group move up the socioeconomic ladder than they are replaced by other aspiring, but very poor, "Americans." In addition, poverty is also associated with America's semi-permanent underclass associated mainly, but hardly exclusively, with our legacy of black slavery.

Marx may have been wrong in his prognosis for capitalism, but history suggests that internal contradictions, albeit of a very different sort, do seem to threaten capitalist societies. If those societies fail they will likely do so not because of the exploitation of labor, but because absolute living standards rather quickly reach such an elevated point that the very character of the societies begins to change, causing them to become almost unrecognizably different from the societies that created the wealth in the first place. Citizens in wealthy capitalist societies, that is to say, gradually become so affluent, so comfortable, that they become more concerned about preserving their living standards than about improving them. When this happens, the vigor of the society quickly diminishes: its citizens demand shorter work weeks, higher wages without corresponding productivity increases, longer vacations, easier jobs, more personal autonomy ("Who the hell is my boss to tell *me* what to do?"), and so on.

Much of this is, to be sure, simple human nature. Decades ago, psychologist Abraham Maslow postulated the existence of a "hierarchy of needs."[26] According to Maslow, human beings are motivated mainly by unsatisfied needs. Moreover, certain lower needs (or, as Maslow called them, "deficiency needs") must to be satisfied before the "higher" needs can be fulfilled, or even aspired to. Subsidiary needs are, in Maslow's terms, "prepotent," powerful and requiring that they be fulfilled before the next need in the hierarchy can be addressed.

"Physiological" needs are basic human needs such as air, water, food, sleep, sex, and so on. If these needs remain long unsatisfied, we experience pain. Once they are satisfied, however, we can begin to think about "safety" needs, which Maslow associates with maintaining stability and consistency in a world that otherwise appears to us as chaotic and uncontrollable. Only then can we aspire toward love, esteem and, ultimately, self-actualization, the highest level in Maslow's hierarchy of needs. Self-actualization has to do with the desire to become all that we are capable of becoming, to maximize our potential, whatever it may be. We may seek oneness with our God, personal peace, knowledge of various kinds, and so on.

Whether or not Maslow's hierarchy holds water in every detail, it seems intuitively correct and in any event accurately describes the behavior of people in societies that offer them the opportunity to satisfy increasingly complex needs. Many forms of social organization can satisfy most of the "deficiency" needs. Indeed, some societies that seem in many ways appalling to us came to

---

26 Abraham Maslow, *Motivation and Personality* (Harper, 1954).

exist precisely because they at least supplied these basic, deficiency needs of their citizens better than whatever (often chaos) preceded them.

But "love" needs require a sense of belonging, the opportunity to associate with and communicate openly with other human beings. And they require a society open enough to permit such associations—in other words, a largely democratic society. "Esteem" needs require that we master increasingly complex tasks for which we are naturally suited (self esteem) and that we be viewed positively by our peers for our accomplishments (esteem by others). These are needs best addressed by a society with an open, competitive economic system that provides an enormous range of employment, volunteer and other options, ensuring that virtually everyone can find something to be competent at—in other words, a free market economic system.

But here is a critical point: self-actualization—"the desire…to become everything that one is capable of becoming," in Maslow's words—is fundamentally different from the other needs. Self-actualization does not occur naturally among individuals whose previous needs have been satisfied—satisfaction of those needs may be a necessary condition for the achievement of self-actualization, but they are not a *sufficient* condition. Assuming that the society in which we live offers the possibility to do so, we progress naturally up the hierarchy from the deficiency needs through love and esteem; these seem to be true needs to which human beings naturally aspire. But to make the leap to full self-actualization requires intense individual effort and, therefore, intense desire. Free market democracies are forms of social organization that can provide the platform that makes the leap possible, but it will not occur automatically. Indeed, once the incentive to become rich is eliminated, the tendency to become complacent dominates.

Thus, to a very considerable extent the comfort that advanced post-industrial civilizations offer us seems positively to interfere with the further development of our potential. With all our other needs satisfied we tend not to gather our courage for yet one more struggle—the extraordinary leap to self-actualization. Instead, the lure of becoming everything we are capable of being is lost amidst the creature comforts of our lives. Worse, our desire for continued progress is overwhelmed by the fear of losing what we have already attained. Hence the odd result that societies that appear to be ideal platforms for the full expression of humanness tend at some point in their development to impede further achievement—by producing citizens who are no longer willing to strive for it, to take the risks upon which all significant achievement depends. Instead, these societies produce citizens who spend most of their time building walls around what they have. The fear of losing ground dominates all else.

Capitalist societies, then, begin as robust, competitive communities, rapidly moving their citizens up the socioeconomic ladder (and, if you will, the Maslovian hierarchy). But all too often they decay into what appears to be middle class comfort, but which is really a surface calm underlain by apprehension. As we decline to risk our current, admittedly high, level of comfort, we forfeit any possibility of achieving more. We build walls around our prosperity, and those walls ultimately stifle us.

Because they are so wealthy, it is not immediately apparent how weak many formerly robust capitalist societies have become. But as productivity declines, fewer and fewer of those societies' products can compete internationally. Formerly free market governments must now impose high trade barriers or other forms of subsidy in order to continue to produce goods and services that were formerly competitive.[27] Inefficient industries are thereby walled off from more efficient competitors elsewhere, excused from the competition that would make them more efficient.

And if we decline to place our jobs or our social status at risk, how must we feel about placing our very lives at risk, as, for example, in the defense of our country? Societies that become risk-intolerant in the economic sphere tend to become risk-intolerant in many ways. The emphasis on keeping what we have, rather than incurring risk to achieve more, softens the society, allowing it to become cautious, effete. To paraphrase Louise Bogan, these formerly vigorous capitalist societies now "have no wilderness in them, they are provident instead."[28]

Providential Societies

Providential societies, as we might call them (with apologies to Ms. Bogan)—societies that no longer have the stomach for economic, social, cultural or military risk—are analogous to investors who have lost their tolerance for market risk. It is an iron law of modern portfolio theory that rewards are, at

---

[27] The delivery of services, as opposed to goods, has historically been a local phenomenon, largely impervious to remote competition. But just as the production of goods has long been internationally competitive, so too has the delivery of many services recently become subject to international competition. This occurs as the result of the ease of travel, communications, electronic delivery mechanisms, and the consolidation of service businesses (e.g., law firms, accounting firms, travel agencies, etc.) In addition, improvement of services in one society provides a powerful, if indirect, incentive for service quality to improve in other societies.

[28] Louise Bogan, "Women," *Blue Estuaries: Poems 1923–1968* (Farrar, Straus and Giroux, 1968).

least within reason, positively associated with the risks incurred. Investors can avoid risk quite easily: by, for example, putting all their money in Treasury bills. But this is the investment equivalent of sticking one's head in the sand and hoping to become invisible. Progress marches on, carrying along with it its handmaiden, inflation. Investors who own only Treasury bills become a little poorer every day in real terms. If those investors are unfortunate enough to have to pay taxes on their meager interest,[29] their backward progress accelerates profoundly. Investors who cannot tolerate risk therefore die a little bit each day investment-wise, becoming slightly poorer than they were before, a process that leads inevitably to economic death, that is, to poverty.

Like risk-averse investors, societies that become unwilling to take risk also die a little bit each day, becoming a little poorer relative to societies that are more vigorous. It is essential, for example, that individuals be willing to take entrepreneurial risk—otherwise, new businesses will not be formed. But taking entrepreneurial risk means accepting the risk of personal failure and the risk that cushy jobs provided by existing firms will be eliminated. It is essential that businesses be exposed to competition, including competition from foreign firms and from hostile takeovers of poorly managed businesses. Otherwise, businesses become complacent and inefficient. Societies that find themselves so risk-averse that they can longer start new businesses or permit open competition for existing businesses are societies whose growth begins, imperceptibly at first, to slow and ultimately to stop. Opportunities for further advancement begin to disappear for already-affluent citizens, but also for citizens and immigrants who have the bad luck not to be already affluent. The slowing growth of these societies also imposes severe burdens on the development of emerging economies that depend on exports for their own economic growth.

And, like it or not, it is essential that societies be vigilant in their own defense, notwithstanding the economic costs and, of course, the risk that citizens may die in battle. Indeed, this is probably the ultimate touchstone for societies that have entered a terminal stage of decline—remarkable as it may seem, societies caught in the throes of providentiality simply cannot bring themselves even to take on the costs and risks of their own defense.

This is precisely the condition in which most of the advanced post-industrial societies of Europe and Scandinavia have found themselves. Our first glimpse of European ineffectuality came in Kosovo and Bosnia in the 1990s, when, among other atrocities, a tinpot dictator named Slobodan Milošević slaughtered thousands

---

29 Yes, high-income investors typically own tax-exempt municipal bonds, not taxable bonds. But the same phenomenon prevails: municipal bonds yield less than taxable bonds, the difference being roughly equal to the amount of the taxes saved.

while (European) United Nations troops stood by and watched the carnage. Only when American troops entered the fray—very much against the wishes of the Europeans and the UN—was the murderous rule of Milošević brought to an end, peace imposed and the dictator brought to trial for war crimes.

The Balkan conflict was, to some extent, a (messy) tempest in a teapot. But if the Europeans were incapable of mounting a credible military operation in their own backyards, where they faced an obvious threat to European peace and stability, what possible chance was there that they could mount credible military operations against more distant threats, such as those posed by Iraq or North Korea? The answer, of course, is none at all. In the 1991 invasion of Iraq, despite United Nations approval of the attack, the contribution from most of Europe was almost risible.[30]

In the run-up to the 2003 Iraq invasion, so-called "old Europe" was solidly opposed to the attack. While there were certainly important reasons to examine the American case for an invasion, the Europeans were transparently opposed to the war for other reasons altogether. Some of those reasons had to do with a natural fear of massive American military and economic power and the desire to band together to limit it. Other, more selfish, reasons had to do with (legal and illegal) trade relations with Iraq. But the fundamental fact of the matter was that no European country (except Britain, which joined in the attack) had any military capacity to wage a war in Iraq, and hence the notion of a "United Nations" coalition was a hollow joke from the beginning.[31]

---

[30] As a random example, the French sent a few jet aircraft to Iraq, but these Mirages were so out of date that their antiquated radar left them dangerously vulnerable to Iraqi anti-aircraft fire. No doubt the French pilots of these planes were as brave as their American counterparts. But their service on behalf of such an enfeebled society meant that they had to be escorted through the battle zone like non-combatants. The French were simply no match for a second-rate, Third World power like Iraq.

[31] See, generally, the hilarious and sad article by Philip Shishkin, *How the Armies of Europe Let Their Guard Down: Guaranteed Jobs for Soldiers Leave Little Room to Train; Battle of the Belgian Bands* (Wall Street Journal, February 13, 2003), p. 1, 7. The main point of Shishkin's article is that "Europe's military muscle has grown soft" mainly because "so much money is spent on pay and benefits that there is less left for the technology, weapons and other gear that modern forces need." This, of course, is my point exactly: a providential society doesn't maintain a military force as a serious deterrent against possible aggression or to maintain their own security and integrity, but rather as an instrument of social policy to reduce unemployment, provide a social safety net and respond to citizen demands for less-work-and-more-pay.

A society that possesses an imposing military force can make the decision to use it or not, and, like America, it might make those decisions wisely or unwisely. But at least the choice is there. Europe had no choice. Despite their incredible wealth, despite being vastly more advanced socially, economically and technologically than Iraq, the European nations were no match, individually or collectively, for Iraqi power. Hence, the European rationale for opposing the war proceeded not from substance but from a kind of disease—the disease of providentiality.

Risk and Strength

Ironically—just as in the investment world—the willingness to tolerate a reasonable amount of risk actually reduces overall systemic risk in a society, because the assets of the society become diversified, more robust. The existence of a powerful military force—and the will to employ it—means that the society is less likely to be attacked, not more likely. Exposing a society's business enterprises to foreign competition means that, overall, those enterprises will be stronger, not weaker. The knowledge that we can be fired for incompetence or indolence makes for better, not worse, employees. Thus it is that risk-averse societies are more risky overall than non-risk-averse societies, in precisely the same sense that risk-averse investors end up holding portfolios that are more risky than those of non-risk-averse investors.[32]

Of course, there is no gainsaying that costs are paid by societies that expose themselves to risk. In my own city of Pittsburgh, years of inefficient management, obsolete plants and a legacy of powerful, militant and unaccountable unions destroyed the Pittsburgh steel industry in one generation. A city that, during World War II, produced more steel than all of Germany and Japan combined, produces, today, not one ton of steel. In barely more than a decade, nearly 100,000 steelworkers lost their jobs. These were men (almost all were, in fact, men) wholly unsuited by training or culture for any other remotely equal employment. Thousands of businesses that relied on the steel industry also collapsed. The pain caused by this dislocation can hardly be overestimated. But

---

[32] Relative to investors holding "risk-free" portfolios, investors holding fully diversified portfolios, subject to many offsetting risks, will face greater short-term risks (in the sense of price volatility), but fewer long-term risks (in the sense of becoming poorer over time). And so it is with non-risk-averse societies, which experience short-term loss of jobs and industries because they aren't protected, but experience long-term growth in wealth as a result of their far greater competitiveness.

the consequences for American competitiveness of propping up the Pittsburgh steel industry—by, for example, imposing high tariffs on imported steel[33]—would have been far worse. It was crucial that other American industries (the auto industry, for example), and the investors in those industries, observe what was likely to happen to them if they failed to remain competitive.

In a very important sense, risk-averse societies—providential societies—are opposed to the idea of progress itself. In effect, these societies are saying, "I am now rich and comfortable enough that further progress is unnecessary, since it brings risks, and to hell with the consequences for others of this attitude." As noted above, we needn't look far to observe this phenomenon in full flower in much of Western Europe and Scandinavia.

It is important to keep firmly in mind that it is not that Europe lacks the inherent capability to build a strong military force or to create a more vigorous economy. The European Union encompasses twenty-five nations and is the single richest and largest organized bloc of nations in the world. Europe's population is, in the aggregate, more than 100 million people larger than that of the US.[34] What so many in Europe (and elsewhere) lack is the *will* to do those things.

One hundred and forty years ago, Abraham Lincoln understood this point quite precisely. Speaking at the great cemetery at Gettysburg, a place as haunting today as it was in 1864, Lincoln articulated the reason why the United States would not allow democracy to die. It was not because the US had the military power to enforce its wishes against the Confederacy—in 1864 that was still very much unclear. Nor was it that the US possessed the industrial might to dominate the Confederacy. Nor was it, even, that God was on the side of the North. The United States would not allow democracy to die simply because we *willed* it to remain alive. Democracy would prevail as the result of a collective act of American resolve: "We here *highly resolve*...that government of the people, by the people and for the people shall not perish from the Earth."[35] Nearly

---

33 Tariffs have, in fact, been imposed on imported steel from time to time, most recently in 2002 (they were removed in 2003). However, these tariffs have been more about warning other countries against subsidizing their own inefficient steel industries than about subsidizing our own. Even so, tariffs are generally counterproductive because, among other things, while they may temporarily maintain employment in the targeted industry (i.e., steelmaking), they reduce employment in all the industries that must now pay more for steel.

34 When ten former Soviet satellites joined the European Union in early 2004, the population of that trading bloc rose by another 100 million people.

35 See Paul Berman's discussion of the role of resolve in the preservation of democracy. *What Lincoln Knew About War* (The New Republic, March 3, 2003).

a century and a half later, Lincoln would still recognize, in an America otherwise formidably changed, the collective American resolve to preserve democracy, a resolute will that is determined to prevail despite almost unanimous opposition from our friends and our foes alike.[36]

America and Decline

Why is it, we might ask ourselves, that America seems to have been largely (albeit certainly not completely) immune to providentiality? Virtually since the United States appeared on the world stage there have been confident predictions that the country would soon enter a period of inexorable decline. Some of these predictions were based on the view that all successful civilizations pass through various stages, with a robust, dominating stage certain to be succeeded by a self-indulgent, dissipated stage, followed by collapse in the face of challenges presented by more vigorous civilizations. Other predictions have been based on underestimations of American society, estimations based on the assumption that American society is just like European society, or on peculiar conditions in America that seemed to threaten its preeminence.

After World War I, for example, most Europeans—and, for that matter, most Americans—assumed that the old order would quickly reassert itself, with London as the capital of the Anglo-Saxon world and Paris and Berlin vying for control of the Continent. America was seen as too insular to succeed to world dominance. Indeed, the German high command in World War I had made the crucial, and fatal, assumptions that America would not enter the war until it was too late and that the admittedly imposing American economy could not switch to war production quickly enough to affect the outcome.[37] But in fact America had become the dominant world economy long before the war began, and its preeminence afterward was due only in part to the devastation the war caused to Britain and the Continental powers.[38] By 1918 the dollar had replaced sterling as the world currency, a role the dollar continues to

---

[36] Our friends would prefer America to be as irresolute as they; our enemies would prefer us to be as irresolute as our friends.

[37] In fact, however, "By the war's end, the United States had an arms-making capacity that eclipsed that of England and France combined." Ron Chernow, *The House of Morgan* (Simon & Schuster, 1990), p. 189.

[38] In 1914, Britain accounted for 8.3% of the world's GDP. It is interesting to compare Britain's pre-World War I "dominance" with America's dominance today: in 2000, America accounted for fully 23% of the world's GDP. John B. Judis, *Decline and Fall*, New York Times Book Review (May 12, 2002).

play today, more than eight decades later. World War I certainly accelerated the rise of American dominance, but it was already preordained.

If affluence alone were sufficient to convert America into a provident society, one would have expected to see signs of it long, long ago. It was, after all, way back in the mid-eighteenth century that America surpassed all other regions of the world in living standards. Surely 250 years as the world's richest country ought to be enough to corrupt us. And, as everyone knows, the United States is not merely the world's oldest democracy—it is the world's oldest continuing government of any kind, operating under the same Constitution since 1788. That, my friends, is a long time for any kind of government to persist, notwithstanding the confident prognostications of cyclical decline theorists.

And, though it is difficult to prove, it seems likely that, by the middle of the nineteenth century, America was already the world's foremost military power. During the American Civil War, for example, the two most powerful armies on earth were both American. 150 years of such power ought, surely, to have been long enough for America's military to fall into over-confidence, complacency, corruption, lassitude. But in the early twenty-first century America is more dominant militarily than any civilization has ever been. Granted, America did not begin to project its economic, political and military power globally until World War I, but even that is now nine long and action-packed decades ago.

But the pundits never give up. Every time America stumbles—and we certainly stumble at least our fair share of the time—we hear that this time the final decline has begun. From the late 1940s through the 1970s, the virulence of anti-communism in America was accounted for in part by the fear that the Soviet Union had invented a more powerful military-industrial engine, that American was too free and disorganized to compete against such a disciplined juggernaut. Yet it was primarily the imposing economic and military strength of America that ultimately caused the USSR to collapse.[39]

As recently as the 1980s it was fashionable to argue that a bloated America could not possibly compete with such vigorous economies as Japan and Germany. These powerhouse societies, it was said, possessed more efficient decision-making cultures, more homogeneous populations all pulling in the same direction, more civilized labor-management relations, and were unhampered by legacy industrial plants, having been completely rebuilt after World War II primarily with American aid. But what a difference a decade or so can

39 Even Ilya Zaslavsky, the main Gorbachev advisor during Perestroika, admitted that it was Reagan's policy of "negotiating through strength that brought the Kremlin to its knees." David Remnick, *Lenin's Tomb: The Last Days of the Soviet Empire* (Vintage Books, 1994), p. 323.

make! Today, Japan is mired in a fifteen-year economic malaise, while the German economy is virtually stagnant, weighed down by high wages, short workweeks and stalled productivity. The American economy, far from succumbing to the competition, is more dominant than ever: total US GDP today is nearly twice that of Germany and Japan combined.[40]

Yet even today, with American economic, cultural and military power astonishing (and frightening) the world as never before, we continue to read of our imminent demise. A representative example is Kevin Phillips' *Wealth and Democracy*,[41] in which Phillips argues that, like Spain, Holland and Britain before it, America exhibits all the classic symptoms of cyclical decline: a preoccupation with finance, technology and services rather than basic manufacturing; capital markets prone to bubbles and speculation; the export of jobs and capital; the import of cheap foreign labor to do jobs Americans don't want; a growing inequality of income and wealth; frequent and incipient wars.[42]

But Phillips has it exactly backwards: whether or not these were symptoms of decline in societies hundreds of years ago, they are, today, symptoms of vigor, of continued dominance. Since Phillips' view of the world is widely held, let's examine each of his "symptoms of decline." In brief:

- Contrary to Phillips' view, in the early twenty-first century it is important that simple ("basic") manufacturing take place in societies where less expensive labor can produce goods more cheaply and efficiently. This not only contributes to economic progress in those countries, but the resulting, less expensive goods are then more affordable not merely to rich post-industrial populations, but also to people in developing societies.
- Bubbles will always be a part of capital markets because they reflect not markets but human nature. What is important is not that America experienced a bubble market in the late 1990s, but that the bubble was quickly and relatively painlessly punctured—demonstrating the relative efficiency of the US markets and the resilience of the economy.[43]

---

40 Judis, op. cit., note 38.

41 Op. cit., note 20.

42 Phillips, op. cit., note 20, p. 389 ff.

43 The bursting of the bubble certainly caused pain to the investors who caused it, but that is as it should be. The point is that the market collapse had relatively little long-term impact on the American economy. Indeed, the bubble market collapse of the late 1990s led to the mildest American recession of the twentieth century. By contrast, the "tulipmania" bubble (1636–37) so devastated the economy of Holland that the country entered into a generation-long economic recession and stock markets were banned in Holland for half a century.

- Yes, America exports capital, but that capital is used by less developed economies to build economic capacity, reducing global poverty and, ultimately, enlarging the markets for American goods and services—in addition to making the world a safer, more just and more stable place.
- The "cheap foreign labor" that America imports (legally and quasi-illegally[44]) doesn't stay cheap very long. Within a few generations, immigrants, like those who came before them, tend to become productive citizens even by Phillips' narrow standards.
- I have already addressed the inequality of income and wealth in America—it is not the size of the disparity that matters, but the absolute level of affluence of the non-wealthy, as well as the ability of the non-wealthy to become rich.
- I have also briefly addressed the delicate issue of war. It is undoubtedly true that a warmongering America bent on world domination by military might would present a serious and undoubtedly effective means of engineering our ultimate decline. But that is a far different America from the one that stands vigilant over the free world, its vigor as the world's wealthiest and most powerful country undiminished, very much as though it were still a youthful, struggling country, rather than the world's oldest government.[45]

Similarly, we hear virtually every day about other evidence of our decline. Not long ago, for example, a friend pointed out to me that the average Japanese high school math student would rank in the top 1% of American high school math students. This is certainly an alarming statistic (if true), but there is a problem with such statistics—namely, that we have been hearing them year-after-year

44 Illegal immigrants have so often been granted legalized status that the phrase "illegal immigrant" has little meaning.

45 The issue of American unilateralism in the early twenty-first century is sometimes evoked as evidence of an American arrogance that will precipitate our decline. This is a serious issue, but the conclusions of most commentators strike me as alarmist. My own view is that unilateralism is not a permanent characteristic of American policy, but simply a natural reaction to the ineffectiveness of multilateral action in the Balkan conflict, in Iraq, in North Korea and elsewhere. If international cooperation in the rebuilding of Iraqi civil society after the 2003 invasion proves successful, that alone is likely to reduce inclinations toward unilateralism on the part of the US.

since at least Sputnik,[46] and, so far, at least, America has only become ever more dominant. (Indeed, the society whose educational prowess was so superior to ours in 1957 no longer exists.) A well-educated population is certainly a useful thing to have, but as in so much of life it isn't "what you've got," but "what you do with what you've got" that matters. A truly uneducated America would undoubtedly be a recipe for disaster. But a reasonably well-educated America motivated to deploy every ounce of its competitiveness is an unstoppable juggernaut.

There are, in other words, conditions that could cause America to begin an inexorable decline into mediocrity, and it would be interesting and instructive to consider what those conditions might be. But Phillips' (and others') focus on the specific conditions of the distant past, rather than on the effect of those conditions, has led the pundits far astray. Indeed, many of the conditions that were symptoms of decline in past civilizations are now, given the dramatic change in economic and political conditions, symptoms of continued vigor.

American Distinctiveness and Private Wealth

Which raises again the crucial point: how is it that America has avoided becoming a providential society? Surely we are affluent enough that, long ago, we ought to have begun building post-industrial walls around our prosperity, ought to have begun to fear progress, competition, to worry more about losing what we have than about producing ever more; we ought to have reduced our military spending and avoided confrontations that might endanger the lives of our citizens. America ought, in short, to have led the headlong rush into providentiality, but we haven't. Well past two centuries old, America acts more like a young economic stallion, posting economic productivity numbers that look suspiciously like those of emerging economies, demanding ever more, not less, competitiveness from our corporations, expecting ever smarter work, ever longer hours, from our workforce. And no one on earth has the slightest doubt that, when freedom is attacked, America will respond swiftly and massively, and that the cost in dollars—and, unfortunately, in lives—will be paid as necessary.

Far from succumbing to providentiality, America, even in the minds of its detractors, seems if anything to have evolved too much in the opposite direction: we are too aggressive, too independent-minded, too bold, "interventionist

---

46 For those of my readers who are too young to remember, Sputnik 1 was a Soviet satellite that successfully achieved an earth orbit in October of 1957. Sputnik launched the Space Age, beating America into space and inaugurating the first of the long succession of lamentations about the poor quality of American scientific and technical education.

bullies with no regard for the sovereignty of [other] countries."[47] America, it is argued, ought to grow up, to settle into a kind of sociopolitical middle age, to become softer, more malleable, more predictable. This is, after all, what has happened in every other advanced post-industrial free market democracy. Why hasn't it happened in the United States?

Continuing American vigor is accounted for principally by the ongoing competitive spirit that animates a society in which virtually anyone can become rich by doing something spectacularly useful for the broader society. If that spirit were to become constrained by political or cultural mechanisms, America would rather quickly come to resemble its European cousins. In order for the lure of wealth to be meaningful, America must be willing to tolerate the consequences of competition, including the possibility that some people will lose in that competition and *including the possibility that some people will become very wealthy*.

Most free market economies long ago placed serious constraints on the ability of citizens to prosper. In effect, these societies have said, "Up to this point we want you to work hard and work smart, to ensure that our society remains competitive. But beyond this point we want you to stop working hard and working smart, and if you don't we will confiscate the fruits of your labors." However well-motivated this approach might be, it simply can't work. One reason it can't work is because the truly spectacular ideas that drive civilization and that lead to dominance are invariably snuffed out by economies that confiscate wealth above a certain point.

More fundamentally, no society can know at what point the tradeoff between the desire to "eliminate the rich elite" begins to conflict with the desire to remain competitive. Sure, we could go ahead and place Bill Gates and Warren Buffett into the category of "Evil Rich to be Liquidated." But what about Dan and Eve Eckels, who used their (paltry) life savings to organize the Eckels Steel Fabricating Co. in 1950 and sold it for $45 million in 1998? Eckels Steel Fabricating Co. didn't have anything like the impact on national productivity and competitiveness that Microsoft had. But the Eckels Co. did have an important impact on competitive conditions in its own industry (which is why it flourished), and, while there is only one Microsoft, there are thousands of Eckels.

The fact is that constraining the fruits of hard and smart work have the same effect on a society as blowing up a balloon that has a hole in the other end. Competitive societies recognize the contributions of the Bill Gateses of the world by showering them with billions of dollars, and competitive societies

---

[47] William Safire, *Myth America 2002*, New York Times, July 8, 2002, p. A21.

recognize the contributions of the Dan and Eve Eckleses of the world by showering them with millions of dollars. And so on in a seamless parade of extraordinary contributions to remarkable contributions to useful contributions to no contributions to negative contributions.

It is only a kind of shorthand, therefore, to say that America dominates other free market economies because of the contributions of wealthy families to its competitive spirit. The profuse creation of private capital through the intense pursuit of the best business ideas is what distinguishes America from other capitalist systems. The possibility of becoming wealthy motivates millions of Americans to take risks and to work harder than they would otherwise be inclined to do—and than they would do if they lived in other countries.

Moreover, the competitive spirit that animates the most successful Americans creates a culture that is internalized by almost all Americans, even those who have virtually no chance of becoming wealthy. In an open society, citizens will eventually internalize the values that they observe to be legitimate and valuable.[48] If a society claims that it wishes its citizens to be competitive, but then discourages the pursuit of wealth (via taxation or cultural disapproval, for example), citizens in that society will internalize not the message to be competitive but the message not to be too competitive. As the most successful people in America become rich, other citizens observe the legitimacy of that activity and its value to themselves, and they internalize the competitive spirit that led to those riches. At length, all of American society is permeated with the spirit of hard work, smart work, competition, and progress. Other societies can only watch in astonishment.

* * *

If the sheer economic vigor of a society were the sole measure of its success, that would be the end of the story. We could all see clearly that America's economic success is driven by the wealth creation process, and that the possessors of that wealth are the key to understanding American competitiveness. But the lure of wealth and its impact on economic vigor is only half the story. The other half is the creative use of private capital after it has been earned. Let's turn to that subject in Chapter 2.

48 In a closed society, citizens can be taught to internalize almost any values, however venal. North Korea is a case in point.

One

Chapter 2

Creative Capital

It is as impossible for a society to be formed and lasting without self-interest as it would be to produce children without carnal desire or to think of eating without appetite.
—Voltaire, On the *Pensées* of Pascal (1734)

It is not enough that an economic system be successful economically. American-style capitalism has astonished the world, to be sure. But if we really want to observe a powerful economy in action, we need only look at the Soviet Union between 1917 and 1935. In barely a generation, Soviet-style communism transformed a backward, peasant, agrarian society into the second largest economy in the world, an economic triumph that seems unlikely to have been surpassed by any nation in history.

The trouble with the Soviet system was that it was not a morally legitimate form of social organization. It could be sustained only by the extravagant use of state power to maintain an entrenched elite. Tens of millions of Soviet citizens would die to accomplish the remarkable economic outcomes produced by the USSR, the Soviet natural environment would be destroyed, human freedoms would be eliminated, and the moral nature of Soviet citizens would rot. Held in check by American military might for seven decades, the Soviet Union would eventually implode.

The lesson of the USSR, and of the decline of many other once-powerful civilizations, is that, ultimately, it is the moral basis of a society that matters. Remarkable as the accomplishments of the American free market might be, those accomplishments would not have persisted unless Americans in particular, and other citizens of the world in general, perceived the American system to be operating on a legitimate ethical basis. Human beings are both economic and moral creatures—that is, we are both selfish and selfless—and the organization of successful societies must recognize and nourish both aspects of our being. Thus, to fully understand the role of private capital in America's success, it is necessary to take a small detour and—briefly!—examine the moral dimension of capitalism.

A (Brief) Moral History of Capitalism

Even those few of my readers who have studied economic theory or the history of economics probably studied them long ago and not entirely voluntarily. As a result, names like Adam Smith have a musty scent to them, suggesting something that happened long ago and far away and that couldn't have much relevance to 21st century America. Whatever capitalism might have meant in the early days before the Industrial Revolution, we think, surely it means something quite different today. But in fact the fundamental tenets of market theory are as profoundly important to modern economies as they were profoundly important to economies two or three centuries ago.

And what is of central importance today, as it was three hundred years ago, is the *moral* character of capitalism. Serious critiques of the effectiveness of market economies versus other forms of economic organization have almost completely disappeared, buried by the stunning success of capitalism. To argue, early in the 21st century, that some other system might produce superior economic results would be to mark ourselves as serious ideologues. But moral critiques of capitalism have always been with us, and probably always will be. It simply can't be denied that market economies are designed in part to appeal to aspects of human nature that don't exactly represent our proudest moments. If human beings weren't selfish, weren't inclined to be lazy, didn't instinctively mistrust anyone outside our own families, didn't love power and luxury—well, in that case other, gentler, more charming economic systems would certainly be preferable.

Nor can it be denied that capitalism forces wrenching changes in traditional ways of life. If the craft guilds of Germany couldn't compete with the vast new industrial enterprises in England, the craft guilds would disappear, and along with them would disappear an entire, traditional way of life. If family farms in the American Midwest can't compete with "factory" farms, family farms will disappear, and along with them will disappear hundreds of small towns that once represented the backbone of America. To argue that nothing is lost in such transitions would be harsh, indeed.

Finally, capitalism always and everywhere results in unequal economic outcomes, with some citizens becoming remarkably wealthy while others remain poor and most end up in middle income categories.

But it is possible to mount a thoughtful defense of the moral properties of capitalism, and it is useful to remind ourselves of this fact. Indeed, virtually all the early proponents of market economies were drawn to them *precisely because they were perceived to be morally superior to other systems.* Let's briefly focus on this moral dimension of free market systems.

The Ancients

The more men value moneymaking,
the less they value virtue.
—Plato, *Republic* (quoting Socrates)

Do not lay up for yourselves treasures on earth,
for where your treasure is, there will your heart be also.
—Jesus, *Sermon on the Mount*

We could go on and on with anti-capitalist quotes from the ancients ("It is easier for a camel to pass through the eye of a needle than for a rich man to enter into the Kingdom of Heaven," etc.) From Greek and Roman times through the Late Middle Ages, the world was burdened by the notion that whatever wealth existed was fixed and immutable. Only in heaven could riches be created anew, and then only by God Himself. Therefore, if one man enriched himself, another man must inescapably become poorer. In such a world any sort of market activity would naturally be considered immoral:[49] "*Si unus non perdit, alter non acquirit.*"[50]

By the 12th century, however, modern-style cities had begun to appear, commerce began to thrive, and even a hidebound Church hierarchy could not

49 In a sense, these societies can be viewed as profoundly hypocritical. The Greek ideal could not abide trade or commerce, and yet the Greeks could not even feed themselves without importing vast amounts of grain. See Paul Rahe, *Republics Ancient and Modern: Classical Republicanism and the American Revolution* (Univ. of North Carolina Press, 1992), especially chapter 3, "The Political Economy of Hellas." In the quote from the *Republic*, Socrates was speaking to and thinking of that tiny fraction of the Greek population that were free citizens, ignoring the fact that those citizens could avoid participating in commerce only because all their material needs were provided by slaves.

50 St. Augustine (354-430); essentially, "If no one loses, then no one gains."

fail to notice the dramatic improvement in the condition of men. The Church was thus faced with a serious dilemma. On the one hand, commercial activity was clearly a profound social good. On the other hand, all the Church's founding documents and theories—written when the world was a more static place—had heaped scorn on this very activity. Thus began a slow and careful "reinterpretation" of Church gospel, led by such thinkers as Thomas Aquinas. Aquinas and other Scholastics marshaled religious arguments for the social necessity of private property, concluding that market systems themselves were morally neutral and their consequences socially beneficial, and focusing their scorn only on characteristic abuses of commercial activity, such as dishonesty, sharp dealing, fraud and, of course, usury.

Indeed, nowhere was the struggle to accommodate religion to capitalism more complex and strained than on the question of usury. The lending of money at interest had always been a mortal sin—had not Jesus himself cleared the temple of moneylenders? Yet commerce could not flourish without the willingness of people with capital to lend it to people with productive ideas. The Lateran Council had banned usury in 1139—right in the teeth of the early growth of commerce and hence the need for loans. In effect, the Church had agreed that wealth in general was not a fixed commodity, but rather something that could be created by the efforts of men. The earlier, static notions now clung only to the object of money itself, which was considered sterile and incapable of growth—money does not beget money. This final dilemma was resolved not theologically, but by the expedient of creating a monopoly for Jews, who dominated moneylending for centuries.[51]

Moral Arguments for Capitalism[52]

Voltaire. By the time *The Wealth of Nations* appeared in 1776, capitalist economies had already flourished for more than a century. Hence Smith and his fellow "economists"[53] were not speculating about a type of political economy that might prove fruitful—they were describing and praising a system

---

51 It was not only the Jews who practiced moneylending, however. Famous figures like Voltaire himself found ways to lend large sums of money, especially to the royal houses, through the ruse of "donations" made in return for a lifetime stream of payments.

52 Much of my argument in this section of the book follows the fascinating account of Jerry Z. Muller, *The Mind and the Markets* (Alfred A. Knopf, 2002).

53 The notion of economists as a separate profession did not exist in the 18th century. Adam Smith was a professor of moral philosophy.

that had existed for many decades and that had proved itself remarkably adept at improving the condition of men and women.

Well before *The Wealth of Nations* appeared, the earliest and most prominent proponent of capitalism was Voltaire, who had moved to England in the 1720s to escape persecution by the French Catholic Church and government. The first public intellectual in the modern sense of the word, Voltaire was immeasurably impressed by the accomplishments of the market economy that had transformed the lives of ordinary people in Britain. Compared to the traditional French, the population of England was better dressed, better fed, and better housed. Material objects that the English considered no more than absolute necessities were still almost unknown among the mass populations on the Continent.

But what really captured Voltaire's attention was the moral impact of capitalism. He had been appalled by the almost continuous warfare on the Continent, the dreadful political machinations of the Church and the royal parties, the religious zealotry that dominated every aspect of society. Such strife had seemed to be inherent in the human condition. Say what you will, Voltaire pointed out, men will act, and the only question is whether their energy will be directed toward discord and chaos or toward more constructive ends. For Voltaire, the great thing about the market economy of Britain was that the extraordinary energy of men was put to work constructively. Not only was human energy absorbed by the pursuit of wealth through commerce, but the outcome of that pursuit was the improvement of the condition of all men, not just those who proved most successful in the competition. Referring to the London Stock Exchange, Voltaire observed, "Here the Jew, the Mohametan and the Christian deal with one another as if they were of the same religion, and reserve the name 'infidel' for those who go bankrupt."[54]

Voltaire met head-on the charge that capitalism relied on selfishness, while a stable social order must be based on altruism. Blaise Pascal had powerfully argued this point, writing, "Each of us tends toward himself. That is against all order. We must tend toward the whole; and the tendency toward self-interest is the beginning of all disorder in war, in government, in economy, etc."[55] Absent a market economy to channel the self-interest of men, Pascal was probably correct. But in the context of capitalism, self-interest was transformed from a source of unrest to a source of concord and progress.

---

[54] Voltaire, *Philosophical Letters* (1734), quoted in Muller, *The Mind and the Markets*, op. cit., note 52, p. 35.

[55] From Pascal's *Pensees*, quoted in Muller, *The Mind and the Markets*, op. cit., note 52, p. 35.

One key problem with the pursuit of self-interest in a free market economy was that it clashed with medieval and religious notions of "luxury." One person's luxury is, of course, another person's necessity—better yet, an earlier generation's luxury is almost always, in market societies, a later generation's necessity. But in the later 17th and early 18th centuries, luxury was a charged word. Static notions of social order reserved luxury goods for the upper echelons of society—royalty and the aristocracy. For the masses to aspire to material wellbeing wasn't viewed as a natural, human inclination, but as a dangerous threat to social and religious order. Instead, Church and State encouraged monkish "virtues" such as self-denial and asceticism.

Voltaire attacked these static ideas, and glorified the struggle for material well-being, in his controversial poem "The Worldling," and its successor, "The Defense of The Worldling." The first poem—published in Paris without Voltaire's permission—caused him to flee France again, this time to Russia (where he wrote "The Defense of the Worldling"). Centuries before Abraham Maslow developed his "hierarchy of needs," Voltaire asserted in these poems that prosperity was an absolute prerequisite to the progress of civilization. Voltaire even defended the "conspicuous consumption" (as we would call it) of the affluent, pointing out that demand for luxury goods increased the need for labor, which ultimately improved the lives of the non-affluent.

In short, Voltaire correctly saw capitalism as the only serious antidote to anti-rational forces such as religious zealotry and absolutist governments, forces that had led to constant strife and warfare. Capitalism worked its magic, undermining extremist, anti-human forces, by refocusing the attentions and energies of people into constructive, rather than destructive, activities. As the pursuit of those constructive activities raised the material welfare of the population, people began to see themselves not as helpless victims of larger forces, but as serious, independent actors, responsible for their own fate. They became far less susceptible to extreme forms of thought, religious or otherwise, and far less tolerant of being dictated to by arbitrary governments.

Adam Smith. We tend to think of *The Wealth of Nations*—then and now the finest book ever written about market economies—as a dry economic text. But it was not so perceived by Smith's contemporaries, who made the book an instant sensation and Smith an instant celebrity. Much of Smith's book is devoted to a brilliant analysis not just of what free markets can accomplish, but precisely how and why such accomplishments occur. Smith spoke not just at the level of economic theory, but at the level of the factory floor. He described in detail how the individual self-interest of workers led to greater productivity, how the division of labor allowed production to increase geometrically without longer hours or harder work. He demonstrated over and over again how capitalism rewarded efficiency, and how efficiency drove living standards.

Smith was a Scot, and he lived at a time when he could not fail to be impressed by the differences in conditions between the north and south of Scotland. In the Lowland industrializing cities of Glasgow and Edinburgh, market forces had so rapidly improved living standards that ordinary workers could, for the first time in human history, support their families on one job. In the backward Northern Highlands, however, the primitive clan culture still dominated, local chiefs wielded absolute power,[56] market forces had not yet penetrated, and the population lived in medieval conditions.

But mere material progress was not what really impressed Smith. A Professor of Moral Philosophy at the University of Glasgow, he was far more impressed with the ethical progress that capitalism promoted among the population. Pre-capitalist societies were marked by superstition, a conviction of powerlessness, suspicion of anyone outside the family, an indolence that had to be overcome by force.[57] But populations subject to market forces quickly developed a far different character. Citizens developed behaviors characterized by fundamental decency: nonviolence, prudence, openness to the opinions of others, the ability to postpone gratification and to work for long-term objectives. These were, perhaps, modest enough virtues. But compared to the condition of men in pre-capitalism societies, they were cause for celebration.

Capitalism, Smith argued, encouraged good behavior because, in a market society characterized by trade and exchange, each person was dependent on others. This dependency was utterly unlike the dependence of a serf on the protection of his lord. It was a dependency of equals on equals, intermediated by the use of cash as the medium of exchange. Thus, if I treat people fairly and deliver value, people will treat me fairly in return and my living standards will rise. If I don't treat people fairly, they won't treat me fairly in return—indeed, they will refuse to deal with me at all—and I will therefore fail in my endeavor to improve conditions for myself and my family. For Adam Smith then, what Muller calls the "moral balance sheet" of capitalism[58]—its dependence on innate selfishness on one side of the ledger, versus its ability to improve living conditions and the quality of human interaction—fell solidly into the black.

---

[56] Following the Jacobite rebellions that consumed Scotland between 1708 and 1746, the British government forced the breakup of the clan system in the Highlands. But what replaced the clans was not capitalism, but chaos.

[57] These are, of course, precisely the conditions that continue to dominate societies that have not adopted free market systems.

[58] Muller, op. cit., note 52, page 72.

What organized religion had failed to do for thousands of years, capitalism had succeeded in doing in a few decades, namely, enabling masses of people to live "a morally decent existence."[59]

Hegel. Adam Smith published *The Wealth of Nations* roughly half a century after Voltaire moved to England and began his observations of the British market economy. Half a century after Smith's book appeared, the moral character of capitalism was taken up in turn by Georg Wilhelm Friedrich Hegel, the German philosopher who was perhaps the most influential thinker of the 19th century (at least, now that Marxism[60] is largely dead). The moral attraction of capitalism, for Hegel, lay in its ability to reify the dignity of men without resort to some higher power. In the *Philosophy of Right* (1820), and especially in the student lectures that preceded and followed publication of the book, Hegel contrasted the failure of the French Revolution with the success of capitalism.

Hegel pointed out that the leaders of the revolution had failed because they had profoundly misunderstood the nature of liberty, considering all institutions to be impediments to human freedom. In fact, freedom cannot exist, cannot have any meaning, outside the context of institutions that are broadly accepted by members of society. If someone asserts, "I am a separate and independent person, fully entitled to all the dignity of a free man," what can that mean? What are the characteristics of such a freedom? Where does it begin and end? Absent an acknowledgement from the rest of society, such a person is not really free but only, at best, a deluded slave and, at worst, a madman.

The great thing about capitalism for Hegel was that its institutions—especially private property, the sanctity of contracts, and the need for citizens of market societies to engage in mutually beneficial trade and exchange—reify men's assertions of their separate existence, their dignity, their freedom.[61]

---

[59] Muller, op. cit., note 52, page 76.

[60] Marx was one of the so-called "leftwing" followers of Hegel, part of a group of atheists who accepted Hegel's historical dialecticism but replaced Hegel's philosophical idealism with materialism. They were contrasted with the "rightwing" Hegelians, who found Hegel's thinking to be consistent with Christian beliefs and who tended to be politically orthodox. In addition to Marxism, Hegel's work profoundly influenced phenomenology and, via Kierkegaard, existentialism.

[61] Throughout Hegel's philosophy runs the argument that human states of mind remain stable only when their abstractness is manifested outside themselves in some concrete way—in material objects, in rules of social and organizational conduct, in social patterns. Possession of property, and the recognition by others in society that this particular property is ours, is an important external reinforcement of our sense that we are separate individuals with our own wills and our own dignity.

When a person asserts, "This is my property, no one can take it from me except with my consent and for value delivered," it may not have the same noble ring as the assertion of freedom, but in fact it is a far more profound and meaningful affirmation. Because other members of society acknowledge the institutions of private property and fair exchange—not out of some abstract benevolence, but because it is in their own interests to do so—the assertion has meaning and permanence. And because the institutions that grow up in market economies—courts, for example—define the meaning and limits of concepts such as private property, contracts, and what constitutes fair trade, there is broad understanding of and agreement about what those concepts signify.

In the Hegelian market economy, then, citizens achieve their dignity not via supplication to some higher power (a lord, the State, the Church) but by what amounts to common consent. The morality of property arises out of this common consent: men in market economies are equal, despite the fact that wealth outcomes will differ, because they are mutually acknowledged to be equal in dignity.

Contemporary discussions. Modern discussions of the ethical nature of capitalism have strayed far from the realities of the lives of human beings, tending to turn on complex philosophical concepts such as "freedom" versus "unfreedom."[62] Perhaps this was a natural response to the horrific reality of Communism under Stalin and Mao—real-world free market societies proved to be so clearly morally superior to real-world Marxist societies that the discussion could continue at all only at a theoretical level far removed from our actual experience.

Nonetheless, what all the critiques of the moral basis of capitalism have in common is their scorn for the market's focus on mankind's selfish instincts; their concern about capitalism's tendency to pull down traditional societies; and, of course, the unequal economic outcomes that occur in market economies. The defenses of capitalism respond by noting that the market's focus

---

62 This happens to be the formulation of the Marxist philosopher G. A. Cohen. In other words, while it may be true that everyone in a capitalist society has the opportunity to become wealthy, since we know that only a small percentage actually will become wealthy, the opportunity is illusory: it's not a freedom but an "unfreedom." See G. A. Cohen, *Self-Ownership, Freedom, and Equality* (Cambridge University Press, 1995). The trouble with such discussions, aside from their eerie other-worldliness, is that they don't particularly distinguish capitalist societies from other kinds of societies. Since no one in a Marxist society is allowed to become wealthy, it is difficult not to view that also as an "unfreedom."

on selfish instincts is simply a realistic view of the dual nature of humankind; that traditional societies restrict the ability of people to achieve their full potential; and that unequal outcomes are acceptable in capitalist societies because the *average* outcome is far higher than in other economic communities.

* * *

What keeps the moral balance of capitalism in the positive zone is this emphasis not on what capitalism does for successful capitalists, but what capitalism does for the rest of society—"the greatest good for the greatest number." Thus, let's ask ourselves the following question. We know (see Chapter 1) that private capital is at the very center of the remarkable success of the spectacularly vigorous American version of capitalism. But what is the moral argument for private capital once it has been earned and is no longer contributing directly to economic progress, no longer building new companies?

That capital is now likely to be invested passively, in portfolios consisting mainly of stocks and bonds. It might be invested wisely (see Chapters 3 through 17) or unwisely. What role does this capital play? This is, after all, the wealth that supports the lifestyles of generations of members of wealthy families, most of whom had nothing to do with the hard work of earning the wealth in the first place. Is it simply a deadweight on the American polity, an unfortunate legacy of an otherwise useful capitalist economy? Or is it perhaps a neutral element, supporting the economy's need for capital,[63] but not contributing anything of a positive nature?

My conclusion is that it is neither. This wealth—what I will call "creative capital"—is deployed in ways that enrich human lives far more than any other civil institution anywhere in the world. Creative capital—capital that has already been earned and that is being stewarded either by the founders or by subsequent generations[64]—is so critical because it is used overwhelmingly to support ideas. Ideas drive the destiny of mankind and capital is the essential nourishment that allows ideas to flourish.

---

[63] Capital invested in Treasury securities supports the government's borrowing needs. Capital invested in corporate bonds supports the borrowing needs of corporate enterprises. Capital invested in equity securities supports the equity base of corporations, providing long-term growth capital and allowing them to borrow money as necessary (from banks or via the bond markets).

[64] As I note elsewhere, this capital might still be in private hands or it might be held in the form of a charitable foundation or a nonprofit endowment. But all these holding structures trace back to the original wealthy families who deployed their capital so creatively.

Having money available to people and institutions with interesting ideas is important in two ways. First, an idea that can't be deployed, that can't be implemented or tested, is an idea that is useless to society. But it costs money to test a new idea, whether that idea is for a new business, a new arts organization, or a new intellectual journal. Creative capital supplies that money. Second, the knowledge that money is available to support new ideas encourages ideas to be generated—creative capital acts like rainwater in the desert, encouraging that proliferation of ideas in all fields of human endeavor that is so characteristic of American society.

Let's take a look at how creative capital works and why it is so central to American preeminence in so many fields wholly unconnected to business competitiveness.

Creative Capital in America

Invention is the mother of necessity.[65]

The worst way to organize an economy is for the central government to amass all the capital—by taxing its citizens heavily or by owning all enterprises itself—and then for that government to decide how the capital will be deployed. The Soviet Union paid with its life for its stubborn commitment to a centrally planned economy, and Maoist China was headed down the road to the same hell in the same handbasket until Mao's successors, terrified by what was happening to the USSR, began to convert their centrally planned economy to a more capitalist-oriented economy. On a smaller scale, the economies (and, to a considerable extent, the societies) of Cuba, much of Central and South America, and most of Africa were destroyed by top-down economic systems.

The best way to manage an economy is to allow it to manage itself as freely as is possible without tolerating monopoly profits or other forms of illegal or predatory activity. In such a society, decisions about the use of capital—before and after it has been earned—will be pushed down as far as they can go. In terms of the deployment of wealth after it has been earned, those decisions are made in the US at the individual wealthy family level. Wealthy families are, by definition, the only ones who possess "excess" capital, that is, wealth far beyond what will be needed to provide comfortable lives for themselves.[66]

---

[65] David Owen, *Copies in Seconds* (Simon & Schuster, 2004), referring to the invention of the plain paper copier.

[66] Middle income families, by contrast, have "savings," capital that is not needed today, but that is expected to be needed by those families in the future.

The effectiveness with which a society deploys its privately accumulated capital will in important part determine its competitive success against other societies. This is nothing more than a special case—though a very important one!—of the rule that the most successful societies will be those which most effectively maximize the talents and capabilities of their citizens. Private capital, in other words, is one of the important competitive strengths of a nation, like extensive natural resources, a democratic political system, or the vigor of its population.

Creative capital in America is a force for vitality, change, and competition in virtually every aspect of American society, from the arts to the academy to intellectual leadership to the formation of new businesses—in short, for every worthwhile endeavor that cannot support itself financially *ab initio*, if ever. We tend to recognize the role of private capital in philanthropy, but it is worth repeating: no arts or cultural organization,[67] no institution of higher education (or lower education, for that matter),[68] no journal of ideas, no small press,[69] nor most other worthwhile social and cultural activities[70] are able to support themselves financially without the assistance of charitable contributions.

All these activities depend on the existence of private capital and the willingness of the owners of that capital to put it at risk by supporting those activities. I say "at risk" both because there is rarely any assurance that philanthropic dollars will be used effectively, but also because it is often the case that support for cultural, intellectual and educational activities winds up being support for individuals and ideas that are hostile to everything that allows private capital to be

---

67 If a cultural organization is able to cover half its budget from "earned" income (ticket and gift shop sales, for example), it is doing pretty well. At one US "top ten" symphony, the average ticket price for a performance is between $50 and $60. But the actual all-in cost of putting on that performance is *eight times* that much. The balance is covered by private contributions—creative capital at work.

68 So-called "full-pay" students at private colleges, universities and prep schools are actually paying about half of what it actually costs to educate them. The same is true of public institutions, which are heavily subsidized by taxpayers and, increasingly, private donations.

69 Virtually every journal (whether on the political left, right, or center), virtually every small press in America is subsidized by wealthy backers, and when that backing is withdrawn they cease to exist, along with the ideas they espoused.

70 Notice that I did not mention religion, the one activity that is able to attract enough mass support to underwrite most of its costs. Even so, some wealthy churches and synagogues rely on periodic capital campaigns to finance buildings and other activities.

generated and deployed. This willingness to have the system constantly subjected to criticism and evaluation by its own dependents is one of the most astonishing things about vigorous free market democracies, and it is an aspect of the system that keeps it fresh and dynamic.

Most Americans are at least vaguely aware that our system of private philanthropy is dominated by wealthy families, but few realize just how dominant the role of those families is. There are roughly 280 million people in America. But 7% of all charitable giving—including middle class giving, which goes overwhelmingly to churches—comes from a mere 400 families. To save you from doing the math, this means that roughly 0.0002% of the people give 7% of the money. Looked at another way, the wealthy are roughly 36,000 times more important to American philanthropy than is the average American. And if we eliminate from the notion of private philanthropy any giving that goes to religious organizations—which accounts for the overwhelming proportion of middle class giving—the dominance of the wealthy would be vastly greater.

This phenomenon can also be demonstrated by looking at how American nonprofit organizations raise the capital necessary to fund their operations. Let's look specifically at a college that has decided to mount a $100 million capital campaign. Any fundraising professional could sit down and in five minutes draw us a "capital campaign giving pyramid" showing how many and what size contributions the college will have to raise to be successful in such a campaign. Specifically, the college would have to receive:

- 3 contributions of $10 million each
- 4 contributions of $5 million each
- 5 contributions of $2.5 million each
- 8 contributions of $1 million each
- 15 contributions of $500,000 each
- Many, many smaller contributions

We can easily do the math to see that contributions from wealthy donors will represent $78 million of the $100 million campaign. In other words, out of the thousands of contributions the college hopes to receive, only 35 really matter.[71] Indeed, unless and until the college receives about 60% of the total

[71] This isn't intended to be as elitist as it sounds. The support of thousands of small donors who are enthusiastic about the mission of the college is a good part of what justifies the campaign in the first place. In addition, of course, some smaller donations represent sacrificial gifts by donors with modest resources.

needed—probably from no more than a dozen people—it won't even announce the campaign publicly.

The point here is not that the wealthy are necessarily more or less generous than other citizens,[72] but simply that the American system of private philanthropy could not persist without the creative capital of the wealthy. Our vaunted philanthropic system would not just shrink—it would collapse altogether if creative capital ceased to exist.

Certainly we could raise taxes substantially and leave it to the central government to decide which cultural activities are deserving of support, which ideas should be backed and which extinguished, who should be educated and how, which religions are legitimate and which aren't. We could, but we don't, and as a result of the richness of the millions of individual decisions made by individual families, America dominates the world of arts and ideas, and its higher education system is not merely the envy of the world, it is the only higher education system globally that is worthy of the name.[73]

If for no other reason than this extraordinarily successful system of private charity, we ought all to care a very great deal about the quality of the stewardship of private capital in America. If we cease to allow private capital to be produced, or if we place serious constraints on how that capital can be spent, or if we allow the stewardship of private capital to be so poor that it withers or disappears, much of what makes America successful, and most of what makes the American version of capitalism so singular, will wither along with it.

Consider that at the very moment that Marxist doctrine was fueling the anger that led to the Russian Revolution, the wealthiest man in the world—Andrew Carnegie[74]—was giving away all his money. Carnegie was an extraordinary person in many ways, but he was hardly the exception that proves the rule. In other words, Carnegie was not a gentle, soft-hearted fellow who somehow managed, in

---

[72] The most recent data, gathered by the NewTithing Group, suggests that the rich give away roughly twice as much as less affluent people measured as a percentage of investable assets. But of course the rich can afford to give away more. See "The Generosity of Rich and Poor: How The Newly Discovered "Middle Rich" Stack Up," *NewTithing Group* (April 22, 2004).

[73] If the two best non-American universities in the world—Oxford and Cambridge—were suddenly transported to the US, they would rank roughly with one of our better public university systems, the University of Minnesota, let's say. Even today, it is virtually impossible for a talented poor or lower middle class student to be admitted to Oxcam.

[74] In 1901, Carnegie sold Carnegie Steel Company to a group led by J. P. Morgan for $250 million, forming the United States Steel Corporation.

competition with the most ruthless industrial captains in the world, to become the wealthiest living human. Carnegie was, in fact, a barracuda. Among other things, he was capable of ordering an end to the Homestead Steel Strike in 1892 no matter what the cost in lives,[75] then slipping out of the country so that the blame would fall on his friend and colleague, Henry Clay Frick.

Carnegie would turn out to be not an isolated example of extraordinary benevolence, but a role model for the millions of wealthy Americans who made their money in ways that benefited the society and then gave it away in ways that benefited the society yet again. Carnegie in effect invented the idea of creative capital, an idea that continues to be the definitive role of wealthy families in America to this day.[76] Bill Gates, for example, is now the wealthiest living American, and the William and Melinda Gates Foundation is America's largest grantmaking foundation. That foundation will, no doubt, get much larger when Gates dies. Warren Buffett, the second wealthiest American, has already announced plans to leave all his money to charity.

Carnegie, Rockefeller, Mellon, E. I. du Pont, Gates, and Buffett are examples of creative capital on a very grand scale, but, as we will see, there are innumerable examples of creative capital being deployed on a smaller, but still important, scale. Let's take a look at the role of creative capital in several spheres of American life by examining specific examples of important ideas that would not have survived but for the support of private capital.

Higher Education: The Case of St. John's College

In the 1930s, tiny St. John's College was an institution on the ropes. Founded way back in 1696—only Harvard and William and Mary are older—

---

[75] The violence was supplied by an army of Pinkerton detectives hired by Carnegie Steel Company, as well as members of the Pennsylvania National Guard. The workers' strike failed and the union was virtually destroyed. On Carnegie generally, see the compelling recent biography by Peter Krass, *Carnegie* (John Wiley & Sons, 2002).

[76] Creative capital barely exists in other free market democracies, even ones that seem very much like our own. As an amusing example of how different the philanthropic cultures of other free market democracies are, consider the request by a group of Canadian fundraising executives that the Canadian Federal government declare November 15 National Philanthropy Day (as in the US). The request was denied on the ground that, "the concept of philanthropy [is] too closely tied to money." See Ian MacLeod, "Philanthropy Day Too Rich for Canadians," Edmonton *Journal* (April 11, 2004).

by the middle of the Great Depression the College saw its enrollment declining, its small endowment rapidly disappearing, and its ancient physical plant crumbling. The College certainly would have disappeared altogether had not a group of radical educators, led by Scott Buchanan and Stringfellow Barr, arrived at St. John's and instituted an entirely new educational program. This program eliminated faculty departments, instituted an all-required curriculum heavy on math and science, built its courses around the classic works of Western Civilization, and taught its students in seminars, not lecture halls.

The intellectual seriousness of the St. John's approach landed like a mortar round in the increasingly feeble American university world. The new program, launched in 1937, very quickly challenged other colleges and universities to examine what they were about. While few institutions were likely to institute as rigorous a program of liberal education as St. John's, the College nonetheless established itself as the conscience of American higher education. Other institutions measured themselves against St. John's, almost always to their acute embarrassment.

But powerful and important as the idea of St. John's was, the College had a serious problem. Alumni of the "old" St. John's had little interest in the new program—as far as they were concerned, St. John's was now a completely different institution. And alumni of the "new" St. John's were few, young, and generally impecunious. In fact, when a new college is started, it takes roughly half a century for its alumni base to mature to the point where the college can count on support from that quarter. How was St. John's to bridge that 50-year gap?

The answer, of course, was creative capital, in this case largely in the person of Paul Mellon. Mellon had matriculated at St. John's after having already graduated from college, starting over as a freshman "to get the education I should have gotten at Yale." His new education was interrupted by World War II, but Mellon never lost interest in St. John's—or, more precisely, in the College's vision of what a liberal education could be. For three decades Mellon's financial support allowed the College to survive, and in several cases saved it from almost certain ruin.[77] And when Mellon finally handed the reins to younger patrons of the College—led by people like Stewart H.

---

[77] On the subject of the early decades of St. John's College under the new program, see the superb account of Charles A. Nelson, *Radical Visions: Stringfellow Barr, Scott Buchanan, and Their Efforts on Behalf of Education and Politics in the Twentieth Century* (Bergin & Garvey, 2001).

Greenfield[78]—the job of these younger supporters was not to save the College but to help it to flourish.

The ideas behind St. John's were not created by Mellon, Greenfield and the other patrons of the College, nor did they do the hard work of teaching and running the College. And yet, the idea that is St. John's—the idea that a serious liberal education can and should be offered to American young people—survived and flourished only because creative capital was available to support it.

Politics: The Conservative Resurgence

Not so long ago, the American Republican Party seemed destined for the garbage dump of history. Both houses of Congress were controlled by large Democratic majorities, virtually all state legislative houses were dominated by Democrats, moderate Republicanism—"Rockefeller Republicanism"—bored everyone stiff, and the one-note anti-Communism of the Goldwaterites had been soundly rejected by the broad voting public. Yet, within a few decades Republicans would control the House and Senate, most state legislatures, most governorships, and the entire American South, which had been Democratic (or Dixiecratic) for generations, would turn solidly Republican. What happened?

Many things happened, of course, but what mainly happened was that creative capital entered the political sphere on the side of the Republicans. Two individuals in particular—Joseph Coors and Richard M. Scaife—decided that the Republican party needed a whole bevy of new ideas, and they began quietly supporting young conservative thinkers wherever they could find them. At first, to be sure, they were decidedly hard to find—young Americans had been radicalized in the Sixties and most of them had nothing but scorn for Republicans in general and conservatives in particular. But Coors and Scaife, working largely independently, relied on a core group of "talent scouts" (mainly older conservative thinkers) operating at colleges from Dartmouth to Stanford. When a young man or woman showed promise, financial support was made available. Conservative (and neo-conservative) journals were launched with support from Coors, Scaife and others (most prominently, *The New Criterion*). New conservative think tanks were formed (the Heritage Foundation, and the

---

78 Though less well-known than Paul Mellon, Greenfield is a remarkable man in his own right. After graduating from St. John's in 1953, Greenfield built a career as a venture capitalist successful enough to make him a legend in that field. Apparently under the impression that that was not enough accomplishment for one lifetime, Greenfield then launched a highly successful hedge fund of funds, which he continues to manage with his partner, David K. Storrs.

Manhattan Institute, for example) and older think tanks (like the American Enterprise Institute and the Hoover Institution) were reinvigorated.

No single thing that Coors and Scaife did shook the world, but the mere existence of the creative capital they supplied encouraged more and more conservative thinkers to rise to the surface and to continue to think and publish and teach other thinkers.[79] Ultimately, their disciplined deployment of creative capital over a long period of time would revolutionize American politics and American political ideas, for better or worse.[80]

New Business Ideas: Venture Capital in America

In most circumstances, free market economies allocate capital through the mechanism of supply and demand. But how does capital get attracted to *new* ideas, that is, to the development and distribution of products and services that don't yet exist and for which there is, consequently, no demand, no supply, and hence no price? This is a critical question for an economy that wishes to be more than static, and it is the central question for an economy that wishes to lead the world in innovation, efficiency, growth and power.

When Bill Gates and his team began to mess around with something called Windows, for example, few of us owned computers or could imagine why we might want to. And those few of us who did own them were using DOS and were perfectly happy with it.[81] Gates figured that computers were the future, and that if massive numbers of people were going to use computers, something far simpler

---

[79] Although the giving capabilities of left-of-center foundations are roughly fifteen times the giving capabilities of right-of-center foundations, there are a few foundation funders of conservative ideas: the John M. Olin Foundation (which is in the process of liquidating), the Smith Richardson Foundation, and the JM Foundation, for example.

[80] I want to emphasize that I am not endorsing the ideas of the conservative wing of the Republican Party—or of any wing of any party. I am simply pointing out what a relatively small amount of creative capital, intelligently deployed, can accomplish.

[81] For those of my readers who are too young to remember the halcyon days of DOS (disk operating system), DOS commands were the language we used to communicate with our computers. DOS was, in effect, a piece of computer software that allowed us to control our computer hardware. Today, for example, if we want to backup a few files, it is the work of an instant. But in the good old days we would go to our DOS screen and type something like, "BACKUP a:[path][filename] a:[/S][/M][/A][/F:(size)] [/P][/D:date] [/T:time] [/L:[path]filename]." I'm being perfectly serious about this…

than DOS had to be developed. He turned out to be right, but he could easily have been wrong. Where did he get his early capital for this odd idea?

The answer is the venture capital industry—in its broadest sense—which has a much longer history in America than is generally supposed. When we think back to the period between about 1870 and 1930, we tend to think of the great Captains of Industry (or, depending on our point of view, the Robber Barons): Carnegie, Morgan, Ford, Rockefeller, and so on. These men accumulated vast fortunes[82] putting together the industrial enterprises that were required to meet the huge appetites of a rapidly industrializing United States. But, in retrospect, we can see that such figures could exist only during a brief period of time, a mere speck in the great sweep of history. Very quickly, the requirements for capital to build railroads, highways, steel mills, oil refineries, iron ore and coal mines, and other industries far outstripped the financial capacity of any one family. Only firms that could gain access to the *public* equity and debt markets could hope to continue to compete effectively. The Captains of Industry were, in effect, spectacular dinosaurs.

But something else was going on at about the same time that would persist far longer, namely, the support for new ideas and enterprises provided by wealthy individuals in the form of what we now think of as venture capital. The best known of these early venture capitalists was Andrew W. Mellon, then and now perhaps the greatest venture capitalist who ever lived. Mellon was one of the great industrial titans of the day (he controlled the Pennsylvania Railroad, for example), but he made his lasting impact on history through his support for new, startup enterprises. Operating from the platform of the family bank (then known as T. Mellon & Sons, now Mellon Financial Corp.), Mellon listened to many entrepreneurs pitch their ideas and when he found one he liked he backed the venture. Since these new enterprises were far too risky to justify a simple loan, Mellon took stock in the ventures as additional compensation.

Many of the new businesses failed, of course, but others grew into industrial behemoths that changed the landscape of American industry. Mellon's major venture capital successes included Gulf Oil Corporation, which rivaled Rockefeller's Standard Oil Co. for control of the world oil markets; ALCOA,

---

[82] As noted earlier, in 1901 Andrew Carnegie sold Carnegie Steel Company for $250 million, allowing J. P. Morgan and his group to form the United States Steel Corporation (now USX Corporation). At the time, United States Steel Corporation was the largest industrial enterprise ever formed, and Carnegie was the wealthiest man in the world.

founded by Charles M. Hall, the inventor of the process to convert alumina to aluminum, and then and now the world's largest producer of aluminum; Carborundum Company, founded by Edward Goodrich Acheson, the first manufacturer of synthetic abrasives, which were and are critical in the mining and extraction industries; and H. Koppers Company, founded by coke oven inventor Heinrich Kopper, which created an entire industry by transforming industrial waste into usable products such as gas, tar, and sulfur.

Beyond these spectacular and enduring venture capital successes, Mellon was also instrumental in the organization or growth of many other young enterprises, such as Standard Steel Car Co., McClintic-Marshall Co., Pittsburgh Coal Company, Pittsburgh Plate Glass (now PPG Industries), Crucible Steel Corp. and so on. Mellon also founded the Union Trust Company and, of course, dominated Mellon Bank. Other companies controlled by Mellon, or in which he exercised substantial influence, included Eastern Gas and Fuel Associates, Brooklyn Union and Brooklyn Borough Gas, Duke-Price Company, Pullman, Inc. (into which Mellon merged Standard Steel Car), Bethlehem Steel, United States Electric Power Corporation, United Light & Power, United Light & Railways, American Light and Traction, Westinghouse Electric Corp., Niagara Hudson Corporation, the Pennsylvania Railroad, the American Rolling Mill Company, and the Philadelphia Company, which controlled Pittsburgh's public utilities.[83]

Andrew Mellon's eye-popping success in his venture capital activities, and the lasting impact of his investments on the American economy, did not go unnoticed, and the venture capital industry as we know it today gradually evolved as other wealthy investors attempted to emulate Mellon's triumphs. As the industry matured, the players in the industry began to specialize, with some being responsible for identifying and nurturing new ventures (the general partners of venture capital partnerships), while others were responsible for providing the capital (the limited partners). For decades, these limited

---

83 This quiet "venture capital" activity contrasted strongly with the flamboyant activities of other industrialists of the day. Thus it was that despite Mellon's extraordinary success, and despite the fact that he had pioneered an investing technique that would prove far more lasting than those of the industrialist dinosaurs, Mellon remained largely unknown outside Pittsburgh until he was tapped by Warren Harding to be Secretary of the Treasury in 1921. Mellon served in that role under three successive Presidents—Harding, Coolidge, and Hoover. Late in life, Mellon gave his personal art collection, plus $10 million, to the United States to form the National Gallery of Art in Washington, DC.

partners were virtually all wealthy families. As the industry continued to mature, however, institutional investors got into the action.

Today, however, the well-known VC partnerships are not really in the business of backing true startups, which are far too risky for most of the institutional limited partners. In addition, startups don't require enough capital to attract the attention of major VC partnerships, which these days command hundreds of millions or even billions of dollars of capital. Instead, business startups in America[84] continue to be underwritten almost exclusively by creative private capital. Initially, entrepreneurs seek the earliest, smallest amounts of capital from the proverbial "friends and family" equity round: money is raised by maxing out the entrepreneurs' credit cards and by tapping the capital of wealthier friends, neighbors and family members. If all goes well, the fledgling business will seek out "angel" investors, wealthy individuals who enjoy backing and working with new businesses and with young (and not so young!) entrepreneurs.[85] The next step may be to send a business plan to one of the many regional venture capital funds that almost every sizeable city boasts. Only when the business has passed all these hurdles is it likely to find favor with one of the larger VC partnerships.

Thus it is that from the founding of the venture capital business to the support for new business ideas being developed today, the only source of capital is the "creative" private capital that is made available, and that can only be made available, by wealthy investors. But notice one very odd aspect of the use of creative capital: it almost never provides a satisfactory return on investment in the usual sense of the word. This is obvious in the case of private philanthropy—however happy we might be with our "investment" in a nonprofit organization, we will never receive a return on our investment in the traditional sense. Our "returns" will come to us in other, non-financial ways.

And the same is generally true of the use of creative capital in the sense of backing for new business enterprises. At the most mature level of the VC industry, it turns out that only a tiny fraction of the hundreds of VC partnerships—the so-called top-tier funds—will ever produce an investment return

---

84 I am not including the launch of thousands of traditional small businesses that are not intended to become big businesses. Most of these local enterprises are launched by "sweat equity" rather than true financial capital.

85 There are nearly 200 formally organized angel groups in the US, in addition to the thousands of individual angel investors. There is even a national association for angel investors, the Angel Capital Association, organized with the assistance of the Kauffman Foundation. See Tom Stein, "Angels or Devils?," *Venture Capital Journal* (April, 2004), p.30.

that truly compensates investors for the risks they are assuming.[86] And few investors will ever have the opportunity to invest with these top-tier firms. As we go down the VC ladder towards the regional venture capital partnerships,[87] to the activities of angel investors, to the hapless "friends and family" who are the reluctant backers of most true startups, we find that almost no one receives even a positive return, much less a return that could begin to compensate for the risks. Indeed, many VC angels can spend a lifetime backing startups and never hit a double, much less a home run. For every local angel who backs a Microsoft or a Yahoo!,[88] there are tens of thousands whose returns come, if at all, only in non-financial terms.

But, in both the case of private philanthropy and private venture capital, there is all the difference in the world between the return to the providers of the capital and the returns to society at large. The great good that accrues to society as the result of private charity and as the result of successful venture capital investments is obvious. But the same outcome results from the use of creative capital to back new business ventures that don't necessarily succeed in financial terms: the collective losses experienced by the providers of the capital are vastly—vastly—outweighed by the enormous good that redounds to society from these activities. Let's look at a few examples of how "unsuccessful" venture activities benefit society.

Missing the entrepreneur's second good idea. Many entrepreneurs have to cut their teeth on a venture or two before they get it figured out. After all, making a success of a startup enterprise is a complex undertaking, requiring a wide variety of skills, most of which aren't normally found in one individual. The backers of an entrepreneur's first idea will often lose everything and will be reluctant to touch the entrepreneur's second idea: once burnt, twice shy. Yet, it's often the second idea that proves successful, and it couldn't have happened without the learning experience of the first idea. Society is grateful for the backers of the first idea, but those backers lost their entire capital.

---

[86] This is not to say that most limited partners actually lose money investing in VC funds. It's just that the return, however satisfactory it might be in an absolute sense, doesn't justify the risks assumed.

[87] Most of these funds can be more accurately thought of as analogous to nonprofit, public service organizations, rather than to true investment vehicles. They tend to be established by general partners who simply enjoy working with new ventures, and tend to be capitalized by wealthy individuals who want to be sure that a source of local capital exists for local good ideas. While an odd regional VC fund or two will sometimes prove financially successful, most will have to measure their contributions in other ways.

[88] Google and Cisco Systems also got their start thanks to angel backing.

The idea that's ahead of its time. Many ideas are good ones at one point in history, but bad ones at another point. If an idea is too far ahead of its time, it will not be financially successful, and its backers will lose their capital. Later, society will resurrect the idea and put it to good use—but this will be too late for the creative capital providers of the earlier era.

The idea that pans out too late. Back in 1980, a group of young entrepreneurs launched a computer company in Wisconsin. The initial capital they needed was provided by a wealthy relative. The company puttered along for years, always just breaking even but never really flourishing. In the mid-1990s, the relative died, leaving his interest in the company to a favorite charity. In 1999, the company hit paydirt with a hugely successful software program. Everyone got rich except for the initial provider of the risk capital.

The idea that just breaks even. Imagine a startup company that raises seed capital, grows to a reasonable size, makes a smallish profit, and is eventually sold to a much larger company for a sum that, on a time-weighted basis, essentially allows the original backers to break even. The capital providers got their money back, but the opportunity costs to them were huge—they could have earned 10% per year just by buying an S&P 500 index fund. But think of the benefits to society that were provided—and continue to be provided—by this relatively "unsuccessful" investment: several hundred new jobs were created and the people who held those jobs gained important work experience; several million dollars worth of goods and services were purchased by the company and by the employees; taxes were paid by the company and its employees; the technology the company developed has been pushed forward and will be further developed by the company and others; the company continues to operate (under new ownership), so all those benefits will continue indefinitely; and so on. The company was not a good deal for the backers, but it was a great deal for the society that encouraged those backers.

The poor-returning idea that revolutionizes a field. Consider a firm that introduces a new idea into society. The idea is a good one and people adopt it readily. Alas, existing firms in that field are not brain-dead and they quickly adopt the same, or a similar, idea. The first firm never flourishes and its backers are disappointed in a financial sense. And yet, as far as the broader society is concerned, the world is a far better place (more efficient, less expensive, fairer, whatever) because of the activities of the poorly-returning, but visionary firm.

Bad ideas are useful, but not to the provider of the capital. Of course it is useful to a society for good ideas to receive backing and to be implemented. But it is also useful for societies to know that bad ideas are bad—no further time, energy or money need be expended in that direction. Hence, the backers of bad ideas are performing a service to society, albeit at their own cost.

We could continue with examples for many more pages, but you get the idea: there is no necessary relationship between the value of a new business venture to the creative capitalists who support it and the value of those ventures to society. America's economy would be as static as that of France or Germany (or as static as those economies would be if they weren't able to benefit from the new ideas developed in America) if it weren't for this incredible, versatile power of creative capital.[89]

Creative Capital and Vibrant Societies

Ideas drive civilization, and capital is the rocket propellant behind ideas. Therefore, societies that encourage the production of wealth and its creative deployment will be far better off, far more vibrant and resilient, than societies that discourage these activities.

In America, entrepreneurs are heroes, daring individuals who incur great personal risks to pursue ideas that will make America a better place. Most of them fail, suffering the consequences of their boldness without experiencing any of the rewards. But others quickly take their place, lured by hopes of wealth and by the availability of the creative capital that makes possible even the most Quixotic of dreams. Yet, how different matters are in most other free market democracies! Throughout most of Western and Northern Europe,[90] entrepreneurs are viewed as troublemakers, arrogant iconoclasts who care more about their own potential wealth than about the welfare of their fellow citizens. These are the individuals, after all, who are advocating ideas that may render existing businesses—and the cushy jobs they provide—obsolete.

Providential societies attempt to discourage entrepreneurship by taxing away most of the gains, by imposing crushing death duties that attempt to eliminate industrious families after one generation, and—most devastating of all—by developing cultures that discourage entrepreneurship, enterprise and innovation. Thanks to policies and cultural attitudes, little private capital is produced, and little of that can be used creatively. The ultimate result is the creation of calcified economies and, ultimately, calcified societies.

---

[89] A BankBoston study conducted in 1997 documented the extraordinary impact that one American institution (MIT) has had on the US economy: MIT faculty and alumni have founded more than 4,000 companies with global sales of $232 billion. The British government recently launched a partnership between MIT and Cambridge University (the Cambridge-MIT Institute) whose aim is to improve the dismal level of entrepreneurial activity in Britain.

[90] Britain, again, is something of an exception, but only since the Thatcher era (1979–1990).

Why Do Creative Capitalists Persist?

As I have noted, there is no financial return in the usual sense from the deployment of creative capital in philanthropic ventures, and very little in the deployment of creative capital in venture capital activities. Why, then, do creative capitalists persist in putting their money out in this way? The answer is undoubtedly complex, but I suggest that it has much to do with the peculiar conditions created by societies that are both capitalistic and democratic. Free market economies allow wealth to be created. Wealthy families in democratic republics internalize the ideals of democracy, of the dignity of every citizen, and behave accordingly. This creative use of capital after it has been earned validates the soundness of the American idea. American families who have become wealthy have richly deserved that wealth, enriching all our lives. But it is the ongoing deployment of private capital in creative ways that validates the moral acceptability of capitalism in America and that ensures the continued importance—indeed, the decisive importance—of wealthy families to America's sustained preeminence.

The Indispensable Nation

The distinct American version of free market democracy, with wealthy families at its indispensable center, is crucial not just for Americans, but for the world at large. And not just in ways that might immediately come to mind. Yes, American economic vigor, and the resulting gigantic market we represent to other economies around the world, is certainly the main engine of global economic growth and therefore the main hope for people everywhere for material improvement in their lives. Yes, American democracy is the most widely admired form of political organization in the world and therefore represents the main hope for freedom among people everywhere. And, yes, American military might is the main guarantor of peace globally and the main fear of despots everywhere; as well as—let's face it—the main source of fear even among our allies.

But my argument goes beyond these issues, important as they are. When former Secretary of State Madeleine Albright insisted that the United States was the world's one "indispensable nation," European statesmen engaged in paroxysms of sputtering outrage. But Albright was transparently correct. Let's examine why.

In the famous "Kantian paradox," Emmanuel Kant pointed out that the only solution to constant warfare among the aggressive and all-too-adjacent European powers was the creation of a world government. But since such a government would have to be all-powerful to enforce a "state of universal peace," the world government would represent a threat to human freedom far greater than even the Hobbesian world of brutal competition and international disorder that it was intended to replace.[91] Yet, today, most European leaders seem to feel that Europe has resolved this paradox, that the European Union and its associated institutions (the United Nations, the World Court, the Court of International Justice, etc.) have created, in Kagan's words, "a post-historical paradise of peace."[92] This "paradise" is contrasted starkly with the supposed mindset of the United States, which, it is argued, remains mired in a Hobbesian world where might makes right.

But like all paradises that are supposed to exist in a world of imperfect human beings, the European "paradise of peace" is a chimera, a frail orchid of a paradise that could not, and cannot, exist outside the protective American military hothouse. Europe is, indeed, at peace, and has been for more than half a century—a happy miracle, certainly, if not a paradise. But, as Kagan points out, peace in Europe was launched not by post-historical moral progress on the part of enlightened Europeans, but by the applied and brutal and sometimes morally ambivalent[93] use of historical military power by America in twice crushing an aggressive Germany. And European peace was further enabled by America's willingness to fund the rebuilding of Europe and to fund its military defense, especially against the USSR, leaving Europeans in the privileged, but hopelessly unrealistic, position of having little to worry about but getting along with each other.

If, at any moment during the Cold War, the US had withdrawn its military protection from Europe, the Red Army would have overrun the Continent in a few weeks, converting our enlightened European friends into inmates in a vast

---

[91] In this discussion, I am following the argument elegantly set forth in Robert Kagan's celebrated essay, "Power and Weakness," which appeared in June, 2002 in *Policy Review* (No. 113). Kagan expanded the article into his brief but powerful book, *Of Paradise and Power: America and Europe in the New World Order* (Alfred A. Knopf, 2003). Although my argument differs on several points from Kagan's, his article and book represent the best thinking on either side of the Atlantic on global power relationships following the collapse of the Soviet Union.

[92] Kagan, "Power and Weakness," ibid.

[93] The carpet bombing of German cities like Cologne and Dresden occurred because bombing technology was too imprecise for allied air forces to take out critical urban war plants without taking out entire cities. But it is certainly true that very little ethical hand-wringing took place over a strategy that was certain to, and did, lead to tens of thousands of civilian deaths and to painfully few military gains.

Stalinist gulag. Even today, if every other free market democracy on earth disappeared, the continuing existence of the United States would ensure that the candle of freedom would continue to burn, and to burn fiercely. But if the US disappeared, leaving all the other democracies intact, civilization would mount a deathwatch for human freedom.

European nations find themselves, in short, in the paradoxical position of having to be militarily weak in order to cooperate with each other. It's a paradox because, being weak, they are easy prey to aggressive nations who have very different (and, to European minds and our own, very much worse) visions of how societies should operate. In order to avoid being destroyed by such unpalatable societies, Europe must seek the protection of a country it identifies not with its own post-historical ethical vision, but with the very Hobbesian vision that led to all of Europe's problems, i.e., the United States.[94]

But what both Europeans and Americans seem to miss in this picture is that Europe and America, and free countries and countries struggling toward freedom everywhere, *already* exist in a world that bears at least a distant resemblance to Kagan's (and Kant's) "paradise of peace." In this ersatz version of paradise, one party—America—preserves the peace. The other party—mainly, but not exclusively, Europe—drives the search for mechanisms that might ultimately eliminate the need for a militarily-enforced peace.

This circumstance doesn't *seem* like a paradise to either party, because neither party can fully participate in the activities of the other. As the guarantor and enforcer of the peace that allows our friends to work toward happy coexistence, the United States cannot fully participate because the reduction in sovereignty these experiments require would eviscerate our role as the global "hyperpuissance."[95] And as I have noted at great length in Chapter 1, our European friends cannot much participate in their own defense without first becoming as competitive and vigorous as the US—in other words, without risking another European arm's race. This odd circumstance requires each party to trust the other to do the right thing, a trust that is extraordinarily difficult to manage.

---

[94] Paul Berman has pointed out that peaceful republics quite similar to those of modern-day Europe have existed before—Florence and the other economically powerful city-states that arose in the late Middle Ages, for example. These republics "blossomed splendidly for a few decades and then, in their defenseless condition, were invariably crushed under the heel of some marauding army." Paul Berman, "What Lincoln Knew About War," *The New Republic*, March 3, 2003.

[95] Former French Foreign Minister Hubert Védrine's term for the US. He did not, however, intend it benignly.

Fortunately for Europe, America is largely a *benign* hyperpuissance, a democracy with long-term interests closely aligned to those of Europe. And fortunately for America, European traditions and views on crucial issues of culture and human dignity are largely aligned with our own. Europe will never be content with America's vast military power and will always feel that we are abusing it. And America will never concede that our European friends are doing essential work that we cannot do ourselves. But, like it our not, Europe needs the US and the US needs Europe. One can imagine far worse outcomes than to have the most successful, the most civilized, and the most advanced societies guiding the fate of the world.

* * *

We instinctively favor the underdog in every circumstance. We boo Bluto and cheer when Popeye, having downed his trusty can of spinach, knocks the brute into orbit. If Goliath had defeated David the story would have ended there, but Goliath's defeat by the puny David created a legend that has persisted for thousands of years. In its early history, Israel was widely perceived as a small, embattled nation surrounded on all sides by large and aggressive enemies. But Israel's very success in war after war—to say nothing of having the United States in its corner—has caused this perception to change. Israel is now widely perceived around the world as the neighborhood bully—a serious political problem for the Israelis. And then there is the United States itself. Worldwide we are feared and loathed not for what we stand for or the policies we advocate. We are hated simply because we are bigger and stronger than anyone else—indeed, stronger than everyone else combined.

And this is as it should be. We can imagine a world in which we instinctively cheered for the powerful as they smashed the powerless into dust, but it is not a world most of us would like to live in. Nazi Germany was such a world—Germans still embittered by the terms imposed on them at the end of World War I cheered Hitler when he overran Poland and Czechoslovakia, and all-too-many Germans applauded when the Nazis hunted down and murdered Jews, even then a small, persecuted minority in Germany.

Like America itself, wealthy families will never be perceived as underdogs whose interests need to be protected. Whenever politicians can't think of principled reasons to oppose a policy or program, they can always denounce it as a sop to the rich. This is simply a fact of life and it will never change—indeed, we ought to hope it never changes, because the world that such a change would presuppose would be a world that would be anathema to most of us.

Still, the trouble with our instinctive reaction in favor of the underdog is that it sometimes interferes with cogent thought. Because we sympathize with the struggles of the American poor, because we extol the middle class as the backbone of America, we can easily forget that it is not these groups that distinguish America from other nations, or that account for its success. The poor, after all, are everywhere, and every developed society has at its center a solid middle class whose interests must be protected.

What distinguishes America is the presence, in very large and ever-growing numbers, of the rich. It is the prevalence of the rich—as a demonstration to the poor[96] and middle class that wealth is achievable—that distinguishes us from other free market democracies and that has enabled us to grow to a position of such astonishing dominance. And it is the creative use of the private capital of wealthy families that encourages the creation and supports the implementation of American ideas—the ideas that mainly fuel the drive toward a better world.

It is possible, of course, that America will prove to have been an experiment gone wrong, "the only nation that has gone from barbarism to degeneration without the usual interval of civilization," as Clemenceau put it. It is possible, indeed, that civilized behavior will one day prove to be associated entirely with gentleness, with an insistence that every problem can and must be peacefully decided. Until that day arrives, however, civilization will persist only because America's veneer of gentleness and its commitment to peace remains underlain by a hard core of steel, an adamantine resolve.

The role of private wealth in a democratic republic is and always will be a fragile one. But so long as the holders of that wealth accumulate it fairly and use it creatively, America will continue to be the wonder of the world, and, alone among all the countries of that world, the one indispensable nation.

---

96 Several years ago a young busboy in a Chicago hotel pointed to my copy of *Built from Scratch*, Bernie Marcus and Arthur Blank's story of the building of Home Depot, Inc. "Good book," he said in an English so accented I could hardly understand him. "You've read it?" I asked incredulously. "Three times," he replied matter-of-factly. "Some day I build such a company."

PART TWO

The Stewardship of Wealth

Introduction to Part Two

America became wealthy and powerful, far beyond that of any other country in history, because of an economic system that produces private wealth on a massive scale and that then deploys that wealth in creative ways. The holders of that wealth are the natural end result of that system and its most powerful symbol. Wealthy families are therefore central to the American experiment and therefore they are central to what we might call the near-paradise of peace that holds the promise of freedom and progress for all people globally.

As the principal beneficiaries and prime symbols of this remarkable system, wealthy families bear a serious responsibility to manage their wealth prudently, to engage in a level of stewardship appropriate to the important role our capital plays in America and in the world. We now turn our attention to the details of that demanding, and rewarding, task.

In Part Two, I will discuss the broad issues that most directly affect the ability of families to maintain their capital over long periods of time:

- How difficult it is to manage private capital successfully over the long term;
- Understanding and managing capital markets risk;
- The difficulties associated with meshing capital markets theory with real world investment decisionmaking;
- The role of investor trust in investment success;
- The difficulty of finding competent, objective advisors, and the consequences of failing to do so; and
- The complexity of structuring ourselves to make sound and disciplined investment decisions.

Families who come to grips with these broad issues, who internalize the proper mindset of stewardship, will have gone a very long way toward ensuring the preservation of their capital across many generations.

Two

Chapter 3

Hard Slogging: The Challenge of Long-Term Investment Success

If you swallow a toad when the market opens, you will encounter nothing more disgusting the rest of the day.
—Paraphrase of a remark attributed to the famous misanthrope, Nicolas de Chamfort (1741–1794)[97]

John Bogle, founder of The Vanguard Group, and one of the wisest men in the business, once gave a speech entitled, *Don't Count On It! The Perils of Numeracy*, in which he said, in part:

> "My thesis is that today, in our society, in economics, and in finance, we place too much trust in numbers. *Numbers are not reality.* At best, they're a pale reflection of reality. At worst, they're a gross distortion of the truths we seek to measure."[98] [Emphasis in the original.]

Oddly, nearly twenty years earlier the eminent ecologist, Garrett Hardin,[99] had *bemoaned* our lack of numeracy:

> "[L]iteracy is not enough…we also need numeracy, the ability to handle numbers and the habit of demanding them. A merely literate person

---

97 Chamfort's actual remark was, "Swallow a toad in the morning and you will encounter nothing more disgusting the rest of the day."

98 John C. Bogle, *Don't Count On It! The Perils of Numeracy*, keynote address before the Landmines in Finance Forum of the Center for Economic Policy Studies at Princeton University (October 18, 2002).

99 Dr. Hardin is probably best known for his environmental parable, *The Tragedy of the Commons*, Science, vol. 162, pp. 1243-1248 (1968).

> may raise no question when a journalist speaks of 'the inexhaustible wealth of the sea,' or 'the infinite resources of the earth.' The numerate person, by contrast, asks for figures and rates."[100]

Far be it from me to choose sides between such towering *eminences grises*—let's just say that they are both right. Bogle is surely correct: numerate investors have focused so hard on the gross return expectations developed by modern portfolio theorists that we have frequently missed the forest for the trees. But Hardin is also right: frustration with investment results is all-too-often the result of innumeracy, that is, our failure to appreciate the true import of the numbers we are looking at. The long and short of it is that investors who hope to preserve—much less grow!—their capital are faced with enormous challenges.

Let's follow Bogle's calculations,[101] as set forth in his speech, and see where they lead. Imagine an investor—we'll call her Edith—who at age twenty-five is the happy recipient of a $10 million inheritance from her grandmother. Aside from being a very fortunate young lady, Edith is also no fool, having studied modern portfolio theory at Vassar. Edith decides that she would like to do the same for her own grandchildren one day—leave them a handsome inheritance. Noting that the long-term return on stocks is 11.3%,[102] Edith asks her family's long-time advisor, Mildew Trust Co., to invest the entire $10 million in stocks. A simple calculation tells Edith that, fifty years hence, when she is seventy-five, *she should be able to pass on to her grandchildren a trust fund worth a cool $2.8 billion.* This should certainly earn her the distinction of Everyone's Favorite Grandma.

What Edith Forgot

Unfortunately, Edith forgot a few things in her eagerness to generate terrific total returns and become Everyone's Favorite Grandma. Let's observe what is actually far more likely to happen to that wonderful sum of $2.8 billion.

---

100 *An Ecolate View of the Human Predicament.* This article appeared in McRostie (ed.), *Global Resources: Perspectives and Alternatives* (University Park Press, 1985). The essay was expanded into Hardin's book, *Filters Against Folly* (Penguin, 1985).

101 That is to say, I have applied the Bogle total return rates to a different set of dollars, just to make it more interesting.

102 Bogle, op. cit., note 98, p.5.

The First Thing Edith Forgot: Variance Drain

Edith calculated her compound annual return on her trusty financial calculator, but she simply projected an 11.3% straight-line return. Alas, such returns don't happen in the messy real world of the capital markets. In other words, Edith isn't going to get an 11.3% return every year for fifty years. Sometimes her return will be better, sometimes worse. Specifically, assuming that her returns exhibit a Standard Deviation (S.D.) of 16, then two-thirds of the time her return is likely to fall between +27.3% and -4.7%. One-third of the time her return will be higher or lower than that. And this variability in the return series—the price volatility that is inherent in owning equity securities—*will profoundly reduce her terminal net wealth.* Indeed, the greater the volatility of the returns the lower will be her terminal wealth, assuming that we keep the annual compound return constant. If we assume, as we have, an average variability of 16% (roughly the S.D. of US large company stock returns over Bogle's measuring period), we find that the best Edith can hope for after fifty years of compounding is about $1.5 billion.[103] (Not to be an alarmist, but if the S.D. of Edith's returns turns out to be closer to 20%, as has been the case over longer periods of time with US large cap stocks, Edith's terminal wealth will be reduced further, to $1 billion. But let's hope for the best.) We'll forgive Edith for this lapse—her grandchildren will still be billionaires—but variance drain is an issue to which too many investors (and all-too-many investment professionals!) don't pay enough attention.[104]

The Second Thing Edith Forgot: Inflation

As Bogle points out, over the past fifty years inflation has average 4.2%.[105] Therefore, the *real* rate of return on US stocks is not 11.3%, but only 7.1%. Surely Edith doesn't want to leave her grandchildren worthless, inflated dollars, but real buying power. Alas, then, her original dream of leaving several billion dollars to her grandchildren has turned out to be a fantasy. The real

---

103 Variance drain costs Edith 128 basis points of annual compound return, bringing her effective return (for net wealth purposes) down from 11.3% to 10.02%.

104 In adjusting our final wealth calculations for the variability of the returns we have used the simple approximation: $C = R - \sigma^2/2$, where R is the mean return and σ is the variance in the return. See Tom Messmore, *Variance Drain*, Journal of Portfolio Management (Summer 1995), p. 106.

105 Bogle, op. cit., note 98, p.6.

value of her legacy is "only" $182 million. Even so, her grandchildren will be centimillionaires.

The Third Thing Edith Forgot: Investment Costs

Stock market indices produce gross returns, but investors generate only returns that are net of the costs of obtaining them. These costs include investment management fees, brokerage commissions, spreads between bid and asked prices and (something many investors overlook) market impact.[106] Bogle estimates that such costs come to at least 2% per year.[107] While we are confident that Mildew Trust Co. could run that number up considerably higher, we'll settle for Bogle's number. Net of investment costs, therefore, Edith's return is likely to be about 5.1%. This brings her future grandchildren's inheritance down to $67 million. Well, even so, it's nothing to sniff at.

The Fourth Thing Edith Forgot: Taxes

If Edith had been born into life as a pension plan or charitable endowment, she could obtain her investment returns without worrying about having Uncle Sam as her investment partner. But as a taxpaying future grandmother, Edith must pay ordinary income tax rates on interest, dividends and short-term capital gains, and capital gains tax rates on long-term gains. Bogle estimates that, over time, taxes eat up about 2% per year of investment returns.[108] This reduces Edith's annual returns to 3.1% and her grandchildren's inheritance to $25 million. A far cry from $2.8 billion, to be sure, but still better than a poke in the eye with a sharp stick.

The Fifth Thing Edith Forgot: Spending

A girl's gotta live somehow, of course, and while we don't know exactly how much of Edith's inheritance she will spend each year, we have some pretty good yardsticks to use for comparison purposes. The Internal Revenue Service,

---

106 Market impact refers to the fact that, since money managers tend to be huge investors, the mere fact that they are attempting to buy a stock will force the price of that stock up, substantially increasing the cost of the transaction. An identical problem occurs when the manager tries to sell a stock: the large sell order will cause the stock price to decline, reducing the sales proceeds. The combination of buying higher and selling lower has a huge impact on managers' abilities to produce competitive returns.

107 Bogle, op. cit., note 98, p.6.

108 Bogle, op. cit., note 98, p.6.

for example, requires private charitable foundations to spend 5% of their endowment values (on average), and many non-profit organizations also spend roughly 4% to 6% of their average endowment values each year. Of course, these are largely[109] tax-exempt investors. But we also have the Uniform Principal and Income Act, which permits trustees to manage trusts as "unitrusts," adopting total return investment strategies and simply paying out to the income beneficiary a certain percentage of the value of the trust corpus each year. That percentage is fixed at 4%. Indeed, if a trustee wishes to pay out more or less than 4% per year it must seek court approval to do so. While we harbor our private doubts about whether Mildew Trust Co. will spring for the unitrust idea, we'll give them the benefit of the doubt and assume that they do. Her spending brings Edith's annual return down to—oops.

Edith's return has now moved into negative territory: -0.9% per year. In other words, instead of watching happily as her $10 million grows to $2.8 billion over the next half century, *Edith will be lucky to wind up with a bit over $3 million*, roughly 1/10 of 1% of what she hoped to get. Instead of Everyone's Favorite Grandma, Edith is likely to be remembered as That Old Witch Who *%##@! Away Our Inheritance (this is a family publication).

What Should Edith Do?

John Bogle has an answer to Edith's dilemma, and it will surprise no one who knows him: index funds.[110] Perhaps we can be forgiven for suspecting that Mr. Bogle would also view index funds as the cure for world hunger, the solution to the Arab-Israeli conflict, and a handy way to deal with killer asteroids. But in this case he's onto something. If Edith had used index funds instead of Mildew Trust Co., she would have reduced both her investment costs (index fund fees are very low and, given their relatively low turnover, generate lower frictional investment costs than do active managers) and her taxes as well (lower turnover translates into lower taxes).

While we don't subscribe to Bogle's claim that the use of index funds will "reduce both investment costs and taxes almost to the vanishing point,"[111] if Edith could cut her cost- and tax-drag in half she would at least move her long term rate of return back into positive territory. Adding 2% back to her bottom line annual return would bring her overall return to 1.1% and would allow Edith to grow her principal modestly and leave her grandchildren slightly

---

109 Private foundations pay a small excise tax on their investment income.
110 Bogle, op. cit., note 98, p.6.
111 Bogle, op. cit., note 98, p.7.

more money than her grandmother left her. But that's if everything else goes right, including Edith's ability to achieve an 11.3% annual compound return over fifty years. A far more likely outcome, we fear, is the one we reached a few paragraphs ago: Edith's $10 million inheritance will gradually diminish in value, not grow.

One reason we don't share Mr. Bogle's unlimited enthusiasm for index funds is that he was speaking about a retail investor—instead of starting with $10 million for purposes of his calculations, he started with $1,000—while we are speaking about families with a significant degree of affluence. Such families are almost always in far higher (and more complex) tax brackets than retail investors, and hence even the normal turnover and costs associated with the use of index funds will be problematic. Moreover, a US large capitalization index fund is hardly a clever portfolio strategy, nor one Edith—or any other investor—should adopt or stick with through thick and thin.

The point of all this is obvious: investing capital successfully is a gigantic challenge. In fact, for families with significant capital, the stewardship of that wealth is almost certainly going to be the biggest challenge they will ever face. There may be *more important* challenges—raising happy and productive children, finding the right mate and making that relationship work—but we are largely programmed to undertake those challenges. Our everyday experience virtually from birth prepares us for those duties. But almost no one is prepared to invest capital successfully. Our everyday experience is not only not on point, but is all-too-often positively counterproductive—since much about successful investing is counterintuitive.[112] Consider what Edith would have to do—and do it all right!—in order to grow her inheritance over a fifty year period:

- Edith would have to pay close attention to the problem of variance drain, by developing a sophisticated portfolio strategy that maximizes her investment returns while minimizing her risk (that is, the volatility of those returns). (See Chapter 10.)

---

112 An entire branch of modern portfolio theory—behavioral finance—is devoted to studying the counterproductive actions people take when investing capital. In 2002 the Nobel Prize in economics was awarded to Daniel Kahneman for his pioneering work in "having integrated insights from psychological research into economic science, especially concerning human judgment and decision making under uncertainty," as the Royal Swedish Academy of Science said in its public announcement of the award. Much of Kahneman's work was done in partnership with Amos Tversky who, having died, was ineligible for the Prize.

- Since inflation is the insidious cancer of the investment world, quietly but effectively destroying wealth over time, Edith must anticipate this issue in her portfolio. She could permanently add assets to her portfolio that tend to perform well during periods of unexpected inflation—real estate, commodities, inflation-protected bonds—but the problem with this tactic is that it will tend to bring down her long-term rate of return. (See Chapter 12.)
- Like inflation, tax rates come and go, but like death, they will always be with us. Edith will need to adopt tax-efficient strategies *throughout* her investment portfolio, including:
  - ✓ Designing her asset allocation strategy using estimated after-tax (not pre-tax) returns, and adjusting expected correlations and volatilities as appropriate. Otherwise, she will not be deploying her assets efficiently. (See Chapter 10.)
  - ✓ Paying close attention to asset *location* issues. Putting the right investments in the wrong pockets can seriously compromise Edith's returns. (See Chapter 14.)
  - ✓ Developing tax-aware strategies in each asset class. A strategy that works in US large cap, for example, will likely be suboptimal elsewhere in the portfolio. (See Chapters 10, 11 and 15.)
  - ✓ Working with investment managers who exhibit proper awareness of the tradeoffs between alpha generation and tax consequences. The production of alpha generally implies taking investment actions that will cause tax consequences for the investor. If the anticipated alpha isn't great enough to compensate the investor for the tax cost, the actions shouldn't be taken. (See Chapters 13 and 15.)
  - ✓ Aggressively harvesting tax losses throughout the year and across all managed accounts. (See Chapter 15.)
- Edith will need to optimize (not minimize) her investment costs, primarily by (a) being aware of the damage such costs can cause to her portfolio, (b) allocating investment fees to asset classes and managers who actually have a chance to add value (and away from asset classes and managers who have little chance to do so), and (c) keeping portfolio turnover to a minimum. (See Chapter 13.)
- If Edith is anything like the rest of us, her post-inheritance lifestyle will be considerably more opulent than her pre-inheritance lifestyle. But while $10 million (or $100 million, or $1 billion) seems like a lot of

money, there is no amount of money that profligate spending can't decimate over time. If Edith can keep her spending closer to 3% of her principal than 4%, she will have a far better chance to maintain and grow her wealth. (See Chapter 17.)

- Finally, despite the many provocations Edith is likely to face over the course of half a century, she will need to stick to her long-term investment strategy with almost superhuman endurance. (See Chapters 9 and 10.)

Hard Slogging

There is a Chinese parable about the Sage who, having performed an important service to the empire, was asked by the Emperor what he would like as his reward. "All I ask," replied the Sage, "is one grain of rice today, two grains tomorrow, four the next day and so on throughout the remainder of my poor lifetime." "Ah," said the Emperor, "surely you must ask for more than that!" But the Sage was firm in his modesty and the Emperor agreed to the bargain. It was only a few months later that the Emperor learned there was not enough rice in all of China to meet his obligation to the Sage. Whereupon, recognizing that he had been evilly tricked, the Emperor had the Sage executed, bringing to a brutal but effective end this particular episode in the thrill of compound interest.

And that is precisely the point: nothing compounds forever, or even for very long. Trees start from small seedlings but don't grow to the sky. Some species spawn thousands of offspring, threatening to overwhelm the earth, but few of these offspring live long enough to reproduce. Malthusians[113] have warned for more than two centuries that human population growth would quickly overwhelm the world's resources, causing the species to collapse. But it never happens: between disease, famine, war and economic and technological progress, the compounding never comes close to what a straight line projection would suggest.

Einstein is famously supposed to have remarked that, while the theory of relativity is certainly interesting, the most remarkable thing in the world is compound interest. But the truth is (talk about disagreeing with an *eminence grise*!) that the most remarkable thing about compound interest is how frequently its existence tends to be, as Hobbes said of the lives of the English poor, "nasty, brutish and short."[114]

---

113 Thomas Malthus wrote his famous paper, *An Essay on the Principle of Population*, in 1768.

114 Thomas Hobbes, *Leviathan* (1660). "No arts; no letters; no society; and which is worst of all, continual fear and danger of violent death; and the life of man, solitary, poor, nasty, brutish, and short."

We have explored some of the reasons why the magic of compound interest rarely plays out in the lives of investors, but there are others as well: psychological factors, sociological issues, family dynamics, social and economic disruptions, the collapse of civil societies, and so on. But whatever the reasons, managing an investment portfolio in a taxable, family environment is the most formidable intellectual and psychological challenge Edith, or any other family, will ever face. The sad and simple fact is that most affluent families, faced with the challenges identified by Mr. Bogle and those just mentioned, will not grow their wealth over time, or even maintain it, but will watch helplessly as it disappears before their very eyes.

We are all so numerate these days that total return numbers trip lightly off our tongues. But those are sly devils as numbers go, Miltonesque Satans luring us into traps from which, unless we are very wary, there is no escape. And what escape there is involves not just a numerate understanding of how things actually compound and how they don't, but a very large degree of hard slogging, the paying of minute attention to the issues that count—if, that is, like Edith, we hope to pass along our capital intact to a future generation.

Two

Chapter 4

Understanding and Managing Risk

We helped Einstein invest his money.
What makes you think you should do it alone?
—Billboard advertising the services of TIAA-CREF

Once we possess capital of any size, our first duty as the steward of that capital is to preserve it against diminution through inattention, negligence, the ravages of inflation, incompetence or, God forbid, fraud. What we will actually do with our capital is a crucial question, of course, but if we don't husband our wealth carefully this crucial issue will never arise—there won't be enough wealth to worry about.

Families and Investment Risk[115]

Investing is the process of putting out money today in the hope or expectation that we will receive more money in the future. If the expectation that we will receive our capital back is very high, the return we can demand on it will be very low. This is because many, many other investors are happy to take very little risk and still receive a return. Likewise, if the hope of having our capital returned intact is more speculative, we can demand a much higher return, since few other investors will have the appetite or ability to put their capital at significant risk. It's a simple matter of supply and demand, but mainly supply: there is always a great deal of demand for serious risk capital, but rarely much

---

115 One of the best books ever written about risk is Peter L. Bernstein's *Against the Gods: The Remarkable Story of Risk* (John Wiley & Sons, 1998). It is highly recommended reading.

supply of it; there is a fairly static demand for low-risk capital (to finance the routine operations of governments and corporations), but there will always be a large supply of it.

Virtually every American family that is wealthy today got that way because someone in the family at some point took very serious risks. Yes, they also worked very hard and had a good idea. But one can work very hard and not become rich—coal miners, for example. And one can have brilliant ideas and not become rich—tinkerers and dreamers of all kinds. ("In the end, a vision without the ability to execute is probably a hallucination," as Steve Case once put it.) It is the combination of hard work, a good idea and risk that generates wealth on any significant scale.[116] The risk typically involves doing something new and different, or doing something old in a new and different way. The grander the idea the larger the potential wealth—but also the greater the chance of a spectacular failure.

"Low" risk investments. Risk in the context of capital markets is no different—but, one hopes, operates on a more modest and more controllable scale. After all, once an investor has already become wealthy the justification for continuing to take huge risks diminishes rapidly. But large or small, risk is a tricky subject. Consider the safest investment in the world for a US investor—a United States Treasury bill. (I say "a US investor" because foreign investors must take currency risk when they buy US Treasuries.) The likelihood that the US government will default on its promise to pay us back in ninety days is so remote that it is fair to say, for most practical purposes, that US Treasuries are risk-free investments.

Huge numbers of investors like this low-risk alternative, and consequently the US government typically needs to offer a return no higher than the underlying inflation rate to attract capital. Since most buyers of US government paper are tax-exempt institutions, the return on US Treasuries tends to equal the inflation rate *before* tax. Taxable investors who buy Treasuries can therefore expect to receive negative real returns over time.

Hence the odd result that the "safest" investment in the world could destroy vast amounts of wealth if used exclusively in family portfolios over a very long period of time. For example, if a family had invested $100 million in US Treasuries beginning fifty years ago and simply rolled the Treasuries over every ninety days for half a century, that family's wealth would have declined to the equivalent of about $60 million today (net of taxes and inflation, *but assuming*

116 Luck certainly plays a role, of course, though over the course of a lifetime good luck and bad luck tend to even out. In any event, Lady Luck always favors the bold.

no spending). If the same family had put all its money in stocks compounding at 10% fifty years ago, that family would have today—net of taxes and inflation—something like $2.8 billion. The $2.6 billion difference between these two numbers is the long-term consequence of investing exclusively in the safest investment in the world.

"High" risk investments. Let's compare the other end of the risk spectrum: early stage venture capital investing. Venture capital is capital available to very new, untested companies. Early stage venture capital investing involves the funding of new companies shortly after they have started up. Perhaps they have received initial capital from a "friends and family" investment round, or perhaps from a small group of "angel" investors. But the company is still new and untried, almost certainly unprofitable and possibly it even has no revenue stream. To say that such companies are risky investments is simply to state a truism: many will fail altogether, others will sputter along never completely returning their investor capital, a very few will succeed brilliantly.

Three or four decades ago, when America's entrepreneurial culture was in its infancy, a few intrepid investors—mainly families, not institutions—began to seek out and invest in early stage venture companies. In those days the supply of capital for this sort of investing was almost nonexistent, given the huge risks involved and the lack of infrastructure in the industry. Consequently, annual returns could easily reach 40% or even 50%.[117] Huge fortunes were made in this way.[118]

But those kinds of returns began to attract additional capital and talent to the business. As "deal flow" increased—that is, more entrepreneurs with ideas began to come along—investors began to form partnerships to source and nurture these fledgling enterprises, with the objective of eventually taking them public or selling them to larger firms. Today, the venture capital industry is fully developed in the United States, with hundreds of venture capital partnerships offering funding and advice to tens of thousands of entrepreneurs. Billions of dollars are raised every year by these partnerships.

---

117 If you could invest $1 million and compound it at 50% per year for ten years tax-free, your money would grow to $134,000,000. Venture capital profits aren't tax-free, of course, but they are tax-deferred (profits are generated many years after the investments are made) and almost always receive long-term capital gains treatment.

118 As discussed in Chapter 2, Andrew W. Mellon was probably the first American venture capitalist in the modern sense of the term. Mellon and his family and family bank provided the seed capital for such ventures as Alcoa, Koppers, Gulf Oil, and many other firms, as well, of course, as Mellon Bank itself (founded by Andrew's father, Thomas).

But of course the law of supply and demand holds: returns have declined. Investors making diversified investments in early stage venture capital partnerships today can expect to receive returns in the 15% to 35% range, depending on whether they are invested with top-tier or average partnerships. While 20% annual compound returns are nothing to sniff at, given the capital risks and, especially, the illiquidity of these investments, few sensible investors would participate in early stage venture investing in the hope of receiving 15% per year. On the other hand, savvy investors investing directly in deals, or participating in the best partnerships and diversifying by partnership, industry, stage and time, can have a reasonable expectation of achieving 25% to 35% annual compound returns—probably the highest returns available outside the realm of pure speculation.

But whether the returns turn out to be closer to 15% or 35%, these are stunning returns from passive investing, and, given their favorable tax treatment, can easily produce huge increases in wealth for families who take the venture capital investing process seriously. Hence the odd result that, while the safest, low-risk investments will destroy wealth over time, the riskiest investments, properly structured, will almost certainly create significant real wealth.

"Reasonable" risk investments: marketable securities. The core of most wealthy family portfolios will be marketable securities—stocks and bonds—and so I want to spend some time on the nature of risk in this sector of the market.

Stocks are issued by corporations through public or private offerings, but most of us buy stocks not directly from corporations (or, technically, the underwriters of the corporate stock offering) but from other investors, typically through the mechanism of a stock exchange. Indeed, the history of America is virtually coterminous with the history of the New York Stock Exchange, the largest exchange in the world, founded under a buttonwood tree near Wall Street in 1792. (The United States Constitution, you will recall, was ratified in 1788.)

The law of supply and demand (again). As with other investment sectors, stocks follow the laws of supply and demand. When more investors are interested in buying than in selling a stock, the price of that stock will rise, and when more investors want to sell than buy, the price will decline. This is true not only of individual stocks, but of stocks as a whole. When investors are optimistic and in a buying mood, the level of the market itself (the S & P 500, say, or the Dow or NASDAQ) will rise. When investors are pessimistic markets will decline. Note—as we'll discuss in a moment—that individual stocks and entire markets can rise or decline based on fundamental business or economic conditions, but they can also rise and fall simply as a result of investor sentiment, whether that sentiment is factually based or not.

Supply and demand can be confusing in the capital markets context. For example, it might seem sensible to suppose that an investor—a money manager, for example—who wishes to buy a very large supply of a particular stock should get a bargain, a "quantity discount." In fact, most large purchases drive *up* the price of the stock, resulting in the odd phenomenon that money managers attempting to purchase a large block of stock will pay more than investors attempting to purchase more modest positions.[119] Similarly, sales of large blocks of stock will push the price of the stock down, so that a large money manager will receive less for his stock than will a small investor selling only a few shares. As a result, the main cost involved in buying or selling shares for most money managers or other large investors is not commissions or spreads between the bid and ask price—the main cost is "market impact," the increase or decrease in the stock's price caused by the investor's attempt to buy or sell it.

Idiosyncratic ideas about risk. In thinking about the risks associated with investing in stocks, investors tend to think in idiosyncratic terms. What I think of as risk, for example, may be quite different from what you think of as risk. This has partly to do with our individual circumstances and partly to do with our differing natures. It's important, of course, to understand ourselves as investors and to know what we mean by risk. But it's far more important to understand that *the capital markets don't care about what we think of as risk.*

If risk to me means never experiencing a negative return in any calendar year, I can design a portfolio that will be highly likely to avoid that particular risk. But to do so I will have to sacrifice far more return than I probably want to give up. In other words, I'm being pennywise and pound-foolish. If risk to you, on the other hand, means failing to achieve at least a 15% annual return from a traditional stock and bond portfolio, you can probably accomplish that, too. But you will be exposing yourself to breathtaking price volatility, volatility so great that you will almost certainly abandon the portfolio long before it has generated your desired rate of return. And the same is true of other idiosyncratic definitions of risk. Hence, it's crucially important that we understand

---

[119] For this reason, purchases of *extremely* large blocks of a particular stock will often occur not on a stock exchange but in a negotiated transaction. In such a transaction the buyer(s) will often get a bargain, a true "quantity discount" relative to the price at which the stock is selling on the exchange. On the other hand, the seller will also get a bargain, since the discount he will give the buyer will be lower then the discounted price likely to result from the market impact of such a huge sale. In 2001 the Bass family famously negotiated such a sale of Disney stock, a forced sale apparently resulting from margin calls.

the real risks that are embedded in the capital markets. We can still indulge our "eccentric" ideas about risk, but at least we will understand something about the costs associated with doing so.

Recall that in our discussion of investing in Treasury bills we learned that the world's safest investment can, in fact, destroy wealth over time. The very fact of its safety ensures that its return will be too low even to keep up with inflation for a taxable investor. Thus, a family putting all its money in T-bills because their idiosyncratic idea is never to place their capital at risk are in fact placing their capital at enormous risk over time. The cost of indulging the family's peculiar notion of risk is enormous, and they should understand that key fact before undertaking a long-term investment program based on investing in Treasury bills.

Real risks: individual stock risk versus broad market risk. Some risks associated with investing in stocks are unavoidable, while others are relatively easily avoided. The risks that can be avoided do not, except in the hands of geniuses and the very lucky, reward us for taking them. On the other hand, over time we will be rewarded for taking risks that cannot be avoided, that are inherent in the activity of owning stocks, and we should be eager to accept those risks.

The main avoidable risk is *individual stock risk*. If our stock portfolio consists of only one stock, we might make a great deal of money on that investment and we might lose everything. But unless we are Warren Buffett, or unless we know a very great deal about the company (because, perhaps, we own or run it), our investment results are likely to be both random and completely beyond our control. We aren't rewarded for taking the risk of owning one stock any more than we are rewarded for playing roulette in Las Vegas.

The reason we aren't rewarded for this behavior is that it can easily be avoided—by buying more than one stock. Owning even a small handful of carefully selected stocks dramatically reduces the risk of a one-stock portfolio, and owning twenty or thirty carefully selected stocks virtually eliminates individual stock risk. Note the words "carefully selected." This means buying stocks of companies that operate in different industries, industries that are affected differently by the same business and economic conditions. Buying five biotechnology stocks rather than one doesn't significantly reduce individual stock risk because many of the conditions that affect one of those companies will also, and similarly, affect the others.

The main risk we cannot avoid when we buy stocks is broad market risk, the risk inherent in owning equity securities. Even if we owned every stock listed on the New York Stock Exchange we would still be exposed to market risk. On the other hand, we are compensated for accepting broad market risk, compensated by receiving a "risk premium" over the risk-free rate (typically the interest rate on Treasury bills). Over a very long period of time the risk premium for US large company stocks has been about 7%. Hence, if Treasuries have yielded roughly 3% over time, US large company stocks have returned roughly 10% compounded over time. The size of the risk premium changes over time, but only glacially, since the risk premium seems to be imbedded in the very concept of broad ownership of productive assets on a large scale—that is, on a scale sufficiently large to be importantly affected by the growth of the broad economy. It would not surprise me to learn that Ancient Egyptians were earning a risk premium of something like 7% when they put their capital at risk in various and sundry Egyptian enterprises.

Real risks: price volatility. The trouble, of course, is that the risk premium we earn through broad stock ownership isn't a fixed rate of return like the return on a Treasury bill. Instead, our return fluctuates, sometimes wildly. This fluctuation is known as *price volatility,* and it is a key concept for anyone even thinking about investing in equities.

Let's take numbers roughly close to the actual numbers to illustrate how price volatility works in the marketplace, how it affects our returns and why it is so important. As noted above, over time US large company stocks have compounded at an annual rate of about 10%. But if we looked at the actual year-by-year returns over, say, 75 years, we would see that stocks almost never return 10% in any particular year. Instead, stock returns have occurred across a wide spectrum, from a high of +53% in 1954 to a low of -35% in 1937. In other words, stock returns fall into the familiar bell-shaped curve we all know and love.

If we assume that the annual Standard Deviation of stock returns—the group of outcomes that encompasses two-thirds of all annual returns—is about 20, then we would expect, two-thirds of the time, to experience returns between -10% and +30%.

This exercise illustrates several crucial points about the experience we are likely to encounter if we invest in stocks—regardless of our idiosyncratic notions about risk. The first important point is that, as discussed above, our average rate of return is likely to be about 10% over a very long period of time. Investors who expect better returns than this, perhaps because recent market returns have been higher, will be sorely disappointed.

The second important point is that we will rarely receive exactly 10% in any one year; instead, our actual annual return from equity investing will fluctuate very widely. Two-thirds of the time, as noted above, we can expect our results to be somewhere between +30% and -10%. An investor who focuses on the 10% average return of stocks without taking into account the Standard

Deviation of their returns is likely to abandon stocks well before the long-term average return has been achieved.

Third, note that the range of +30% to -10% explains only two-thirds of the annual expected price volatility of the stock markets. One-sixth of the time our results will be better than +30% and one-sixth of the time our results will be worse than -10%. If we are invested over a period of ten years—and no one should think about investing in stocks with much less of a time horizon—the odds are that in three or four of those years our results will fall outside this range, either on the upside or downside. And over an investment lifetime it is virtually certain that we will experience many years in which our investment returns will be better or worse than the standard range. Hence, as investors we simply have to understand that we will in fact experience extreme markets and that that experience is as much a part of stock investing as getting our long-term 10% return.[120]

Assuming that we own properly diversified stock portfolios, it is this phenomenon of price volatility that is the key risk we are exposing our assets to. Except under very specific conditions, price volatility can't be avoided without significantly reducing the return we can expect to receive. For example, we can reduce the price volatility of a 100% equity portfolio by converting it into a portfolio consisting of 60% stocks and 40% bonds. But we will have dramatically reduced the long term return that portfolio will generate.

Price volatility is also symmetrical, that is, if US large cap stocks have a characteristic price volatility of 16%, that is 16% on both the upside and downside, around the 10% average return. It simply makes no sense to say, as many investors do, that "upside volatility" isn't risk, only "downside volatility" is risk. If you own an equity portfolio that has 20% upside volatility, you also own an equity portfolio that has 20% downside volatility, as investors in technology, growth and momentum stocks learned after the first quarter of 2000.[121]

---

120 Even more extreme events are also characteristic of capital markets behavior, as I discuss later.

121 The only exceptions to this iron law of investment risk have to do with manager talent: a very few extremely talented managers appear to be able to generate excess upside price volatility (that is, excess positive rates of return) without concomitant downside price volatility. This trick seems to be easier to achieve in extremely inefficient sectors of the markets and where the manager is able both to buy stocks long and sell them short. But as we will see, it is extraordinarily difficult to identify these managers in advance. Moreover, adherents to the "strong" version of efficient market theory would argue that most "talented" managers are really just "lucky" managers. If you flip hundreds of thousands of pennies, a very few, very "talented" pennies will come up heads twenty times in a row!

As we will see when we discuss asset allocation, the price volatility of investment portfolios can be reduced by thoughtfully combining asset classes in a fully diversified portfolio. For example, simply adding small amounts of diversified international stocks to a US stock portfolio will simultaneously reduce the price volatility of the resulting portfolio and modestly increase its expected return—a rare "free lunch" in the investment world. Of course, it's not really a free lunch. Both the domestic and international portfolios will be as volatile as they ever were, and as investors we will experience (and heartily dislike) that volatility. It's just that the price volatility of the blended domestic-international portfolio will be lower than a simple average of the two would suggest, due to the fact that the returns of the two asset classes aren't perfectly correlated.

The implications of price volatility. The phenomenon of price volatility has momentous implications for investors. The first of these implications I will call "idiosyncratic," and the second I'll call "fundamental." That is, the first is avoidable (albeit not easily) while the second is embedded in the nature of capital in a market economy.

The "idiosyncratic" problem presented by price volatility affects investors who simply cannot emotionally abide the ups and downs of the market. In other words, although there is no need for these investors to remove their capital from the equity market during negative periods, they nonetheless do so out of fear, and to their serious detriment. Unfortunately, this category includes the vast majority of investors, since it requires a strong stomach, an iron will, or a professional discipline to deal with the sometimes breathtaking ups and downs that are an ordinary feature of equity markets.

But there is also a "fundamental" problem with price volatility, namely, that capital—which is what the market is made up of—hates illiquidity. Capital needs to be deployed and redeployed in a vigorous economy, and the timing of the redeployment is usually unknown in advance. Unfortunately, however, capital deployed in an equity portfolio can't simply be redeployed willy-nilly. If our redeployment opportunities require us to put capital into a market near the top and take it out for redeployment elsewhere near the bottom, then we are being forced to adopt the worst possible equity investment strategy. The phenomenon of price volatility requires that capital held in equity portfolios be withdrawn only at certain optimal points in time, and those optimal times will often be inconsistent with capital redeployment opportunities elsewhere.

Real risks: wildness in the tails. As I discuss in Chapter 10, bell curves seriously underestimate the frequency and extreme nature of events that occur in the "tails" of the bell curve. What, for example, must be the odds that the stock market will decline by 20% in two days? As noted in Chapter 5, if capital markets events were randomly distributed, such an event would be unthinkable—if we had begun investing in stocks at the time the universe was born, it would still be extremely unlikely that we would ever experience such a dramatic decline. Yet, as we all know, such a decline occurred in October, 1987. Thus, we can't specify exactly what will occur or when it will occur, but we know for certain that if we invest long enough, bizarre events will decidedly occur and we had better be ready for them. There is, as someone has appropriately put it, "wildness" in those tails.

Other examples of "wildness in the tails" would include the 1929 Stock Market Crash (when the markets declined by 89% from the 1929 peak to the 1932 trough), the abysmal markets of 1973 and 1974 (when the markets declined in real—net of inflation—terms by 50%), the collapse of liquidity in the third quarter of 1998 (associated with Russia's default on its sovereign debt and the collapse of the Long Term Capital Management hedge fund), and the stock market gyrations that followed the September 11, 2001 terrorist attacks. These extreme events can be truly threatening, not only to individual investors but also to markets as a whole. For a time during the 1998 liquidity crisis, for example, the Federal Reserve feared that Long Term Capital's collapse might lead to a collapse of the entire market system.

Real risks: investor behavior. One of the most natural, but nonetheless frightening, aspects of investing has to do with the fact that, capital markets theorists notwithstanding, investors do not behave rationally, at least not in the short term. I've just cited the example of October of 1987. Can it actually have been possible that American corporations were worth 20% less on October 19 than they were on October 18? It's ludicrous on its face. Either investors were irrational on October 18 or they were irrational on October 19 (or, more likely, both), but they can't have been rational on both dates.

We observe the same phenomenon over longer periods of time in bear and bull markets. Stocks rarely go from over-priced to fairly priced, or from under-priced to fairly priced. Instead, they almost always go from over-priced to under-priced, and from under-priced to over-priced. When bear markets occur, investors quickly become overly pessimistic, concluding that the world is going to hell in a hand basket (for example, 1973–74, 2000–03). When bull markets are roaring, investors become overly enthusiastic, convinced that stock prices will rise forever (for example, 1998–99). For truly rational investors, these periods of emotionalism represent tremendous opportunities, either to sell to the enthusiastic crowds at inflated prices or to buy from the terrified rabble at artificially deflated prices. Unfortunately, few of us have the moxie to take advantage of the opportunities, for the simple reason that we are *part* of the emotional crowd, not *apart* from it.

No one knows how much price volatility results from factors inherent in the capital markets and how much results from the fact that investors are human and therefore imperfect, though the work of behavioral finance experts is beginning to shed light on these issues.[122] At the margin, however, near market peaks and bottoms, it seems apparent that it is almost entirely human emotion that is driving prices. We need to realize that investors—including ourselves—aren't rational, at least over relatively short periods of time or during extreme markets, and to take that fact into account as we consider the risks of investing.

---

[122] Several Nobel Prizes have been awarded for work in the field of behavior finance, including the 2002 award in Economics, which went to Daniel Kahneman.

Two

Chapter 5

Investment Theory and Investment Success

Markets can remain irrational
longer than you can remain solvent.
—John Maynard Keynes

Modern Portfolio Theory

The year 2002 marked the 50th anniversary of the publication of Harry Markowitz' seminal paper on mean variance optimization,[123] a then-obscure event which nonetheless inaugurated what we now know as modern portfolio theory (MPT). Over the following five decades, Markowitz and his followers[124] have contributed enormously to our understanding of the behavior of capital markets and of the nature of risk and its relationship to investment returns. MPT has, in a broad way, allowed us to model how markets are likely to behave over very long periods of time, and has therefore allowed us to base the design of investment portfolios on principles that are at least in some fundamental way related to likely market behavior. For investors born after MPT concepts were incorporated into real-world investment portfolios, it's hard to believe what a revolutionary change MPT has occasioned.[125]

---

123 Harry Markowitz, "Portfolio Selection" (*Journal of Finance*, 1952).

124 Among the more prominent contributors to MPT were James Tobin, Franco Modigliani, Merton Miller, William Sharpe, Robert Merton, Myron Scholes and Eugene Fama.

125 These days, when we encounter financial advisory firms that still manage money in pre-MPT ways—mainly stockbrokers, trust companies and regional banks, where individual relationship officers still (amazingly) buy stocks and bonds for their clients—they seem amusingly quaint anachronisms.

The year 2002 also marks the 100th anniversary of Lord Kelvin's articulation of the atomic model, launching what we now know as quantum mechanics,[126] the branch of physics that deals with the behavior of matter and light at the atomic and subatomic scale. Like MPT, quantum theory has also proven to be both accurately descriptive—in this case of how particles behave in the natural microcosm—and also remarkably predictive, enabling scientists, for example, to predict the existence of infinitesimal[127] particles long before physical evidence of their existence could be detected.

But physicists also understand that quantum mechanics has its limits. Under certain prescribed conditions—namely, the world of infinitely small particles—quantum mechanics "works." But events that occur at the level of the visible world we actually inhabit—the world of ants, humans, buildings, planets, solar systems, galaxies—are not merely events that fall several standard deviations outside what quantum theory would predict. Instead, they are events that have nothing whatever to do with quantum mechanics, but that are governed instead by very different rules that can be understood only by reference to very different theories. Indeed, the Holy Grail of physics these days is the attempt to construct a "unified theory," one that will reconcile quantum mechanics with relativity theory.

Likewise, modern portfolio theory is useful under certain prescribed conditions, some of which we know about and some of which we don't. We know, for example, that MPT assumes continuous pricing, a world in which markets are free, societies are free and stable, and investors are rational wealth-maximizers. Events that occur outside these conditions are not merely events that fall several standard deviations outside what MPT would predict. Instead, they are events that have nothing whatever to do with MPT, but are governed instead by very different rules that can be understood only by reference to very different theories. Indeed, the world of behavioral finance has blossomed in

---

126 Many physicists will be surprised to learn that 2002 marks the 100th anniversary of quantum theory. More likely dates for the theory's origin would be 1897 (Thompson's discovery of the electron), 1900 (Max Planck's development of the concept of the "quantum," or fundamental increment of energy), 1905 (the year of publication of Einstein's three seminal papers on the photoelectric effect, the special theory of relativity and statistical mechanics), 1913 (Niels Bohr's proposal of the quantitative shell model of the atom), or even 1926 (Heisenberg's uncertainty principle).

127 The term "infinitesimal" is relative, of course, but by way of example a single cubic centimeter of air contains roughly 10,000,000,000,000,000,000 atoms.

response to our recognition that at least one of the prescribed conditions—that investors behave rationally—rarely holds true.

We also know that other prescribed conditions are often absent. Prices are never—not rarely—continuous, for example,[128] and sometimes the discontinuity can be breathtaking. Consider Black Monday in October 1987, when, two-thirds of the way into an otherwise unremarkable year, a year in which the markets would ultimately rise 5%, the US markets suddenly plummeted 23% *in one day*. Viewed in modern portfolio theory terms, this event simply cannot be understood. Indeed, financial economists have calculated that,

> "on the basis of the market's historic volatility, had the market been open every day since the creation of the universe, the odds would still have been against [the market's] falling that much on a single day. In fact, had the life of the universe been repeated *one billion times*, such a crash would still have been theoretically 'unlikely.'"[129] (Emphasis in the original.)

Two standard deviations, indeed!

Or consider an especially sophisticated German investor who, just after World War I, designed his portfolio in accordance with the tenets of MPT, carefully balancing German large, mid and small cap stocks with a sensible allocation to German bonds and a reasonable allocation to international stocks. By the end of the Weimar Republic in 1933, our savvy investor would have been bankrupt.[130] His mistake was to assume that MPT governed all

---

128 Consider as one minor example the need to price securities at an arbitrary moment in time—the "close of business." In an era when securities are traded virtually 24/7, this alone injects an element of arbitrariness and discontinuity into securities pricing. "Understanding Tracking Error: Advanced Comments," *Research Brief*, Parametric Associates (1999), page 2, note 3.

129 These calculations were prepared by Jens Carsten Jackwerth and Mark Rubinstein, "Recovering Probability Distributions from Option Prices," *Journal of Finance*, 51, no.5 (December 1996), p. 1612. The illustration was cited by Roger Lowenstein in *When Genius Failed* (Random House, 2000), p. 72. Yale professor Benoit Mandelbrot has calculated the odds of three major daily market declines in August 1998 at one in 500 billion, and the odds of three large declines in July 2002 at *one in four trillion*. Benoit Mandelbrot and Richard L. Hudson, *The Misbehavior of Markets* (Basic Books, 2004), p. 4.

130 By that date hyper-inflation gripped the German economy. Prices rose hourly and at the end it cost $1 billion German marks to send a letter to the US. Capitalizing on public outrage and resentment against the terms imposed on Germany by the Allies after World War I, Hitler came to power in 1933 and promptly suspended the Weimar Constitution.

events in the capital markets, when in fact, under the conditions of post-World War I Germany, MPT was completely irrelevant.

MPT professionals proceed on the assumption that financial theories, like physics theories, must be formulated in terms of numbers, equations and mathematics. But mathematical analyses only provide an abstract framework within which scientific conclusions can be drawn without direct reference to the actual reality of the capital marketplace. And that actual reality is not merely quirky and messy, it is a reality that frequently behaves according to rules quite different from, and bearing no relation to, the elegant but sterile equations of the MPT gurus.[131]

The point of all this is simply that, while modern portfolio theory is an essential tool in the design and management of intelligent portfolios, it cannot be blindly relied upon for the simple reason that market events will occur, and with alarming frequency, which have nothing to do with MPT. MPT holds such sway in the United States because, by a considerable margin, US stock prices are the most continuous, its markets are the most free and efficient, US society is the most free and stable, and US investors are the most knowledgeable and rational in the world. Elsewhere around the world these conditions are largely or wholly absent, and investors in those parts of the world would be foolish, indeed, to own MPT-designed portfolios. But even in America our stock prices are not truly continuous (see above), our markets are not perfectly free and efficient (witness insider trading, questionable accounting practices,

---

[131] One possible reason why modern portfolio theory is simultaneously an elegant explanation of market behavior under a set of very simple rules and also completely clueless about market behavior under most real-world conditions is this very insistence on explanation-by-mathematics. It makes financial economics seem more scientific—more like physics and less like psychology, for example—but it misses the big picture: MPT cannot explain much of what happens in real, operating markets and simply avoids such questions. But investors must place their capital at risk in real markets, not abstract frameworks. One possible way out of this dilemma has been proposed by physicist Stephen Wolfram, who, working with relatively simple cellular automata (patterns created by simple computer programs), has managed to create enormously complex systems that are not necessarily continuous or smooth, but that look remarkably like living, breathing stock markets. Stephen Wolfram, *A New Kind of Science* (Wolfram Publishers, Inc., 2002), p. 429-32. See also the interesting work of Benoit Mandelbrot, employing fractal geometry to propose a more accurate way of describing market behavior. Mandelbrot and Hudson, *The Misbehavior of Markets*, op. cit., note 129.

conflicted analysts, corrupt executives), US society is not perfectly free and stable (witness race riots, terrorist attacks, controlled markets for many goods and services), and US investors are not perfect wealth-maximizers (consider daytrading, the bubble markets of the late 1990s, the dot.com foolishness, and the huge difference among virtually all investors between their *theoretical* time horizons and risk tolerance and their *real* time horizons and risk tolerance).

What are the implications of recognizing the limits of modern portfolio theory? The main implication is that advisors who rely blindly on MPT to design client portfolios are ill-serving those clients. Such portfolios will work well when the special conditions relevant to MPT are operable, but will perform very poorly—indeed, disastrously—on the frequent occasions when those conditions are inoperable. Financial advisors must understand that events will occur in the capital markets that are not predictable by—indeed, that are irrelevant to—MPT, and hedge client portfolios accordingly. In particular, advisors to capital preservation or absolute return-oriented investors,[132] like most families, need to give at least as much consideration to worst case outcomes as to computer-generated "efficient" portfolios. And those advisors must remember that Standard Deviation is not an appropriate measure of worst case outcomes.

Let's consider some specific examples of how a blind reliance on MPT approaches to portfolio design can wreak havoc, and how non-MPT approaches can work in investors' interests.

Developed Versus Emerging Markets

As this chapter is written, it is becoming cutting-edge opinion that the traditional distinction between developed and emerging markets is artificial and should be eliminated. To some extent this is nothing more than a marketing ploy: investors who are terrified of emerging markets and would not consider investing in them may in fact invest in emerging economies if that money is part of an overall international allocation. In other words, the impact of the emerging markets exposure is heavily diluted—and therefore largely invisible—and so the investor goes along with it. But viewed from the point of view of the limits of modern portfolio theory, this cutting-edge opinion is dangerous. MPT largely works in developed markets because the special conditions required are largely present. But in most emerging markets few or none of

---

132 If the S&P 500 Index is down 25% and the domestic equity portfolio is down 20%, a relative return investor is happy, but an absolute return investor is distinctly unhappy.

those conditions are present: capital markets are largely not free, emerging societies are neither democratic nor stable, and investors—both local and foreign—rarely behave rationally in the face of the frequently-bizarre behavior of those markets and societies. Hence, MPT concepts largely prevail in developed international markets and are largely irrelevant to the behavior of international emerging markets.[133] As a result, the distinction between these two asset classes needs to be preserved.

Anchors to Windward

Recently, Greycourt advised a family who had become enormously wealthy as the result of the sale of their company for cash. Aside from investing that cash wisely, our first advice was to take a significant piece of the capital, invest it in a very solid, core fixed income portfolio, and surround that portfolio with a sophisticated asset protection strategy. No tenet of modern portfolio theory would have suggested such a strategy, and no soundly-designed asset allocation model would have demanded such a move. Our advice was informed in part by principles of behavioral finance, of course, but it was also the result of our recognition that MPT concepts simply don't operate at many times and in many places for reasons that no one fully understands, and that this fact of investment life should be acknowledged in this particular client's portfolio.

Treasury bonds for taxable investors. Sophisticated advisors sometimes recommend that wealthy investors own non-callable, long-term Treasury bonds even though a soundly-constructed portfolio of intermediate-term municipal bonds would generate more after-tax income with lower price volatility. In part, such a recommendation results from the recognition that the strategy represents the only assured hedge against a deflationary economic environment. More broadly, however, it is a recognition that MPT concepts don't apply in many kinds of unusual market environments, one of those being deflationary markets.

---

133 I don't mean to imply that investors should avoid emerging markets, or any other markets where MPT concepts rarely operate. I do mean to imply that investors who put money into emerging markets expecting that MPT concepts of risk and return will prevail are likely to be sorely disappointed. Note that since the MSCI Emerging Markets Free Index was constructed, emerging markets returns have not begun to compensate investors for their risks (S.D.), another clue that something other than MPT is going on here. Another important point is that, as American-influenced free markets' ideas have permeated the world, the number of "emerging" markets has declined and the number of "developed" markets (or quasi-developed markets) has increased.

Hedge funds. For the better part of a decade, and in rare cases for much longer, investors who have constructed thoughtfully diversified hedge fund portfolios have achieved something quite remarkable: equity-like returns with bond-like price volatility. According to MPT, this is impossible: risk and return must be positively related. An MPT-friendly explanation of this phenomenon might go something like this: Hedge fund investment results are a transitory phenomenon resulting from the obscurity of hedge funds until recently; as more and more investors and money managers enter the hedge fund world, returns will decline, volatilities will rise, or both.[134] An MPT-unfriendly explanation might go something like this: talented managers can hedge out directional market risk (hence the bond-like volatility) while still identifying promising investment opportunities (hence the equity-like returns).

Asset returns. Everyone "knows" that stocks generate 10% to 12% annual compound rates of return over time, while bonds will generate considerably less and cash even less than bonds. The reason we "know" this is because of the good work of Roger Ibbotson and Rex Sinquefield, who have produced very accurate reports on *Stocks, Bonds, Bills and Inflation*[135] beginning with the year 1925, updating the numbers annually. In addition, the theoretical underpinning of modern portfolio theory supports analytically what the actual results suggest empirically. I have already addressed some of the issues surrounding over-reliance on MPT in designing portfolios, but let's also take a look at problems with the actual numbers:

- First, it is important to acknowledge that the Ibbotson/Sinquefield numbers are the best we have and, as with MPT generally, we would be foolish not to work with them in our portfolio design work. That said, the question is how confident we should be in those numbers, an issue that will affect the portfolios we recommend to our clients.
- On this subject, the "strong" version of MPT would argue that returns of 10% to 12% are core investment wisdom, that there is something inherent in the ownership of a diversified portfolio of large company stocks that

---

134 Actually, I agree that something like this MPT-friendly outcome is highly likely to occur. A huge amount of inexperienced money is pouring into hedge funds, with the result that new-and-unsophisticated hedge fund investors and rapacious-but-inexperienced hedge funds-of-funds vendors are likely to be bitterly disappointed in their investment results. But I also believe in the MPT-unfriendly argument: thoughtful investors working with talented hedge fund managers will continue to achieve very un-MPT-like results.

135 Roger Ibbotson and Rex Sinquefield, *Stocks, Bonds, Bills and Inflation 2000 Yearbook* (Ibbotson Associates 2000).

produces such returns over time. The "weak" version of MPT would acknowledge that absolute levels of returns are unknowable (based on this data), but that over time stocks will outperform bonds which will outperform cash. Investors would do well to adhere to the "weak" version.[136]

- Although three-quarters of a century may seem like a long time, it's actually a relatively short period of time in terms of the degree of confidence we can have that the Ibbotson/Sinquefield data have much useful predictive power. There are simply not enough observations in a seventy-five year period to allow us to say with confidence that the next seventy-five years will turn out the same way.
- If seventy-five years isn't a long period of time confidence-building-wise, consider the time horizon of the typical wealthy family. Most families design portfolios for ten-to-twenty year periods,[137] but in virtually no ten-to-twenty-year period did US large caps produce 10% to 12% returns. Sometimes they produced more, sometimes less. Over periods of time that short, it's anybody's guess. (And, as noted above, there is a considerable difference between most families' theoretical time horizon—the ten-to-twenty-years referred to above—and their actual time horizon—about thirty-six months.)

Hard assets. Many families own so-called "hard" assets: gold, timber, crude oil, directly placed real estate, etc. Advisors sometimes treat these assets as

---

136 It may seem inconceivable that, over a long span of time, bonds could outperform stocks. But imagine a world in which the yields on stocks rose significantly (before the 1960s, stock yields were always higher than bond yields) and in which equity investors demanded some sort of senior claim on the assets of the corporation (say, by restricting its borrowing power). Such a world may not be a likely one, but it is a possible one, and in it bonds might well outperform stocks. It is also interesting to note that between 1800 and 1900 stock and bond returns were close: 6.51% for stocks and 4.99% for bonds. It was only in the 20th century that stocks significantly outperformed bonds: 9.89% for stocks and 4.85% for bonds. See Jeremy J. Siegel, *Stocks for the Long Run: The Definitive Guide to Financial Market Returns and Long-Term Investment Strategies*, 3rd ed. (McGraw-Hill, 2002), 5-18.

137 The "objective" time horizon for most multi-generational families is actually much longer than this. However, the *actual* time horizon for many family investors is much shorter. After observing family investors in action for nearly thirty years, it is clear to me that for many families invested during very difficult market periods (1973–74 and 2000–01, for example), the true time horizon is less than three years.

though they were no different than other investment assets—that is, that they have expected rates of return, price volatilities, and correlations with other assets—and design the portfolio accordingly. But hard assets are best viewed as true hedges against MPT-designed portfolios, not as a part of them. Applying MPT concepts to gold-as-an-asset-class (for example) is like applying quantum mechanics concepts to black holes.

"Fat tails." Financial advisors sometimes casually note that while their models assume a normal distributions of events, in practice "fat tails" are often encountered.[138] But a distribution that has fat tails is by definition not a normal distribution, and the consequences for the management of real world portfolios of this casual fact are momentous.[139]

Risk. In modern portfolio theory terms, the risk associated with owning capital assets is measured by the price volatility of those assets. In some ways, that makes perfect sense, but in other ways it is simply too silly for words. To see why, let's look at volatility in a different context: the risks associated with weather. Imagine that climatological scientists were to argue that weather risk can be defined by the volatility—that is, the changeability—of weather. In some ways, that makes sense. Whether the weather is good or bad, if it is consistent enough that we can plan ahead for it, then we can deal with the risks. But if volatility is too high—if weather changes from good to bad to good too frequently and unpredictably, then we can't plan ahead. But this is almost a trivial consideration—what really matters is the risk of extremely damaging weather: hurricanes, tornados, lightning, powerful thunderstorms, hail, etc. And the same is true for the price volatility of investment assets: the natural, and even occasionally extreme, oscillations in the price level of securities should be a trivial consideration for most investors. We know from long experience that good markets follow bad and vice versa, just as good weather follows bad, and vice versa. What really matters is that we not employ strategies

---

138 In a perfectly normal distribution, two-thirds of all observations fall within one Standard Deviation. Two Standard Deviations (actually, 1.96 S.D.s) would encompass 95% of all observations, and so on out to an infinitely rare set of observations at the tail end of the curve (on each side). But when we plot real-world capital markets events we don't get a normal distribution. Instead we get a distribution with "fat tails" on both ends of the curve. What this means is not that Standard Deviation methodology is fundamentally right but slightly wrong. What it means is that Standard Deviation is not the correct measurement of risk in the real world because the real-world distribution of events is not "normal."

139 In case you want to impress your friends, distributions with fat tails are technically known as leptokurtic distributions.

that destroy capital so permanently as to change fundamentally the investor's economic circumstances. Such strategies are easy to identify and avoid, although, unfortunately, many investors fail to avoid them:

- Significant capital can, and very likely will, be *rapidly* destroyed by (a) holding concentrated positions in individual securities or industries, no matter how sound those companies seem today;[140] (b) getting caught up in bubble markets or trendy investment themes (dot.coms, daytrading, tech, telecom, momentum stocks, etc.); structuring a portfolio that contains far more imbedded risk than you can tolerate, so that you bail out immediately after incurring large losses.
- Significant capital can, and will, be *slowly* (but equally surely) destroyed by (a) owning a portfolio that is too cautious relative to your spending; (b) not paying attention to the costs of investing: (in this order) taxes, transaction costs (including market impact), and advisory fees; and (c) constantly changing your investment strategy.

These are the real risks of investing, and most of them have nothing to do with portfolio volatility, and hence with MPT.

Behavioral Finance

Traditional finance assumes that we are rational, while behavioral finance simply assumes we are normal.

Meir Statman[141]

There is nothing quite like a Nobel Prize to focus the investing public's attention. As noted above, Harry Markowitz developed the concept of mean

---

140 Whenever I mention this to people, they always point out the (very rare) exceptions: wouldn't Greycourt have advised the early Microsoft employees to diversify their Microsoft positions? By holding onto that one stock, they became millionaires. Well, yes and no. Greycourt rarely advises diversifying completely away from a concentrated position in which the client has confidence. In the exceptional cases (like Microsoft), diversifying enough of the position to ensure future wealth regardless of what happens to the company will result in investors being less rich than they would have been, but still very rich. In all the other cases, diversifying a portion of the position will avoid a possibly catastrophic loss of capital.

141 Statman is the Glenn Klimek Professor of Finance at Santa Clara University. Quoted in Jean Brunel, "Revisiting the Asset Allocation Challenge Through a Behavioral Finance Lens," *The Journal of Wealth Management*, Fall 2003, p. 10.

variance optimization in the early 1950s,[142] but it wasn't until he was awarded the Nobel Prize in Economics in 1990 that most investors began to develop a keen interest in efficient frontiers. In 2002, Daniel Kahneman won the Nobel for his work in behavioral finance, and suddenly investors everywhere are looking at behavioral finance techniques to improve their risk-adjusted performance. In fact, Kahneman (and his colleague, Amos Tversky[143]) did their key work back in the 1970s.[144]

Well better late than never. The fact is that Markowitz' work revolutionized the way the capital markets operated and what the implications of that knowledge might be for the design and diversification of investment portfolios. And while it is too soon to say with certainty, it seems likely that the work of the behavioral finance professionals will similarly revolutionize the way we think about the design and management of our portfolios. Since Markowitz won the Nobel in 1990, we have tended to design our portfolios as though we were all mean variance optimizers, perfect little economic beings who always made the "right" decision in our own interests. The work of Kahneman, Tversky, *et. al* has blown this cozy little conceit to pieces. Sometimes, it true, we behave as perfect economic beings. But other times we behave like, well, human beings. We make decisions on the basis of biases that don't reflect real world facts. We allow our responses to decisions to depend on how the questions are framed. We engage in complex mental accounting, ignoring the fact that our various asset baskets are all interrelated. We allow ourselves to be driven by hopes and fears, rather than facts.

So which is better—modern portfolio theory, which describes how markets work, or behavioral finance, which describes how people work? The answer, of course, is that we need both. MPT and behavioral finance are both important tools in helping us design and manage successful investment portfolios. Both have advantages and disadvantages, however, and it is useful to review those pros and cons before we proceed to think about how combining the two approaches might work.

---

142 Harry Markowitz, "Portfolio Selection," *Journal of Finance*, 1952.

143 Tversky had the misfortune to die in 1996. Nobel Prizes can only be awarded to living persons.

144 See, e.g., Daniel Kahneman and Amos Tversky, "On the Psychology of Prediction," *Psychological Review*, 1973, 80:237-251; Amos Tversky and Daniel Kahneman, "Availability: A Heuristic for Judging Frequency and Probability," *Cognitive Psychology*, 1973, 5:207-232; Amos Tversky and Daniel Kahneman, "Judgment under Uncertainty: Heuristics and Biases," *Science*, 1974, 185:1124-1131; Daniel Kahneman and Amos Tversky, "Intuitive Prediction: Biases and Corrective Procedures," *Management Science*, 1979, 12:313-327.

Limitations of Modern Portfolio Theory

The heart has its reasons,
of which reason knows nothing.
Pascal

I have discussed above the many issues presented by modern portfolio theory, especially when we try to apply its theories to the real world of investment portfolios. Suffice it to say that MPT is a theoretical construct that attempts to describe how capital markets operate, not a recipe for designing investment portfolios. In other words, MPT is descriptive, not prescriptive. And even insofar as MPT can be said to be prescriptive, its predictive accuracy about how markets will behave in the future is unusably low within any kind of time horizon relevant to human investors. Finally, MPT's assumption that we are all and always rational wealth-maximizers is clearly incorrect.

As a result of these issues, when financial advisors attempt to communicate with clients about their portfolios using MPT constructs, communication largely ceases. As Meir Statman hilariously puts it:

> Conversations with clients often resemble the Gary Larson cartoon in which the man says to his dog, 'Ginger, I have had it! Stay out of the garbage, Ginger. Understand, Ginger? Stay out of the garbage, or else!' And Ginger hears: 'Blah blah blah, Ginger. Blah blah blah, Ginger. Blah blah blah, Ginger.' Financial advisors say, 'High returns cannot be guaranteed. No one can guarantee that high risk will bring high returns. No guarantee, you understand?' And clients hear: 'Blah blah blah high returns. Blah blah blah no risk. Blah blah blah guaranteed!'[145]

Limitations of Behavioral Finance

In a sense, behavioral finance picks up where modern portfolio theory leaves off, completing the circle. It describes how investors actually behave, rather than how they should behave. It recognizes that we sometimes act in our own best economic interests, and that we sometimes don't.[146] Assuming that modern

---

145 Meir Statman, "Financial Physicians," *AIMR's Investment Counseling for Private Clients IV* (No. 4, 2002), p. 5.

146 In other words, there is a sense in which utility maximization—the basis of modern portfolio theory—is a tautology. However we behave, and no matter how bizarre or "irrational" that behavior appears, it must be in our interests or we wouldn't behave that way. See Richard H. Thaler's very interesting book on economic anomalies, *The Winner's Curse: Paradoxes and Anomalies of Economic Life* (Princeton University Press, 1992), p. 2.

portfolio theory largely correctly describes the way markets operate, behavioral finance describes how we might best profit from that knowledge.

The foundations of behavioral finance were established by the work of Daniel Kahneman and Amos Tversky, the founders of "prospect theory."[147] Prospect theory suggests that, in making decisions (especially, but not exclusively, financial decisions), we tend to "irrationally" favor long-shots, to avoid near certain gains, to buy insurance against losses that are quite unlikely to occur, and to take large risks to win back large losses. The theory focuses especially on the fact that our attitude toward the risks associated with obtaining gains may be quite different from our attitude toward risks associated with losses.[148]

But there are serious issues associated with behavioral finance, just as there are with modern portfolio theory. Before proceeding, let's examine some of them.

Weather patterns don't know they are being studied. Behavioral finance shares with other forms of psychological research the challenge of dealing with sentient research subjects. If a scientist is studying weather patterns, the weather patterns don't know they are being studied and don't change their behavior as a result of being involved in a research project. But human research subjects are maddeningly more complex. The very fact of knowing that we are involved in an experiment causes us to behave differently than we would behave outside the laboratory context. Maybe we are answering questions honestly and without guile. But maybe we are trying to give the investigator the answer she wants to hear. Maybe we are annoyed at having been "strong-armed" into participating in the experiment (to pass Psychology 101, for example). Maybe we are nervous about appearing stupid and hence inadvertently give answers that we wouldn't give in another context.

Human subjects don't always play by the rules. Imagine that CNN has just reported the results of a large, longitudinal[149] study of 10,000 subjects showing

---

147 The term "prospect theory" apparently derives from one's prospects of winning a lottery. Most people believe, however, that Tversky and Kahneman adopted the term mainly because it was catchy and would raise the profile of their work. See, e.g., Daniel Kahneman and Amos Tversky, "Prospect Theory: An Analysis of Decisions under Risk," *Econometrica*, 1979, 47:313-327.

148 The most extensive treatments of behavioral finance are probably Hersh Shefrin's *Beyond Greed and Fear: Understanding Behavioral Finance and the Psychology of Investing* (Oxford University Press, 2002), and Richard H. Thaler's earlier *Advances in Behavioral Finance* (Russell Sage Foundation, 1993).

149 A "longitudinal" study is one that continues over time, rather than being a one-off project. At one extreme, a large population may be studied over decades. At the other extreme, a longitudinal study might follow a relatively small group of subjects for a few days or weeks.

that people who ate bran muffins everyday doubled their chances of developing brain tumors. Before we eliminate bran from our diets, we might be interested to know that since the study went on for ten years, almost everyone in both groups cheated. In other words, those in Group A, who were supposed to eat bran muffins everyday, didn't—possibly because they got sick to death of bran muffins. And those in Group B, who were never supposed to eat bran muffins, did in fact eat them regularly—possibly because they liked bran muffins and possibly because they figured that since bran muffins were the subject of the research study they must be good for you. In other words, the two groups were a lot more like each other in their bran muffin habits than the researchers assumed.

The phrase "statistically significant" doesn't necessarily mean much. Referring back to the study of bran muffins, when CNN tells us that the results of the study were "statistically significant," we tend to hear "the results were valid and we should stop eating bran muffins." Actually, there is a subtle but important distinction between statistical significance and, say, the likelihood that the results of the study can be applied to us. Statistical significance is a measure of the randomness of the data in a study. If the sample itself (the subjects selected to participate in the study) is biased in some way, the statistical tests for significance will be meaningless. Thus, it would be important to know that all the subjects in the bran muffin study were middle-aged female residents of the San Francisco Bay area who were paid to participate and who were unlikely to move away during the ten-year period of the study. In other words, "statistical significance" with respect to the bran muffin study probably means nothing more than that similar results would likely be generated if the study were repeated using 10,000 middle-aged female residents of the Bay Area (etc.). The relevance of the study to the rest of us remains a major unanswered question.

What about the other 40%? If the results show that 60% of the subjects in a behavioral finance experiment made the "wrong" choice on a financial test, what about the other 40%? As investors and financial advisors, can we simply assume that all our clients fall among the 60% who got it wrong?

Experience and education matter. All of us make bad decisions in areas we know little about, but that doesn't mean that we will continue to make bad decisions once we have learned something about the subject. I might be a lousy bridge player, making one bad decision after another. But that's because I don't know much about bridge. If I played more often and studied the game, I would likely make much better decisions. And the same is true of many of the findings of behavioral finance theory: once investors understand that their decisions are bad ones, and why, they are likely to make much better decisions in the future.

Having something really at stake matters. It's one thing to pop off with a quick answer in a laboratory setting. That answer might even be the "natural" answer we would make. But it's another thing altogether to make a decision that affects, say, a $100 million investment portfolio. In the latter case we are far less likely to "pop off," or shoot-from-the-hip. We are far more likely to think hard about what the right answers might be and to get some advice about them.[150]

Experimenters' expectations affect the outcome of their studies. Our worst fears about research studies have proven to be correct: researchers' *expectations* of what they will find profoundly affect what they actually find. In one study, a group of teachers was told that the members of their class had scored in the "near genius" range on a set of aptitude tests. Members of that class subsequently got excellent grades. A second group of teachers was told that members of their class had scored well below average on aptitude tests. Members of that class subsequently got poor grades. Needless to say, the members of both classes were the same. And this phenomenon of "finding what we expect to find" (or worse, finding what we *want* to find) extends even to non-human subjects. In another study, one group of experimenters was told that the strain of mice they were using had been bred to be especially intelligent. Those mice turned out to learn their way through mazes very quickly. Another group of experimenters was told that the strain of mice they were using was particularly dense. Those mice turned out to learn their way through mazes very slowly. The strains of mice in both groups were, of course, identical.[151] Thus, while experimenters do their best to structure their experiments carefully and to avoid allowing their own expectations to affect the results, investigator bias is always an issue.

Employing Iterative Combinations of Both Theories

MPT can be thought of as the "rational" approach to portfolio design. Despite its limitations, it looks unblinkingly at the way capital markets operate and suggests how we might optimally exploit those markets to our own advantage. Unfortunately, the investment strategies suggested by MPT are often unpalatable to investors, even when they are correctly understood.

---

150 See, generally, Gerald Marwell and Ruth Ames, "Economists Free Ride, Does Anyone Else?" *Journal of Public Economics*, vol 15, pp. 295-310 (1981). This article also politely suggests that the only people who behave like utility maximizers are economists.

151 These studies were reported in the Wall Street Journal. See Sharon Begley, Science Journal, "Expectations May Alter Outcomes Far More than We Realize," *Wall Street Journal*, November 7, 2003, p. B1.

Behavioral finance can be thought of as the "arational" approach to portfolio design. An "arational" approach is not necessarily "irrational." Indeed, the "wrong" choices we make as investors may be suboptimal from a purely economic perspective, but those choices often serve deeper emotional needs.

It is interesting to speculate about the possibility of combining "rational" MPT and "arational" behavior finance approaches into one integrated advisory process. Suppose, for example, that we were to design the client's portfolio in the traditional manner, using MPT-based strategic asset allocation techniques. At the same time, we can design the client's portfolio using techniques informed by behavioral finance. We can then compare the two results in an instructive way.

Step One—Design the Traditional MPT Portfolio

Strategic asset allocation[152] represents the state of the art in MPT-influenced portfolio design, although in reality it is practiced by a surprisingly small group of elite advisory firms.[153] In Chart 1, the column labeled "MPT" suggests a portfolio that might have been designed using strategic asset allocation techniques. This portfolio is based on a forward-looking view of capital markets expectations and the degree of risk required to grow our asset base faster than inflation, spending, taxes, and so on. It has the advantage of being likely to succeed in pure financial terms if we will stick with the strategy.

But that is precisely the rub. The portfolio is "uncomfortable" for us, partly because of the inclusion of asset classes we may not completely understand (emerging markets, directional hedge), and partly because the portfolio will likely incur periods of short term underperformance that will sorely test our investment patience. For these reasons, the likelihood that we will, in fact, stick with the portfolio is small. Indeed, there is a serious possibility that we will abandon the strategy at the very worst time. The MPT portfolio elevates risk-return optimality over investor comfort, with the result that we are unlikely to meet our long term needs.

---

152 Defined by Brunel as an approach that "should cover all the multiple locations…through which a wealthy family holds their assets and be formulated through a multi-period process driven by after-tax results." Brunel, op. cit., note 141, p. 10.

153 A serious drawback of strategic asset allocation, insofar as the financial industry is concerned, is that it can only be accomplished by very senior investment professionals working one-on-one with clients in a highly customized manner. This is exactly the opposite of the mass approach that maximizes the profitability of the global financial giants.

Step Two—Design the Behavioral Finance Portfolio

Despite the thirty-year history of behavioral finance, few investigators have suggested concrete ways to implement the learning of that branch of economics. Traditionally, in trying to get a sense of a client's tolerance for investment risk, financial advisors have engaged in rule-of-thumb exercises or even more bizarre techniques. There was, for example, the approach we might call your-age-is-your-fate: subtract your age from 100 and that's what your equity exposure should be. There were the pre-designed portfolios assigned to clients according to their age range: if you were between 30 and 40, you got Portfolio A; between 40 and 50, Portfolio B, etc. My personal favorites were the bizarre questionnaires investors were asked to complete: "Would you rather curl up with a good book or go bungee jumping?"

Recently, however, two more promising approaches have been suggested:

- Meir Statman has suggested that an investment portfolio be viewed as a pyramid, with the lowest-risk goals (and associated investments) at the broad bottom and the highest-risk goals (and associated investments) at the narrow top.[154]
- Jean P. Brunel has elaborated on Statman's suggestion by converting Statman's pyramid into a more traditional portfolio design framework: Brunel invites the investor to quantify the relative importance of the four traditional investment goals: liquidity, income, capital preservation and growth.[155]

In Chart 1, the column labeled "Behavior Finance" suggests a portfolio that might result from the use of the Statman/Brunel approach. It is a cautious portfolio, reflecting behavioral finance's findings about loss aversion. Since three of the four investment goals (liquidity, income, capital preservation) tend to lead inevitably toward cautious strategies, and only one goal (growth) tends to lead toward more aggressive strategies, the behavioral finance portfolio has the likely disadvantage of growing too slowly to preserve our wealth over the years. But it has the advantage of being "comfortable" for us, and representing a strategy we are likely to stick with at least until we realize that our asset base hasn't kept pace with their expectations. In other words, our behavioral finance portfolio has indulged our inherent biases, but it may have resulted in a suboptimal portfolio that elevates comfort over investment success.

---

[154] Meir Statman, "Behavioral Finance: Past Battles, Future Engagements," *Financial Analysts Journal*, November/December 1999, pp. 18-28.

[155] Brunel, op. cit., note 141, pp. 11-18 passim.

Merging the two approaches

Given this dilemma, how can we reconcile the capital markets strength of MPT portfolios with the human-centered strength of behavioral finance portfolios? One suggestion is to evaluate both portfolios simultaneously, being honest about the advantages and disadvantages of each. Our game plan would be to start with a portfolio that is closer to the behavioral finance model, but with the expectation that, over time, we would move iteratively evolve toward the MPT model.

Thus, we might begin with the behavioral finance portfolio but with a five-year plan (or even longer) to move toward the MPT portfolio. The column in Chart 1 labeled "Difference" shows what we would have to do to make this transition. Thus, we will have to decrease the portfolio's exposure to "comfortable" asset classes like US large cap, bonds and cash, and we will have to increase its exposure to less comfortable asset classes like emerging markets, directional (long/short) hedge, absolute return hedge, private equity and real estate. In addition, when the spreads between high yield bonds and Treasury bonds reach extreme levels, we will opportunistically gain exposure to junk bonds, moving gradually out of that asset as spreads narrow.

To make this transition palatable, it is necessary that we gain experience with less comfortable asset classes gradually. If the transition is expected to occur over a five year period, for example, it may make sense for us to adjust asset class exposures at the rate of 20% per year. Thus, each year 3% of the beginning US large cap exposure will be sold off and invested in asset classes that need to grow.

The beauty of making the transition over time is that, while the initial goal may be to have made the complete transition in five years, there is no reason why this decision can't be revisited. If we find that we are especially concerned about a particular asset class, investments in that category can slow down. If we find that we are particularly comfortable with a particular asset class, investments in that category can speed up.

Challenges Associated with Making the Transition

The challenges associated with the transition from a behavioral finance portfolio to an MPT portfolio are the same as the challenges associated with any significant portfolio transition, namely, taxes, market timing issues, and minimum account size problems (for smaller families). Regarding taxes, it is fortunately the case that most behavioral finance portfolios will prove to be too cautious. Therefore, we will tend to be moving from lower-growth assets to higher growth assets, minimizing problems associated with having to sell low tax cost basis investments. In Chart 1, for example, we will need to reduce the bond and cash portfolios most significantly, and that transition is unlikely to incur serious tax problems.

Market timing is always an issue in transitioning an investment portfolio. But by making the transition over an extended period of years, we are not only getting used to uncomfortable assets, but are able to average-in and out of asset classes over time, minimizing the risk of bad market timing calls. More sophisticated families, of course, may wish to key the portfolio transition not to "time" but to "valuation," i.e., moving toward needed asset classes as they become under-valued and moving out of unneeded asset classes as they become over-valued.

Minimum account size issues can also arise, of course. If our asset base is not large, it may be difficult to gain a small, starting position in certain asset classes. If we have $10 million of investable assets, for example, it should not be difficult to put $1.5 million productively to work in directional hedge (via a fund of funds, for example). But if we are moving from a 0% directional hedge exposure to a 15% exposure over five years, it may be more problematic to put $300,000 to work productively each year. Fortunately, minimum account sizes are falling, even among some of the better hedge funds of funds, and in other asset classes it will be relatively easy to find an institutional mutual fund (or Delaware business trust) to invest in until we meet the minimum size for a separate account.

Summary

Modern portfolio theory represents the best learning we have about how capital markets actually operate, while behavioral finance offers the best insights into how investors actually behave. But markets don't care what investors think of as risk, and hence idiosyncratic ideas about risk and what to do about it are bound to harm our long term investment results. On the other hand, Daniel Kahneman, Amos Tversky and their followers have demonstrated beyond doubt that we all harbor idiosyncratic ideas and that we tend to act on them, regardless of the costs to our economic welfare.

By combining both MPT and behavioral finance models as we design our portfolios, we stand the best chance of designing, implementing and maintaining portfolios that will prove to be both acceptable to our peace of mind and productive to our wealth.

CHART 1

Asset Class	*Behavior Finance*	*MPT*	*Difference*
US large passive	30.0%	15.0%	15.0%
US small passive	5.0%	5.0%	0.0%
Non-US active	5.0%	5.0%	0.0%
Emerging markets equity active	0.0%	5.0%	-5.0%
Directional hedge	0.0%	15.0%	-15.0%
Absolute return hedge	5.0%	15.0%	-10.0%
Private equity/venture	5.0%	10.0%	-5.0%
Real estate passive	5.0%	10.0%	-5.0%
High yield debt	NA	*	*
Bonds	35.0%	17.0%	18.0%
Cash	10.0%	3.0%	7.0%

*Opportunistic

Two

Chapter 6

Financial Crooks and Investor Trust

The Corporate Scandals

Corporate America has got to understand there's a higher calling than trying to fudge the numbers.
—President Bush, June 28, 2002

For a considerable period of time during the first few years of the 21st century it had gotten to the point where we were afraid to turn on the news or pick up a newspaper. Appropriately enough, we are all deeply disturbed by the chicanery and outright fraud that have come to characterize too much of corporate and financial America. But before we give in to despair and take investment action that could be damaging to our capital, let's step back and try to put the situation in perspective. While it is too early for any of us to understand all the implications of the Bubble Markets of the late 1990s and the resulting corporate scandals, some of those implications are already apparent. Not all of them will be palatable to investors, but the willingness to stare unpalatable truths in the eye is one of the hallmarks of successful investing. Here is a summary of those implications:

- First, whether we like it or not (and we certainly don't), periodic epidemics of bad corporate behavior are an inevitable part of the price we pay for the benefits of a free market economy.
- Second, the seeds of the current crop of corporate scandals were planted not by corrupt executives but by greedy investors and their Wall Street cheerleaders.

- Third, while the scandals have involved a small minority of companies and executives, a fundamental change has occurred—namely, the acceptance and, indeed, encouragement of "earnings management" by corporations. This change has important implications for investors, the main one being that the dangers associated with holding concentrated securities positions is now extreme.
- Finally, on the bright side, corporate scandals, collapsing markets, and investor fear and distrust are likely to present a once-in-a-lifetime opportunity for thoughtful investors to create wealth.

Bad Behavior and Free Markets

Starting with "first principles," let's not forget that free capital markets require that we trust individual corporations and their executives to make decisions that, within reason, are in their own best interests. We know perfectly well that executives will sometimes make wrong or socially undesirable decisions, particularly when faced with considerable temptations. As a result, we establish constraints—civil, criminal, and cultural—on individual decision-making at roughly the point where we feel that the undesirable consequences overwhelm the importance of individual decision-making. Because we know that millions of individual decisions will produce better outcomes than one state-imposed decision, we tend to err on the side of giving people more, rather than less, discretion.

One result of this free market approach is that, periodically, we will experience epidemics of bad corporate behavior. These epidemics peak at exactly the point where the incentives for self-enrichment at the expense of the broader good are at their greatest—in other words, during Bubble Markets. The names of the miscreants of the modern era resonate with the tenor of their times: Robert Vesco, Michael Milken, Marc Rich, and, of course, Enron, Tyco, WorldCom, *et al.* Today's epidemic is certainly the worst of our professional lifetimes, but then the Bubble Market and Cinderella Economy of the late 1990s was the most extreme since the boom of the 1920s. (After the Stock Market Crash of 1929, the Pecora Hearings in the early 1930s shocked and titillated Americans with tales of astonishing greed, brazen stock price manipulation, insider trading, incredible interlocking trusts that controlled vast industries, and similar exposes.) The bigger the boom, the bigger the bust.

Still and all, while criminal corporate behavior needs to be appropriately punished and the constraints we impose on individual decision-making need to be re-examined, we shouldn't forget that periodic bad behavior is part of the cost we bear for the benefits we derive from a free market economy.

Investor Complicity

While politicians have made hay with voters by criticizing executive greed, there is plenty of blame to go around, and some of it lies at our feet as investors. For example, during the peak of the Bubble Market (roughly 1998–1999), companies were brutally punished for missing consensus earnings targets by mere pennies.[156] CEOs who missed targets two quarters in a row were summarily fired, to the loud applause of enraged investors. Moreover, companies who consistently met consensus earnings expectations saw their share prices soar, and CEOs of those companies were rewarded beyond the dreams of Croesus. Faced with the choice of being fired or getting unimaginably rich, how surprised ought we to be that most CEOs began to "manage" corporate earnings?

Of course, there is a big difference between "managing" earnings and "manipulating" earnings. (Think of this analogy: it is acceptable for individual taxpayers to arrange their affairs so as to *avoid* payment of income taxes, but it is a criminal act to arrange our affairs so as to *evade* payment of taxes.) Since investors prize consistent earnings growth, sensible CEOs "manage" company earnings to ensure quarter-over-quarter growth. The earnings they are reporting are real and accurately reflect the fundamental value of the company, but those earnings would not have arrived on so conveniently consistent a schedule without substantial attention to earnings management techniques.[157] The most talented of these earnings managers—Jack Welch at GE, Lou Gerstner at IBM, Bill Gates at Microsoft—have become icons, and their strategies are studied by other executives and at every business school in the world.[158]

But note what a change this represents from the way CEOs operated a mere decade ago. In those days, Old School CEOs followed conservative accounting

---

156 According to the New York Times, companies that missed analyst estimates often lost 10% of their market value. Alex Berenson, "Tweaking Numbers to Meet Goals Comes Back to Haunt Executives," New York *Times*, June 29, 2002, p. A1. In a desperate attempt to meet consensus earnings expectations, one company (WorldCom) cooked its books sufficiently to meet expectations by 1/100 of one cent (twice)!

157 "Did Microsoft manage earnings? Does GE manage earnings? Sure, we all know that." Jon Brorson, who oversees $65 billion in equity investments at Northern Trust Company, quoted by Alex Berenson, op. cit. note 156, p. A1.

158 Even the icons can sometimes step over the line, however. One abusive technique is to create accounting reserves that can be released later when they are needed to boost earnings. Microsoft engaged in exactly this behavior, and was fined for it by the SEC.

practices and let the earnings chips fall where they may. In some quarters their companies' earnings greatly exceeded consensus expectations and in some quarters they fell far short. Those practices passed muster in the 1980s, but in the 1990s, and especially during the Bubble Market, Old School CEOs either changed their stripes or were summarily fired, usually just ahead of investor lynch mobs.

Now let's turn to earnings *manipulation*. Most modern CEOs are pragmatic folks who understand that an important part of their jobs is to produce strong and consistent quarter-over-quarter earnings growth. As noted, they are willing to engage in legal and (for the most part) ethically acceptable accounting techniques to accomplish that goal. But they draw a line in the sand somewhere, beyond which they simply will not go, no matter how loud the howls of protest may be from Wall Street and the investor community. But Bubble Markets and greedy investors also produce a different kind of CEO, the kind who believe their job is to give investors whatever they want and to engage in whatever accounting techniques are necessary to do so.[159] These CEOs are not engaged in managing real earnings to ensure that they occur at the right times, but in *creating earnings where none exist.* These are the executives who have created the scandals we read about every day.

In any event, the larger point is that, whenever investors demand the impossible, there will be companies around willing to deliver exactly that. Politicians can rage all they want about the need for conservative accounting practices and higher ethical standards, but the Old School CEOs long ago fell by the wayside—at investor insistence—and their type has all but disappeared from the corporate gene pool.

Implications for Investors

What used to be a conflict is now a synergy.
—Jack Grubman, former telecommunications analyst at Citigroup Salomon Smith Barney, during the Bubble Market, mid-1999

Distressing as the corporate scandals of the early twenty-first century may be, they represent both an important lesson for investors and, ironically, a very

---

[159] Some common abusive accounting techniques involved capitalizing costs that should have been expensed (WorldCom); creating incentives for wholesalers to purchase far more product than the wholesalers believed they could resell to retailers, in effect, cannibalizing future sales to push them into the current year (Bristol Myers Squibb), and engaging in undisclosed off-balance-sheet financing (Enron).

rare opportunity for sophisticated investors to create significant, permanent wealth. Here are some of those implications.

Conflicts of interest matter. When markets are so strong that any daytrader can easily select stocks that are certain to appreciate handsomely, concern about conflicts of interest can seem quaint, or even a sure mark of unsophistication. Indeed, now-disgraced Salomon Smith Barney telecommunications analyst Jack Grubman used to brag that it was precisely his conflicts of interest that made him useful to investors. Because Grubman was so close to Bernard Ebbers at WorldCom, for example, Grubman claimed that, "What used to be a conflict is now a synergy. They [investors] know I'm in the flow of what's going on."[160]

The trouble was that, while "everyone knew" that research analysts were really just a sales force for their firms' investment banking services, no one dreamed how much wealth could be lost by relying on their analyses. Similarly, "everyone knew" that public accounting firms considered their auditing functions to be nothing more than loss leaders for the sale of far more lucrative consulting services. But no one imagined that the enfeebled auditing function would one day be the last, hopeless line of defense between corporate fraud and massive investor losses. And, of course, "everyone knew" that the huge stock options packages granted to corporate executives badly misaligned executive and shareholder interests.[161] But no one could have foreseen how dramatically this conflict would enrich executives while investors lost billions.

---

160 That was Grubman speaking in mid-1999. After WorldCom collapsed, Grubman was singing a different tune about being "in the flow of what's going on." Interviewed on CNBC, he claimed that, "I am as shocked about this as everybody else." See Patrick McGeehan, "Timing of a Rating Shift Is Raising Some Questions," New York *Times* (June 28, 2002), p. C5. Citigroup would eventually pay WorldCom shareholders $2.65 billion to settle claims that Citigroup and Grubman had misled them about WorldCom's prospects.

161 When an investor owns shares outright, he or she loses money when the stock price declines. But when an executive simply owns an option, he or she has only upside potential, with no downside exposure. (Indeed, if the stock price goes down and stays down, the executive knows that the board of directors will eventually re-price the options.) Once the options are vested and in the money, the executive will exercise the options immediately—there is no advantage to delay, since the stock price could decline below the exercise price at any time. But once the executive exercises, tax rules force him or her to sell the stock immediately in order to raise cash to pay the taxes. Hence, the executive has every incentive to take whatever action is necessary to raise the stock price in the short term, no matter how unsustainable that price may be. He or she will exercise the options, sell the stock and put the cash in the bank, leaving longer term shareholders holding the bag when the stock price eventually collapses.

The simple fact is that conflicts of interest matter. They matter during bull markets and bear markets. They matter whether the conflicts are large or small. They matter because an advisor is either working for you or against you. There is no "synergy" between an investor and an advisor who is working the other side of the street: you are either a guest at the dinner or you are the main course.

Diversify, diversify, diversify. The important lesson is this: earnings management is here to stay, and it is virtually impossible for any investor to know in advance the difference between a company that is managing its earnings and a company that is manipulating its earnings.[162] As a result, no one can know for sure that any company, no matter how squeaky-clean its current reputation, won't be the next Enron, WorldCom, Tyco, Global Crossing, or Bristol Myers Squibb. As a result, having any significant part of your wealth concentrated in one or two companies, always a risky business, has become immeasurably more perilous. Here is a simple test: if a concentrated security position represents so much of your net worth that if its stock price went to zero your lifestyle would be seriously impaired, *you need to diversify, and promptly.*

CAUTION: Competent advisors have determined that taking precipitous investment action in revulsion against appalling corporate behavior could be hazardous to your wealth.

Opportunities to create wealth. Sensible investors recognize that the equity markets are likely to generate returns far lower than those of the 1980s and 1990s, and that the techniques that worked in those days—indexing, focusing on mega-cap, Blue Chip names, employing momentum-based strategies—are likely to prove disappointing. But there is a silver lining inside every black cloud. Many inexperienced investors are likely to follow the (among other things, preposterously tardy) advice of self-help gurus and abandon stocks. After the markets turned in April, 2000, investors have lost literally trillions of dollars. Many no longer trust corporate financial numbers and no longer believe anything corporate CEOs, research analysts or public accounting firms have to say. These investors have absolved themselves of complicity in the post-Bubble debacle, and may abandon the stock market for a generation. In other words, not since 1974 will savvy investors have faced such an extraordinary set of opportunities in the American capital markets. Those opportunities will have to be exploited thoughtfully and over time, of course, but at least the raw

---

162 And given the appalling conflicts of interest among research analysts, investors can expect no help whatever from this quarter.

material for once-in-a-generation creation of permanent wealth lies before us, in the very rubble created by the market collapse and the corporate scandals.

The Mutual Fund Scandals[163]

In 2003 and 2004, our attention was diverted from the corporate scandals by a series of scandals that hit even closer to home, at least for some investors—namely, the mutual fund scandals. The odd thing about many of the activities that led to regulatory action against individuals and firms in the mutual fund industry was that almost everyone who was paying attention knew they had been going on for years. Indeed, certain of the activities—rapid mutual fund timing trades, for example—had even had scholarly articles written about them. Still, even grizzled veterans were surprised at the scope and depth of the activity. More important, the world had changed, post-Enron, and behavior that was formerly winked at suddenly came to be perceived as highly unethical, perhaps even criminal.

How Mutual Funds (Are Supposed to) Work

A mutual fund is nothing more than a special type of corporation. Instead of building factories, it buys securities. Therefore, it is categorized as an "open end investment company" and is regulated accordingly. (Mutual funds that issue only a limited number of shares are "closed-end investment companies.") Although mutual funds have many, many public shareholders, the disclosure rules that apply to public non-investment company corporations do not apply to mutual funds. Instead, corporations that are mutual funds are regulated under the Investment Company Act of 1940. They are regulated so as to ensure that they will operate in the interests of the mutual fund shareholders, as opposed to the interests of asset management firms, brokers, insiders and so on. Indeed, the preamble to the 1940 Act specifically notes that funds are to be "organized, operated [and] managed" in the interests of the mutual fund shareholders, as opposed to the interests of "directors, officers, investment advisors" and others.

To examine how mutual funds work, let's examine a typical, but simplified, situation. Combustible Asset Management is a money management firm specializing in micro-cap technology stocks. Combustible decides to form a mutual fund. It does so by setting up a corporate entity and registering it with the SEC as

163 This portion of the chapter originally appeared, in a slightly modified form, as an open letter to clients and friends of Greycourt, dated November 13, 2003. Important contributions to that letter were made by several Greycourt Managing Directors, especially Gregory R. Friedman and Mark Laskow.

an open end investment company. The Combustible Fund will launch itself by selling a certain number of shares, probably purchased by Combustible Asset Management and its principals. The shareholders of Combustible Fund will then elect a board of directors, and that board of directors will, in turn, engage a money management firm to buy and sell micro-cap stocks. Unsurprisingly, the board, which consists entirely of Combustible Asset Management principals and their friends, engages Combustible Asset Management.

Let's assume that micro-cap tech stocks perform quite well. In a few years, Combustible Fund will have a nice track record to advertise, and many investors who have nothing to do with Combustible Asset Management will buy shares in the Combustible Fund. Indeed, eventually, the "public" shareholders will own all but a tiny fraction of Combustible Fund's shares. These "public" shareholders will now elect a board of directors every year, and it is the responsibility of that board to engage, negotiate a fee with, monitor and terminate the fund's manager, Combustible Asset Management.

What actually happens is that the fund's shareholders don't think of themselves as the owners of the Combustible Fund. True, every year they receive a proxy statement asking them to vote for board members nominated by the insiders, but most shareholders throw the proxy material away without even opening it. And those who do return the proxy materials vote overwhelmingly for the nominated candidates—what choice do they have?

After five years or so, let's suppose that Combustible Fund has produced a lousy track record. Combustible's benchmark is up 14%, the average micro-cap fund is up 12%, and Combustible Fund is up 7%. Shouldn't Combustible's board fire Combustible Asset Management and hire a better management firm? Of course it should—it is required by law to act in the interests of the fund's shareholders—but will it? Of course not—Combustible Fund and Combustible Asset Management are "controlled" by the same people, and as long as Combustible Asset Management can make a nice profit on the fees Combustible Fund is paying it, we can be certain that Combustible Asset Management will be reengaged every year, no matter how poorly they perform, no matter how much the "public" shareholders in Combustible Fund are harmed—in short, no matter how much the plain terms and clear intent of the 1940 Act are ignored. The problem, as discussed below, is that the interests of the shareholders of Combustible Asset Management and the interests of the shareholders of Combustible Fund (the mutual fund) are very, very different.

By keeping in mind the distinction between how mutual funds are supposed to operate and how they actually operate, it will be easier to understand how the trading scandals could have occurred.

What Activities Caused the Scandal?

Regulators are examining a variety of improper activities, some of which have bedeviled the mutual fund industry for years, while others are disturbingly new. The traditional problems included:

- Brokers selling "A" shares of mutual funds to larger investors without giving the investors the benefit of lower loads, called "breakpoints." According to the SEC, one in every five investors entitled to lower loads failed to receive them.
- Brokers selling "B" shares of mutual funds as "no load" shares, even though B shares impose loads when the shares are sold.
- Brokers holding sales contests to push in-house mutual fund products.

But what has really fueled the current scandal is a series of activities that, at their best, constitute serious breaches of trust with fund shareholders, and, at their worst, represent criminal activities. The main culprits have been late trading of mutual fund shares and mutual fund timing trades:

- *Late trading.* At 4:00 p.m., most mutual fund shares close for trading, and the fund's shares are priced at that time.[164] Anyone who sends in an order to buy shares after 4:00 p.m. on, say, Monday, will end up buying those shares at the 4:00 p.m. closing price on Tuesday. If an investor could somehow send in a late (post 4:00 p.m.) order on Monday evening and still get the Monday price, that investor could take advantage of late-breaking news that would almost certainly cause the Tuesday price to be higher. This version of insider information is illegal. Nonetheless, firms like Bank of America allowed Canary Capital, and perhaps others, to engage in illegal late trading, and BofA even set up special software for Canary, at Canary's office, to ease the process of illegal trading.
- *Mutual fund timing.* Unlike stocks, most mutual fund shares are priced only once a day, at 4:00 p.m. This feature of mutual fund pricing can be "gamed" by investors who trade rapidly into and out of fund shares.[165] From one point of view, such investors are simply engaging in traditional

---

164 Some mutual funds, such as the Fidelity sector funds, are priced every hour.

165 One frequent type of "gaming" occurs because foreign exchanges close, and hence closing stock prices are known, long before US-based international mutual funds are closed and priced. Suppose that NatWest closes in London at 11:30 a.m. New York time on Monday. US mutual funds that own NatWest are likely to use that closing price in pricing their own fund shares at 4:00 p.m. New York time on Monday. If something happens at 1:00 p.m. New York time that

arbitrage activities, identifying mis-priced securities and profiting from that knowledge. But there are several problems with this point of view. In most arbitrage situations, the arbitrageur is performing a public service—his activities cause mis-pricings to narrow or disappear, making markets more efficient. But when a trader buys into and sells out of mutual fund shares rapidly, he isn't causing the prices of the mutual fund shares to become more accurate—those prices don't change based on the volume of activity in them. Instead, they change only in response to changes in the prices of the underlying securities owned by the mutual funds. In effect, therefore, the rapid trader in mutual fund shares is making his profit at the expense of other, more patient shareholders. Worse, these rapid traders know perfectly well that the mutual fund companies have policies prohibiting rapid trading, and the traders know they are violating those policies. (Some traders have conspired with brokers to trade in many different names, in an effort to avoid detection by the fund companies.) Nonetheless, there is undeniably a difference in culpability between investors who try to time mutual funds, on the one hand, and employees of the mutual fund companies, who owe a duty of loyalty to their fund shareholders. This rapid trading works to the disadvantage of traditional fund investors, since the rapid trader is co-opting for himself profits that rightly belong to the shareholders who are playing by the rules, and since those investors must bear all the costs of the rapid trading. In addition, rapid trading disrupts the fund managers' jobs, as they must constantly be raising cash to meet the needs of redeeming investors and constantly putting new money to work. As a result, as noted, most mutual fund firms actively discourage rapid buying and selling of their shares. The firms set up mechanisms to identify rapid traders and bar them from buying into their funds, and the prospectuses for the funds make it clear that rapid trading will not be tolerated.

Unfortunately, in some mutual fund organizations there was one set of rules for ordinary investors and another set of rules for favored investors. At firms like Janus, Bank of America, Strong, Alliance and others, certain

---

seems certain to boost NatWest's price when it opens on Tuesday, gaming becomes possible. US mutual funds that own NatWest will likely price it at its closing price in London, even though the subsequent news makes it likely that NatWest will close higher on Tuesday. If it does close higher on Tuesday, everything else being equal, the Tuesday price of the mutual fund will also be higher. By buying the fund's shares at the Monday price and selling them at the Tuesday price, traders are profiting from the post-London-closing information.

investors were permitted to trade rapidly in fund shares, while all others were prohibited from such trading. The rapid trading was conducted in secret and only came to light when New York Attorney General Eliot Spitzer exposed the trading programs at Canary Capital Partners, a hedge fund managed by Hartz Mountain heir Edward Stern.

Though rapid trading is not, strictly speaking, illegal, especially from the point of view of the trader (as opposed to the fund), it constitutes a serious breach of trust between the mutual fund firms and their fund shareholders. Mutual funds are stewards for the investor capital entrusted to them, and when a fund permits rapid trading in return for other considerations that duty of stewardship has been breached. Spitzer and others believe that criminal charges can be based on this breach, and they have publicly announced that they are considering charges against, for example, Richard Strong, who traded rapidly in his own companies mutual funds.

Who Were the Worst Offenders?

The industry itself. While the current scandal has focused investor attention on abuses in the mutual fund industry, the simple fact is that many, perhaps most, mutual fund firms have been abusing investors for many years. Though regulators have focused on brokers who sell A and B shares, for example, those shares were invented by mutual fund firms, not brokers.

Or consider the unconscionable level of fees and expenses fund firms have charged over the years. According to Morningstar, the average US large cap mutual fund boasts an annual expense ratio of roughly 1.5%—versus the 5 to 18 basis points charged by the Vanguard index funds, which have outperformed at least three-quarters of all actively managed mutual funds. Munder NetNet Fund, as Morningstar has pointed out, allowed its expense ratio to rise to a hilarious 3.2% while its performance declined 89%. Georgetowne Long-Short Fund charges 3.25% a year and is run by an inexperienced former White House intern. Who buys this stuff?

Or consider the sorry record of fund companies launching trendy new funds at the tops of markets. According to John Bogle, founder of Vanguard, more than 440 tech funds were launched in the 1990s, taking in over $500 billion. The tech funds, the dot.com funds and so on that were launched during the height of the bubble market hysteria fed the foolish enthusiasm of unsophisticated investors, almost all of whom lost big.

Or consider the appalling state of governance among mutual funds. Mutual funds are required by law to have a board of directors responsible for looking out for the interests of fund shareholders. These directors are usually appointed by the managers—very often they are the managers. Instead of looking out for the fund shareholders' interests, highly compensated directors have done essentially nothing for decades.[166]

I could go on and on, but my point is that the mutual fund industry very badly needs to be reformed and in many ways. Focusing on rapid trading and late trading is terrific if it leads to other reforms, but otherwise we will simply halt a few abuses while leaving the many to flourish.

Specific offenders. So many new revelations tumble out everyday that it is impossible to keep up with the pace of the scandal. At this writing, the following firms have been implicated:

- *Putnam.* Putnam traces its name back to Mr. Justice Putnam, author of the famous "prudent man rule," promulgated by the Massachusetts Supreme Court in the Harvard College case in 1830. But modern-day Putnam is famous mainly for its aggressive marketing strategies and poor-quality funds. Putnam CEO Lawrence J. Lasser, has been fired, but repairing Putnam's reputation will be a gigantic challenge.
- *Strong.* While the actual scale of the offenses at Strong was relatively modest—Strong allowed Canary and others to engage in rapid trading—the revelation that Richard Strong himself had engaged in rapid trading sends a message of corruption that investors fear may permeate the entire firm.[167]
- *Bank of America (Nations Funds).* At BofA, CEO Ken Lewis has long made it clear that he intends to make the bank one of the top money managers in the world. To accomplish such a feat in what is essentially a commodity business required BofA to engage in across-the-board aggressiveness that might actually have been in the interests of BofA shareholders, but that was directly opposed to the interests of investors in its mutual fund products.
- *Janus.* Although it is easy to forget, Janus was once a fine, well-managed firm, chock full of talent like founder Tom Bailey, Helen Young Hayes, Tom Marsico and Jim Craig. But during the bubble market Janus lost its way, jumping into virtually every over-valued security on the market, ensuring that its fund shareholders would get badly hurt. (Janus was, let's remember, the largest single shareholder in Enron.) From that point it was all downhill for Janus, as management turmoil followed

---

166 Rules adopted in mid-2004 require the chairs of mutual fund boards to be independent of the mutual fund.

167 In mid-2004 a crippled Strong was sold to Wells Fargo & Co., Inc.

management turmoil, culminating in Janus's involvement in the latest Canary episode. One supposes that it is technically possible for Janus to recover from all this, but it is difficult to understand why investors should care one way or the other.

- *Others.* Many other fund firms have been implicated in major or minor ways. Banc One has already admitted permitting Canary to execute market timing trades in its funds with the full knowledge of senior managers; Prudential brokers (Prudential is now Wachovia Securities) allowed market timing trades despite receiving many letters from fund companies protesting their activities; Alger allowed illegal late trading in its funds; Alliance permitted market timing by a broker and Canary; and the SEC has suggested that as many as 30% of mutual fund companies may have permitted improper trading and that 10% may have permitted illegal late trading.

What Should Investors Do?

Many investors, including several state pension funds, have been so outraged by the scandals that they have simply terminated the involved firms without regard to the possible consequences. But for more prudent investors, here are some thoughts.

Separating bad apples from good apples. First, whatever we do, we shouldn't be giving more money to firms that have demonstrated their complete disregard for our welfare as investors. New money should be placed with firms that have not been implicated in the recent scandals and that have conducted themselves honorably and in the interests of their fund shareholders for many years (e.g., American Funds, Dodge & Cox, Fidelity, T. Rowe Price, Vanguard, etc.)[168]

Separating bad apples from sort-of-good apples. Regarding termination of accounts with funds embroiled in the controversy, it's worth taking the trouble to distinguish between fund companies where the culture that led to the improprieties was established right at the top, versus companies where the improper trading activities may not have permeated the entire firm. Consider the knotty problem of AllianceBernstein. In mid-2000, Alliance Capital, a go-go, sales-oriented, growth stock firm, bought Sanford C. Bernstein, a sedate, research-driven,

---

168 Of course, we can't know for a fact that no illegal or unethical activity has taken place at these firms, but based on their investor-friendly policies over many years, we would be very surprised to see any of them embroiled in the current scandal.

value stock firm.[169] No doubt from the point of view of the marketing team this combination made sense, but it was almost comical miscegenation to anyone familiar with the wildly different cultures of the two firms.

Almost immediately following the acquisition, Alliance's growth approach fell off a cliff. The extremely poor performance, plus what looked like overly cozy relationships between Alliance's senior managers and the companies whose stocks they bought, led to terminations of Alliance by pension funds, and even some lawsuits. Now the same aggressive marketing and asset growth culture has led Alliance into trading improprieties serious enough that the SEC has issued a "Wells" notice[170] to the firm, making it the only firm other than Putnam to receive such a notice. Alliance President and Chief Operating Officer, John D. Carifa, and the chairman of the Alliance mutual fund distribution unit, Michael J. Laughlin, have resigned.

And yet, and yet—Bernstein, though legally part of Alliance, remains a different kind of culture and a different kind of manager. So different that AllianceBernstein has made Lewis Sanders, a Bernstein executive, its Chief Executive Officer, in the hope of cleaning house and establishing a more investor-friendly attitude. When Alliance executives Carifa and Laughlin were asked to resign, they were replaced by Bernstein people: Gerald M. Lieberman and Marc O. Mayer.

Thus the odd case that investors remaining in most Alliance products probably need to have their heads examined, while investors remaining in most Bernstein products are probably acting wisely.

Mutual funds aren't stocks. If the CEO of a listed company were about to be indicted, investors might well decide to bail, expecting the stock to be trashed. But mutual funds aren't stocks—regulatory action, or even criminal action, shouldn't affect the value of the stocks held in the mutual fund's portfolio. Ultimately, of course, if many investors bail out the remaining investors will bear the expenses and taxes associated with the fund's sales activity, but that is something that will happen, if at all, only over time. Hence, there is generally no emergency attached to investor decisions.

Finding a replacement fund. If the offending fund plays an important role in your portfolio, finding a very similar fund is important. Selling an Alliance aggressive growth fund and buying the Vanguard 500 Index Fund represents a

---

[169] Thus, Bernstein is owned by Alliance Capital, which is controlled by AXA Financial, Inc., which is in turn controlled by AXA, SA, based in Paris.

[170] A Wells notice informs a firm that the Commission is prepared to recommend regulatory action.

change in your strategy, and one that might overload your portfolio with value and core stocks, leaving you under-exposed to growth. Hence, before you sell, it's a good idea to know what you're going to buy.

Considering taxes. Mutual funds are required to distribute out to shareholders 95% of realized gains and income. Between that rule and the bear market, most fund investors won't have huge untaxed appreciation in their equity funds. Indeed, long-term investors in bond funds may find that they have a lower cost basis than most equity investors. But if you do have a substantial tax liability, that might outweigh a good bit of moral outrage.

How good are these funds, anyway? I've always wanted to believe that the investment firms with the most integrity are also likely to be those with the best products. This isn't as Pollyanna-ish as it sounds. Consider the kinds of investor-unfriendly actions I discussed above: high fees, high turnover, huge asset bases, launching trendy funds, heavy sales pressure, poor governance. These aren't just disreputable activities, they are the very activities that lead to poor results for investors. Sure, the most ethical fellow in the world can still be a lousy money manager, but it doesn't work the other way around.

And now that the trading scandals are out in the open, it appears that my belief has been confirmed—the fund companies that have made headlines are those that have the most undistinguished groups of funds: Putnam, Alliance, BofA, Alger, Banc One, Prudential. Given the thousands of solid mutual fund products offered by ethical firms, there is really no reason for any investor to buy a fund from these vendors.

Serving two masters. The fundamental problem with mutual fund companies is that they are trying to serve two masters at once. On the one hand, mutual funds exist to serve the needs of investors for sound risk-adjusted returns, and from a regulatory perspective the funds are supposed to be managed in those investors' interests (this is why mutual funds have their own boards of directors). On the other hand, the real money in the mutual fund business comes from the management fees, and it is therefore in the interests of the management company's corporate shareholders to maximize those fees. Thus, fees are way too high and asset bases are way too large. Vanguard avoids this problem by being owned by its own investors: the Vanguard mutual fund shareholders and the Vanguard corporate shareholders are the same people. But short of forcing the Vanguard model on the entire industry, it is interesting to think about how regulators should deal with this dilemma.

What Should the Regulators Do?

It's interesting to report on what one of the main experts on mutual funds has to say. Here, in summary form, are the recommendations made by Don Phillips, a managing director at Morningstar, Inc.:[171]

- Apply the same disclosure standards to investment companies as to publicly traded operating companies. As I noted above, mutual funds are corporations whose stock is held by thousands of "public" shareholders. Yet the disclosure rules that apply to other publicly held corporations don't apply to corporations operated as mutual funds. As Phillips says, "[B]ecause equity shareholders [of publicly held corporations] have historically had a louder voice than have fund shareholders, it's not surprising that disclosure standards for stocks remain far higher than those for funds in many areas. It's time for someone to speak up for fund shareholders and level the playing field."
- Bring more visibility to the corporate structure of funds and the safeguards it provides. At the beginning of this letter I outlined how mutual funds are organized. Though it seems simple and straightforward, as Phillips points out, "The typical fund investor is largely unaware of the corporate structure of funds. Few investors in, say, Fidelity Magellan think of themselves as the owners...of the fund." Phillips also recommended that (a) the chair of the mutual fund board be independent; (b) that the chair of the board write to the fund's shareholders every year to "address the steps the board takes each year in reviewing the manager's performance and the contract that the fund has with the fund management firm;" and (c) that the board be far more active in reviewing marketing materials and other communications between the money manager for the fund and the fund's shareholders.
- Insist that fund management companies report to fund shareholders as they would owners of the business. In particular, Phillips points out that the practice of stating fund costs as a percentage of the assets in the fund, rather than as a percentage of the investor's gain, means that "the real toll of fund fees is dramatically understated."
- Ensure that all shareholders are treated fairly. This is Phillips' response to the current trading scandals. He recommends wider use of "fair

---

171 The full text of Phillips' testimony can be found on the Morningstar Web site, www.morningstar.com.

pricing"[172] and more and higher redemption fees to discourage mutual fund timing.

It would also be useful if we all became far better consumers of mutual fund products. Someone once pointed out that when we are born we get the face we inherited, but that ultimately we end up with the face we deserve. Ultimately, it's a free country, and, ultimately, mutual fund investors will get the mutual fund industry they deserve. The best way to enforce ethical behavior is to stop rewarding unethical behavior. In other words, don't buy expensive funds, don't tolerate high turnover, don't invest in trendy new products, don't put up with lousy returns.

What Should Financial Advisors Do?

Financial advisors are not regulators, and if we spent much of our time trying to ferret out fraud we would never get anything else done. Now that we know about the pervasiveness of trading problems in the mutual fund industry, of course, advisors should inquire specifically about it when possible. For example, when evaluating mutual fund products we can specifically make such inquiries as:

- Have you ever marketed or otherwise offered capacity to do late trading or market timing trades?
- Have you permitted any late trading, either overtly, through manipulation of the timing of orders by brokers, or by other means?
- What have been your policies on market timing trades? Have you ever granted exceptions to these policies?
- What policies and control procedures do you have in place today to prevent any of this?

What financial advisors can certainly do is to focus on the factors described above that tend to label a mutual fund organization as one focused on investor interests or as one focused on the interests of its corporate shareholders. By avoiding the latter, we are highly likely also to avoid most of the problems associated with ethical and compliance lapses.

---

172 "Fair pricing" refers to the practice of some mutual fund companies in using more realistic prices, rather than actual closing prices, in pricing mutual fund shares. Thus, if after the markets closed in Europe something has occurred that is likely to affect the prices of all or some specific listed companies, the mutual fund will adjust those prices upward or downward in pricing the mutual fund shares.

The SEC Inquiry into Pension Consultants

In December of 2003, the SEC sent a 12-page letter to a group of well-known investment consulting firms primarily serving the pension plan industry. (I will refer to those firms as "pension consultants.") The letter requested massive amounts of data about the level of independence of the firms, whether their advice to pension funds might have been compromised by payments from money managers, and similar matters. The deadline for responding was January 12, 2004.

I think the SEC's concerns are valid and that investors of all kinds, as well as advisors to those investors, can learn a great deal by understanding the nature of the inquiry. In addition, recent mainstream press coverage[173] may have raised questions in the minds of many investors about the quality and independence of the advice they are receiving.

Who Were the Subjects of the SEC inquiry?

The Commission has not made public the names of the firms that received its letter, and some firms have declined to comment about the inquiry. Nonetheless, press reports make it clear that a number of the major pension consultants were involved, including Callan Associates, CRA Rogers Casey, Frank Russell Co., Mercer Investment Consulting, Segal Advisors, Strategic Investment Solutions, Summit Strategies Group, Watson Wyatt, Wilshire Associates, and so on.[174]

What Information Is the Commission Seeking?

I have not seen a copy of the Commission's letter, but industry press coverage has suggested that the SEC is interested mainly in "practices with respect to advice regarding the selection of investment advisers to manage plan assets; selection of other service providers such as administrators, custodians, investment research firms and broker-dealers; and services other than investment consulting provided to plan sponsors, investment advisors and mutual funds."[175]

---

173 Mary Williams Walsh, "Concerns Raised Over Consultants to Pension Funds," New York *Times* (March 21, 2004), p. 1.

174 See, e.g., Barry B. Burr, "Consultants Under the Gun with SEC Probe," *Pensions & Investments* (January 12, 2004), p. 1, 25; Arden Dale, "SEC Looks at Pension-Fund Advisers," *Dow Jones Newswires* (February 11, 2004); Mary Williams Walsh, op. cit., note 173; John Wasik, "Pension Consultants Need to Come Clean on Conflicts," *Bloomberg.com* (February 23, 2004).

175 Quoted in Arden Dale, ibid.

In other words, the SEC is concerned that money managers and other vendors to pension plans are being recommended by pension consultants based on payments from the vendors to the consultants, rather than because they are best-suited to the pension plans' needs. This kind of conflict of interest goes to the very heart of the integrity of the investment advisory business, and to the trust that investors can have in their advisors.

Why Is the SEC Acting Now?

Most of the practices the Commission is looking into have bedeviled the pension consulting community for decades. Hence, it is interesting to wonder out loud why the SEC is moving now, and why, if the practices are so malign, the Commission didn't act many years ago.

I am speculating, but I believe that there are three answers to this question:

- First, during the very long Bull Market that persisted from 1982 until 2000, even investors with poor or conflicted advice experienced reasonably good outcomes in absolute terms (though not, of course, in relative terms). It was only when the very difficult markets of 2000–2002 came along that the fault lines in the pension consulting business became obvious. Many pension funds lost hundreds of millions of dollars during this period, and states, municipalities and corporations found themselves in the unwonted position of having to make huge contributions to their pension plans. Conflicted advice caused losses to be larger than they would otherwise have been (just as conflicted advice had caused gains to be smaller than they would otherwise have been in earlier years), and the howls of protest from mayors, state legislators and corporate executives and shareholders were hard for the Commission to ignore.
- The prominence of the folks whose oxen had been gored also made it difficult for the SEC to turn a deaf ear. While pension plan trustees—themselves deeply implicated in the conflicts (see below)—might have been willing to look the other way, state legislators who had to vote to contribute cash to under-funded pension plans were demanding action.
- Finally, some of the practices that led, at least indirectly, to losses are relatively new. Only in recent years, for example, have pension consultants brought in truly marquee talent (Bill Clinton, for example) to their

conferences in an attempt to distract pension plan trustees from the conflicts of interest that were eating away at their assets.[176]

What Practices Is the SEC Concerned About?

Lori A. Richards, director of the SEC's Office of Compliance, Inspections and Examinations, has pointed out that the Commission's inquiry is still in progress and that no conclusions have yet been drawn. However, there is no mystery about the kinds of activities that ought to concern the regulators, as they have been the subject of widespread press coverage (see, e.g., note 21):

- Believe it or not, some consultants are engaged in the most egregious and straightforward type of "pay-to-play:" money managers pay the consultants to recommend them to clients.[177] Although not (yet) illegal, one would have thought this practice would have died of shame long ago.
- Many pension consultants require their money managers to pay for the consultants' marketing activities. The most common examples are the many conferences sponsored by pension consultants. These conferences have little purpose beyond advertising the consultants' (and money managers') services and cementing relationships between the consultants and the trustees who are supposed to be looking out for their plan participants' interests (but who are clearly looking elsewhere). The conferences are paid for not by the consultants, and not by the plan trustees (through registration fees), but by the money managers the consultants are recommending.
- Many pension consultants have broker/dealer affiliates. By channeling client trades through these affiliates, the consultants supplement their incomes, sometimes very substantially.[178] Exactly how this practice

---

[176] Other luminaries who have appeared at pension consultant conferences recently include retired General Norman Schwarzkopf, Colin Powell (before he became Secretary of State), political strategist Mary Matalin, former New York Comptroller H. Carl McCall, and former Israeli Prime Minister Ehud Barak. Mary Williams Walsh, op. cit., note 173, p. 16.

[177] Sometimes the payment takes the form of sharing investment advisory fees that would otherwise be paid to the manager—wrap accounts usually work this way.

[178] The New York Times cites one case in which UBS PaineWebber misled the city of Nashville into such an arrangement, which ended up costing the city $60 million. UBS eventually paid $10 million to the city as part of a settlement agreement. Mary Williams Walsh, op. cit., note 173, p. 16.

comports with the requirement to obtain best execution is a mystery to many people, including me.

- Many pension consultants are engaged in businesses other than providing investment advisory services to their clients. Most of these businesses involve selling services to—surprise, surprise!—money management firms.[179] While the consultants claim that the managers are always told that buying services won't necessarily lead to being recommended to clients,[180] money managers might very well believe that if they *don't* buy the services, they will *never* be recommended.
- Many consultants actually compete with money managers for business by having their own asset management arms. These asset management units typically market funds of funds products, in which the consultant bundles several managers into one product.[181] Exactly how the consultants decide when to recommend an outside money manager and when to recommend their own products is a deep mystery.
- Many consultants have cozy relationships with managers, especially alternative managers like private equity partnerships. Consultants often serve on the advisory boards of PE firms. A close look at such consultants almost always reveals that their clients have suspiciously high exposures to PE.[182]
- Pension consultants spend huge sums of money (sometimes their own, most times that of money managers) entertaining pension plan trustees and employees. This entertainment occurs at conferences held in fashionable locations, at sporting events where tickets are hard to come by (the Masters gold tournament, the NCAA basketball tournament), and via direct gifts at holidays.

---

179 These services typically involve selling advice to money managers about how to market their products, or perhaps selling strategic planning advice to money managers.

180 The New York *Times* cites the case of a Hawaii pension fund that learned that 14 of 16 managers recommended by Callan Associates were paying Callan for marketing advice and other services.

181 Until recently, Wilshire Associates consolidated both its asset management and consulting units under one executive. After the SEC inquiry was launched, Wilshire separated these two units and the executive left the firm.

182 At one point, the Louisiana teachers pension fund had 42% of its assets committed to alternative investments, according to the New York Times. Mary Williams Walsh, op. cit., note 173, p. 16.

- Public pension plans are controlled by elected officials who appoint all or most of the trustees. Those trustees then decide which pension consultant to engage. Consultants who wish to be considered had best be prominently listed among the financial supporters of the officials who appoint the trustees. Consultants who wish to remain engaged had best respond enthusiastically when the arm is put on them for additional contributions. This is the original pay-to-play problem, and it remains amazingly widespread.

Why Reform Is Important

Let's take a moment to reflect on why it is so important to reform the pension consulting business. A few pension funds, it is true, are prodigious in size, heavily staffed with experienced investment professionals, and altogether well able to fend for themselves. Those funds, however, are the exception, not the rule. Most pension funds are unstaffed or have modest staffs with little investment experience. Trustees are often retired teachers, firefighters, bus drivers, or political appointees selected for their political loyalty, not their investment knowledge.

Thus it is true that, legally speaking, pension consultants are only advisors and all important investment decisions are made by the trustees. But the more important reality is that the decisions on which the retirement security of millions of Americans depends are made by pension consultants whose competence and, especially, integrity, are open to question. If we ignore this truth we are elevating a legal formality over the retirement security of millions of working Americans.

How Not to Reform the Pension Consulting Industry

To its credit, the first instinct of the SEC when it encounters a problem is to deal with it through improved disclosure. This notion, that "sunshine is the best disinfectant,"[183] comports with the free market idea that informed consumers will make better decisions than government regulators. The problem here, as with the mutual fund scandals, is that there are very few consumers around who can be informed in any useful sense of the word. The more disclosure we put in mutual fund prospectuses—which are already virtually unreadable even by professionals—the less likely it is that mutual fund investors will

---

[183] Actually, as disinfectants go, sunshine leaves much to be desired. Otherwise, instead of scrubbing up before operations, surgeons would simply stand out in the sun for a few minutes.

read them. And the same phenomenon occurs in the pension fund industry: adding ten more paragraphs on page 68 of the pension consultant's Form ADV won't improve the knowledge of most pension fund trustees.

There is another parallel with the mutual fund scandals: the very folks who are supposed to protect consumer interests are the folks who are least likely to do so. With mutual funds it was the mutual fund boards of directors. Notwithstanding the intent of the Investment Company Act of 1940, mutual fund boards serve the interests of the investment advisors to the funds, not the interests of the investors in those funds. Similarly, in the pension industry it is the plan trustees who are supposed to be looking out for the interests of the plan participants. But, notwithstanding the provisions of ERISA, even if those trustees were capable of understanding what was going on (as noted above, most aren't), they are the very people who have been most compromised by the pension consultants.

Pension consultants claim that their judgment is not affected by the payments they receive from money managers, and plan trustees claim that their judgment is not affected by the boondoggles and gifts they receive from the consultants. Even if this were mainly true, there would still be an unsavory odor rising out of the pension consulting business that more disclosure won't cover up. What is needed is substantive reform.

What Should be Done?

I'm not an expert on the pension consulting business, and I don't have enough detailed knowledge of that business to offer concrete suggestions about how the pension consulting mess should be cleaned up. However, the general outlines of what needs to be done to restore confidence in the management of America's public and private pension fund assets are pretty clear:

- First, the open architecture concept badly needs to be introduced into the pension consulting business. Open architecture requires the elimination of conflicts of interest between advisors and their clients. If the pension consultants were required to operate in an open architecture manner, most of the unsavory practices in the industry would disappear overnight.
- Second, the regulators should recognize that a bribe is a bribe is a bribe. Pension plan trustees should be prohibited from taking anything of value from pension consultants, and pension consultants should be prohibited from offering anything of value to trustees. Consultants should also be prohibited from making political contributions to the campaigns of government officials that oversee plans they are advising or wish to advise.

- Finally, I recognize that regulating the practice of pension consultants accepting value from the money managers they recommend is a complex problem. No sooner would the regulators outlaw existing practices than many others would crop up. Moreover, it would be difficult to regulate this issue in the pension consulting industry without undercutting other practices—such as wrap fee accounts—elsewhere in the financial services industry. Here, perhaps, is an area where disclosure can play a role—but it would have to be real disclosure. Taking as an example the "red herring" language of preliminary prospectuses (and the cancer warnings on cigarette packages!), I offer the following disclosure suggestion only partly tongue-in-cheek. Pension consultants who have taken anything of value from a manager they are recommending to a pension fund might be required to state, on the front cover of the recommendation, in red text, something like this:

  SOME OR ALL OF THE MANAGERS RECOMMENDED IN THE FOLLOWING MATERIALS HAVE PAID US TO RECOMMEND THEM TO YOU. WE DO NOT BELIEVE THAT THESE PAYMENTS HAVE COMPROMISED OUR JUDGMENT. REASONABLE PEOPLE MAY DISAGREE WITH THIS VIEW, HOWEVER.

Two

Chapter 7

Facing Off Against the Financial Industry: Conflicts of Interest and the Destruction of Wealth

---

So act that your principle of action might safely be made a law for the whole world.[184]

Mark Twain tells the story of the fly that attempted to settle on a tempting pot of hot milk. Only at the last instant did the fly realize just how sticky the surface of the milk was. He struggled mightily and, at the very last instant, tore himself loose. As he flew off the fly reflected on what an instructive experience he had just had, but that, on the whole, he would prefer not to do it again.

Twain's story pretty well summarizes investor reactions to the first three years of the 21st Century: damned instructive, but on the whole we'd prefer not to live through them again. The story also makes the important point that, even though we may understand an issue intellectually, sometimes we don't fully appreciate its implications until disaster stares us in the face.

Consider the problem of financial conflicts of interest—a perfect example of our ability to understand a concept intellectually but fail to grasp its full significance. During the bubble markets of the late 1990s only the brain-dead could have failed to be aware of the many conflicts of interest that pervaded the financial world. And if we couldn't see them for ourselves, scolds like then SEC Chairman Arthur Levitt, then Vanguard Chairman John Bogle and many others were happy to point them out to us. The problem was that we didn't listen, and the reason we didn't listen was that no one told us (who knew?) just how much of our wealth was about to be destroyed as a result of these conflicts.

---

184 Kant's categorical imperative.

Let's look at some examples of conflicts of interest we knew existed, but the consequences of which were monstrously underestimated.

The Destruction of Wealth: 2000–2002

Analyzing what went wrong in the '90s,
we can identify two specific elements:
a decline in professional standards and
a dramatic rise in conflicts of interest.
—George Soros[185]

The Destruction of Wealth by Financial Analysts

Throughout the 1990s the prima donnas of the investment world were the superstar financial analysts at global financial powerhouses. Analysts like Jack Grubman (Citigroup/Salomon Smith Barney), Henry Blodgett (Merrill Lynch), Mary Meeker (Morgan Stanley) and Frank Quattrone (Credit Suisse First Boston)[186] commanded enormous power and influence (to say nothing of compensation). We all knew, if we bothered to think about it, that most of these analysts were inherently compromised. They were attempting to serve both investors (who paid them nothing) and investment banking clients of their firms (who paid them millions). What we never quite internalized, until it was hammered home to us in the most brutal manner possible, was just how much investor wealth could be destroyed by relying on the recommendations of financial analysts who were *known* to be compromised. The losses on investments in dot.coms, telecoms and technology stocks are now measured in the trillions of dollars.

---

185 "Busted: Why the Markets Can't Fix Themselves," *The New Republic* (September 2, 2002), p. 19.

186 Quattrone was not technically an analyst, but the head of CSFB's technology investment banking group, to whom all the tech and dot.com analysts reported. Many investigations of Quattrone's activities have been launched and he has been placed on administrative leave by CSFB.

The Destruction of Wealth by Accountants

Everyone knows that capital markets cannot operate unless investors have confidence in the financial numbers published by corporations. And we all knew, if we bothered to think about it, that the accounting firms that blessed these numbers were hopelessly compromised. These firms, or at least the big global accounting firms, made far more money selling consulting services to corporations than they did selling auditing services.[187] When the latter was endangered by the former, which was likely to prevail? What never quite penetrated, at least until Enron, Global Crossing, and so many others, was just how much investor wealth could be destroyed by relying on audits blessed by accountants who were *known* to be compromised. The answer, it turned out, was billions and billions of dollars.

The Destruction of Wealth via Executive Stock Options

During the 1990s corporations showered top executives with massive stock options packages, arguing that it was important to align executive interests with those of shareholders.[188] But we all knew, if we bothered to think about it, that stock options don't align executive and shareholder interests at all. For one thing, option holders have no downside exposure if stock prices fall, while investors, as we learned to our horror, decidedly do. For another, most executives must sell their stock once the options have been exercised in order to pay taxes, making them extremely short-term owners. Thinking this misalignment through, perhaps we ought to have been able to see that unscrupulous executives could game the system powerfully against us, boosting short-term financial results to prop up stock prices, then exercising their options and selling out before the inevitable price collapse. We were left holding the bag—instructive, all right, but not an experience we'd like to repeat.

---

187 Even in 2000 and 2001, 72% of the fees corporations paid to accounting firms were for non-auditing consulting services, according to the Investor Responsibility Research Center. Cited in Gretchen Morgenson, *On Reform, It's Time to Walk the Walk*, Wall Street Journal (October 6, 2002), Section 3, p. 1.

188 These options packages also resulted in massive increases in CEO pay. According to William McDonough, President of the Federal Reserve Bank of New York, CEOs earned 42 times the pay of the average production worker twenty years ago, but earn 400 times that pay today. Greg Ip, *New York Fed President Chides CEOs on Hefty Compensation* (Wall Street Journal, September 12, 2002), p. A2.

We could go on and on analyzing conflicts of interest and the disastrous consequences for investor wealth: the practice of "spinning:" allocating hot, no-risk IPOs to powerful CEOs;[189] the collaboration between rogue corporations and banks that enabled the former to post hyped earnings through off-balance-sheet financing using special purpose entities while the latter kept quiet;[190] the use of armies of brokers to push technology and dot.com stocks into investor portfolios and to keep them there, even when the investors wanted to sell.[191] But the point is clear: investors chronically and dramatically underestimate the wealth-destroying consequences of relying on compromised advisors.

The Destruction of Wealth: 2003–200-?

For an integrated investment bank like Goldman Sachs, conflict management is a core competence.
—Goldman CEO Henry Paulsen[192]

---

189 Charles Gasparino, "Salomon's Grubman Resigns; NASD Finds "Spinning" at Firm," *Wall Street Journal* (August 16, 2002), p. 1. Wall Street's response to the outrage over spinning is to assert that every industry favors its best customers: allocating no-lose IPOs to CEOs of its best investment banking customers was nothing more than sound business practice. But this is disingenuous at best. The "customer" was the corporation, not the CEO. The huge investment banking fees came out of the shareholders' pockets and the hot IPO proceeds should have gone into the shareholders' pockets. Moreover, investment banks routinely underpriced IPOs in the late 1990s, transferring billions of dollars from investment banking clients and their shareholders to CEOs and the investment banks themselves. Sanford C. Bernstein & Co., for example, estimates that IPOs were underpriced, on average, by 30% in 1999. See Gretchen Morgenson, *Another Slap at Democracy on Wall Street*, New York Times (September 1, 2002), section 3, p. 1.

190 Martin Mayer, *Banking's Future Lies in Its Past*, New York Times (August 25, 2002), section 4, p. 9; Julie Creswell, *Banks on the Hot Seat*, Fortune (September 2, 2002), p. 79.

191 Bruce Kelly, *Merrill a "Boiler Room" during Tech Boom*, Investment News (August 19, 2002), p. 1.

192 Mark Gimein, *The Enforcer*, Fortune (September 16, 2002), p. 84.

A conflict of interest is a conflict of interest.
—New York Attorney General Eliot Spitzer[193]

It is too soon to know whether the conflicts of interest described above will be eliminated or at least dramatically reduced, but certainly important efforts are underway. Consider: the most conflicted of the superstar financial analysts have resigned in disgrace and face both civil and criminal sanctions; Arthur Andersen, once the most respected of the big accounting firms, is dead; billionaire CEOs are forced to endure "perp walks," arrested, handcuffed and paraded before the media; the pressure to expense stock options is intense, even in the technology industry; the practice of "spinning" is under intense scrutiny in the press, in Congress, and by the New York Attorney General; executives at major banks have been forced to appear before Congressional committees to defend their practice of making off-balance-sheet loans to the likes of Enron; the Sarbanes-Oxley Act is now the law of the land;[194] and tens of thousands of investor lawsuits and arbitrations have been filed against financial firms in an effort to hold them accountable for the wealth they destroyed through conflicts of interest.

Another Conflict: Compromised Wealth Advisory Services

But, terrible as these conflicts were, there is another conflict of interest that has resulted in the destruction of far more wealth among affluent investors, but which has been largely underestimated by the investors that are victimized by it: namely, the conflicts of interest that infest the financial advisory business. As with the conflicts discussed above, it is not that investors are unaware of the conflicts. The real problem is that investors dramatically underestimate the wealth-destroying *consequences* of these conflicts.

Let's be clear about this issue: I am talking about financial firms that undertake to advise a wealthy client *generally*, not about firms whose relationship with a client is solely that of product vendor. We don't expect the Ford dealer to be objective about Chevrolet and we shouldn't expect Morgan Stanley's product sales team (i.e., the brokers) to be objective about Goldman's products. But when a firm is advising a family generally, as Morgan Stanley, Goldman and many others frequently do—so that the quality of the advisory firm's advice on strategies, products and services will profoundly affect the

---

[193] Mark Gimein, *op. cit.*, note 192, p. 82.

[194] Among other things, the law establishes a new accounting oversight panel, the Public Company Accounting Oversight Board.

family's wealth and happiness—objectivity and very high professional standards are essential.

And yet, objectivity and high professional standards are perhaps the rarest of all qualities to be found among financial firms. Instead, what we almost universally encounter are hucksters for lousy products,[195] advisors with little experience advising wealthy families, limited product and service lines, aggressive sales tactics, and no concern whatever with the consequences of these conflicts on investor wealth.

Examples of wealth destruction on a grand scale resulting from conflicted advice are so common they go almost un-remarked-upon. I have now been advising wealthy families for almost three decades, long enough to watch substantial fortunes diminish into ordinariness through nothing more than a conflicted advisor's determination to keep family wealth in its own uncompetitive and over-priced investment products. "Shirtsleeves to shirtsleeves in three generations" occurs far more often as the result of poor financial advice than as the result of foolish behavior on the part of families. (Unless we count the use of conflicted advisors as foolish behavior, which it most certainly is.)

But the destruction of wealth can also occur in brief, spectacular fashion as the result of conflicts of interest. In late 2002, for example, two such cases were much in the news.[196] But we all know of many, many other examples over the years.

I have emphasized the fact that the conflicts of interest among financial analysts, accountants and CEOs were generally well-recognized by investors, and the same is true of conflicts in the wealth advisory business. Indeed, many financial professionals make no bones about them. The now-retired head of private banking for a major investment bank, when presented with the myriad conflicts of interest his firm brought to the process of advising wealthy clients, didn't waste his breath with denials. Instead, he had an effective rejoinder: "The people we are dealing with," he would say, "are consenting adults."

This may be as cynical a *caveat emptor* as an investor could wish to hear. We can re-phrase the banker's remark to say, "My job is to transfer wealth from your family to my firm. Your job is to look out for your own interests." But cynical or not, our tough-minded banker knew whereof he spoke. Wealthy

---

195 "Almost everything Wall Street does is inefficient and benefits select insiders at the expense of regular investors. Many of its services aren't just useless, but damaging." Shawn Tully, *Is Wall Street Good for Anything?* Fortune (September 16, 2002), p. 33.

196 *Ex-Northpoint Exec Charges Goldman with Conflict of Interest*, Private Asset Management (August 19, 2002), p. 1; Susanne Craig, *Merrill Is Told to Pay Couple $7.7 Million Sum*, Wall Street Journal (August 28, 2002), p. C1.

investors are not the widows and orphans of the investment world, but substantial players with respect to whom sophistication is assumed,[197] whether it exists or not. When wealthy investors lose capital, no one outside the family mourns. And no one can be expected to come to the rescue.[198]

But, with rare exceptions, wealthy investors are no match for the top firms in the financial business. Few families made their capital in the financial industry, and hence they are Johnnie-Come-Latelies to the business. The best financial firms, by contrast, have been in the business for many decades—several centuries in a few cases. They employ smart, aggressive, well-trained, highly incentivized professionals who are relentless in their sales efforts. These firms deploy massive capital in an attempt to distribute their products as widely as possible. Families, by comparison, tend to be thinly-staffed and reactive, forlornly hoping that their advisor has their best interests in mind. As a result, in the competition between financial firms intent on selling inferior advice, products and services and families intent on preserving capital, families will always finish second.

Given the almost daily horror stories, why do families continue to rely on advice they know to be chock full of conflicts of interest? To help us gain a perspective on this puzzling phenomenon, let's take a very quick look at the history of independent advice in the financial services industry.

The Compleat[199] History of Objective Advice

Thirty years ago—in 1974, to be exact—Congress passed the Employment Retirement Income Security Act, or ERISA. Among other things, ERISA applied the Prudent Investor Rule to pension plans and made it clear that plan trustees faced personal liability for violations of the Rule. Since few, if any, pension plan trustees knew anything about modern portfolio theory concepts of risk, return, diversification and so on, and since none wanted to risk incurring personal liability, a mad rush ensued to hire firms that did understand these concepts. Thus began the investment consulting business. Trustees of endowed institutions, who were also fiduciaries, weren't slow to follow suit, and today it

---

197 For example, the definition of an accredited investor is anyone with $5 million in investable assets. For some purposes, the threshold is as low as $1 million.

198 The Securities and Exchange Commission, for example, does not consider investors with more than $5 million when it counts the "clients" of an investment advisory firm.

199 Compleat, but not, of course, complete. Compare *The Compleat Angler*, by Izaak Walton; *The Compleat Cat*, by Cleveland Amory; and, best of all, *The Compleat Guide to Day Trading Stocks*, by Jacob Bernstein.

is difficult to find a sizeable pension plan or endowment fund that doesn't work with an independent advisor.

Roughly ten years later, retail investors got into the act. In the mid-1980s, burned by churning of their accounts and propelled by a constant barrage of publicity in the mass media about the dangers of using commission-based advisors, retail investors began to move in overwhelming numbers to fee-only financial planners and discount brokerage firms. Firms like Charles Schwab & Co. rode this wave to great success—today more than half the assets at Schwab are accounted for by financial planners.

So where are the wealthy families? That leaves only one large group of investors still depending mainly on compromised advisors: wealthy families. In one sense, this phenomenon is easy to understand. Families often have legacy relationships with conflicted financial firms that are difficult to break, emotionally if not legally. In addition, at least until recently, wealthy families tended to be relatively isolated. The mass media had no interest in discussing issues of importance to only a few Americans (even though they controlled massive wealth), and privacy issues often prevented families from networking effectively.[200]

But in a more important sense the continued dependence on conflicted advisors is unfathomable given the critical importance of capital to wealthy families. Consider that if a pension plan loses capital due to conflicted advice or otherwise, the main consequence is that the plan sponsor (a corporation or public entity) simply has to increase its contribution level. If an endowed institution loses capital, the main consequence is that the fundraising staff has to redouble its efforts. Even for retail investors, private capital is typically far less important than earned income and retirement plans. But if a wealthy family loses its capital an irreplaceable loss has occurred that will affect the happiness of the family for generations to come. Family members responsible for the stewardship of family wealth—and, therefore, in some very large measure responsible for the future happiness of family members—would do well to consider the examples of pension plans, endowment funds and retail investors and to demand high quality, objective advice.

---

200 The media continue to express little interest in the management of significant wealth, unless it involves a major investment disaster or family squabble. However, the relative isolation of wealthy families has been effectively shattered by the good work of intermediary groups such as the Family Office Exchange, the Institute for Private Investors, the CCC Alliance, and the many seminars and conferences for families sponsored by Lido, IIR and others.

How Compromised Advice Harms Wealthy Investors

We all know intuitively that investment advice that is compromised is harmful, but how many of us have thought through exactly why this is the case and how the harm occurs? When we think about conflicts of interest, we typically focus on the problems that arise when an advisor is both attempting to give sound advice and also to sell an investment product (or, sometimes, a service). Because of the advisor's financial interest in making the sale, he or she is likely to over-estimate the value of the product and to underestimate the negative consequences for the investor's wealth of buying it, rather than buying a more competitive or appropriate product from another vendor—or simply doing nothing.

But this is only the tip of the conflict iceberg. I suggest that most of the wealth destruction caused to families by conflicts of interest arises out of the failure of the financial industry to acknowledge and respect the nature of families as clients, particularly the enormous *complexity* of families as investment entities. Consider that families: pay capital gains and ordinary income taxes at different rates; must separate long and short term gains for tax purposes; live with enormously complicated estate, trust and tax planning strategies resulting in entities with wildly differing tax treatments and investment planning considerations; often own complex operating businesses; sometimes hold their assets inside a C corporation which is classified as a personal holding company; sometimes hold their assets in an S corporation that was formerly a personal holding company; sometimes own very substantially appreciated (legacy) securities that are exposed to price declines that could devastate the family's wealth; employ investment decision-making strategies that are complicated and very different from those of institutional or retail investors; face intergenerational and other family-specific concerns that have deep emotional and psychological roots; are often focused as a family on matters other than wealth management (such as philanthropy). And this merely scratches the surface of family complexity.

Even the greenest broker cold-calling from his lonely cubicle is subject to the "know your customer" rule: generally speaking, he shouldn't be selling IPOs to elderly widows or fixed annuities to thirty-year-olds. Yet, when financial firms target affluent private clients—as virtually all financial firms do—they make little effort to know their customers. More typically, a firm goes after the private client business not by considering the needs of family investors but by focusing on distribution, asset gathering and cross-selling. The firm will organize a "wealth management group" consisting of a few retreads from the asset management division, some under-employed investment bankers and a large helping of brokers. And voila!—they are in business.

Instead, financial firms who wish to advise private clients should be attempting to match their services to the complex needs of family investors. The first need that comes to mind is the one cited by George Soros in the quote that appears earlier: very high professional standards. Newly minted MBAs, brokers, reassigned professionals from investment banking and asset management groups, and similar personnel have little business advising family investors. It requires many years of experience to navigate the complex challenges presented by family investors, and therefore Rule #1 for financial firms wishing to build a private client business ought to be to recruit only the most senior professionals who have worked with complex, substantial families for many years. And Rule #1 for family investors ought to be to demand nothing less from their advisors.

As a result of the daunting complexity of family investors, the second need that comes to mind is the need for access to an enormously wide array of competitive products and services—that is, not products so much as *solutions* for the many challenges family investors will face over time. Yet, no small or medium-sized firm can possibly have, in-house, all the products and services families are likely to need, and no large firm can possibly have *competitive* products across such a broad landscape. Hence, Rule #2 for financial firms wishing to advise large families ought to be that some form of an open architecture service platform should be made available to family clients. And Rule #2 for family investors ought to be to demand no less from their advisors.

Roughly 98% (my rough estimate) of the financial firms seeking to advise affluent family investors fail both of these tests—they don't employ professionals experienced in advising large families and they don't have access to a broad array of competitive products and services. These firms—smaller trust companies, regional banks, most asset management firms and investment banks—simply should not be in the wealth advisory business. Despite the apparent temptations of the business, their participation is likely to result in damage to their reputations, damage to the wealth of their clients, and potential legal liability. Let's take a brief look at how the limitations of these firms damage investor wealth:

- The first step in the advisory process for most wealthy clients is making the crucial decision about how to deploy the family's capital. But a firm that fails Rule #1 will have little capacity to develop sound after-tax, after-fee, multi-investor, multi-period asset allocation strategies, or even to understand the necessity for such a complex approach to asset allocation.

If they take the trouble to purchase software that allows capital allocation decisions to be modeled on such a basis (an extraordinarily rare step for such a firm), their brokers will not understand how to use it or what its limitations may be. Moreover, because the firm violates Rule #2, it will have access to only a limited line of investment products. Hence, whatever asset allocation strategy is recommended will be based not on the family's needs but on what the firm happens to have handy.[201] The net result of violations of Rules #1 and #2 is that clients of these firms have their interests compromised from the very beginning of the advisory relationship. At the very least, they will end up with portfolios characterized by far too much embedded risk for the returns they can expect. At worst, the clients will experience dramatic and unnecessary destruction of their net wealth as the result of portfolios that are far too concentrated in too few asset classes and investment styles.[202]

- Because Rule #2 has been violated, the investment products placed in the family's portfolio will be limited to those offered by that firm alone. Since no firm has a monopoly on quality, these products are likely to be largely non-competitive: over-priced, under-performing, possibly even inappropriate for the family's needs.[203] Compounding these disadvantages over time is one of the prime reasons for the decline of family wealth.
- As the relationship continues, the complexity of the family's needs will continue to tax the financial firm's capabilities. Can the firm recommend cutting-edge estate planning strategies to the family? If not, the family's wealth may disappear in unnecessary taxes. Can the firm recommend appropriate strategies to hedge appreciated securities positions in the

---

201 Following are examples of investment products most smaller and mid-sized firms frequently don't have access to and which are therefore not included in portfolio design work done for their clients: different investment styles (growth, value, momentum, tech, top-down, bottom-up, etc.), US mid-cap stocks, US small cap stocks, international stocks, international small cap stocks, emerging markets stocks, international fixed income, high yield debt, directional hedge, absolute return-oriented hedge, venture capital, private equity, real estate, etc.

202 A distressingly common example involves firms—including some large, global firms—that concentrate most of their clients' wealth in US large cap growth stocks. Net wealth declines in the 30% to 50% range have been suffered by many of the clients (or ex-clients) of such firms over the past few years.

203 See the amusing article, "Can't Anyone Here Play This Game?" by Tom Lauricella, *Wall Street Journal* (July 8, 2002), p. R1.

family's portfolio? If not, the family's wealth may be reduced unnecessarily. Can the firm tax-manage the family's portfolio? If not, the family will simply pay more taxes than necessary. Can the firm recommend possible solutions to a personal holding company problem? Can the firm help the family deal with intergenerational tensions? Can the firm offer solutions designed to improve the family's satisfaction with its philanthropic activities? Such questions become more and more embarrassing for firms that violate Rules #1 and #2.[204]

Since violations of Rules #1 and #2 cause such harm to wealthy clients, why would financial firms persist in violating them? The answer is conflicts of interest. Most firms don't employ investment professionals experienced in advising wealthy families (Rule #1) because such people are expensive, independent-minded, reluctant to sell uncompetitive products and generally difficult to manage. The fact that these are precisely the kinds of advisors wealthy clients need is a fact that is quickly lost in the firms' focus on their own short-term bottom line.[205] Most firms don't offer their clients access to a broad array of products, services and strategies (Rule #2) because they lack the expertise or capital required to do so and because they can't get paid to offer such advice. The fact that families need these products, services and strategies to avoid destruction of their wealth appears to be a matter of little concern to the industry.

Conflicts Presented by Even the Best Financial Advisory Firms

Let's assume either that the firms discussed above leave the wealth advisory business or that most families have the good sense to avoid them. Unfortunately,

---

204 It is true, of course, that it will be a rare family that will need all of these services. But the point is that virtually every family will need some of them as the years go by, and the failure to offer them in a competitive manner will have dramatically negative consequences for the family's wealth.

205 Remarkable as it may seem, one occasionally encounters exceptional individuals working inside "closed architecture" firms who, somehow, find ways to insulate their personal clients from their own firms' conflicts of interest. These professionals manage to deliver largely objective and helpful advice, but unfortunately they are working very much at cross-purposes with their own employers. Many pay a price for focusing on clients rather than products. Faced these days with constant publicity about their firms' investor-unfriendly behavior, many of these individuals are bailing out—setting up their own shops, joining open architecture firms, or, unfortunately, leaving the industry altogether.

families aren't home free just yet. Of the (roughly) 2% of financial firms that don't violate both of our rules for advising wealthy families, half violate one of the rules and the other half violate the other. Let's examine how this works out in practice by considering a very common situation. We'll imagine a wealthy family headed by one N. Nelly. As a result of the capital markets environment we have all experienced over the past decade—a bull market followed by a bubble market followed by a bear market—Ms. Nelly, like many investors, holds a portfolio of substantially appreciated securities that are exposed to possible declines in value. Not being a sophisticated investor herself, Ms. Nelly conducts a search for a competent financial advisor. She is astute enough to avoid the 98% of firms that violate both our rules, so let's see what is likely to happen to her in the hands of the remaining 2%.

The smaller firm problem. Ms. Nelly has been recommended to Patina Trust Company, a posh[206] mid-sized firm in New York that has been advising wealthy clients for many years. She visits the firm's offices and is immediately impressed by the marble entry, the wood-paneled lobby, the thick carpets, the old prints, the fine china in the private dining room. Everything about the place speaks of Old Money Well Managed. Over lunch she meets her relationship manager, a cultured gentleman who has obviously been advising affluent families for decades. The president of the company stops by to say hello. She is assured that the firm has seen every issue a family could possibly face and that her wealth will be in good hands. Deeply impressed, Ms. Nelly engages Patina as her general financial advisor. Over the next year or so her relationship manager is attentive, promptly returning phone calls and getting her monthly account reports out on time (usually). He is a charming lunch companion when she is in New York. He understands the benefits of diversification and attempts to educate Ms. Nelly about the importance of a sound asset allocation strategy.

Unfortunately, however, what Ms. Nelly most feared has begun to happen—her very large, concentrated securities positions begin an implacable decline. She is reluctant to sell her stock and incur large capital gains taxes, and her relationship manager, charming as he is, has no further suggestions. But Ms. Nelly is nothing if not persistent. She checks with several other financial firms and learns that complex hedging strategies can be employed to protect her appreciated stock positions. She engages in such a transaction with another firm, but

---

206 Posh—or POSH—was originally the designation for the most desirable staterooms on transatlantic cruise ships embarking from Southampton: Port Out, Starboard Home.

not before she has lost millions of dollars of value. She fires Patina and brings a legal action in an attempt to hold Patina responsible for her losses.

From the point of view of the trust company, the lawsuit is unfair in the extreme. Patina doesn't offer complex hedging strategies and hence can't make a profit on them. Because such strategies are not part of the firm's product line it has not, naturally enough, bothered to educate its relationship managers about them. There are, Patina points out, a great many investment products, services and strategies that it does not offer and hence cannot possibly be held accountable for. The lawsuit should be dismissed for failure to state a claim on which relief can be granted. The entire financial services industry would agree with Patina's position—would, indeed, consider it to be self-evident.

But Ms. Nelly sees the matter rather differently. In her eyes Patina has engaged in a simple bait-and-switch tactic. When Patina was competing for her business, it regaled her with its vast experience and capabilities, and she relied on Patina's representations. It may be true that Patina never directly stated that they understood securities hedging strategies, but they certainly left the impression that there was little or nothing about managing wealth that they didn't understand. And, as we know, the need for hedging strategies is a very common need. But now that much of her wealth has disappeared, Patina has taken the position that it is merely a small firm with limited capabilities and that Ms. Nelly's expectations, if they were otherwise, were unreasonable.

Unfortunately for Patina, the judge is inclined to agree with Ms. Nelly. After all, no one told Patina that it had to go into the business of advising complex, affluent families. If it decided to enter that business but not to bother gaining access to advisory services wealthy families were likely to need, it did so at its peril. When Patina was competing for Ms. Nelly's business, did it misrepresent its capabilities? That is clearly a matter for the jury to decide. The court denies Patina's motion to dismiss the complaint and Patina quickly, and wisely, settles the case.[207]

The lesson of the Patina example is that smaller firms invariably violate Rule #2: they have limited product and service lines, and hence virtually every complex family that engages a smaller firm will, sooner or later, come face-to-face with a compelling need the firm can't meet. In many cases, the family won't even recognize that it has such a need until it is too late, since the advisory firm either won't recognize the problem itself or won't mention it to the client (since it can't profit from a resolution of the problem).

---

207 The "facts" of the Patina case have been invented by me, of course. But see *Levy v. Bessemer Trust Company*, (SDNY, July 30, 1997), which involved a similar set of facts.

The larger firm problem. Let's rewind our advisory videotape and assume that, instead of focusing her advisor search on small, exclusive firms like Patina Trust Company, N. Nelly had instead focused her search on large, integrated, global financial powerhouses. Ms. Nelly contacts Global Integrated Powerhouse, Inc., a fully integrated financial services firm with capabilities in banking, asset management, trust services, custody, lending, insurance and investment banking, among others.[208] She is invited to visit the firm's New York headquarters, where she is introduced to Global's senior officers and spends many hours with the firm's private wealth management unit. The firm demonstrates beyond any doubt that it has products, services and strategies that can address every conceivable investment challenge a wealthy family might face. Deeply impressed, Ms. Nelly engages Global as her general advisor.

Global assigns Ms. Nelly's account to a broker who operates out of Global's local office in Ms. Nelly's home town. This broker has little experience advising complex families, but he is an excellent golfer and proceeds to develop a personal (albeit strictly business!) relationship with Ms. Nelly. Unfortunately, however, what Ms. Nelly most feared has begun to happen—her very large, concentrated securities positions begin an implacable decline. She is reluctant to sell her stock and incur large capital gains taxes, and her broker has no further suggestions. But the decline in her stock value accelerates, and Ms. Nelly ultimately suffers losses measured in the tens of millions of dollars. Ms. Nelly terminates her relationship with Global and initiates an arbitration action in an attempt to hold Global responsible for her losses.

From the point of view of Global, the lawsuit is "outrageous." Global insists that, "We met all our duties and obligations as a broker." But from Ms. Nelly's point of view, this merely begs the question: were Global's obligations those of a retail broker, or were they instead directly related to the vast capabilities the firm bragged about when it competed for Ms. Nelly's business?

Unfortunately for Global, the arbitration panel agrees with Ms. Nelly. After all, no one told Global that it had to go into the business of advising complex, affluent families. If it decided to enter that business but didn't bother to hire experienced advisors capable of handling the complicated affairs of the

---

[208] Note that, from the financial industry's point of view, amassing such broad capabilities simply increases the opportunities for cross-selling. But from the client's point of view such broad capabilities merely multiply the conflicts of interest.

wealthy, it did so at its peril. Global failed the "know your customer" rule, and hence the arbitrators hand down a very large award for Ms. Nelly.[209]

The lesson of the Global example is that larger firms invariably violate Rule #1: they work hard to develop a broad line of advisory products and services, but then rely on their existing brokerage armies to advise wealthy families, as though the needs of those families were no greater than the needs of retail investors. These global, integrated financial firms are all about product distribution and cross-selling, not about the needs of complex family investors. The failure to employ professionals experienced in advising wealthy clients ensures that virtually every complex family a large firm will advise will, sooner or later, have a compelling need the firm's brokers can't meet—or even recognize.

The best of all possible worlds? Let's suppose that Global Integrated Powerhouse and Patina Trust Company were to merge. Global Patina now appears to offer "the best of all possible worlds:"[210] a firm that employs Patina's experienced wealth advisors (Rule #1), who now have access to Global's vast product line (Rule #2). But this Panglossian world is less ideal than it appears. While it is possible for a small firm to focus on a few things and to do them quite well, a large firm that strives to do everything will invariably do them poorly. Hence, if the former Patina advisors are going to do a good job for their clients, they will have to recommend that the clients use products of firms other than Global Patina. In other words, even in the best circumstances imaginable, firms that wish to advise wealthy families will have to introduce some form of an open architecture service. And we may wish to keep in mind that these "best circumstances imaginable" are just that: imaginable, but not real.

---

209 The "facts" of the Global case have also been invented by me. But see *Millar v. Merrill Lynch*, in which a San Francisco panel of arbitrators handed down what was reportedly the largest arbitration award ever rendered. The decision is reported by Suzanne Craig, *Merrill Is Told to Pay Couple $7.7 Million Sum*, Wall Street Journal (August 28, 2002), p. C1. The quotes from "Global" in the preceding paragraph are from Merrill.

210 This immortally ironic phrase was uttered (again and again) by that eternal optimist, Dr. Pangloss, a character in Voltaire's comic masterpiece, *Candide.* Voltaire, incidentally, was one of the earliest and most powerful advocates of free market economic systems, even pre-dating his younger friend Adam Smith. Voltaire popularized two ideas that continue to be of importance to wealthy families: the political legitimacy of the pursuit of wealth through market activity, and the moral legitimacy of the consumption of wealth. See Jerry Z. Muller, *The Mind and the Market: Capitalism in Modern European Thought* (Alfred A. Knopf, 2002), p. 20 *et seq.*

Introducing Objectivity into the Advisory Process

Let's assume for the moment that it would be a good thing if conflicts of interest were eliminated in the wealth advisory business. In other words, in the future when financial firms undertake to advise a client generally, they will do so from a platform that is largely objective. How could we get from here to there?

What the financial industry can do. Despite the increasing clamor for objective advice, the industry has approached the provision of open architecture services with all the enthusiasm of a condemned man approaching the gallows. But in a world in which financial firms are determined to sell inferior products and investors are determined to preserve their wealth, financial firms and investors are natural enemies. Worse, in this worst of all possible worlds, financial firms are predators and families are the prey. This vicious cycle needs to be broken, and—long term—it is as much in the interest of the financial services industry as it is in the interests of families.

Why would a supposedly sophisticated industry be so tentative in responding to an obvious client demand from such an attractive[211] sector of the market? The reasons are complex, but they have mainly to do with three factors, none of which is incapable of being overcome: entrenched corporate cultures, an understandable-but-bogus fear of disintermediation, and a misunderstanding of the economics of the open architecture business. Let's examine each of these issues briefly.

Cultural issues. Since the development of the modern financial services industry early in the twentieth century, financial firms have evolved into aggressive, sales-oriented cultures. This was not an outcome that was engraved in stone, but one that was prompted by the fact that investors have historically been unskilled, passive consumers of investment products. That is to say that investors have not traditionally shopped proactively for investment products and services—they don't typically sit down and determine what products and services they need, then go out and search for the best vendors. Instead, investors sit back passively and allow themselves to be sold various products and services, ending up not with an ideal constellation of products for their

---

[211] Wealthy families represent by far the most attractive target market for the financial services industry today. Pension plans and endowed institutions long ago switched to independent advisors, and retail investors are in the process of abandoning the capital markets, perhaps for a generation. Affluent families, however, are hugely under-advised and represent an ever-increasing proportion of the world's wealth. This gives families enormous clout in the struggle to get objective advice.

needs, but instead with those products sold by the most persuasive salesmen. Clearly, investors have been complicit in their own demise.

Hence, virtually from the beginning of the industry, if a financial firm was going to survive it had to develop an effective sales culture. Asset gathering has been the name-of-the-game forever, and the financial professionals who are able to gather the most assets are the most prized employees. At the top of every financial firm are the most able salesmen,[212] not the employees who have given clients the best advice. (The latter long ago migrated away from the sell side of the business.)

Corporate cultures are notoriously difficult to change,[213] but if ever a time was auspicious for a change in the culture of financial institutions, that time is at hand. I described above the many conflicts of interest among financial firms that have led to Congressional, SEC and even criminal investigations. But what I haven't discussed is the almost universal outrage among investors.[214] This outrage has had tangible results, such as the pummeling of stocks of firms like Citigroup and JP Morgan Chase, despite financial results that have been positive, and tens of thousands of lawsuits and arbitrations. Less obvious consequences include private clients who are migrating to independent firms and the quiet but determined decisions of many of the best financial professionals to leave the compromised, sell-side firms because they have concluded that they cannot, in good conscience, advise their clients effectively from those platforms.

In the occasional instances where an integrated financial services firm has acquired or built an "open architecture" unit,[215] the exercise has been

---

212 In fully integrated financial services firms, the top officers may also come from the banking, lending, or investment banking sides of the business, and hence are likely to know very little about the financial advisory business.

213 In the financial world, only Charles Schwab has demonstrated the repeated ability to cannibalize its most profitable products in order to move to an even more profitable strategy.

214 Several recent studies have documented the increasing restiveness of affluent investors who are advised by conflicted firms. See, for example, *Corporate Scandal and the Lack of Advisor Objectivity*, The Spectrum Group, Inc. (2002). The study is described in "Investors Prefer Brokers' Advice to be Free of Conflict," *Wall Street Journal* (September 10, 2002), p. D2, and "HNW Investors More Leery of Investment Bank-Affiliated Advisors," *Private Asset Management* (September 16, 2002), p. 1.

215 I put the term "open architecture" in quotes because these units range from truly open to semi-open to semi-closed architecture platforms.

compromised from the beginning by a refusal to understand that the culture of the firm has got to change to accommodate an objective, client-centered advisory approach. If the open architecture unit is simply appended to the existing firm without changes in compensation programs and reporting lines and without committed support from senior management, as though it were no different from, for example, asset management, the experiment is doomed to failure. For one thing, the employees in the open architecture units and the sales units will view each other with unrestrained hostility.[216] Open architecture professionals tend to view brokers[217] as venal predators, all-too-willing to compromise their clients for the sake of their own bottom line. Brokers tend to view open architecture advisors as supercilious Milquetoasts wholly unsuited to the rough and tumble world of private client work. (Ok, I exaggerate for effect. These points of view are caricatures, but only just.)

The fear of disintermediation. It seems logical to suppose that if an open architecture alternative were made available to the clients of a financial firm, those clients would, in overwhelming numbers, demand that their portfolios be advised from that platform. This would result in thousands of clients dropping out of uncompetitive proprietary products and strategies and migrating to best-in-class products and strategies, with dramatically negative financial consequences for the firm. But in fact there is no evidence that this sort of disintermediation represents a danger. Indeed, when financial firms have offered something resembling an open architecture option, disintermediation hasn't occurred at all, except in a positive way: clients who would have left the firm to seek an open architecture alternative in fact stay in-house but move to the open architecture platform.

This counterintuitive phenomenon occurs because, as noted above, investors are poor consumers of investment services. Although they may be invested in inferior proprietary products and may be receiving compromised advice, most private clients won't act until their investment results are truly

216 The head of one open architecture unit appended to an integrated financial firm admitted that fewer than 5% of the brokers in the firm had ever—*ever*—referred a client to the open architecture unit. (Personal communication to the author.)

217 When brokers are assigned to private client work they are almost never called "brokers," of course. But salespeople whose financial incentives encourage them to push product regardless of quality and client need are brokers, whatever the firm calls them. One happy result of a broad move to objective advisory platforms will be a reduction in the number of over-compensated, over-testosteroned high net worth brokers.

horrific—in other words, until it is too late.[218] Unfortunate as this may be, it gives financial firms the luxury of offering open architecture alternatives without suffering what, in a more just world, would be a serious penalty.

The economics of open architecture. Finally, financial firms don't offer open architecture options because they fundamentally misapprehend the value of an open architecture unit. Open architecture fees are typically lower than asset management fees (*everything* is lower than asset management fees), and therefore if a financial firm simply assumes that open architecture clients will substitute for asset management clients, the firm would never offer open architecture services.

But there are many defects in this line of reasoning. The first is making a straight-line projection based on current revenue growth and profitability levels of asset management services. Asset management generally, and especially asset management as it is practiced by larger financial firms,[219] is rapidly becoming commoditized. Fees are being driven down and competitive standards are rising, resulting in a significant decline in both revenue and profitability of asset management services at large institutions. Therefore, if a financial firm compares the *future* value of asset management services against the *future* value of open architecture services, the latter will appear far more appealing.

But the value of open architecture services for an integrated financial firm doesn't stop there. Because the open architecture unit will be working with the

---

218 "Too late" because the mathematics of very negative investment results are lethal. A portfolio that is down 50% must appreciate 100% simply to get even—a highly unlikely proposition. Consider, in light of this fact, the fate of clients who owned tech and dot.com securities that declined in price by 90% or more. These investors would have to achieve appreciation of 1,000% *merely to get their capital back.* Such investors are, in other words, permanently impoverished. Losses on this order were common among investors working with compromised advisors, but such losses are virtually inconceivable for investors working in an open architecture environment.

219 Large firms tend to be inhospitable environments for talented money managers. With rare exceptions, money management units at large institutions are simply pale, over-priced, lower-returning versions of the superior products offered by smaller, boutique money management firms. See Lauricella, "Can't Anyone Here Play This Game?" *op. cit.*, note 203. Large institutions tend to be competitive in products that require large scale (such as index products) or where buying power can be especially important (as in cash and fixed income management, where the cost-to-potential-return ratio is daunting).

world's largest and most demanding investors, that unit's professionals represent a kind of early warning radar for the kinds of strategies, products and services that investors will be demanding in the future. This will give the financial firm a large competitive advantage in the race to develop products for which there will be an assured market. Finally, because open architecture professionals are in the business of evaluating investment products, they possess the intellectual capital required to design and build best-in-class products across the capital markets. Large firms that have more competitive products and fewer uncompetitive products will prosper versus their more traditional competitors. In short, the first financial firms to offer truly open architecture services will quickly come to dominate the private client business.

Two

Chapter 8

Finding the Right Advisor

We didn't underperform.
You over-expected.
—Financial advisor to his client

Not so long ago, finding an overall financial advisor was like falling off a log: most families engaged the local bank trust department. A few larger or more sophisticated families might wind up at one of the national trust banks—Bessemer, US Trust, Northern Trust, Wilmington Trust. But that was about it. It wasn't until about thirty years ago that even the very largest American families began to migrate out of the trust department backwaters and into a world that resembled what today we would call an open architecture approach to wealth management.

But what a change a generation or two can make! Today, the problem for families is not lack of choice, but too many choices. The traditional banks and trust companies are still around, though many are unrecognizably changed.[220] Investment banks, insurance companies, and brokerage firms have gotten into the business of advising wealthy families. Larger money management firms

---

220 Most of the changes have been associated with the extraordinary consolidation that has occurred in the banking business. But, in addition, some of the old line trust companies are attempting to move toward open architecture, or semi-open architecture, anyway. United States Trust Company is an example of a traditional firm that is trying to change its culture and advisory platform. Wilmington Trust Co. has adopted a different strategy aimed at the same end: it acquired a consulting firm (Ballantine & Co.) and is now offering "open architecture trust services."

have begun to target substantial families. And, of course, there are the various open architecture competitors that have come along in the past five years or so (including my own firm, Greycourt & Co., Inc., just so my biases are on the table).

Given the huge range of choices, the primary challenge for families is how to narrow the field down to a manageable group of finalists. Let's think about how we might accomplish this.

Dimensions of the Problem to Focus On

While every family will have its unique needs, most families will find it useful to focus on the two main dimensions along which advisors fall. These are what we might call the "bundled-versus-unbundled" spectrum and the "open-versus-closed architecture" spectrum. Finding the right place for our families on these two dimensions will very substantially simplify the challenge of finding the right advisor.

Bundled-versus-unbundled. An advisor who bundles its services is mainly selling convenience, simplicity, and one-stop shopping, but at the cost (usually) of quality and family knowledge (we'll discuss why in a moment). At the extreme "bundled" end of the spectrum, the advisor might already have in place such services as custody, brokerage, asset allocation, money management, performance reporting, fiduciary services, and a broad range of "softer" services some families will need, such as check-writing, intergenerational counseling, and so on. These services might all be performed by the advisor itself, or some or all might be outsourced.

At the extreme "unbundled" end of the spectrum, an advisor is mainly selling best-in-class services across the board, but at the sacrifice (usually) of simplicity. An unbundled provider will wait until it understands the family's needs before recommending custodians, brokers, asset allocation strategies, money managers and so on. Even performance reporting can be outsourced, though that would be rare.

Extreme bundled advisors tend to be closed architecture, while extreme unbundled advisors tend to be open architecture, but that is not universally true. In particular, as we move along the spectrum from completely-bundled to completely-unbundled, we will encounter every possible variety of bundling and unbundling mixed up with every possible variety of open and closed architecture.

Open versus closed architecture. A purely closed architecture advisor will employ a service platform that relies on its own in-house capabilities, sometimes across-the-board, sometimes only in money management. A purely open architecture advisor will employ a service platform that offers no products of its own; instead, it will search for the best and most appropriate products for its clients across-the-board. As with the bundled-versus-unbundled dimension, advisory firms can fall anywhere along the spectrum from completely closed architecture to semi-closed architecture, and from semi-open architecture to completely open architecture.

To illustrate how we might approach the problem of locating the optimal position on the bundling and architecture dimensions, let's look at the experience of the Schulberg family.

What Business Are We In?

In 1995, the Schulberg family had liquid assets of $23 million. In absolute terms, of course, that was a large sum of money. But as a percentage of the total wealth of the family, the liquid assets were dwarfed by the value of the family's operating business: a regional cable television company that was growing very rapidly and was already worth, in 1995, an estimated $100 million.

In looking at the range of advisory options available to it, and in trying to reduce the sheer number of possibilities to a manageable few, the Schulberg family asked itself two very simple questions (the answers to which, however, are not always simple). The first question was, "What business are we in as a family?"

Since the ultimate destiny of the Schulberg family would be far more dependent on how well the family managed the cable TV business than on how well the family managed its liquid wealth, the family sensibly concluded that it was in "the business of business." It was important that the family apply all its time and talents to the cable business to ensure its success. That didn't mean that the family would ignore what was happening with the liquid assets, but it did have important implications for the kind of advisor the family would need.

Since the family would have little time to devote to the management of its liquid assets, the Schulbergs realized that they needed an advisor that fell toward the "bundled" end of the business. Such an advisor would take most of the complexity and most of the time-consuming activities associated with wealth management off the family's shoulders, leaving the family free to focus on the operating business. This one important decision eliminated many possible competitors for the family's advisory business.

How Do We Feel about Conflicts of Interest?

In terms of the open-versus-closed architecture spectrum, the Schulbergs asked themselves a second question: "How do we feel about conflicts of interest?" Some families will be very sensitive about conflicts, seeing them as going to the very heart of the issue of trust, without which no advisory relationship can flourish. Other families will see conflicts as an inherent part of the advisory business, and as an issue to be managed, not avoided.

The Schulbergs fell into the former category, partly because, in the early 1990s, the family had experienced a brush-up with conflicts of interest in the investment banking business. The family's investment banker had recommended that the cable TV company issue junk bonds as a way to gain access to the financing it needed to propel its growth. This turned out to be good advice, except for one problem: another unit in the investment bank was buying up smaller issues of junk bonds (like those issued by the Schulberg's company), gaining leverage over the company and trying to force a sale of the company or a buyback (at a premium) of the bonds.

This experience had sensitized the Schulbergs to the dangers of conflicts of interest, and consequently they decided to limit themselves to the "open architecture" end of the advisory spectrum. This eliminated many competitors and, combined with the family's decision about bundling, allowed the family to focus on a very small group of appropriate advisory firms. It was to this limited group of four or five firms that the Schulbergs sent a request for proposal designed to assist them in distinguishing the strengths and weaknesses of these few remaining competitors.

Defining (and Redefining) the Definition of the "Right" Advisor

Ultimately, the Schulbergs selected a firm that offered what it called "outsourced chief investment officer" services. This firm bundled most of the services the Schulbergs would need to manage their $23 million: asset custody, asset allocation, manager selection and performance reporting. All the family needed to do was review the periodic performance reports to monitor the portfolio. The advisor was also mainly open architecture in the sense that it selected providers of these services in a best-in-class manner, taking nothing of value from any vendor.[221]

All went well for seven years, at which point the Schulberg family sold its cable television company to Adelphia for cash and stock. The family could simply have continued with its existing advisor, but the Schulbergs didn't

---

221 Much later, the Schulbergs would realize that "taking nothing of value" didn't eliminate important conflicts of interest between its advisor and itself. The "outsourced CIO" firm, for example, took nothing of value from the vendors (custodians, money managers, etc.) it selected. On the other hand, those vendors were selected not because they were the best for the Schulberg family, but because they were the best for the "outsourced CIO" firm.

become wealthy by allowing inertia to dictate their fate. Instead, the family convened a series of family meetings, including the family's key advisors, at which it re-asked the two key questions: "What business are we now in as a family?" and "How do we feel about conflicts of interest?"

Obviously, the family's situation was now—mid-2002—quite different than it had been in 1995. Back then, the family had been deeply involved in building a strong regional cable TV business. Now, the Schulbergs were sitting on a pile of cash and securities—including a concentrated position in Adelphia stock—of nearly $300 million dollars.

Family intellectual capital. Thus, when the Schulbergs re-asked themselves the question, "What business are we in as a family?" the answer was quite different. The Schulbergs were now no longer in "the business of business," but in the "business of managing liquid wealth." These are very different activities, and the consequences for the Schulbergs were momentous.

A few pages above, I mentioned that bundled advisors offer simplicity "at the cost…of…family knowledge." During the almost eight years that the Schulberg's liquid wealth had been managed by its bundled advisor, the Schulbergs had learned almost nothing about the business of managing wealth. Their investment results had been satisfactory, but the family's advisor had made all the decisions and therefore the results in terms of the family's human capital had been unsatisfactory, indeed. The family knew nothing about the role of an asset custodian, knew nothing about how brokerage was handled in their account (the answer to this would not please them), understood nothing at all about the very complex business of selecting money managers, and they viewed the asset allocation process as a black hole. The Schulbergs reviewed their performance reports regularly, but exactly what those reports meant had never been very clear to them. In effect, the family had become an intellectual ward of their advisor during those years.

At the time, that sacrifice in the family's intellectual capital had been worth it—the Schulbergs had been focusing on larger issues and their liquid wealth had been mainly a sideshow. But now the management of the liquid wealth was the entire ballgame for the Schulberg family—screw that up and it would all be over. What the Schulbergs badly needed was to become as good at managing liquid wealth as they had been at managing a cable TV business. And just as it had taken many years for them to learn the ropes and become adept at the one business, it would also take many years to become adept at the other. But the family needed to start learning right away.

Consequently, the Schulbergs decided to terminate their bundled advisor and to engage an advisor whose services would be as unbundled as possible. The family had a lot to learn, and the best way to start the learning process was to participate with a good, unbundled advisor in making decisions about every aspect of the wealth management process.

"Conflicts really matter now." Even before the cable business was sold, the Schulbergs were sensitive to the issue of conflicts. But back then advisor conflicts would at least compromise only a small portion of the family's wealth. Now financial conflicts of interest would go right to the heart of what the family needed to do. As a result, the family was now much more focused on identifying advisors who were located on the extreme open architecture end of the open-versus-closed architecture spectrum.

Gathering Names

Back in 1995 it had been relatively easy for the Schulbergs to gather up a small handful of names of firms that offered bundled services from a largely open architecture advisory platform—there were only a few such firms in the United States and they were reasonably well-known. But by 2002, as I mentioned above, the choices available to families had grown exponentially.[222] But this is where the process of narrowing the advisory choices down to those that are likely to be most appropriate comes in. The Schulbergs knew that they wanted an unbundled relationship, and they knew that they wanted an open architecture relationship. Hence, they were in a position to be specific when they asked around for recommendations.

The sources for advisory recommendations used by the Schulbergs were the ones most families would use. They spoke to their legal and tax advisors, their bankers and trustees, families in similar circumstances. They also used the resources of intermediary membership organizations such as the Family Office Exchange[223] and the Institute for Private Investors.[224] FOX and IPI have had

---

222 Technically, of course, "exponential growth" means no more than that a quantity grows at a rate proportional to its value. In other words, a snowball rolling downhill grows "exponentially:" as it grows twice as big, it gathers snow twice as fast. Growth can be exponential-and-slow or exponential-and-fast. But inasmuch as exponential growth of any kind will always overtake linear growth of any kind, we can perhaps be forgiven for using "exponentially" in the sense of "surprisingly fast growth."

223 100 South Wacker Drive, Suite 900, Chicago, IL 60606, (312) 327-1200. FOX was founded by Sara Hamilton, one of the pioneers in the field of helping substantial families preserve their wealth.

224 74 Trinity Place, New York, NY 10006, (212) 693-1300. IPI was founded by Charlotte Beyer, the other great pioneer in working with substantial private investors.

long relationships with many different types of advisors, and also have had the benefit of feedback from their family members about which advisors do what, who is doing a good job and who isn't, etc. Finally, the Schulbergs spoke to members of their regional family office networking group.[225]

When the family had a list of four or five advisory firms that met its unbundled/open architecture requirements and that came highly recommended, they were ready to circulate an RFP (request for proposal)[226] to those firms.

The RFP Process

Until a few years ago it was almost unheard-of for a family to use an RFP as a tool in its advisor selection process. But as families have become more serious about engaging advisors who are both appropriate and first rate, it was natural that we would borrow a tool from the institutional world. Still, the RFP process is fraught with dangers and difficulties. Let's examine some of the major pitfalls.

Mimicking Institutions

Unfortunately, by the time families began to use RFPs, the institutional RFP process had become seriously calcified. Initially, of course (we are talking fifteen or twenty years ago), institutional investors such as pension plans and endowments used the RFP process as a sensible and focused tool that was part of a larger process designed to identify an appropriate financial advisor (typically a pension consultant). But by the time families began to use RFPs, and to look to the institutional world for models, the RFP process was often a sham. There are only a limited number of serious pension consultants in the US, and after a couple of decades everyone knew everything about all of them. Thus, the RFP process was little more than an attempt to demonstrate diligence where none actually existed: institutions already knew which firm they were going to engage long before they sent out the RFP.

As an example, I know of one public pension plan that has religiously distributed an RFP to consulting firms every three years since at least the mid-1980s. But that pension plan is still working with the same consultant it was

---

225 Many large cities have informal (or, sometimes, more formal) groups of families that meet periodically to network and discuss matters of mutual interest. These groups often go by cute acronyms such as CAFE (Cleveland) and PALS (San Francisco).

226 RFPs are also sometimes called RFIs—requests for information. That is actually a more appropriate, though less common, term.

working with in 1985. It's possible, of course, that in every case the plan trustees carefully evaluated their existing consultant against others, and that in all six searches they concluded that the existing consultant was the best choice. But given the fact that the existing consultant has changed unrecognizably over those eighteen years, and given the regular and loyal payment of campaign contributions the consultant has made to the public officials who appoint the trustees of the pension plan, we might be forgiven for being suspicious.

In point of fact, the RFP process in the case just mentioned is and for many years has been a joke. And this is true of all-too-many supposedly honest advisory searches in the pension plan world, and, increasingly, in the endowment world (which, like families, mimicked the pension plans' use of RFPs). As far as families are concerned, the important point of this is that no one in the institutional world has given much thought to the RFP process for many years. Therefore, simply mimicking the institutional approach—or, God help us, using the same forms and questions!—is likely to lead us into trouble.

The RFP Is Only a Tool

Even the best-designed RFP has to be viewed not as a magic bullet but as one tool among many to be used in identifying an appropriate advisor. In the institutional world, the RFP often represents the entire diligence process, except possibly for the final "beauty contest," at which the two finalists present. Since most pension plans are seriously understaffed on the investment side and have trustees (policemen, firemen, teachers, bus drivers, political appointees) who know nothing about the investment process, this may be the only way they can proceed. But for families, where our own private capital is at stake, using the RFP as the only—or even as the principal—tool in the advisory selection process is a serious mistake.

Instead, the family process should begin (as described above) by asking the key questions that will dramatically narrow down the field of possible advisors to a few who are likely to be appropriate. The family should then seek comments about those advisors from people in the business who are likely to know them: money managers, other families, other financial institutions, FOX, IPI, etc. Only then should we begin to think about using an RFP.

Preparing the RFP

Referring back to our friends the Schulberg family, we will recall that the family had narrowed its advisory search to a small handful of firms that offered unbundled, open architecture services. The family had asked around to get informed feedback on this group of firms, and that feedback had eliminated one of the firms. (That firm had recently been acquired by a larger firm and, in the process, the firm's founders had left.) The Schulbergs were ready to prepare an RFP to the four remaining firms. There were a number of mistakes the family could have made in preparing the RFP, including those discussed below.

Mistake #1: Copying an institutional RFP. This is almost always a gigantic mistake, partly because no one in the institutional world has taken the RFP process seriously for many years, and partly because institutions are very, very different from families. After examining a few samples of institutional RFPs, the Schulbergs tossed them in the circular file, thereby dodging this particular bullet.

Mistake #2: Copying another family's RFP. While this is not as big a mistake as copying an institutional RFP, it is still a mistake. No two families are alike, and even families with identically-sized asset bases can have wildly differing investment needs. The Schulbergs were unable to find a family RFP specifically seeking unbundled, open architecture services, so they were able to dodge this bullet as well.

Mistake #3: Making the RFP too detailed. In the course of constructing an RFP, it is always a temptation to ask just another few questions, to bore in just a little more specifically on this point or that point, to ask this or that question in several different ways. We can easily convince ourselves that we are simply exercising our stewardship obligations, making certain that we aren't overlooking anything of importance. If we are working with outside advisors in the search process (legal, tax, etc.), they will all want to demonstrate their own knowledge and diligence by suggesting numerous areas of inquiry. Soon, counting subparts and sub-subparts of questions, we will find that we have created the Frankenstein Monster of All RFPs, with several hundred questions.

Keep in mind that we are sending this RFP not to one firm, but to several. No two firms will answer *any* of our questions, much less all, in the same way, or will even approach their answers in the same way. What we will receive back for our efforts will be thousands of pages of completely incomprehensible, radically inconsistent, totally incompatible responses. We will now have to engage McKinsey & Co. to make sense of it all (and McKinsey will charge us far more than the advisor would have charged us).

If we keep in mind that the RFP process is simply one of many tools we are using to find the right advisor, we will recognize that what we need to do is focus the RFP on a few key areas that are of intense concern to us. At this stage of the process we are not interested in the *esoterica* of how Advisor A (versus Advisor B versus Advisor C versus Advisor D) balances turnover versus tax lot accounting in assessing the tax-awareness of money managers. Instead, we want to focus on key differentiating features of the advisors we are looking at evaluating.

In the case of the Schulbergs, the family's main concerns focused on these issues:

- which services are bundled and which are unbundled?
- what kinds of financial and non-financial conflicts of interest exist at each of the advisory firms?
- which professionals would be assigned to the Schulberg account?
- how would the family's fees be calculated?
- how would the advisor's success or failure be measured?
- how was the portfolio design process approached at each firm?
- how did each firm identify, evaluate and monitor money managers recommended to their clients?
- what kinds of performance reports would the family receive?

Sure, there were a million other things the Schulbergs could have asked about in their RFP, but each additional area of inquiry would, in fact, have compromised their ability to focus on the key factors that were of most importance. Later, when the field has been narrowed to two final firms, the Schulbergs will inquire orally or in writing into these other issues. In other words, the Schulbergs recognized the RFP for what it was: merely one tool among many in a well-designed advisory search process.

Mistake #4: Allowing ourselves to be "gamed" by the advisors. Like money managers, financial advisory firms can be divided into those whose business success is based on giving sound advice and those whose business success is based on asset gathering. If we aren't careful—if we don't control the process tightly ourselves—we will find that we have been "gamed" by advisors who are far better at the RFP process than we are. Most families will be lucky (well, unlucky) to send out one or two RFPs in an entire investment lifetime. Advisory firms receive hundreds of RFPs every year. If we aren't careful, then, we will find that we have engaged a firm that is good at responding to RFPs, rather than a firm that is good at giving us advice.

Where Is the Sample RFP?

In other chapters I give examples of forms I discuss in the text: investment policy statements, manager guidelines, etc. So where is the sample RFP? I have in my files dozens of examples of RFPs, some of which I consider to be quite well done, very focused and useful to the families who circulated them. Why not attach one or two samples to this chapter?

The reason is that I want to emphasize the point that there is no such thing as a "good" RFP in the absence of detailed knowledge about the family that is conducting the search. Sure, there are better and worse ways of inquiring into specific issues, but that's a detail. The important point is that a terrific RFP for the Schulberg family might well be a terrible RFP for the Greene family, and vice versa. The time we devote to custom-designing our own RFP will be time very well-spent, since it will require us to focus on those few areas that we really care about. And by keeping the RFP focused, we will also be able to make sense of the results we receive, even if we are sending the RFP out to five or six firms.

Final Diligence

Once we have received and reviewed the responses to our RFP, the next step is to conduct telephone conferences with each of the firms that is still in the running. The point of these calls is simply to go over responses that weren't completely understood by us, or responses in which the advisor seemed to have missed our point.

Next, if at all possible, we should visit each of the remaining competitors in their home offices. It might be the case, for example, that the individual professional(s) to be assigned to our account might be terrific—very people-oriented, very charming, very experienced and knowledgeable. But who is working behind these people? If the home office is staffed by former brokers and insurance salesmen whose sole mission in life is to improve the profitability of our account, we should probably know about that before we sign up. If the RFP response is warm and fuzzy, but the home office is clearly an impersonal bureaucracy, that is also something we should know. If the individuals we have met are organized and focused, but the home office is disorganized and confused, that is likely to say something important about the experience we are likely to have as clients of the firm.

Finally, we should invite *no more than two* firms to meet with all important family members and any key outside advisors. *We*—not the advisors—should prepare the agenda for these meetings, and that agenda should focus on the issues that are most important to us. If this is the first time we have met face-to-face with the advisors' personnel, they will want to make a pitch for their firms. This is fair enough, but the "pitch" should be limited to no more than five minutes.

Why meet with no more than two firms? Two reasons. The first is that if we have truly done our diligence well, we should be able to identify the top two candidates at this point. If there are still four or five firms under serious consideration, we simply haven't done our job. The second reason is that having more than two firms present to our families will only generate massive confusion. It's reasonably easy to compare Firm A with Firm B. But start adding Firms D, E and F and everyone's head will be spinning. If a decision is made at all, it will be made out of sheer exhaustion.

Where Does Diligence Leave Off and Psycho-Drama Begin?

Wife: I think we should have a child.
Husband: Why bring strangers in the house?
—Comedian at a comedy club

For families looking to engage an overall advisor for the first time, or when families have worked with an advisor but new family members have been charged with replacing that firm, the decision can be excruciatingly difficult. After all, we are talking about turning our hard-won family fortune over to people who are essentially strangers. Not only that, but we are not buying a technology, we are engaging specific human beings with whom we will be working. Many people who are otherwise decisive find "personnel" decisions to be very difficult. On top of everything else, most people would rather discuss their sex lives than their personal financial affairs.

This difficulty tends to play itself out in the form of endless diligence, as we inquire intensely into ever-less-important issues. We eliminate firms from consideration for reasons that are, objectively speaking, silly. Anything to avoid or postpone making a decision. It's all perfectly understandable, but also perfectly deadly. Short of engaging a completely incompetent or fraudulent advisor, the worst decision a family can make is to do nothing. Even a marginally competent objective advisor, while he or she might not grow our wealth at the rate we were hoping for, will at least stand as a bulwark against the kinds of bad decisions that will destroy our wealth.

Recognizing that advisor decisions can be difficult ones to make, it may help families who are having trouble bringing their search to a conclusion to ask exactly what it is that we fear.

What's the Worst That Could Happen? [227]

Realistically speaking—again, short of engaging incompetent or fraudulent advisors—there are only a few serious mistakes we can make in our advisor search process.

Mistake #1: Engaging an advisor who pushes narrow strategies. Some advisors—mainly, but not exclusively, closed architecture firms—advocate strategies that are very narrowly focused on individual asset classes and/or individual investment styles. Many of these narrow strategies would be imprudent per se in most fiduciary portfolios, and as families we should heed that message. Examples include advisors who advocate any of the following:

- *Portfolios consisting only of US large cap stocks and municipal bonds.* Many banks, especially, fall into this category. This strategy is so simplistic, and is so likely to underperform badly, that there is little point in paying someone to recommend it to us.
- *Portfolios consisting only of deep value or aggressive growth strategies.* Many money management firms and investment banking houses tend to fall into this category. There is nothing wrong with deep value or aggressive growth *as part of a much broader, diversified strategy*. Indeed, firms that follow narrow strategies probably have a better chance of outperforming benchmarks than their more cautious brethren. But hidden beneath a track record that shows long-term outperformance will be many years of terrible underperformance. It is during those years that families are likely to abandon their strategies and advisors, right at the bottom of the market. It's important for us to keep in mind that these strategies underperform badly while other strategies are doing quite well, thank you. In other words, no one likes a bear market, but at least everyone is in the same boat. The worst case is for our portfolio to be down 30% or 40% while other families' portfolios are *up*.[228]
- *Portfolios overly focused on specific asset classes or sectors.* Some advisory firms specialize in hedge, private equity, technology, real estate, and so

---

227 The book of the same name, though it has nothing to do with investment matters, is highly recommended: *What's the Worst That Could Happen?* by Donald E. Westlake (Warner Books, 1997), featuring the endlessly amusing and hapless crook, John Dortmunder. Westlake also writes, in a much darker vein, as Richard Stark.

228 This happened to deep value investors in the late 1990s and to aggressive growth investors in the early 2000s.

on. If we engage these firms we can be virtually certain that our portfolios will be heavily over-weighted in whatever the advisor's specialty is. But our advisors should be designing our portfolios in ways that are in our interests, not theirs.

Mistake #2: Engaging an advisor who possesses conflicts of interest we can't manage. Even families who are not terribly sensitive to conflicts of interest can easily underestimate the consequences of those conflicts. In Chapter 7, I pointed out that conflicts of interest among accountants, corporate executives, stock analysts, etc. were well understood by investors who nevertheless lost billions of dollars. The problem was that those investors didn't quite realize just how badly they could be hurt by conflicts. Some conflicts don't get properly managed because we don't know they exist (i.e., we haven't done our diligence). Some conflicts don't get properly managed because we underestimate their danger to us (i.e., we placed ourselves on the wrong end of the open-versus-closed architecture spectrum). And sometimes we simply overestimate our level of sophistication relative to the financial services professionals who are bringing their conflicts to our table. If we have doubts about our ability to recognize, manage, or understand conflicts of interest, the best course is to engage advisors who don't have them.

Mistake #3: Not engaging an advisor at all. This is the biggest mistake of all. As families we are often quite experienced, sophisticated, smart. But our smarts will have been honed in a world quite different from the investment world. Just because we have been wildly successful at business, real estate, oil and gas, technology, whatever, doesn't have any implication at all for our ability to compete successfully in the world of capital markets. As I mentioned above, even a moderately competent advisor can serve as an important shield against the horribly bad decisions that can devastate our wealth. Competent advisors, properly selected for our needs, will virtually assure the preservation of our wealth across the generations.

Two

Chapter 9

Making Family Investment Decisions

When you come to a fork in the road, take it.
—Yogi Berra

A "Model" Investment Committee

In 1975, at the ripe old age of thirty, Jack "Jackie" Gleason became the head of his family, the head of his family office, and the permanent chair of his family's investment committee. Over time, Jackie would build a family governance structure that could be the envy of families everywhere. But there would be more than a few bumps in the road, several unexpected detours, and even some serendipitous good fortune along the way. Let's take a look at how one very wealthy family, largely stumbling along in the dark without models, managed, in time, to create a sound governance and education structure that helped the family dodge almost certain disaster. But we're getting ahead of ourselves.

Back in the 1920s, Jackie's grandfather, "Old Jack" Gleason, had launched a steel foundry and built it into an industry powerhouse during World War II and the post-war era of rapid economic growth. Jackie's father, "Jack Two," had become skeptical of the foundry industry's future, and had launched a steel scrap business that had morphed into a substantial electric steelmaking enterprise. When Old Jack died in 1959, Jack Two promptly sold the foundry business, netting more than $50 million. Jack Two himself died suddenly in 1970, and Jackie's mother, Esther, became head of the family.

Jackie had joined the steelmaking business right out of Case Western Reserve, but after a few years of working for his dad—Jack Two, according to Jackie, made crusty Old Jack look like a cream puff—Jackie had quit in a huff and joined a local Cleveland stock brokerage firm. That didn't work out, and Jackie had just signed on with a commercial insurance broker when his father, Jack Two, died. Jackie took over the steel business, but liked it no more then than he had when Jack Two was alive. No one else in the family was active in the business (other than Esther, who served on the board), and so Jack and Esther determined to sell the company. Their timing was perfect, and the business netted an additional $100 million for the already-wealthy Gleason family.

This was in 1973. The stock market was in its worst Bear phase since the Depression, but Jackie hardly noticed. The bank handled the family's enormous wealth, and Esther watched over the bank. Jackie was busy wondering what to do with his life when Esther suffered a stroke. Esther's mind was not affected, but she couldn't speak or walk. Confined to a nursing home, she went downhill rapidly and died in 1975—thus launching, prematurely, Jackie's career as head of the family.

Many family members had been deeply alarmed by the Bear Market of 1973–74, and with Esther ill, the bank had succumbed to family pressure and largely bailed out of the markets in mid-1974. The bank's timing could hardly have been worse—the market bottomed that summer and then took off. The Gleason family had managed to ride the Bear Market all the way to the bottom, and had then compounded their error by missing the entire recovery of 1974–75–76.

Deciding that it was time to take his responsibilities as "head of the family" seriously, Jackie asked the family's long-time legal counsel and the head of the bank's personal trust group to sit in with him when the bank presented its investment results. Jackie wanted to work with these two "gray hairs" and the bank to try to develop strategies that would prevent the disaster of 1973–76 from happening again. (It would be 1985 before the Gleason family was as wealthy as it had been in 1973.) Not much progress was made for several years, as this small group struggled to figure out what to do during an era of Stagflation and flat markets.

The Group of Three, as other members of the Gleason family called them, not entirely fondly, was burdened by some serious problems. Problem Number One was that the head of the bank's personal trust group had a serious conflict of interest when it came to evaluating the bank's investment performance and proposed strategies. Problem Number Two was that the lawyer member of the group had been a long-term advisor to Jack Two and had even known Old Jack; he simply could not consider Jackie as anything other than a wet-behind-the-ears pup who mainly needed to be protected from himself. The lawyer invariably sided with the bank on every issue, much to Jackie's frustration.

Someone once said that scientists never change their minds about anything, and that scientific progress only occurs because scientists get old and die and new scientists come along with new ideas. In the early 1980s, both the family lawyer and head of the bank's trust department retired, and Jackie seized the opportunity to replace them. At first, it appeared that Jackie had frittered his opportunity away, as his selections for replacements were underwhelming at best. Jackie picked his Uncle Milton, a terminally sweet old fellow who had always doted on Jackie, but who knew precisely nothing about financial matters and who had even less interest in them. His second choice was Billy Rice, an old pal of Jackie's and a former stockbroker at the firm Jackie had (briefly) worked for. Billy now operated as a money manager for a firm he had started, and while he certainly knew something about investments, most folks in the Gleason family saw Billy's selection as rank cronyism.

But all's well that ends well. Uncle Milton had the good grace to fall off his horse, landing head first on a rock. Though he lived another twelve years, he was in a different universe from the rest of us. Milton was succeeded on the "investment committee"—still not called by that name—by his widow, Sarah, Jackie's favorite aunt. Though Sarah had not a drop of Gleason blood in her, she was the most astute member of the family, and things promptly began to look up for the struggling Gleason family investment committee.

That was in 1984, but let's jump ahead to 1995. By that time, Jackie, his aunt and Billy Rice had made so much progress that the family had long forgotten Jackie's rocky start as head of the family. Of course, it didn't hurt that Jackie was now fifty years old, not thirty. He had largely outlived the people who thought of him as an erratic kid, and was now something of a gray-hair himself, respected by his own generation in the family and looked up to by younger family members. The fact that much of Jackie's progress had been due to the quiet, effective counsel of Aunt Sarah didn't undercut the quality of Jackie's success—after all, he put her on the committee and had the good sense to take her advice.

By 1995, the old "Group of Three" had morphed into the Gleason Family Investment Committee, which was, and is, organized as follows:

- The Investment Committee consists of seven members.
- Jackie, as head of the family and head of the family office, is a permanent member of the Committee and its chair.
- There are three additional family members on the Committee, serving staggered three-year terms.
- There are three non-family members on the Committee, also serving staggered three-year terms.

- Family members of the Committee are elected at the annual Gleason family meeting. Candidates nominate themselves. In order to get on the ballot, candidates must prepare a one-page (one-page only!) statement in which they answer two simple questions: Why do I wish to serve on the Investment Committee, and What skills will I bring to the job?
- Only family members aged thirty or older are entitled to vote on the election of Investment Committee members. The family feels that children take a lot longer to grow up than they used to.[229] Interestingly, there is no minimum age limit for members of the Committee itself. This is not as odd as it seemed. The family's view (apparently) is that, while on average people under thirty were not yet full adults, an occasional youthful "star" might be helpful on the Committee at a younger age. (No one under age forty-five has actually been elected so far.)
- Non-family members of the Committee are elected not by the family at large, but by the family members of the Committee. However, the non-family members of the Committee attend portions of each annual family meeting, so family members can meet them, size them up, and (presumably) lobby for or against their reelection.
- The non-family members of the Committee are compensated at the rate of $25,000/year. Family members are not compensated, but have their expenses paid.
- After being elected by the family, family members of the Committee serve two three-year terms. Reelection is by the Committee, not the family, and is largely taken for granted. (A family member would have to screw up royally to fail to be reelected after his or her first term.) After completing a second three-year term, the family member must rotate off the Committee for at least one year.
- Non-family members are also elected (by the Committee) for three-year terms and must also rotate off the Committee for one year after serving two terms.
- Two additional family members, chosen by lot, are invited to join meetings of the Investment Committee for two-year terms, serving ex-officio:

---

229 Many members of the Gleason family in their late twenties were still single and still in graduate school. That contrasted sharply with the growing up of Old Jack Gleason who, at age twenty-one, had seen combat in World War I, had married and had had a son (Jack Two).

they are invited to the meetings, receive the agenda and all materials, and may participate in all discussions but have no vote.

- Any family member aged thirteen or older is welcome to attend any Investment Committee meeting as an observer (no agenda, no materials, no deliberation, no vote).
- The Chair (Jackie) can move the meeting into executive session at any time, requiring everyone except the seven Committee members to leave the room.
- The Investment Committee has formal bylaws and follows an operating manual very similar to the one reproduced at the end of this chapter.
- The Committee has engaged an independent advisor that works with the Committee on strategic and tactical asset allocation issues, manager selection and monitoring, and performance review. The advisor also participates in designing the agenda for the annual family meetings, especially the educational component of those meetings.
- The Committee is "staffed" by members of the Gleason family office, but relies mainly on the staff of the advisor for actual implementation of decisions the Committee makes.

Advantages of the Gleason Investment Committee

Let's consider some of the advantages of this structure.

Family control. First, because family members outnumber non-family members on the Committee, and because the family elects the non-family members, the family is appropriately in control of how their wealth is managed. In truth, however, it would probably be more accurate to say that the family has ultimate control but only the illusion of day-to-day control. Except for Jackie and Aunt Sarah, turnover among family members on the Committee has been high, while turnover among non-family members has been largely nil. (This is probably because good outside members of the Committee are hard to find.) In addition, family members, other than Jackie and Sarah, have tended not to vote as a bloc, but to be divided about issues, while the non-family Committee members tend to see alike on most matters. Finally, the non-family members tend to be older and somewhat more knowledgeable about investment matters than family members of the Committee. The fact remains, however, that if push came to shove, the family would prevail.

Seriousness of purpose. Second, the formality of the Committee's structure and proceedings, and the presence in the room of non-family members, lend its deliberations a seriousness of purpose and gravitas that a less formal governance mechanism might not. In particular, family dynamics issues, which can be disruptive in other contexts, have been almost completely absent on the Committee.

Size. The Committee is large enough to ensure that diverse views are brought to the table, but not so large that its proceedings are unwieldy or that replacing members becomes a serious challenge. The family has discussed enlarging the Committee from time to time (as the size of the family itself has grown), but nothing has happened.

Education. As is the case with most family investment committees, there is an important nexus between the existence of the Gleason Investment Committee and the education of family members about their stewardship obligations. Families without some structural form of governance find that they have to conduct family education on a makeshift basis, and all too often nothing much gets accomplished. The Gleason Committee leverages its existence to help educate family members in several ways:

- Family members with a serious interest in investment matters are able to serve on the Committee and they generally learn a great deal during their term of service.
- Family members who may have little interest in investment matters are specifically invited to attend Committee meetings as ex officio members, on a randomly selected basis. While it is true that many individuals fail to take advantage of this opportunity (they simply never show up), others do show up and a few find that the management of the family's wealth is more interesting and challenging than they imagined. Even those who never serve on the Committee tend to recognize how complex the management of wealth is, and to be more patient when markets are weak. Jackie's cousin Edward, currently a Committee member, originally gained knowledge about the Committee as an ex-officio member.
- Since the Committee meetings are open to any family member aged thirteen or older, even younger family members can attend out of curiosity or budding interest. The Committee has already identified half a dozen younger family members who have shown an interest in investment issues.

Transparency. The existence of the Committee, and the openness of its membership and deliberations, demystifies the wealth management process at the Gleason family. There is no secret "cabal" arrogating power over the money to itself. Even family members who have never attended a Committee meeting know that they *can* attend. Like people who hardly ever vote, knowing that they can vote makes them far more comfortable with the process.

Process. Working with the family's financial advisor, the Investment Committee has touched all the important bases procedurally, ensuring both that "fiduciary"[230] type prudence has been employed and that the family's wealth will be managed in a disciplined way. For example, the Committee has:

- Developed an overall strategy for the family, including asset allocation approaches for the family as a whole and for individual family units. These strategies are reviewed periodically.
- Adopted a written investment policy statement for the family.
- Considered and adopted optimal strategies in each investment category in the family's portfolio.
- Carefully reviewed "asset location" issues, i.e., which investments should be placed in which of the family's many investment "pockets." (Like most wealthy families, the Gleasons have multiple holding structures such as lead trusts, generation-skipping trusts, foundations, intentionally defective grantor trusts, variable life insurance contracts, IRAs, private accounts held in the names of different individuals, different family units, and different generations, GRATs, CRUTs, CRATs, NIMCRUTs, Flip CRTs, family and non-family partnerships, LLCs, privately held corporations, and so on.)
- Established guidelines for each manager engaged by the family.
- Conducted studies to determine optimal spending levels for the family as a whole and for specific family units.

Staying near the cutting edge. Because the family has a structure whose mission it is to ensure the sound management of the family's wealth, the family never risks falling behind as new strategies are developed, new investment opportunities come along, and long-used techniques are shown to be suboptimal. As noted below, the Gleasons were early adopters of alternative investment techniques. They were among the first large families to employ aggressive loss harvesting strategies. Equally important, the Gleasons were early abandoners of strategies that proved unproductive, such as active management in efficient market sectors, designing asset allocation strategies on a pre-tax basis, and so on. It's not necessary for every family to invest exactly at the cutting edge of best practices—the Gleasons certainly do not—but it is necessary for

---

230 The Investment Committee is not technically a fiduciary with regard to individual family members, family trusts, or other entities. Where fiduciaries are required, trustees have been appointed. Nonetheless, the Committee generally behaves as though it were a fiduciary.

families to know where that cutting edge is and to position themselves appropriately with respect to it.

Solid performance. Since the Committee assumed approximately its current form in 1995, the Gleason family's investment performance has been quite solid. Part of this strong performance has been generated by the care and attention the Committee has paid to the investment management function, and part has to do with the fact that the Committee has stayed close to the cutting edge as new strategies and techniques have come along. The Gleasons were one of the first large families to move from a traditional wealth advisory firm (the bank, which used mainly its own investment products) to what today would be called an "open architecture" advisory firm. (See Chapter 8.) They began investing in alternative assets long before that strategy became fashionable. Throughout the portfolio, the family's strategies and practices have generally been thoughtful, patient and disciplined.

Disasters avoided. Every bit as important as the solid performance the Gleasons achieved were the investment disasters they dodged. In the later 1990s, when the Bull Market morphed into a Bubble Market, the Gleasons were sorely tempted—like everyone else—to jump on the tech-growth-momentum bandwagon. Several family members were involved in daytrading, racking up huge gains on almost a daily basis. A small commitment to a technology stock manager seemed to triple in value almost overnight. The idea that the US stock market had used the Goldilocks Economy as a platform to launch itself into a New Paradigm seemed plausible. And, indeed, the family did bend on occasion. The family's equity allocation was allowed to drift to its maximum exposure, and occasionally beyond. Although the Committee had initially agreed (in 1996) to commit no more than 3% of the family's assets to technology stock managers, that limit was raised to 5% in 1998. In its single worst decision, the Committee terminated its deep value manager in mid-1999, moving those funds to an S&P 500 index fund.

But bending is not breaking. The Committee avoided the real disasters that befell so many families in the late 1990s—they never changed their allocation to US large cap stocks, they never fundamentally changed their long-term strategies (we'll ignore occasional tinkering here and there). Despite many intense discussions and more votes in a few years than had occurred in the entire history of the Committee (which usually acts by consensus), the Committee generally held to its course in the face of the strongest investment storms since 1973–74. In other words, the Committee had succeeded in accomplishing precisely the goal it was created to accomplish—avoiding the failure of nerve that had so devastated the family's wealth in the early and mid-1970s.

And it is worth noting that this enviable record of patience and steadiness continued throughout the Bear Market of 2000–2002. Again, the family bent but didn't break. Its equity allocation gradually drifted toward minimum ranges, and the family pulled in its horns, failing to take advantage of tactical opportunities as they presented themselves. In mid-2002, for example, the Committee seriously considered taking a substantial (10%) position in high yield bonds at a time when spreads between junk bonds and Treasuries were at all-time highs. But, having been battered on virtually all fronts (other than investment grade bonds), the Committee couldn't work up the nerve to be proactive. Still, simply staying the course during the long Bear Market allowed the family to participate fully in the powerful rebound that occurred in 2003.

Issue and Challenges

Gleason family investment governance is hardly perfect. Here are a few areas where the structures in place could be improved.

Who runs the family? While the structure, membership and operations of the Gleason family Investment Committee are clear and function well, there is no similar clarity associated with broader issues of family governance. Jackie is the head of the family, the head of the family office, and (therefore) chair of the family Investment Committee because, well, because he's Old Jack's grandson and Jack Two's son. But there is no Jack IV in the picture, and even if there were it's unlikely that the family would automatically consider him to be the next head of the family. There is no formal mechanism for electing a head of the family, and when something happens to Jackie, no one really knows what will happen. This issue of succession is one that the family will have to come to grips with, and soon.

Replacing non-family members of the Committee is a constant challenge. There has been little turnover among non-family members of the Committee, in part because they are so difficult to replace. Since 1995, when a non-family member has completed his term (they are, so far, all males), there has always been a scramble to decide what to do. In one case, a "temporary" replacement was elected, with the clear notion that that individual would serve only one year, allowing the former member to return after his sabbatical year. In another case, the non-family member wasn't replaced at all—the Committee simply operated for a year with one less member until the former member returned from his sabbatical. Clearly, this is unsatisfactory, and Jackie and Aunt Sarah have launched a determined effort to identify potential non-family committee members. So far, however, there are no strong candidates in the offing.[231]

The uncertain role of the family office. The Gleason family office employs twelve people. Jackie heads the office, but day-to-day matters are handled by his "chief of staff," Steffie, who was formerly the family's account administrator at the bank. (When the family moved its investment accounts into an "open architecture" structure, Steffie moved from the bank to the family office.) The family also employs a chief financial officer, an attorney who works part-time, and a young investment analyst—a position that turns over fairly frequently. Because there is so little investment talent in the family office, the activities of the Investment Committee and the family's investment advisor often seem remote from the activities of the family office. Steffie, the CFO and the investment analyst attend most Investment Committee meetings, but other than identifying cash flow issues, they are not active participants. The family does not employ a chief investment officer because Jackie (and others) believe that a truly first-rate CIO either could not be hired or would not stay long. This may change when Jackie is finally replaced as head of the office.

Compensation of the Committee members. This has been a controversial issue from the beginning. Many family members, including Aunt Sarah, opposed compensating non-family Committee members on the ground that those individuals should be serving out of loyalty to and concern for the welfare of the family, not because they are paid to do the job. Other family members support paying Committee members, but feel that family members should also be paid for their service on the Committee. Jackie pushed the compensation issue through the Committee and the family mainly because, in his mind, non-family Committee members had *always* been compensated. The family lawyer—an original member of the Group of Three—had always charged his regular hourly fee for reviewing materials and for attendance at the Committee meetings, and the head of the bank's trust department—the other original member of the Group of Three—was, in effect, being compensated via the fees the family paid to the bank. As the recruitment of non-family Committee members has become more difficult, the notion of compensating

---

231 This is actually an area that might become easier to deal with in the future. More and more professional advisors with long experience working with families are now reaching an age where they are interested in slowing down. Families are seizing on these individuals as potentially valuable investment committee members.

non-family Committee members is gaining converts, and it would not be surprising to see even Aunt Sarah throw in the towel one of these days.[232]

Attendance at Committee meetings. Until recently, this has been a problem on the Committee. The non-family Committee members are all very busy people, and as time went by, their attendance began to be spotty. Something always seemed to come up that caused one or two of them to miss a Committee meeting, or to have to participate by conference call. Observing this behavior, even family members of the Committee began to miss meetings. In 2002, however, Jackie took the bull by the horns and demanded better attendance. In return, he agreed to schedule meetings up to two years in advance and to permit any Committee member to participate in one meeting per year by conference call. He also announced, informally, that any Committee member who missed two out of any six meetings would be dropped from the Committee. It is possible that this rule will eventually be incorporated into the official bylaws of the Committee, but for now Jackie's wrath seems to have been sufficient.

No coordination of investment decisionmaking with philanthropy. The Gleason Family Investment Committee acts as the investment decisionmaker for the Gleason Family Foundation. The foundation currently has an endowment of just over $30 million, but it is expected to grow substantially when Aunt Sarah dies. While this would seem to constitute an important link between investment decisionmaking and philanthropic decisionmaking, in point of fact there is essentially no link. The Committee's meetings don't overlap with those of the foundation's board (except at the annual family meeting), and the trustees of the foundation—unless they happen to overlap with the Investment Committee membership—have very little idea why the foundation's endowment is invested as it is. This is almost surely a missed opportunity, as some family members (though not Jackie) are coming to appreciate. Many members of the extended Gleason family, especially younger members, have a keen interest in charitable activities but no interest in investment matters. The fact that the former activity cannot flourish without success in the latter is completely lost on these people. By consciously linking the importance of investment success to the ability of the family to make a philanthropic impact, the family could significantly leverage the existence of the Investment

232 As noted above, non-family Committee members are paid only $25,000 a year. While not trivial, this sum is hardly meaningful to any of the current outside Committee members, all of whom are successful, highly compensated professional people. The compensation does seem to have the effect of ensuring that the outside members take their jobs seriously—having accepted the money, they feel obligated to earn it.

Committee and, possibly, engage the interest of a much larger group of family members.

Summary

In the long run, human capital is far more important than financial capital, for the simple reason that if the former is frittered away the latter will soon disappear. By organizing and nourishing a well-functioning family investment committee, families like the Gleasons have taken a giant step toward ensuring that both their financial capital and their human capital will remain robust across the generations. The Gleason model isn't perfect, of course, but it is a work-in-progress and will no doubt continue to improve over time. As long as the family's human capital flourishes—through the education of family members and their deepening experience managing wealth in a serious fashion—the stewardship of the family's wealth will be in sound hands.

If it were simply a matter of forming a family investment committee and then letting it take its course, every family would have one and every family would maintain its wealth indefinitely. It is unfortunately the case, however, that all too often investment committees become part of the problem, not part of the solution. In the next section of this chapter we will examine why it is that investment committees so often fail to accomplish their missions, and what might be done about it.

The Family Investment Committee, Today

As is the case with the Gleasons, many families (along with virtually all pension plans, charitable foundations and endowed institutions) use investment committees[233] to provide oversight of the management of their investment portfolios. Unfortunately, history has shown that most investment committees do a poor job of stewarding the assets entrusted to them. There are many reasons why the investment committee has proved to be such an unreliable tool. Let's take a look at some of them.

The Origin of the Investment Committee

The investment committee originated not out of the investment world but out of the world of board governance. Most boards, rather than acting at all

---

233 Investment committees, of course, masquerade under many other names: finance committee, advisory board, family council, etc. Sometimes the board as a whole acts as the investment committee, particularly when the board is small.

times as a "committee of the whole," delegate much of their important activity to committees—smaller groups of board members that are really subcommittees of the "committee of the whole." This process of delegation improves the efficiency and productivity of a board, and has been enthusiastically supported by "good governance" groups such as the Association of Governing Boards of Universities and Colleges (known as the AGB).[234]

The trouble is that the investment committee is fundamentally unlike other board committees. Virtually any board member, no matter what his or her professional background, can be a productive member of such committees as nominating (sometimes called the "committee on trustees"), executive, advancement, buildings and grounds, presidential search, and so on. Our general experience of life and business suit us well for service on these committees. Even the finance committee, while more typically requiring some technical knowledge of accounting, bookkeeping and financial statements in general, can be easily mastered by anyone with a desire to do so.

But successful service on an investment committee requires knowledge so specialized and experience so extensive that it will be a rare board that can produce even one or two such people, much less an entire committee-full.[235] This is a point that is usually ill-understood by boards and board chairs, who generally appoint to the investment committee anyone with a generalized background in "finance." Hence, investment committees typically include accountants, attorneys, bankers, investment bankers, brokers and similar professionals, none of whom is likely to possess the specialized skills and experience required to design, implement and effectively monitor an investment portfolio for a substantial pool of capital. That experience would include a sound understanding of modern portfolio theory, asset allocation, manager selection, performance monitoring, and a host of other skills that are very narrowly distributed through the population of any governing board. When families establish investment committees, they tend to follow the institutional

---

[234] The AGB publishes a variety of useful information about the management of endowment portfolios. See, for example, John H. Biggs, *The Investment Committee*. The booklet is available on the AGB Web site, www.agb.org. See also *Endowment Management*, by William T. Spitz.

[235] As we note below, even such a well-endowed institution as Yale University long ago despaired of finding qualified investment committee members among its board membership. Instead, Yale has created a committee of outside experts, each of whom possesses the relevant knowledge and experience to serve effectively on an investment committee, but most of whom are not members of the Yale governing board at all.

model, placing on the committee individuals who are unlikely to possess the appropriate skills.

Hence, the first and fundamental reason investment committees fail is that the demands placed on them are fundamentally incompatible with their capabilities. The demands on investment committees are different than the demands on other board committees, and yet the investment committee is assembled and operated as though it were no different than any other board committee.

Committee Dynamics

Anyone who has served on a governing board is familiar with the often-dysfunctional internal dynamics of committees. Virtually all board committees consist of volunteers devoting their time to board work as a philanthropic endeavor. Hence, committees of such boards necessarily operate largely by consensus. No one wants to make waves or offend anyone else. Decisions almost always reflect the lowest common denominator, because to do otherwise would necessarily offend some committee member. (And that member may be the largest financial contributor to the organization!) Unless the committee chair is highly experienced in managing committees and a good leader, committee meetings will meander here and there, wasting large amounts of time on side issues, running out of time to deal with more pressing matters. Family investment committees operate according to identical dynamics. Indeed, since families don't exactly qualify as charitable enterprises, the challenge of attracting good people and motivating them to do a responsible job is especially perplexing.

In the operation of some committees, this dynamic is something less than disastrous. On the nominating committee, for example, lowest-common-denominator thinking is often the best way to ensure collegiality among board members. Fighting to nominate an individual who is actively disliked by another board member is likely to lead to disruption, not improved productivity. But in other committees the unavoidable process of committee dynamics and decision-by-committee can be devastating, and this is decidedly the case with the investment committee. Successful management of a large pool of capital requires incisive thinking, a willingness to go against the grain of perceived wisdom, an ability to behave counter-intuitively, to avoid acting on the basis of short-term events, to take the long view, and so on.

But, as currently operated, it is virtually impossible for the voting plurality of an investment committee to act in any of these ways, much less all. Instead, investment committees engage in woolly thinking (often because they are not experienced in the management of capital), tend to follow the conventional wisdom in adopting investment strategies, fail to recognize that much of the process of successful investing is counterintuitive, and typically act (usually in at least a mild state of panic) in reaction to short-term market events that will quickly reverse themselves, whipsawing the investment portfolio.

Making an Impact

The natural desire to contribute, to make an impact, means that even when investment committee members are acting on the best possible motives, their impact on the performance of the portfolio is likely to be negative. Consider, for example, an investment portfolio that has been designed and implemented in a first-rate manner. The best thing an investment committee can do with such a portfolio is to leave it alone, perhaps rebalancing it on occasion. But no member of an investment committee wants to be perceived as lazy or lacking in ideas or motivation. As a result, even if each member of the committee tosses out his or her idea only once a year, the aggregate effect is that the portfolio will find itself constantly being re-jiggered. This is the opposite of a sound approach to portfolio management.

Attempts to Deal with the Problem

Asset Allocation Guidelines and Investment Policy Statements

The usual approach to controlling investment committee behavior is for the full governing board or family to adopt asset allocation guidelines and a written investment policy statement, within whose parameters the investment committee is expected to act. Asset allocation guidelines and policy statements are essential tools in the management of capital, but as instruments for the control of investment committee behavior they are wholly inadequate. The reason is simple: whenever an investment committee wants to act outside the constraining bounds of a written guideline or policy the committee simply changes them (or, worse, ignores them). And who is to enforce compliance with these strictures? If the committee simply ignores the restraints, who will know about it? If the committee asks the board to change guidelines or policies, who on the board is going to argue with the investment committee, who are, after all, the anointed experts on such things?

Using Outside Experts to Populate the Investment Committee

Some large endowed institutions and many wealthy families have given up on the in-house investment committee in favor of an outside investment committee or board of advisors populated by experts selected for their skill and experience in the management of large pools of capital. At Yale University, for example, Chief Investment Officer David Swensen has recruited a sizeable group of experts who serve on what is called the Yale Corporation Investment Committee. Only three of the Investment Committee members need be Fellows of the Yale Corporation, Yale's governing board. There are currently eleven members of the Investment Committee (all, by the way, Yale graduates—coincidence?) In other words, instead of accepting full responsibility—and the associated time commitments—of board membership, these experts focus exclusively on the management of the Yale endowment.[236]

Clearly, Yale and the many families who use boards composed of outside experts believe that this approach is far superior to the more traditional investment committee approach. Unfortunately, experts on the caliber of those used by Yale are few and far between (and typically expensive), making it impossible for smaller institutions and families to mimic the Yale approach.

The Separate Investment Management Corporation

Some very large investors—Harvard University, Princeton University, the University of Texas—have abandoned the investment committee approach altogether. Instead, they have established separately incorporated management companies charged with the responsibility of managing the institutions' endowments. These management companies employ many—sometimes, hundreds—of highly compensated[237] investment professionals, and they

---

236 See, for example, *The Yale Endowment 2003,* published by the Yale Investment Office, p. 24. The quality of the Yale Corporation Investment Committee has probably been exceeded over the past decade only by that of the board of directors of The Investment Fund for Foundations (TIFF), which included David Swensen.

237 Although the investment professionals at these management companies are not typically compensated above levels of their investment peers in private industry, their compensation can seem positively breathtaking when compared to, say, the average salary of a tenured professor. The compensation package of Harvard Management Corp.'s Jon Jacobson, for example, was for many years perennial front-page fodder for the Harvard *Crimson.* This unwanted publicity may have led, in part, to Jacobson's decision to leave Harvard Management and form his own highly successful hedge fund (in which Harvard is reputed to be the largest investor).

have typically produced results that are far superior to those achieved by part-time, in-house investment committees. Unhappily for smaller investors, the investment management corporation is not a serious option for anyone managing less than about $5 billion.

The Family Investment Committee, Tomorrow

Like well-crafted riddles, capital markets events are usually perfectly comprehensible after the fact. But while they are happening there is so much "noise," so much emotional resonance (and dissonance), that we can't make out what will later become clear. Most events in the markets, however important they may seem at the time, are merely noise, and attempting to act in reaction to them is a very sound way to reduce our wealth. Thus, it was perfectly obvious in the late 1990s that equity valuations had become disconnected from reality. The "justifications" for those prices—it's a whole New Paradigm; things are different this time—were specious on their face. But there was so much noise and confusion going on, and the short-term pain of missing out on the almost daily price appreciation was so much more intense than the longer term prospect of a market crash, that perfectly sensible people continued to pay higher and higher prices for stocks that were pretty obviously (but retrospectively!) worth only a tiny fraction of those valuations.

Even events that are truly substantive are often not actionable in a way that will improve returns. The valuation disparity between growth and value stocks, for example, became compelling in the mid-1990s, but anyone who attempted to profit from that disparity found themselves hammered by the continued, almost mystical, appreciation among growth and technology stocks. A similar story can be told about the exceptional opportunities in emerging markets equities—a story that has been compelling now for about a decade, without any concomitant return to emerging markets investors.[238] In other words, it is often possible to "know" that valuations in one sector or another are attractive, but it is never possible to know when the value will be recognized.

Thus, the challenge for investment committees is to maintain their discipline and patience when everyone else has long run out of both. Yet, as noted at length above, investment committees are ill-equipped to act in a disciplined manner or to demonstrate patience in the face of capital markets provocations. As we have seen, traditional attempts to control dysfunctional committee behavior—written investment policy statements and asset allocation guidelines—don't work,

---

[238] With the obvious exception of 1999, when emerging markets stocks rose roughly 70%.

and alternatives to investment committees—committees of outside experts and separate investment management corporations—are beyond the reach of most families and institutions. So what can be done? One promising option is the investment committee operating manual.

Why an Investment Committee Operating Manual?

Most families have little choice but to manage their capital by using the traditional vehicle of the investment committee. Moreover, most families have little choice but to populate those investment committees with individuals who, however competent in other areas, are likely to have little experience in the management of large pools of capital. The point of using an investment committee operating manual is to build on the strengths of the traditional investment committee—namely, common sense and a desire to contribute to the sound risk-adjusted growth of the portfolio—while avoiding many of the defects of the traditional investment committee approach (see above).

What Does an Investment Committee Operating Manual Contain?

Since the purpose of the operating manual is to enable an investment committee to manage a large pool of capital even though they are not professionals at the job, one important job of the manual is to remind the committee members of what should be on their agenda, why those activities are important, and which kinds of mistakes are typically made in carrying out those responsibilities. Thus, a typical investment committee operating manual will set out a seasonal agenda for the committee to follow and will cover the following subjects:

- The purpose of the operating manual
- The purpose of the investment committee
- Meetings of the investment committee
- The investment policy statement
- Asset allocation strategies
- Portfolio rebalancing
- Manager selection and monitoring
- Asset custody
- Portfolio monitoring
- Portfolio implementation
- Conflicts of interest
- Review and revision of the operating manual

Why Does the Operating Manual Approach Work?

Operating manuals tend to work because they help investment committee members impose discipline on their deliberations. By referring to the operating manual, following its seasonal agendas for committee meetings, and internalizing its educational messages, investment committees are able to apply a level of stewardship to their portfolios that would do honor to a professional investment consultant. Once an investment committee has a significant amount of experience working with an operating manual, its members will be reluctant to depart from the disciplines that have served them so well.

If we might borrow a technique from David Salem,[239] *il miglior fabbro*,[240] let's listen in on a typical investment committee conversation—pre-operating manual—held in, oh, March of 2000:

> *Mr. Chair*: The Investment Committee meeting will now come to order. I want to thank the committee members for coming out on such a....
>
> *Ms. Stool*: Excuse me for interrupting, Mr. Chair, but I know our time is short and this is important. The stock market has been rocketing upward for years and we haven't been participating as fully as we ought to be. Only 70% of our portfolio is invested in stocks.
>
> *Mr. Chair*: Well....
>
> *Mr. Ottoman*: It's worse than you think, Ms. Stool. Half of that 70% is held by value managers, who have been stinking the place up for years.
>
> *Mr. Chair*: That's all well and good, but....
>
> *Ms. Bench*: I move that we terminate our value managers and transfer half the funds to growth managers and the other half to an S&P 500 index fund.
>
> *Mr. Ottoman*: I second the motion.
>
> *Mr. Chair*: Well, is there any discuss....
>
> *Ms. Stool*: I call the question.
>
> [Motion carries.]

Now let's see how that conversation might have gone had the investment committee had in place an operating manual:

> *Mr. Chair*: The Investment Committee meeting will now come to order. I want to thank the committee members for coming out on such a....

---

239 CEO of The Investment Fund for Foundations.

240 T.S. Eliot, inscribing *The Waste Land* to Ezra Pound, 1922.

Ms. Stool: Excuse me for interrupting, Mr. Chair, but I know our time is short and this is important. The stock market has been rocketing upward for years and we haven't been participating as fully as we ought to be. Only 70% of our portfolio is invested in stocks.
Mr. Chair: Thank you for those cogent remarks, Ms. Stool. We will certainly take them up when we review our asset allocation guidelines later in the year. The agenda for today, according to Section III of the operating manual, is....
Mr. Ottoman: But that could be too late! Ms. Stool's point is that....
Mr. Chair: Are you suggesting that you would like to suspend the provisions of the operating manual that have so successfully guided this committee in its deliberations 'lo these many years?
Ms. Stool: Well, er....
Mr. Ottoman: I, that is....
Ms. Bench: Let's get on with the agenda. I've got a plane to catch.

The Operating Manual Versus the Policy Statement

An operating manual for the investment committee is a fundamentally different document from the investment policy statement. To illustrate the difference, let's imagine that we are thinking of buying an airplane. Working with our aircraft advisors, we can quickly come up with key specifications for the plane: range, capacity, aeronautics, price, safety features, etc. Having done so, we will have a very precise idea of the kind of craft we are looking for. But we will know essentially nothing about how to build, operate or maintain the plane. It is for this reason that our aircraft will come with manuals telling us how to operate, maintain, and refurbish it.

Unfortunately, investment portfolios don't come with operating manuals. Working with our financial advisors, we can quickly come up with the key design features of our portfolio: asset allocation, risk control metrics (e.g., maximum exposure to individual stocks, minimum credit ratings for bonds), and so on. These design features will be incorporated into our investment policy statement, and anyone reading that statement will have a very good idea of what our portfolio should look like. But, purely by looking at the policy statement, neither we nor any other lay person would likely have much of an idea how to build, operate and maintain the portfolio. What should we do first? Second? Third? The answers to these questions can be found not in the policy statement but in the operating manual.

What about Investment Emergencies?

The need to change an investment strategy suddenly can arise from time to time because of changes in the *investor*. For example, there may be a key death in the family or the mission of an organization may undergo a substantial change. In such cases, of course, the investment portfolio should be reexamined *ab initio*, and that would include the provisions of the operating manual.

Short of that however, and assuming the portfolio is properly designed and properly advised in the first place, *there is no such thing as an investment emergency*. As noted above, immediate reactions to market events are almost always misguided, for the simple reason that it cannot be known until long afterward whether the event was significant or transient, and for the additional reason that most events that investors believe to be significant are, in fact, transient.[241] Hence, an important purpose of an operating manual is to help members of the investment committee avoid short-term thinking, to avoid reacting to market events that are meaningless.

A Sample Operating Manual

No, I don't expect that all across America investment committees will rush out and adopt operating manuals. But I do hope that the *arguments* for an operating manual will be internalized by investment committees, and that the resulting, more disciplined approach to portfolio management will materially improve investment returns. Given the damage inflicted on family portfolios by the bear markets of the early twenty-first century, the managers of those portfolios will need to do everything right to rebuild them over any reasonable period of time.

I have attached to this chapter a sample investment committee operating manual. There is, to say the least, nothing sacred about the organization, language, format or even the substance of the attached manual. It is offered simply as an example. I hope you find it useful.

---

241 Ok, we will concede that there are sometimes *minor* emergencies. If a manager blows up, someone should do something, of course. But except in the case of investments in mutual funds (where taxable investors may need to get out quickly before they are left holding the tax bag), all that needs to be done *immediately* is to revoke trading authority on the account.

ADDENDUM TO CHAPTER 9

Operating Manual for the Gleason Family Investment Committee

Adopted by the Investment Committee
on [DATE]

Contents

I. Purpose of this Operating Manual

The purpose of this operating manual is to set forth policies and procedures to guide the deliberations of the Investment Committee of the Gleason family. Among other things, the manual discusses the purposes of the Investment Committee and the relationship between the Committee and the family; the frequency of Committee meetings; the general agenda for such meetings; the role of the Committee Chair; and the duties and responsibilities of the Committee.

The Committee recognizes that long experience has shown that investment committees frequently make sub-optimal investment decisions. This outcome is an almost inevitable byproduct of the part-time nature of the committee's work, the frequent turnover in personnel assigned to the committee, the tendency of all committees to act according to the "lowest common denominator," and the unstructured nature of most investment committee deliberations.

It is the hope of the Gleason family that the existence of this operating manual and the Committee's determination to be guided by its provisions will help improve the operation of the Committee and redound to the benefit of the Gleason family's investment capital and ultimate wealth.

II. Purpose of the Investment Committee

The purpose of the Investment Committee is to evaluate and make recommendations to the Gleason family with regard to the investment policies and strategies to be followed by the family's investment portfolio, as follows:

1. The Committee will, via its own deliberations and through conversations with the family, determine an appropriate risk profile for the investment portfolio. It is understood that the degree of risk assumed will substantially determine the investment return available to the family.

2. The Committee will recommend investment policies to be followed in the management of the investment portfolio. These policies shall include (a) a long-term goal for the performance of the funds, (b) an asset allocation strategy designed to achieve the long-term goal, and (c) asset classes and types of investments which may be used in the investment of the portfolios.

3. The Committee will prepare and recommend to the family a written investment policy statement.

4. The Committee will prepare and recommend to the family a written spending policy. It is understood that spending by taxable families in excess of

4%—and preferably less—will have an important negative effect on the ability of the family to maintain and grow its wealth.

5. The Committee will prepare and recommend to the family written conflict of interest policies.

6. The Committee will recommend a management structure for the investment management and oversight of the family's investment portfolio. In other words, the Committee will recommend whether the family should engage an investment consultant, should utilize the services of a master custodian, should employ independent managers, should manage the funds in-house, or follow some combination of both.

7. The Committee will monitor the level of expenses incurred in the management of the investment portfolio, including management fees, commissions and other transaction costs, and soft dollar arrangements, if any.

8. If necessary, the Committee will recommend a proxy voting procedure to the family.

In carrying out these important responsibilities the Committee will be guided by the operating procedures set forth in this operating manual.

III. Meetings of the Investment Committee

Unless otherwise determined by the Chair of the Committee, the Committee will meet on a quarterly basis, and at dates and times so established as to ensure that the Committee has access to the most recent performance results for the portfolio. This meeting schedule will enable the Committee Chair to report to the family on any important actions or recommendations of the Committee. In an effort to avoid ad hoc decision-making and/or short-term thinking, the Committee will follow a seasonal schedule of meetings which will be conducted according to the agendas set forth below. Minutes will be taken of the decisions made at each meeting of the Committee.

1st Quarterly Meeting. The first quarterly meeting of the Committee will be convened after performance data is available for the prior calendar year. At the first quarterly meeting, the Committee will:

1. Review and approve the Minutes of the 4th quarterly meeting of the Committee held near the end of the prior calendar year.

2. Review the performance of the overall portfolio funds against the custom benchmark established for the portfolio and, when possible, against the performance of similar institutions.

3. Review the performance of each manager engaged by the family against the benchmark established for that manager and, when possible, against the performance of similar managers.

4. Review the compliance of the family's investments with all guidelines set forth in the investment policy statement.

5. Review the compliance of each of the family's investment managers with the specific guidelines created for that manager.

6. Identify any performance issues with regard to any of the family's managers, such issues to be attended to at the next meeting of the Committee.

2nd Quarterly Meeting. The second quarterly meeting of the Committee will be convened after performance data is available for the first calendar quarter of the year. The purposes of the second quarterly meeting are as follows:

1. Review and approve the Minutes of the 1st quarterly meeting of the Committee.

2. To review (briefly) the first quarter performance of the overall portfolio and the performance of individual managers, it being understood that one quarter of performance is far too short a period of time for meaningful data to be generated about manager performance.

3. To attend to performance issues identified at the first quarterly meeting. In the event that the Committee had identified concerns about the performance of any manager or managers at the first quarterly meeting, that manager or those managers will be invited to attend the second quarterly meeting to discuss the issues with the Committee.

4. In the event that no manager performance issues were identified at the first quarterly meeting, the purpose of the second quarterly meeting (in addition to conducting a brief review of first quarter performance) will be to meet with a manager or managers who are investing in a sector of the market that is of particular interest to the Committee at the time.

3rd Quarterly Meeting. The third quarterly meeting of the Committee will be convened after performance data is available for the first half of the calendar year. The main purpose of the third quarterly meeting is to ensure that the members of the Investment Committee continue to learn about the investment process and become ever more skillful at overseeing the family's portfolio. Thus, at each third meeting of the year the Committee will:

1. Review and approve the Minutes of the 2nd quarterly meeting of the Committee.

2. Briefly review the second quarter and first half-year performance of the overall portfolio and the performance of individual managers.

3. Select an area of the investment process or the capital markets to examine in depth, generally with the assistance of an invited expert in the field. For example, the Committee may wish to examine a particular asset class, developments in portfolio design and asset allocation procedures, particular investment styles, the details of performance reporting and monitoring, macro-economic issues, and so on.

4th Quarterly Meeting. The fourth quarterly meeting of the Committee will be convened after performance data is available for the third quarter of the calendar year. The main purpose of the fourth quarterly meeting is to review the asset allocation strategy of the family's portfolio both strategically and tactically. Thus at each fourth meeting of the year the Committee will:

1. Review and approve the Minutes of the 3rd quarterly meeting of the Committee.

2. Briefly review the third quarter and first three-quarter year performance of the overall portfolio and the performance of individual managers.

3. Review the long-term (strategic) asset allocation strategy of the portfolio to determine whether or not changes in that strategy may be merited. Typically, such changes will be appropriate only if (a) there has been a substantial change in the objectives, risk tolerance, or makeup of the family, or (b) the Committee wishes to add or delete approved asset classes, usually as a result of studies undertaken at the third quarterly meeting.

4. Review the tactical asset allocation strategy of the portfolio to determine whether, in light of market conditions and, especially, pricing and valuation considerations, it may be in the family's interest to adjust its asset allocation posture tactically in the direction of assets that appear to be under-priced or where there otherwise appears to be relatively short-term opportunity in the markets. Except in rare circumstances, such tactical moves should not exceed the pre-set maximum or minimum exposures already established for each asset class.

IV. The Investment Policy Statement

The Investment Committee will prepare and present to the family a written investment policy statement. The purpose of such a written statement is to memorialize the policies, strategies and procedures which will be used in the management of the family's investment portfolio. Over time, the reasons behind even the best-designed portfolio can be forgotten or become confused. This is especially likely to be the case during periods of market turmoil, when the temptation to depart from long-term strategies can seem overwhelming. It is crucial that the Investment Committee not succumb to such temptations. A review of the reasons why long-term strategies were adopted can temper the desire to make ill-considered short-term changes in the portfolio and can offer a measure of comfort during times of stress.

V. Asset Allocation Strategies

The first responsibility of the Investment Committee, and, in terms of long-term risk-adjusted performance, the most important responsibility, is to recommend to the family an overall asset allocation strategy for the portfolio.

In developing the asset allocation strategy for the portfolio, the Committee will have in mind the tenets of modern portfolio theory, especially (i) the core relationship between risk and return and (ii) the key insight that the existence of imperfect correlations among asset classes enables investors to reduce the risk level of portfolios without a concomitant reduction in expected return. The Committee will also be mindful of the limitations of modern portfolio theory, especially the imprecision of forward-looking estimates for risks, returns and correlations, and the difficulty of translating theoretically compelling strategies into successful real-world strategies.

Thus, the Committee will:

1. Determine, based on its understanding of the risk tolerance of the family and the return and income needs of the portfolio, which asset classes will be included in the asset allocation strategy. In making this decision the Committee will be mindful of the fact that most investors erroneously prize liquidity over return.

2. Identify several possible asset allocation strategies that are "efficient," that is, which are designed to produce the best possible expected return per unit of risk incurred. (Viewed another way, these strategies are designed to incur the minimum possible risk for any desired expected return.)

3. Select, from among the efficient asset allocation strategies, that specific strategy which seems best to meet the return and income needs and the risk tolerance of the family. That will be the "target" strategy to be presented to the family for approval.

4. Determine, for each asset class incorporated in the selected asset allocation strategy, a maximum and minimum exposure for the asset classes. In other words, the portfolio may be permitted to fluctuate between the minimum and maximum exposures set for each asset class before the Committee will need to consider rebalancing the portfolio. (See "VI. Portfolio Rebalancing," below.) Rebalancing more frequently will tend to increase the investment costs and taxes incurred by the portfolio more than it will add in terms of risk control and enhanced return. The Committee will then present the target asset allocation strategy and exposure ranges to the full family for their review and approval. In the event the members of the family are not familiar with asset allocation exercises, the Committee may wish to make whatever presentations to the family that may be necessary to assist the family members in their understanding of what asset allocation is, why it is important, and how it is done.

5. Develop and present to the family for approval a series of asset class strategies for each asset class to be included in the portfolio. It is understood that each asset class possesses its own peculiar investment characteristics and that, especially for a taxable family, there will therefore be better and worse strategies to follow in gaining exposure to each asset class.

Once an asset allocation strategy and asset class strategies have been approved by the family, the Committee will monitor compliance with the strategy on a quarterly basis and rebalance the portfolio as necessary. (See "VI. Portfolio Rebalancing," below.)

VI. Portfolio Rebalancing

Once an asset allocation strategy has been implemented, it will almost immediately begin to fluctuate with market events. Some asset classes will rise in value, while others fall and still others move sideways. These movements are natural and, given that there is price momentum associated with most capital markets, they are not cause for alarm. However, if the Committee allows the portfolio to drift too far from its target asset allocation policy, it is in effect making a decision to change, sometimes radically, the risk/reward structure of the portfolio. Rather than allow such implicit decisions to occur, the Committee will review the asset allocation structure of the portfolio at the next meeting occurring immediately after any asset class has exceeded its minimum or maximum exposures. At that meeting the Committee will use its discretion to (i) rebalance back to the minimum or maximum exposure, or (ii) rebalance back to the target exposure, or (iii) determine that the costs (especially taxes) associated with rebalancing make the exercise unwise.

VII. Manager Selection and Monitoring

It is an important responsibility of the Committee to select investment managers for the family's portfolio, to monitor the performance of those managers, and to terminate underperforming managers. Regarding manager terminations, experience has shown that most manager terminations are mistakes in the straightforward sense that the replaced manager outperforms the new manager over the following market cycle. This unhappy result tends to occur because of the tendency of investment committees to terminate managers whose investment style has temporarily gone out of favor in the market and to replace that manager with a manager whose investment style has recently been in favor. In effect, committees tend to "sell low and buy high" when making manager decisions. In an effort to avoid this common mistake, the Investment Committee will, in carrying out its manager selection and monitoring responsibilities, typically proceed as follows:

1. Before terminating a manager, the Committee will review the guidelines prepared for that manager to ensure that the manager has been given sufficient time to demonstrate his capabilities. Managers will typically be terminated before the prescribed time period only (i) because of some fundamental change in the manager (e.g., loss of key personnel, overly rapid gain or loss in assets and/or accounts, etc.), or (ii) as the result of a change in strategy on the part of the portfolio.

2. Before engaging a manager in any asset class, the Committee will gather quantitative and, especially, qualitative information about several managers who are believed to be best-in-class in their sector of the market. Typically, the Committee will interview at least two managers before selecting a finalist to be engaged. It cannot be over-emphasized that the engagement of managers who have produced strong recent returns, but who lack the other characteristics of best-in-class managers, will almost always prove to be unrewarding.

3. The Committee will draft and submit to the finalist manager a set of manager guidelines that will be used to monitor and evaluate the manager during the term of its engagement.

4. Before engaging the manager, the Committee will, as appropriate, engage in fee negotiations with the manager. These negotiations may focus on the absolute level of the manager's fee, the structure of the fee, or the minimum account size typically enforced by the manager. As appropriate, the Committee may wish to attempt to structure incentive fee schedules designed to reduce the fee to the family when the manager under-performs and to reward the manager when he outperforms.

5. As noted above (see "III. Meetings of the Investment Committee," above), each manager's investment performance will be reviewed against its benchmark on a quarterly basis. In addition, whenever possible, each manager will be reviewed against a universe of similar managers.

6. The Committee recognizes that individual money managers may be appropriate for carrying out certain strategies in each asset class and may be inappropriate for other strategies. Thus, prior to conducting manager searches, the Committee will settle on optimal strategies in each asset class, having in mind the family's risk tolerance and return objectives, the tax consequences associated with investing in each asset class, the efficiency or inefficiency of the markets through which each asset class is accessed, and the other costs associated with investing in each asset class.

The Committee recognizes, as noted above, that most manager terminations are a mistake and that these mistakes overwhelmingly occur when the manager's investment style is out of favor in the market. In addition, the Committee recognizes that manager terminations tend to be especially costly for family investors, due to the tax consequences typically involved. Consequently, the Committee will proceed with great care in considering managers for termination.

VIII. Asset Custody

The Investment Committee will determine whether or not it is in the interests of the family to select a master custodian to hold the cash and securities owned by the family. If so, the Committee will conduct a search for an appropriate custodian and will recommend a finalist to the family. An asset custodian ensures the safekeeping of the family's investments and also eases reporting and monitoring tasks, and, absent other considerations, using one master custodian is a best practice in the investment management business.

IX. Portfolio Monitoring

The performance of the overall investment portfolio of the family will be monitored and reviewed on a quarterly basis by the Investment Committee, as noted above (see "III. Meetings of the Investment Committee"). To assist the Committee in conducting these reviews, the Committee will create a custom benchmark for the portfolio as a whole. That benchmark will reflect the indices associated with the asset classes contained in the portfolio with each index weighted in accordance with the target asset allocation selected by the Committee.

The Committee recognizes that short-term investment performance is largely "noise" and does not reflect the longer term quality of the portfolio. Consequently, the Committee will have in mind longer term criteria as it reviews the performance of the overall portfolio. Typically, the portfolio as a whole will be expected to achieve its objectives over a complete market cycle, that is, from peak-to-trough-to-peak (or trough-to-peak-to-trough).

In addition to assessing investment performance, the Committee will also review compliance with all guidelines set forth in the family's investment policy statement.

X. Portfolio Implementation

On relatively rare occasions it will be necessary for the Investment Committee to consider how to implement major portfolio changes. For example, if a key advisor has been terminated and the portfolio has been reduced to cash and fixed income, virtually the entire portfolio will have to be re-implemented. Less severe implementations will have to be carried out in the event of significant strategic changes to portfolio strategies or in the event of major rebalancing events.

When a portfolio is being implemented, the Committee must select an appropriate strategy for the timing of the implementation. Possible strategies might include the following:

1. Implement all changes at the same time and immediately.

2. Implement changes on a disciplined basis over time, in order to dollar-cost-average into the markets.

3. Implement those changes first which involve investing in assets that appear to be undervalued or fairly valued, while implementing changes more slowly where they involve assets that appear to be over-valued.

As the Committee considers which of these strategies to use, it will have in mind the family's risk tolerance and the tax and cost impact of each approach.

XI. Committee Membership

The Committee recognizes that institutional memory and experience in the management of the portfolio are important advantages. Therefore, whenever consistent with the overall governance policies of the family, membership terms on the Committee will be staggered so as to avoid significant turnover in the Committee membership occurring at any one time.

XII. Conflicts of Interest

The Committee recognizes that conflicts of interest can be especially destabilizing to an investment portfolio. Therefore, in addition to any conflicts of interest provisions that apply to the family at large, the following policies shall apply to the members of and the activities of the Investment Committee:

1. No money manager, asset custodian, broker or other advisor may be retained by the family if any member of the Investment Committee is an employee of such firm.

2. The family may employ money managers in which a member of the Investment Committee is also invested, provided that the member shall make full disclosure of the member's interest.

XIII. Review and Revision

The procedures set forth in this operating manual may be reviewed from time to time and may be revised by majority vote of the Investment Committee.

PART THREE

The Rich Get Richer: The Nuts and Bolts of Successful Investing

Introduction to Part Three

Great football teams are great because their strategies are better than those of other good football teams—their vision of the game is superior. But football teams have to be good before they can be great, and being good means mastering the rudiments of the game—the blocking and tackling without which even the greatest game plans cannot be carried out.

And so it is with managing a substantial investment portfolio. Whether a family's investment activities turn out to be great or not will depend on a great many factors, including the level of talent and vision the family can deploy. But every family can—and must—be good at the task. And being good means mastering the rudiments of the game—the nuts and bolts of the investment process.

Mastery in this sense doesn't mean mastery at a professional level. I don't expect that many people will read Part Three and promptly go into the business of advising wealthy families on their investment portfolios. But families need to master the nuts and bolts sufficiently to know when they are being competently advised, to ask the key questions, to carry out, in other words, their stewardship duties.

Part Three begins at the beginning—with the question of how taxable investment portfolios are designed—and proceeds through the various steps in the investment process roughly in order: choosing optimal asset class strategies, working with money managers, asset "location" and portfolio transition issues, investment tax management, and performance monitoring and rebalancing. Part Three ends with a long chapter that discusses a variety of investment challenges that seemed, for one reason or another, not to justify full-chapter treatment.

Three

Chapter 10

Designing Taxable Investment Portfolios

I was particularly struck by David Hume's argument that, though we release a ball a thousand times, and each time, it falls to the floor, we do not have a necessary proof that it will fall the thousand-and-first time.
—Harry Markowitz

"The stock markets are a trap for logical investors because they are almost, but not quite, reasonable."
—Paraphrase of a remark by G. K. Chesterton[242]

From earliest times, mankind has attempted to diversify the risks it faced. Shippers in ancient Egypt consigned their goods to several boats and sent them off at different times, presumably to avoid encountering the same storm (or perhaps the same pirates). In the Middle Ages traders sent their goods to the same destinations overland and by sea. The Rothschild dynasty's famously early and accurate news of world events (used by them to trade with very great effect[243]) was made possible in part because the family depended on more

---

242 Chesterton's actual remark was, "Life is a trap for logicians because it is almost, but not quite, reasonable."

243 Perhaps the most famous example of the Rothschild family trading on early knowledge of world events occurred in connection with the Battle of Waterloo. Nathan Rothschild, then head of the English branch of the family, learned early in the day that Wellington had defeated Napoleon and that English securities would rise dramatically when the news was broadly known. You might imagine that Rothschild would use that news to buy. But he knew that Waterloo was a once-in-a-lifetime opportunity and he intended to make

than one method of communication: fast, proprietary ships, but also couriers and even carrier pigeons.

In the first half of the twentieth century, modern investors intuitively understood the principle of diversification. We knew that owning two stocks rather than one would reduce our risk, and that owning ten stocks would reduce risk still further. Moreover, we understood that owning both stocks and bonds would effect a dramatic reduction in risk, albeit at a similarly dramatic reduction in our returns.

But this was what we might call, in hindsight at least, "naïve" diversification. It was naïve because, while it often worked, investors misunderstood the underlying principle of diversification, namely, that what was important was not simply owning more than one security, but *owning securities that are not perfectly correlated in their pricing behavior*. Consider investors who owned both Worldcom and Global Crossing—they fared little better than investors who owned one or the other of those hapless companies. Or consider investors who owned ten—or fifty—dot.com stocks; they were clobbered in the tech collapse virtually as badly as if they had owned only one dot.com. Finally, as noted, investors who added bonds to their portfolios did indeed achieve risk reduction, but they also suffered a proportionate return reduction.

The Markowitz Revolution

It wasn't until the middle of the century that Harry Markowitz, then a young, unknown professor at the University of Chicago, had the fundamental insight that it was correlation that mattered. In a then-little-noticed article published in a then-obscure journal,[244] Markowitz not only demonstrated

---

the most of it. Therefore, he began quietly to sell. Word gradually spread across the floor of the exchange that the Rothschilds were pulling out of the market. Astute traders began to sell also. Rothschild accelerated his selling and soon the exchange was in a panic. Traders, assuming that Rothschild must know of Wellington's defeat, were desperate to get out of the market. Finally, with prices at preposterously low levels, Rothschild swept in and bought, making a vast fortune in a few hours. This behavior, was, to be sure, aggressive and manipulative. But there is little in Rothschild's behavior on that remarkable day that would violate contemporary American securities laws.

244 "Portfolio Selection," *Journal of Finance* 7, no. 1 (March, 1952), p. 77 ff. Markowitz's breakthrough ideas about portfolio design actually had their origin in his earlier insight about the possibility of applying mathematical methods to the capital markets. It was from this inspiration that all else followed.

that correlation mattered (or "covariance" as he put it); he went far beyond that insight to show that by paying attention to correlation investors could create portfolios that reduced risk without necessarily reducing returns. Indeed, in some cases (such as adding international stocks to a US stock portfolio) risk could be reduced while returns actually *increased*. And in every case in which portfolios were sensibly constructed, risk could be reduced faster than returns declined. Markowitz was the Einstein[245] of the financial world, revolutionizing the way we thought about risk and return and making possible all the subsequent advances that have come to be known as modern portfolio theory.

This astonishing idea took more than twenty years to be adopted in the design of actual portfolios. Part of the delay had to do with the inherent time lag between ideas generated in the academy and the adoption of those ideas in the real world. But there was another problem, namely, the cost and unsophisticated nature of computing power. Consider how portfolios are designed using Markowitz's insights.

Asset allocation á la Markowitz seems deceptively simple. We need only know the future risks (expressed in terms of the Standard Deviation of returns) and returns for each asset class we wish to work with, as well as the future correlation of each asset class with each other asset class. This data is programmed into a computer which then chugs away, looking at all possible combinations of these assets.[246] The computer program, which is an "optimizer," is trying to identify those asset combinations which are "optimal," that is, which produce the most return per unit of risk. Depending on how much risk we are willing to take, there may be many optimal portfolios available to us, and those will fall along the familiar "efficient frontier" curve. Possible combinations of assets that fall below the efficient frontier line are undesirable in the sense that they produce less return for the same risk.

Early Problems with MVO

This process is known as "mean variance optimization," or MVO, and so far, so good. But there are serious problems here. The first problem is that there are

---

245 Like Markowitz, Einstein was virtually unknown when he published his seminal papers on the photoelectric effect, the special theory of relativity and statistical mechanics. Indeed, he was not even a practicing academic, but an obscure clerk in the Zurich patent office.

246 Notice that the computer is not trying to solve a complex equation. Instead, it is conducting an iterative process of looking at each portfolio and discarding those that are inferior.

many, many possible asset combinations to be looked at. If, for example, we wish to consider including ten asset classes in our portfolios, our optimizer will have to search through almost thirty-three million possible portfolios even before it begins to think about changing the *percentages* of each asset.[247] Even as recently as the early 1970s it required a computer the size of a large room, two days of computational time, and tens of thousands of dollars to run one mean variance optimization. In other words, the delay in adopting Markowitz's ideas was not entirely due to intransigence on the part of real world investors.

Oddly, however, the unavailability of cheap, massive computational power was in some ways a blessing for investors. Without access to simple optimization tools, investors relied on reviewing portfolio combinations that had been developed by large financial firms and academic institutions, then applied their own judgment to the application of those portfolios to their own circumstances. In other words, they had little choice but to be thoughtful about the underlying theory of mean variance optimization.

Today, however, investors face a very different and, probably, more intransigent problem. MVO calculations are now simplicity itself. Optimization programs are inexpensive and investors have access to massive and cheap computational power. These days any three-pound laptop computer carried around by a college freshman can run an optimization in a few seconds. But as a result, investors have come to rely on the machine, rather than to consider the underlying theory in a thoughtful way. Let's consider ways in which the machine might produce results that are dangerous to our wealth.

Modern Problems with MVO—Garbage In, Garbage Out

I mentioned above the three inputs needed to conduct an MVO exercise: future risks, returns and correlations for each asset to be included in the optimization. The trouble is, we not only don't know what these values are, we don't really have any idea what they are. This is partly because we can't foresee

---

247 Modern mean variance optimizers employ algorithms designed to reduce—drastically—the number of asset combinations that must be reviewed. See, for example, Markowitz's own work on the fast computation of mean-variance frontiers in his book, *Portfolio Selection: Efficient Diversification of Investments* (John Wiley and Sons, 1959), Appendix A. In addition, financial advisors almost always constrain the optimizer—by, for example, requiring that recommended portfolios have minimum or maximum exposures to certain desired assets.

the future. If we could, we wouldn't be wasting our time designing our portfolios—we would simply pick the stock that is going to be the next Microsoft and load up on it. But we can't. The best work on asset class risks, returns and correlations, for example, has been done by Ibbotson Associates, whose annual *Ibbotson Stocks, Bonds, Bills, and Inflation Yearbook* gives values for asset class data on a quarterly basis from 1925 to the present. Yet, when Ibbotson Associates attempted to issue projections for *future* asset class returns their estimates were so bizarrely off the mark that the firm soon stopped issuing forward projections altogether.

But our inability to predict the future isn't the only problem—we also can't know the past. That may seem like an extraordinary remark, especially considering that I have just cited the excellent Ibbotson data. But the problem is one of definition—what past are we talking about? If, for example, we are talking about the returns on stocks since 1925, then we will get one answer. If we are talking about returns in the Post-World War II period, we will get another answer. If we are talking about returns over the past twenty years, we will get still a third answer. Which of these (or many other) pasts is most likely to resemble the future? We can't know, of course.

But if we can't know the future and don't know the past—that is, if we are putting garbage data into the optimizer and are therefore certain to get garbage advice out of it—what good is mean variance optimization?[248] The answer is that, if used thoughtfully and with a clear sense of its limitations, MVO can lead investors toward portfolios that are more efficient and more appropriate for their needs than any other approach known to the financial world. But for MVO to play this role, our financial advisors must work exactly at the cutting edge of knowledge in this area.

Developing Thoughtful Data Inputs

If we are working with competent financial advisors they will not use purely historical returns in their MVO calculations. Instead, they will adjust past returns to meet the conditions existing in the capital markets today and over our effective time horizons as investors. Future returns are extremely sensitive

[248] There are many other problems with using MVO and similar asset allocation techniques. Some of these are discussed above in Chapter 5. See also Gregory Curtis, "Asset Allocation," in *JK Lasser Pro Expert Financial Planning: Investment Strategies from Industry Leaders*, edited by Robert C. Arffa (John Wiley & Sons, Inc., 2001), pp. 327-345. But the best and most popular book on the subject of asset allocation is Roger C. Gibson's *Asset Allocation: Balancing Financial Risk* (McGraw-Hill Trade, 3rd ed., 2000).

to starting values, and therefore, in particular, advisors must give serious thought to the valuations of assets at the time the MVO exercise is being undertaken. Advisors, frankly, tend to be very bad at this exercise, for two reasons. The first is that it is an enormously difficult task—if we really knew which assets were under-valued and (especially!) when those under-valuations were going to be reversed, we would be far wealthier than we are. The second reason is that most advisors are sales-oriented, not advice-oriented (see Chapter 7), and hence they are far better at telling investors what they want to hear than they are at giving their honest opinions about important matters.

Consider MVO analyses performed in the late 1970s—clearly, they should have taken into account the very low valuations of most equity securities at that time. And consider MVO analyses performed in the late 1990s—clearly, they should have taken into account the very high valuations of equity securities at that time. Instead, most portfolios designed during those periods of time used long-term historical returns (or something close to them) and performed miserably. Investors in the 1970s found themselves seriously *under*-exposed to stocks just as the greatest bull market in US history was starting. Investors in the 1990s found themselves seriously *over*-exposed to stocks just as one of the worst bear markets in history was starting.

In addition, in thinking about the investment environment going forward, our advisors must consider not some generic time period that is convenient to the advisory firm, but our own actual investment time horizons. Thus, for example, our advisor might believe that, over the next decade, US large cap stock returns will reflect essentially their long-term averages. But if our real investment time horizon is five years, not ten, the advisor's opinion is largely irrelevant. If we hope to experience any investment success, we will want to work with advisors who can tailor their MVO inputs to our actual needs, rather than employing a central-office approach where one-size-fits-all.

Multi-Period Optimizers

In general, new developments in capital markets theory and new tools for designing portfolios are likely to be adopted as best practices in due course. But this is not necessarily always the case, and the introduction a few years ago of multi-period mean variance optimizers is a case in point. Conceptually, multi-period optimizers (M-POs) make great sense, because they are able to take into account important inputs that are more difficult to work with using single-period optimizers (S-POs).

An S-PO, for example, assumes that the expected risks, returns and correlations that are programmed into the optimizer will not change, even over long periods of time. In addition, S-POs generally assume that the portfolio will never be rebalanced. Finally, S-POs are unable (or are able only using Herculean measures) to take into account the fact that, in taxable accounts, the tax cost basis of the portfolio typically gets lower over time as a percentage of the market value of the portfolio. As a result, account turnover becomes increasingly expensive over time, something S-POs tend to ignore.

Still, I generally don't recommend the use of M-POs, at least as the technology currently exists. The first and main reason for this is that the complexity that M-POs introduce into the portfolio design process far outweighs their conceptually sounder approach. The guts of M-PO programs are mind-bogglingly complex, and far beyond the ability of the typical investor to understand. In addition, the output of typical M-PO programs is efficient frontier lines that are discontinuous and "peaky." Instead of the familiar gentle curves produced by S-POs, M-POs produce lines that begin and end for no apparent reason and that evidence sharp peaks and valleys.

As a result of these complexities, investors who use advisors who employ M-PO portfolio design systems will find themselves completely at the mercy of the advisor and are unlikely to understand why they own the portfolio they have or how it is likely to behave under various conditions.

Another reason for being wary of M-PO systems is that the assumptions that must go into them are even more complex and difficult to produce than the assumptions that go into S-PO systems. If we can't have much of a handle on the expected risks, returns and correlations of assets today or in the past, how good are our opinions likely to be about such things as they change in the future? And is the assumption correct that the difference between the tax cost basis of our portfolios and their market values will always increase? At what rate?

In short, while the use of M-PO programs might possibly be of use to advisors themselves as they conduct what-if exercises, they are best left back in the office when advisors go out to talk to investors.

Taking Taxes into Account

Family investors can't spend gross returns. Like it or not, Uncle Sam is our investment partner, as are the governor and, very often, the mayor. Since that is the case, why do advisory firms persist in conducting MVO analyses using pre-tax returns? The answer is that that's the way it has always been done. The first investors to use (and pay for!) MVO analyses were pension plans and large endowed institutions. When advisory firms began to seek private clients they didn't bother to adjust their analyses to reflect the singular nature of family clients—the most singular feature being that private clients pay taxes and institutional clients don't.[249]

Even if the tax consequences of all investment assets were the same, advisors who use pre-tax MVO analyses with private investors would be seriously misleading those clients. Assuming non-taxable and taxable investors with identical risk tolerances, the returns achievable by the former will be substantially higher than those achievable by the latter. In other words, private investors will either have to accept lower returns than institutional investors owning the same portfolios, or they will have to own different and more risky portfolios to achieve the same returns.

But the tax consequences of owning different investment assets are in fact *not* the same for private investors. Consider this question: would you rather own a well-performing hedge fund that returns 15% per annum or a poorly performing private equity partnership that returns 15% per annum? If you are an institutional investor, the answer is that you would prefer to own the hedge fund—it is less risky and has better liquidity than the private equity partnership, yet generates the same return.

But if you are a *family* investor, the answer is likely to be quite different: you would probably prefer to own the private equity partnership. Why? Because the hedge fund will generate its 15% return primarily through short-term capital gains, while the private equity fund will generate its 15% return primarily through long-term capital gains. Most wealthy investors will pay high taxes on the hedge fund gains, but much lower taxes on the private equity gains. Hence, the question can be rephrased as follows: would you rather get 12% per year or 9% per year?[250]

We can conduct a similar analysis with essentially every asset we might wish to use in our portfolios. We would notice, for example, that "value" stocks will generate much of their return through dividend payments, while growth stocks will generate much of their return through long-term appreciation. We will note that real estate and oil and gas investments offer tax advantages to families. And so on.

The point of all this is simple—our advisors need to conduct their portfolio design studies using *after-tax* returns, not pre-tax returns. The result of such an approach will be that different assets will be used in different proportions than would be the case if the studies were performed using pre-tax data—and

---

249 Private foundations do pay a small excise tax.

250 Yes, private equity is typically a riskier asset class than hedge, but even on a risk-adjusted basis most families would prefer the private equity return.

the portfolios thus designed will be efficient and appropriate for taxable investors, as opposed to nontaxable institutions.

Looking at Outcomes in Dollars

In the process of designing our portfolios, financial advisors generate a substantial collection of modern portfolio theory statistics about the characteristics of various possible portfolios. These statistics are useful to advisors, but they are hardly useful to investors. What we need to see is the range of possible outcomes for various portfolios in dollars—and, preferably, in after-tax dollars. Such outcomes are developed using Monte Carlo[251] or similar simulations. These simulations begin with a portfolio starting value, then run many iterations based on the risk, return and correlation characteristics of the portfolio.

Monte Carlo simulations are not perfectly accurate for several reasons. A principal reason is that what the computer is actually doing is taking a portfolio, holding it for a one-year period and seeing what the outcome looks like. It then runs the initial portfolio for another one-year period and looks at that outcome, and so on. In the real world, our portfolios change every year and it is the range of outcomes associated with those changed portfolios that matter. Note that in reviewing Monte Carlo simulations we will want to observe the range of outcomes for short, intermediate and longer time periods. Because negative outcomes rise much more slowly than positive outcomes over time, if we look only at longer term periods we might be tempted to select a portfolio that will, in all likelihood, prove too risky for us over shorter term periods. It is therefore important that we look at each portfolio over a range of time periods.

The Problem of Fat Tails

Many natural events occur in a similar pattern, namely, a range of outcomes clustered around a long-term average outcome: the height of trees, the weight of small mouth bass, visits of birds to a sanctuary. If you live in a region that, on average, receives 40 inches of rain in a year, the actual pattern may show that, two-thirds of the time, annual rainfall lies between 30 inches and 50 inches. A statistician would tell you that the mean rainfall in your area is 40 inches with a Standard Deviation (S.D.) of 10. Rainfall results therefore distribute themselves along the familiar bell curve.

251 The name is unfortunate, as it connotes gambling. However, as we all know (I hope!), gambling statistics are biased in favor of the house, while Monte Carlo simulations produce a straight-up, unbiased series of possible outcomes.

Knowing this, we can calculate that, 95% of the time, rainfall in the area will be between 20 inches and 60 inches—two S.D.s. It might be *climatically* possible for rainfall in the area to be as low as 5 inches or as high as 75 inches, but those outcomes would be *statistically* almost impossible. We would not expect to observe such outcomes even over many centuries, and hence it doesn't pay us to prepare for or anticipate them in any way. (The so-called "hundred year flood" is really just the most remote of the possible outcomes, the one that falls in the 95th percentile, or two S.D.s. above the average.)

The returns produced by the capital markets also distribute themselves in bell curve fashion. But there is a crucial difference between capital markets and natural phenomena. The example of rainfall is an example of natural behavior largely uncompromised by human interaction. But securities prices don't somehow magically change from time to time—they change only in response to the action of human beings in buying and selling them. And human behavior, as we all know, is at best complex and at worst truly bizarre. We can behave with calm resolution one moment and panic along with the rest of the crowd the next moment. The result is that the bell curve distribution of capital markets performance is skewed badly near the extreme outcomes—it is these extreme examples that constitute the so-called "fat tails" of the bell curve.

Thus, if the mean return on US large capitalization stocks is 10% and the S.D. is 20 (both about right over very long periods), then we would almost never expect to see annual losses of more than about -30%, that is, more than two Standard Deviations below the mean return. Indeed, if we experienced such a loss even once in a lifetime of investing we could consider ourselves to be relatively unlucky.

In fact, however, extremely poor and extremely good returns are far, far more likely to occur than a pure statistical analysis would lead us to believe. When Eugene Fama did his doctoral thesis on price movements of the Dow Jones Industrial Average, he discovered that for each stock in the index there were many more days of extreme price movements than would occur in a normal distribution. Random distribution couldn't explain these outliers:

> "If the population of price changes is strictly normal, on the average for any stock...an observation more than five standard deviations from the mean should be observed about once every 7,000 years. In fact, *such observations seem to occur about once every three to four years[!!]*"[252] (Emphasis and exclamation points added.)

---

252 Eugene F. Fama, "The Behavior of Stock-Market Prices," *Journal of Business of the University of Chicago*, vol 38, no. 1 (January 1965).

And in Chapter 5 I cited the breathtaking market collapse that occurred over two days in October of 1987, an event that would have been statistically unlikely to occur "had the life of the universe been repeated one billion times."[253]

Investors thus face a curious dilemma. On the one hand, we have carefully constructed our portfolios using the best modern portfolio theory techniques, employing the necessary[254] assumption that market events will occur in a normally distributed fashion. On the other hand, we know from examining the actual data that some market events—namely, very bad portfolio performance[255]—will occur far more often than a normal distribution would lead us to expect. We have, in effect, succeeded in controlling a mathematical version of risk—normally distributed price volatility—but we have not adequately addressed the real risk that investors face: the risk that we will depart from our sound strategies in the face of unexpectedly poor results, thus incurring permanent losses of capital.

Price volatility matters, to be sure, and not just in the world of financial theory. Given our druthers, most of us would prefer to obtain a handsome long-term rate of return with little or no price volatility along the way. But we have to live in the real world, and in that world we must choose between, on the one hand, low-price-volatility-and-low-returns and, on the other hand, high-returns-and-higher-price-volatility. Given that reality, most investors can get used to price volatility *so long as it stays within an expected, reasonable range.* It is not price volatility itself that causes us to flee from sensible long-term strategies—it is unanticipated, apparently irrational price volatility.

Stress-Testing Our Portfolios

How can we reconcile the need to employ mathematical models in designing our portfolios with our knowledge that those models don't accurately describe the environment in which we will be placing our capital at risk? My suggestion is that we go ahead and design our portfolios using the models—after all, they are the best tools we have. But once our portfolios have been designed we need to stress-test them. The purpose of stress-testing is not so much to cause us to redesign the portfolios (though that could happen), but to

---

253 Chapter 5, note 110.

254 Necessary because mean variance optimization is a mathematical technique, not a psychoanalytical technique.

255 Our portfolios will also experience unexpected and very good performance, but we are unlikely to complain about that.

alert us to the real, as opposed to statistically likely, outcomes we will experience if we own the portfolios long enough.

Typical tools for stress-testing portfolios include calculations of the likelihood of a loss over any particular period and the "maximum drawdown," that is, the largest peak-to-trough movement the portfolio is likely to experience. Such tools are useful, to be sure, but they suffer from a key defect: being statistical tools, they also assume that outcomes will be normally distributed.

Instead, we might consider subjecting the portfolio we believe is appropriate for our needs to *actual historical results*, especially during negative market periods. How would our portfolio have performed in 1929–32? In 1973–74? In 1987? In 2000–02? Such periods are rare in the capital markets, but they will occur and we will have to brace ourselves to navigate them successfully. If we know that our portfolio will perform well during normal market conditions, and if we also know how our portfolio will work in the worst conditions—the conditions represented by the fat tails in the bell curve—we will be far better prepared to adhere to sound strategies over the long haul.

But a caution is in order about stress-testing. We need to keep in mind that the purpose of stress testing is to alert us to the enormity of the real world difficulties we can expect to encounter, not to panic us into adopting far more cautious strategies. It would be simple enough to design strategies that would have performed reasonably well during the worst market conditions in history. The trouble with these strategies is that they are so cautious—so full of cash and fixed income securities—that they will gradually destroy our wealth even during the normal-to-good markets that will mainly characterize our investment experience.

Occasionally, to be sure, stress-testing will reveal that the portfolio design we have selected as appropriate is in fact inappropriate. That is, stress-testing will demonstrate to us that we cannot live with the negative performance the portfolio is likely to produce at some point. In that case, of course, it will be appropriate to return to our models and select a less aggressive strategy. After all, it is far, far better to own a less-than-ideal portfolio that we can live with for a very long time than to own a "perfect" portfolio that we will abandon at the worst possible moment.

The Yale Approach to Stress Testing

Yale University has subjected its endowment portfolio to a particular type of stress test that is appropriate for Yale's purposes and that may also be worthy of consideration by other very sophisticated investors. Specifically, Yale has adopted an investment strategy that is designed to control the university's "capital impairment risk" and "spending disruption risk." Capital impairment risk is defined by Yale as the likelihood of losing half the endowment's purchasing power over a fifty year period. Spending disruption risk is defined by Yale as the likelihood of a real (that is, adjusted for inflation) reduction of 10% in spending from the endowment over any five-year period.[256]

I won't go into a detailed description of the complex studies required to calculate impairment and disruption risks, in part because they are so arcane, but mainly because the use of these measures will realistically be limited to a very small group of highly sophisticated investors. Yale can calculate these measures and find that they are useful because Yale has a theoretical investment time horizon measured in centuries—the university is already more than 300 years old—and a real time horizon measured in many decades. This very long-term thinking is possible because of the confidence Yale has in David Swensen, its redoubtable Chief Investment Officer, and in the exceptionally strong Investment Committee Swensen has assembled.

Most investors, whether they are endowed institutions or families, will have had much shorter histories than Yale[257] and will have both theoretical and practical investment time horizons far, far shorter than Yale's. Investors' theoretical time horizons relate to the actual period of time over which the capital is expected to be deployed. Even for families, this time period will often be measured in terms of three or four generations, possibly far longer.

But let's be realistic. The real or practical investment time horizons for most investors is a few years at most, because those time horizons are measured by the period of time over which the investors are prepared to endure unhappy results without flinching—without departing from sensible strategies that, inevitably, are going through a bad period of performance. Few investors will tolerate such periods for more than two or three years.

Moreover, as noted above, Yale's ability to think long-term didn't happen magically. It grew over time as Yale recognized that, in CIO Swensen, it had at the helm one of the great investment minds of our era. It is unlikely that Yale will ever find a benefactor who will add as much to its endowment as Swensen has added. But great investors like Swensen don't come along very often, and

---

256 *The Yale Endowment* (Yale University Press, 2002), pp 4-5. If you are interested, Yale estimates its capital impairment risk to be only 7% (versus 40% for the typical endowment) and estimates its spending impairment risk to be 20% (versus 37% for the typical endowment).

257 This is not always the case, of course, even with private investors. The remarkable Rothschild family has been wealthy for more than 200 years, and the Morgans are nearly as ancient.

when they do they are very rarely content to work for one organization.[258] As a result, most family investors will have to be content to stretch their real investment time horizons out past two years. That is one of the principal goals of this chapter and, indeed, of this book.

The Investment Policy Statement

Once we have gone to all the trouble to design a sound investment portfolio, the next important step is to write it all down. An investment policy statement is the written record of the work we have done, and it will serve as a guide to the management of the portfolio over the years. While such policies can always be revisited and modified in light of experience, the development of and adherence to written policies will have several powerfully positive affects.

First, for fiduciary portfolios, in the rare but certain event of extremely adverse investment results, the existence of written policies will demonstrate the thoughtfulness and prudence with which we have approached the challenge of managing capital in a complex world. Modern concepts of prudence, as articulated, for example, in the prudent investor rule, the Uniform Management of Institutional Funds Act, and similar guides, are not outcome-oriented but process-oriented. Virtually any security and any investment strategy can be prudent if it is adopted thoughtfully and with reference to the actual needs and objectives of the particular fund. The fact that the security became worthless or the strategy failed is largely irrelevant. On the other hand, even relatively uncontroversial investment strategies can be problematic if they were adopted with little thought, if they were inappropriate to the needs of the fund, or if the trustees provided little ongoing oversight of their results.

Second, and more important, the existence of and adherence to thoughtfully developed investment policies and strategies that are appropriate to the needs and objectives of a particular fund will help ensure that major investment disasters will be avoided and that the long-term performance of the portfolio will be satisfactory.

Over time, the reasons behind even the best-designed portfolio can be forgotten or become confused. This is especially likely to be the case during periods of market turmoil, when the temptation to depart from long-term

---

[258] According to the *New York Times*, in 2003 Yale paid Swensen roughly $1 million. Compared to what he could earn elsewhere and compared to what he has accomplished for Yale, he is one of the most underpaid employees on the planet. Stephanie Strom, "Some Alumni Balk Over Harvard's Pay to Money Managers," *New York Times* (June 4, 2004), p. 1.

strategies can seem overwhelming. A specific memorialization of the reasons why long-term strategies were adopted can temper the desire to make ill-considered short-term changes in the portfolio and can offer a measure of comfort during times of stress. Moreover, many family portfolios are managed by individuals whose identities change periodically. In such cases disagreements can easily arise regarding the proper course to be taken, the role played by individual investments or the reasons certain policies and strategies were adopted. The existence of a written investment policy statement serves as an objective method of resolving such disagreements, and, indeed, as a way of reducing the likelihood that such disagreements will arise.

While the policy statement can take any form, a good policy statement might address some or all of the following issues:

- A statement of the reasons why the policy statement has been prepared.
- A list of the accounts subject to the policy statement.
- A statement of the investment goals and objectives for the family.
- A description of the roles and responsibilities of asset custodians, money managers, the staff, the board of directors, the investment committee and any other key advisors (such as an investment consultant).
- A description of the asset classes to be used in the portfolio.
- A target asset allocation for the portfolio, along with a full description of the analyses that led to the selection of the target allocation.
- Maximum and minimum exposures beyond which rebalancing will be required, and the timing within which rebalancing must occur.
- Investment guidelines for the portfolio covering such topics as diversification, credit quality limitations and maturity and duration parameters for the fixed income portfolio, any restrictions on the use of derivative securities, portfolio manager guidelines, prohibited assets, custody, proxy voting, directed commissions, securities lending and any other issues appropriate for the family.
- The criteria to be used in selecting money managers.
- How the performance of the portfolio will be measured (that is, selection of appropriate benchmarks and time frames).
- How often the policy statement will be reviewed.

Most financial advisors have forms of investment policy statements, but serious investors will use those forms only as a general guide. If we simply adopt our advisor's form, it is unlikely that we will actually have thought seriously about the issues addressed in the statement. Instead, we should draft our own statements, putting the language in our own words. Some families like to use policy statements that are detailed and extensive, while others prefer a statement that can fit on one page. The important point is not the form or length of the statement, but that we prepared it ourselves to meet our own needs, and that it remain a real, living document. For what it is worth, I have attached to this chapter two samples of policy statements, one a "long form" and one a "short form."

EXHIBIT A-1: Short Version

THE PRUDENT FAMILY

Statement of Investment Objectives, Policies and Strategies

Adopted [month, day, year]

The Statement of Investment Objectives and Strategies will serve as a guideline for the management of the investment assets of the Prudent family and will be reviewed by the family from time to time.

Statement of Investment Objectives

It shall be the long-term objective of the portfolio to meet the financial needs of the Prudent family, providing a permanent, reliable flow of funds to the family to meet its spending needs (as defined in a separate Prudent Family Spending Policy) and to grow that flow of funds at least as rapidly as the rate of inflation as calculated by the Consumer Price Index. More specifically:

1. the primary objective of the portfolio is to earn at least the spending rate as specified in the Spending Policy (currently 3%), plus the inflation rate as measured by the Consumer Price Index, plus 1% real growth, and
2. the secondary objective is to outperform a custom index consisting of [INSERT], net of all fees and costs.

Specific performance goals will be established for each investment manager as the managers are retained. Those goals will be incorporated into written guidelines for each manager.

Statement of Investment Policies and Strategies

The investment objectives of the portfolio as set forth above will be pursued within the following guidelines, which shall represent the approved investment policies and strategies for the family:

A. Asset Allocation

The asset allocation strategy for the family shall be as follows:

	Target Exposure	*Maximum*	*Minimum*
Growth/equity assets	*0%*	*0%*	*0%*
US large/mid-cap equities	0%	0%	0%
US small cap equities	0%	0%	0%

International/emerging equities	0%	0%	0%
International small cap	0%	0%	0%
Private equity	0%	0%	0%
Directional hedge funds	0%	0%	0%
High-yield debt	0%	0%	0%
Hedging/yield assets	*0%*	*0%*	*0%*
Long/intermediate bonds	0%	0%	0%
Inflation-linked bonds	0%	0%	0%
Real estate/energy	0%	0%	0%
Non-directional hedge funds	0%	0%	0%
Operating assets	*0%*	*0%*	*0%*
Cash/short-term bonds	0%	0%	0%

B. Growth/Equity Asset Policies and Guidelines

The following policies and guidelines will apply to the investments listed under "Growth/equity assets," above:

- Investments which do not offer daily liquidity are limited to a maximum of ___% of the growth/equity portfolio.
- Insofar as possible, and consistent with cost considerations, investments in the growth/equity portfolio will be diversified by manager and by investment style: growth, value, top-down, bottom-up.
- No more than ___% of the family assets at cost, or ___% at market value, will be invested in any one industry.
- No security may be purchased which exceeds ___% of the issuing company's total market value on the date of purchase.
- Any securities convertible into common stocks will be considered as common stocks for purposes of these guidelines.

C. Hedging/Yield Asset Policies and Guidelines

The following policies and guidelines will apply to the investments listed under "Hedging/yield assets," above:

- Investments which do not offer daily liquidity are limited to a maximum of ___% of the hedging/yield portfolio.
- Investments in fixed income securities (other than securities held in non-directional hedge funds) will be limited to those with at least an "[INSERT]" rating (or the equivalent) assigned by any generally recognized rating service.

- No more than ___% of total portfolio assets will be invested in the securities of any one issuer, except for debt issued or guaranteed by the United States of America or agencies thereof.
- The average maturity of the fixed income portfolio shall remain at all times within ___% (above or below) the average maturity of the [INSERT] Bond Index.
- Foreign fixed income securities, including foreign sovereign debt, will not exceed ___% of the portfolio assets at market value.

D. General Policies and Guidelines

The following policies and guidelines will apply to all investments of the Prudent family:

- In an effort to maintain the overall risk level of the portfolio within an acceptable range, the relative mix of asset classes will be rebalanced back toward the target allocations as opportunities permit, but in any event not less often than annually.
- Asset class exposures which fall outside their acceptable maximum and minimum ranges will be rebalanced back to within the acceptable ranges at the next meeting of the Investment Committee following the date on which the guideline violation occurs. In the event the Committee shall determine not to rebalance the portfolio, a note to this effect shall be placed in the minutes of that meeting, indicating that the Committee was aware of the violation.
- Funds awaiting investment in real estate and private equity will be invested, respectively, in operating assets and growth/equity assets.
- Investment guidelines will be established by the Investment Committee for each manager retained by the family. Those guidelines will generally be in the form attached to this statement.
- Unless approved in advance by the Investment Committee, in utilizing derivative securities the following guidelines will be applied: (a) The use of futures and options contracts will be limited to liquid instruments listed and actively traded on major exchanges and (except for short-term funds) to over-the-counter options or forward contract positions executed with major dealers. (b) Derivative securities may not be used to effect a leveraged equity or fixed income portfolio exposure—instead, all options and futures positions must be offset in full by corresponding cash or securities. (c) Futures and options may be used to adjust the duration of fixed income portfolios, but only within the traditional

range permitted for physical portfolios. (d) No derivatives strategy may be used if it would subject the portfolios to greater variance than would be the case with the physical portfolio under a worst-case scenario. (e) Short-term funds may use only exchange-traded futures contracts and options—specifically prohibited are any off-exchange instruments and any exotic or structured securities, as well as notes whose interest rate is tied to security with a maturity of more than one year.

Without the explicit written consent of the Investment Committee, the portfolio will not be invested in any of the following assets:

- Limited partnerships
- Individual real estate properties or raw land
- Private placements
- Futures contracts, commodities, or options

EXHIBIT A-2: Long Version

© Investment Policy Statement
Adopted [INSERT]

A Summary of the Investment Policies, Strategies and Procedures to be Followed in Managing the Investment Portfolio of the Prudent Family

Purpose of the Investment Policy Statement

The purpose of a written Investment Policy Statement is to memorialize the objectives, policies and procedures that will be used in the management of the investment portfolio. Over time, the reasons behind even the best-designed portfolio can be forgotten or become confused. This is especially likely to be the case during periods of market turmoil, when the temptation to depart from long-term strategies can seem overwhelming. It is crucial that investors not succumb to such temptations. A review of the reasons why long-term strategies were adopted can temper the desire to make an ill-considered short-term change in the portfolio and can offer a measure of comfort during times of stress.

Most family investment portfolios serve the financial needs of more than one individual. In such cases disagreements can easily arise regarding the proper course to be taken, the role played by individual investments or the reasons certain portfolio strategies were adopted. The existence of a written Investment Policy Statement serves as an objective method of resolving such disagreements, and, indeed, as a way of reducing the likelihood that such disagreements will arise.

Finally, the lives of individual investors change constantly and it may be necessary from time to time to revise or adjust certain aspects of the portfolio. (This is in addition to the periodic thorough reviews that every portfolio should undergo, as discussed below.) Reference to the objectives, strategies and policies underlying the portfolio will make such adjustments much simpler and more straightforward.

Allocation of Responsibilities

The Prudent Family Investment Committee is charged with responsibility for establishing overall financial objectives and investment policies, including the following:

- establishing an asset allocation strategy for the family;
- selecting qualified investment managers, mutual funds or other suitable asset management vehicles for each asset class which has been approved;
- selecting a qualified custodian for the assets;
- structuring an appropriate communications mechanism with any separate account portfolio managers;
- monitoring the performance of each individual account and of the portfolio as a whole.

The investment managers, including mutual funds and any other pooled investment vehicles purchased, will be responsible for security selection (that is, the actual purchase and sale of stocks and bonds) and the timing of purchases and sales.

Investment Objectives, Time Horizon and Risk Tolerance

- The family's investment objective is to [INSERT].
- The family's investment time horizon is [INSERT].
- The family's tolerance for investment risk [INSERT].
- The family is currently in the following tax brackets: [INSERT].

Investment Guidelines

In pursuit of the investment objectives, the portfolio will be managed on a total return basis, consistent with prudent levels of risk. Investment risk in the portfolio will be evaluated in the context of the portfolio as a whole, rather than on the basis of individual security or asset-class risk. It is understood that certain investments that are risky in themselves can add value to the overall portfolio by increasing overall return while actually decreasing overall risk, depending on the correlation coefficients of the asset classes under consideration. As is the case with any portfolio that holds assets other than cash equivalents, the portfolio value can be expected to fluctuate both up and down, depending on market movements from time to time.

Diversification

The portfolio will be broadly diversified to avoid unnecessary exposure to the risks inherent in any individual security, industry group or asset class. Except for passively managed vehicles (such as index funds) and United States

Government securities, the portfolio should own no more than ___% of the outstanding securities of any one issuer, valued at cost. Nor should the portfolio own more than ___% of such securities valued at market price.

Quality

The average dollar-weighted quality rating of the fixed income portfolio shall be ___ or better by Moody's or Standard & Poor's, and in no event shall any individual issue be rated below ___. Exceptions to this guideline, including instances in which the rating of an issue is reduced after purchase, shall be made only after discussion with the investor. (These guidelines will not apply to high-yield securities purchased within the asset allocation guidelines set forth below.)

Maturity

Guidelines, if any, regarding the average maturity of the fixed income portfolio may be established from time to time. No limit is imposed on the maturity of any single issue. However, the investor may impose a maximum weighted average maturity for the fixed income portfolio over a complete interest rate cycle (defined as a period of both rising and falling interest rates and typically corresponding to a general business cycle).

Use of derivative securities

It is recognized that derivative securities, such as options and futures, may prudently be utilized to reduce portfolio risk. However, in utilizing derivative securities the following guidelines will be adhered to: (a) The use of futures and options contracts will be limited to liquid instruments listed and actively traded on major exchanges and (except for short-term funds) to over-the-counter options or forward contract positions executed with major dealers. (b) Derivative securities may not be used to effect a leveraged equity or fixed income portfolio exposure—instead, all options and futures positions must be offset in full by corresponding cash or securities. (c) Futures and options may be used to adjust the duration of fixed income portfolios, but only within the traditional range permitted for physical portfolios. (d) No derivatives strategy may be used if it would subject the portfolio to greater variance than would be the case with the physical portfolio under a worst-case scenario. (e) Short-term funds may use only exchange-traded futures contracts and options—specifically prohibited are any off-exchange instruments and any exotic or structured securities, as well as notes whose interest rate is tied to security with a maturity of more than one year.

Portfolio manager guidelines

Specific guidelines will be developed for each manager selected to manage assets of the portfolio.

Liquidity requirements

Short-term liquidity requirements are assumed to be no greater than are required for ongoing management of the assets. The investor has established a separate emergency cash reserve if appropriate.

Prohibited assets

Without explicit written consent obtained in advance of the purchase, the portfolio assets will not be invested in any of the following assets:

- Limited partnerships
- Venture capital investments
- Private equity ventures
- Individual real estate properties or raw land
- Private placements
- Futures contracts, commodities, or options

In addition, the managers of the portfolio assets will not engage in short selling, nor will securities be purchased on margin.

Asset custody

Physical custody of securities owned by the family shall be maintained with a bank or other suitable custodian selected or approved by the Investment Committee. A suitable custodian shall have a minimum capital of $___ billion and shall carry insurance against fraud, theft or other loss in an amount deemed sufficient by the Committee. In no case shall custody of the family's securities be in the hands of a money manager or other financial advisor. Such advisors shall have only a limited power of attorney to direct the investment and reinvestment of the family's funds, but not to remove such funds from the care of the custodian.

Asset Allocation for the Portfolio

The portfolio will have a target asset allocation strategy, as well as maximum and minimum exposure ranges, as follows:

Asset class or subclass	*Policy allocation*	*Maximum*	*Minimum*
Equities	x%	x%	x%
Fixed income	x%	x%	x%
Cash	x%	x%	x%
Large cap stocks	x%	x%	x%
Small cap stocks	x%	x%	x%
Specialized assets	x%	x%	x%
International stocks	x%	x%	x%
Emerging markets stocks	x%	x%	x%
High-yield bonds	x%	x%	x%
Long-term bonds	x%	x%	x%
Medium-term bonds	x%	x%	x%
Short-term bonds	x%	x%	x%
Cash	x%	x%	x%

The asset allocation strategy should not be completely implemented immediately, but should be viewed as a target toward which the portfolio should move deliberately over time. In order to minimize exposure to short-term market fluctuations, assets should be shifted from current asset classes to new asset classes by making gradual changes over a period of time. Specifically, when redeploying an entire portfolio, assets should be sold and purchased in equal quarterly (or monthly) installments over a period of one year. When simply moving funds from one asset class to another, without making fundamental changes in the portfolio structure, the following "averaging-in" guidelines should be observed:

If moving from this asset class	*To this asset class*	*Make equal periodic moves over this period of time*
Cash	Short-term bonds	Immediately
Cash	Medium-term bonds	2 quarters
Cash	Long-term bonds	3 quarters
Cash	Stocks	4 quarters
Short-term bonds	Medium-term bonds	2 quarters
Short-term bonds	Long-term bonds	3 quarters
Short-term bonds	Stocks	4 quarters
Medium-term bonds	Long-term bonds	2 quarters

Medium-term bonds	Stocks	3 quarters
Long-term bonds	Stocks	3 quarters
Large/mid-cap stocks	Small cap stocks	2 quarters
Large/mid-cap stocks	International-developed	2 quarters
Large/mid-cap stocks	Emerging markets	3 quarters
Small cap stocks	International-developed	2 quarters
Small cap stocks	Emerging markets	3 quarters
International-developed	Emerging markets	2 quarters

Criteria for Selecting Investment Managers and Investment Products

The investment managers, mutual funds and other pooled investment products that are used in the Prudent family's portfolios will be selected according to the following criteria, which are listed in approximate order of importance:

- Managers or investment products which have—and stick to—an investment objective which is appropriate for the portfolio.
- Managers or investment products that have demonstrated a long-term commitment to and competence in understanding and managing the asset class, sub-class and/or investment style for which it has been selected.
- Managers or investment products that have a demonstrated a commitment to keeping investment costs at a minimal level relative to the expected incremental return. Costs include fee levels, portfolio turnover, and costs associated with the quality of execution.
- Managers or investment products which have experienced long-term manager or management stability. (This may not apply to index funds. In addition, managers who are new to a specific fund or product may have long track records elsewhere.)
- Managers or investment products which have long-term (five and ten-year) performance records in the top quartile of managers with similar investment objectives.
- Managers or investment products which have decided, as a matter of policy, not to attract "hot money" or other investors with very short-term time horizons.

Non-Traditional Managers

In the event the investor shall approve the use of non-traditional managers for the portfolio, specific guidelines will be developed for individual managers and for such managers as a class. These managers may include hedge funds, private equity managers, and venture capital managers (including mezzanine funds and leveraged buyout funds).

Performance Measurement and Objectives

The performance of each asset class and investment vehicle in the portfolio will be monitored against indices appropriate for those asset classes or vehicles and against universes of money managers or funds with similar investment objectives. The appropriate period for performance measurement is three years or one complete market cycle, whichever is longer. The indices used will be as follows:

Large and mid-cap U.S. stocks	S&P 500 Index
U.S. small cap stocks	Russell 2000 Index
Specialty assets	Custom index[259]
International stocks	MSCI World ex-US Index
Emerging markets stocks	MSCI Emerging Markets Index
Core U.S. bonds	Lehman Aggregate Bond Index
Municipal Bonds	Merrill 3-7 Year Muni Bond Index
High Yield bonds	Lipper High Yield Bond Index
Equity real estate	NAREIT Equity Index
Cash and equivalents	Merrill Lynch 91-Day Treasury Bill Index

Portfolio Rebalancing

The asset allocation for this portfolio was carefully selected to meet the family's investment objectives, time horizon and risk tolerance, and to accommodate any special circumstances relevant to its circumstances. As various asset classes increase or decrease in value over time, the asset allocation will begin to fall outside the acceptable ranges. This results in a portfolio that is either too risky or too cautious. Approximately annually, therefore, calculations should be

259 The custom index for Specialized Stocks is constructed by selecting certain percentages of the MSCI All Country World Index as follows: 40% Energy Sources, Energy Equipment & Services; 40% Non-Ferrous Metals, Forest Products & Paper, Misc. Materials and Commodities; and 20% Gold Mines.

made to determine whether any asset class falls seriously outside the recommended percentage representation in the portfolios. If so, serious consideration should be given to selling a portion of those asset classes which fall outside the range on the high side and purchasing asset classes which fall outside the range on the low side.

Important as rebalancing is, though, it shouldn't be carried out blindly by taxable investors. The benefits of rebalancing must be greater than the costs of the taxes to justify the rebalancing exercise. This decision must be made based on the facts in each case, but in general rebalancing will be seriously considered whenever our exposure to an asset class exceeds the ranges set forth above, under *Asset Allocation for the Portfolio*. When asset class ranges become this badly out of balance, the long-term investment considerations typically outweigh the short-term tax considerations.

Portfolio Volatility

It is understood that portfolios designed to achieve long-term objectives will contain volatility (short-term increases and decreases in value) which may at times cause discomfort. However, the portfolio has been designed with the understanding that it will occasionally experience declines in value. Indeed, portfolios that are not exposed to risk cannot hope to achieve significant returns. The long-term expected performance on investment portfolios can be achieved only if the portfolios remain invested long-term—including, importantly, periodic rebalancing back to the original target allocations. The chances of achieving the long-term return objectives of investment portfolios are enhanced significantly if the portfolios remain invested for ten years or more. Fifteen years is even better.

The worst possible case for generating acceptable long-term returns would arise if the portfolio allocations are tampered with during periods of serious market turmoil. Anyone can panic and sell out of a declining market, but no one can accurately identify the correct time to get back in. Panicky investors inevitably miss the rapid rallies that characterize market recoveries, reinvesting too late to catch the market upswing. This constant whipsawing of the portfolio is a certain road to poor—indeed, potentially disastrous—returns.

Portfolio Review and Revision

On a quarterly basis:

- The Investment Committee will review the actual results achieved by the portfolio and by each investment manager;

- The Investment Committee will confirm compliance with all guidelines set forth in this investment policy statement and in any specific guidelines established for individual managers;
- The Investment Committee will review compliance with the asset allocation guidelines set forth in this statement.

On an annual basis, the Investment Committee will review this investment policy statement and the guidelines prepared for individual investment managers and determine whether changes may be appropriate. Approximately every three-to-five years the portfolio should be subjected to a thorough review, including attention to the continued accuracy of the investment objectives, time horizon, risk tolerance and special factors appropriate for the portfolio at that time. In the event of a major change affecting the portfolio, it should be reviewed promptly regardless of the intervening time period since the last review.

Three

Chapter 11

Asset Class Strategies—Traditional Investments

In investing money, the amount of interest you want should depend on whether you want to eat well or sleep well.
—J. Kenfield Morley

Once their portfolios have been properly designed, many investors (and, alas, many advisors) immediately move on to the selection of money managers. This is almost always a mistake, because it confounds two allied but distinct issues. Evaluating and selecting managers is one of these issues, of course (see Chapter 13). But a preliminary issue exists, namely, what are the optimal *strategies* that should be pursued in the asset classes that are to be included in the portfolio? In this chapter we will discuss asset class strategies for traditional asset classes—marketable securities. In Chapter 12 we will discuss asset class strategies for alternative asset classes.

Every type of investment asset comes fully accessoried with its own investment challenges, as well as different tax, risk, return, correlation, and other characteristics. And every investor comes fully accessoried with his or her own individual objectives, time horizons, tax issues, and judgments about alpha versus risk premium. Before we turn our attention to the hiring of money managers, we need to give careful consideration to the characteristics of the asset classes we propose to use and to our own specific needs and points of view. We can then structure investment strategies that maximize advantages and minimize disadvantages. Strategies that might be appropriate for non-taxable investors might be wholly inappropriate for taxable investors. Strategies that are appropriate for the US large cap sector might be inappropriate for the international sector, and so on. Once these strategies are in place for each asset class we plan to include in our portfolio, the strategies will themselves point us toward a very small subset of the huge money manager population that is likely to be of interest to us.

Let's now take a look at strategies that are likely to prove productive for taxable investors in each of the main traditional asset categories: US large and mid-cap stocks, US small cap stocks, international stocks (including international small cap and emerging markets), and fixed income.

US Large and Mid-Capitalization Stocks

The first thing to notice about US large and mid-capitalization stocks, that is, stocks in companies whose names are likely to be familiar to us, is how extraordinarily efficient this category of assets is. These companies are so large and important to the US economy, so many money managers and investors are buying and selling them, and so many analysts are following them, that it is virtually impossible for any one money management firm to gain *and sustain* a competitive advantage over its peers. When we consider the burdens that managers bear—the costs associated with their management fees, trading commissions, spreads between bid and ask prices, the market impact of their trading activity[260] and the "opportunity costs" associated with making buy and sell decisions[261]—it is easy to understand why it is so difficult to find US large cap managers who will add to our wealth beyond what we could obtain by investing passively, through index funds, exchange-traded funds, or similar vehicles.

As a result, many family investors will find that the most attractive approach to the US large cap sector will be to create a core position with a passive, tax-aware manager, and then supplement that position with more modest commitments to boutique or hedge fund managers selected for their ability to

---

260 "Market impact" refers to the fact that when a money management firm buys or sells a stock that very activity affects the price of the stock. When a manager buys, the increased demand causes the price of the stock to rise slightly, meaning that the management firm pays more for the stock than the market price before it placed its order. Similarly, when a manager sells a stock, that activity depresses the price of the stock slightly, causing the manager to receive less for the stock than the prevailing market price before it placed the sell order. For most large money management firms in the large cap sector, and for most managers of any size in the small cap sector, market impact will cause a far greater reduction in returns than will commissions and spreads. In some cases, market impact will even overwhelm the cost of the manager's fees.

261 Opportunity cost refers to the loss of value that occurs between the time a manager decides to buy or sell a stock and when the transaction actually occurs.

deliver after-tax alpha. A passive, tax-aware manager is simply a management firm that, rather than attempting to own securities that will outperform the index, attempts instead to make intelligent tradeoffs between matching the index performance and minimizing investor taxes.

The best way to understand how passive, tax-aware management works is to compare it with purely passive investing, as through an index fund. If we buy an index fund our manager will purchase a portfolio of securities designed to replicate the performance of the benchmark index, typically the S&P 500 Stock Index. The manager will simply hold those securities passively until the makeup of the index changes. (Periodically, Standard & Poor's will remove some stocks from the index and add others in an attempt to keep the index current and representative.) The manager will then sell those stocks that have been removed from the index and buy the stocks that have been added.

That selling and buying activity will cause us to incur taxes, even though we have done nothing but passively own the index fund. Worse, over time and assuming the stock markets go up, our interest in the index fund will be worth far more than our tax cost basis. When we wish to sell our interest we will face a big capital gains tax bill. Some investors who have owned index funds for decades have built up such huge embedded gains that the tax cost of selling the account becomes prohibitive—the investment is frozen, even though it may no longer be appropriate in purely strategic terms.

A passive tax-aware manager starts out in the same way, purchasing a portfolio of securities designed to replicate the performance of a benchmark index. However, the manager then begins to tax-manage the account. Every day, some stocks in the index will appreciate in price and others will decline. When individual stocks have declined sufficiently in price to justify the costs of the trade, the manager will sell them, "capturing" the losses. The manager will then either wait thirty-one days[262] and buy the stock back or, more commonly, replicate the position derivatively. Over time, the manager will have created a basket of losses that can be used to offset the inevitable gains that occur when the makeup of the index is changed. More important, by capturing losses consistently, the manager is ensuring that there will never be a huge difference

---

262 Investors cannot simply sell a stock on day one and buy it back on day two—the so-called "wash sale rule" prohibits such purely tax-motivated selling. The rules require investors to wait a minimum of thirty-one days before buying back the same stock they have just sold. There are, however, many ways to maintain essentially the same investment exposure without actually owning the stock—by buying a very similar stock, for instance, or buying an exchange-traded security that is highly correlated with the stock.

between the tax cost basis of the account and its market value. Thus, the investor can liquidate the account without incurring a large capital gains tax.

The main downsides of passive, tax-aware investing are the costs of trading and the increased tracking error against the benchmark caused by the tax-management of the account. "Tracking error" simply refers to the difference in the performance of the account and the performance of the benchmark index. A true index fund should evidence extremely small tracking error, while a tax-managed index fund will inevitably show slightly larger tracking error. However, the savings in taxes will almost certainly compensate the investor for this downside. The goal of a passive, tax-aware manager is not to outperform the index on a gross basis, but to outperform it on an after-tax basis.

Once the passive, tax-managed core position is in place—typically 50% to 75% of the entire US large cap stock allocation—we can then turn to filling out our large cap position by hiring the best managers we can find. Recognizing that persistent outperformance in the large cap space is extraordinarily difficult, we will tend to look for such managers among boutique firms and hedge fund managers. (See Chapter 12.) Even if we make mistakes, as we are likely to do, we will at least have reduced the impact of those mistakes on our net wealth.[263]

US Small Capitalization Stocks

In stark contrast to the efficient nature of the large and mid-cap stock markets, the small cap sector is intensely *inefficient*. There are thousands of small companies in scores of different industries, scattered all across America and frequently located in smaller, out-of-the-way communities. Investment banking firms cannot make much money on these firms, and hence investment analysts don't cover them. The only way to learn anything useful about such companies is to engage in very hard work: traveling to their locations and talking directly to the management teams, the suppliers to the companies, the customers of the companies and the competitors of the companies. This isn't what most people think of as fun, and consequently managers who are willing to do it end up in the possession of information about small companies' prospects that is of considerable value, since it is not widely known. Indeed, history shows that, over time, smaller capitalization stocks significantly outperform larger capitalization stocks.

---

263 See Chapter 12 for a discussion of the use of directional (long/short) hedge funds as the high-alpha component of a US large cap asset class strategy.

But before we leap to the conclusion that we should load up on small cap stocks, let's look at the dark side of this picture. The first negative is the high price volatility historically associated with owning small cap stocks. As we know from reading Chapter 10, investment assets that exhibit high price volatility must produce much higher returns than low volatility assets to achieve the same terminal wealth. Hence, the higher historic returns of small caps is to some extent negated by their higher price volatility.

The second problem with small caps is that, even if they ultimately produce returns superior to large caps, they can go for very long periods of time (e.g., virtually the entire 1990s) without doing so. Small cap investors, in other words, must be prepared to be patient.

Finally, there is a body of thought that argues that the superior return historically produced by small cap stocks is a product of the fact that small cap indices (such as the Russell 2000 Stock Index) are not traded. Trading smaller securities, it is argued, is so expensive that it completely negates the superior returns offered by the asset class. A representative example is a memorandum sent by Aronson + Johnson + Ortiz, a (large cap) money management firm, to its clients and friends in the spring of 2003. AJO commissioned Wilshire Associates to examine trading costs and returns across different capitalization sectors of the stock market. Wilshire concluded that the largest quintile of stocks by capitalization returned, between 1974 and 2002, only 13.0%, versus 17.6% for the smallest quintile. However, Wilshire also estimated round-trip trading costs for the largest quintile of 31 cents, or 0.8% of the average share price of $41. By contrast, Wilshire estimated that roundtrip trading costs for the smallest quintile of stocks to be 91 cents, or an astonishing 6.1% of the average small stock share price of $15. This caused small cap returns, on a net basis ("Real World Returns," in AJO's terms), to fall below large cap returns, 11.5% to 12.2%.[264]

There is clearly something to this argument. Commissions and spreads on smaller company stocks are much higher than on larger, highly liquid stocks. But the crux of the issue is market impact. Many small companies have limited stock issues and quite small floats.[265] As a result, when a large money manager attempts to purchase a useful position in such a company, its interest causes

---

264 Aronson+Johnson+Ortiz, *Small Cap Stocks Are **Sometimes** Cheap But They're **Always** Expensive* (April 24, 2003) (emphasis in the original).

265 "Float" refers to the amount of a stock issue that is actually traded. Many smaller companies, even publicly held ones, are owned primarily by one family or by the management team. As a result, only a portion of the stock actually "floats," that is, is available for purchase.

the stock price to rise significantly. Similarly, when a manager believes that a small company stock has reached its full potential, the manager's desire to sell the stock seriously depresses its price. Unless the manager is very careful, the trading costs incurred in buying and selling a small cap stock will completely offset the superior return of the stock.

My own view falls somewhere in-between the argument that "small caps will always outperform in the long run," and the argument that "the small cap effect is completely illusory." A small group of small cap managers have mastered the art of trading smaller company securities, accumulating positions very slowly over time and liquidating positions slowly and carefully. They limit turnover severely and will avoid even attractive stocks if they cannot find a way to trade them efficiently. These managers can deliver significant alpha, even net of their trading friction. On the other hand, the notion that we can simply invest in smaller stocks and sit back and watch our wealth increase is clearly delusional.

As a result, a sensible strategy in the small cap space may be to ask our passive, tax-aware manager (see the discussion, above, under *US Large and Mid-Capitalization Stocks*) to manage our money not against the S&P 500—a pure large and mid-cap index—but against, say, the Russell 3000, which includes smaller cap stocks. That will give us roughly a 7% to 8% exposure to small caps on a passive basis. We can then consider doubling that exposure by identifying one or two boutique or hedge fund managers who specialize in small caps.

A final issue to keep in mind in the small cap space is that there is a huge difference between small cap value and small cap growth. Yes, these designations are, as noted above, largely the invention of pension consultants. But in the small cap space they are distinctions with a real difference. A small cap growth company is likely to be a budding technology company that could either become the next Microsoft or the next Wang (which went bankrupt). A small cap value company is likely to be making iron castings in Duluth. These are very different enterprises, needless to say, and hence when we look for small cap managers we will probably want to diversify our exposure between growth and value.[266]

International Stocks

Most of what was said above about small cap stocks goes equally well—except more so—for international equities. The sector is a vast and inefficient

---

266 An increasingly troublesome issue for small cap managers is the crowding-out factor caused by hedge fund activity in the small cap space. A few long-only small cap managers have actually exited the business because hedge funds were, in their view, causing chaos in the pricing of small cap stocks.

one, and hence manager skill and hard work can pay off handsomely. On the other hand, trading costs (and custody costs[267]) can be extravagantly high, bleeding away much of the advantage of international investing. Fortunately, as free market economic systems gradually spread throughout the world, the most bizarre and inefficient local market practices are fading away, to be replaced by trading institutions and mechanisms that look more like those in the US and Europe. This is, however, a slow process, as older, inefficient players continue to exercise enough political clout to slow their own march toward oblivion.

There are many criticisms of international diversification. Some investors believe that international diversification is unnecessary, pointing to the very high correlations between the US markets and international developed country markets that have persisted in recent years. Other investors concede the long-term benefits of international diversification, but point out that during very negative periods in the US markets the international markets are also highly likely to be weak, rendering international diversification useless just when you need it most. Finally, some investors, even those who recognize the benefits of international diversification, simply distrust foreign markets (and foreign governments) and advocate gaining international exposure mainly through ADRs.[268] Let's examine these criticisms one-by-one.

International diversification is unnecessary. It is certainly true that, from time to time, the correlations between US equity markets and foreign equity markets increase. But to argue from this that international diversification is unnecessary is to drive by looking in the rearview mirror. Correlations among equity markets change slowly over time, but they are not mono-directional. During some market periods—especially those that are powerfully directional (up or down)—correlations will increase and we will conclude that international diversification provides no benefits. But no sooner will we eliminate our international exposure than—voila!—correlations will move the other way and we will have forfeited the benefits.

It can, to be sure, be maddening to own international stocks during periods when they are both under-performing US stocks and providing little diversification (as was the case during much of the 1990s). But since it is impossible to time correlation changes and investment return leadership, the only way to

---

[267] See the discussion in Chapter 17.

[268] ADRs are American Depository Receipts, securities issued by foreign companies that trade on US stock markets. A foreign company that wishes to list its ADR in the US must comply with certain rules, mainly regarding US-type financial disclosure and financial reporting.

gain the long-term benefits of international diversification is to own international equities as a permanent core position in our portfolios. Thus, in constructing our portfolios we should establish a range for international exposure and remain near (but not below) the bottom of that range when correlations are high. As correlations decrease, our exposure to international stocks will typically rise of its own accord and it will now be our job to keep that exposure near (but not above) the top of the range.

Just when you need it, diversification doesn't work. This is, alas, all-too-true, at least if we think of our need for diversification as a short-term requirement. When the US equity markets collapse, we can be certain the international developed country stock markets will also collapse. But if we wish to succeed as investors, we simply have to accept the fact that we cannot design portfolios that are both bullet-proof and wealth-creating. If we try to do so, we will end up failing as investors, mainly by consistently buying into markets at the top and selling out of them at the bottom. Bad markets—bad markets globally—are simply a part of the investment experience, just as bad periods are a part of any good marriage. The only way to make our portfolios bullet-proof is to put all our money in US Treasury bills and become slightly poorer every day.

More important, our diversification needs aren't short-term at all. The point of diversification—including, especially, international diversification—is to reduce the long-term price volatility of our investment portfolios. The main reason to do this is not so that we can be more comfortable holding those portfolios. The reason we do it is because the more volatile our returns, the lower our terminal wealth will be. (See the discussion of "variance drain" in Chapter 3.) Thus, it is precisely when we don't seem to need it—when the price volatility of our portfolios is being modestly suppressed by our international diversification—that diversification is doing its job. Yes, it would be nice if collapsing US markets were always offset by rising international markets (or vice versa), but it doesn't happen that way. More important, it isn't necessary for it to happen that way for diversification to work its wealth-creating magic for us.

It's easier and safer to gain international exposure by investing in ADRs. It's easier and safer, to be sure, but it's also mainly a waste of time. ADRs are issued mainly by gigantic multinational foreign corporations whose prospects are affected in the main by exactly the same factors that affect the prospects of gigantic multinational domestic corporations. Buying ADRs of BP isn't going to gain us any more diversification than buying Exxon Mobil. There is nothing wrong with buying ADRs if we think the issuer is a good investment bet, but there is no point in buying them to obtain international diversification.

The best way to gain international diversification for most family investors is to look for international equity managers who are truly exposing their portfolios to regional, national and even local factors. Some of these managers will be focused on smaller capitalization companies whose prospects are inherently more likely to be dominated by non-global factors, while others will be buying larger capitalization companies focused heavily on local and regional foreign markets. Owning these kinds of companies will, over the long-term, tend to provide both diversification against a US stock portfolio and also slightly higher returns—one of the few "free lunches" in the investment world.

As with US managers, some international managers will tend to have a growth bias and some will have a value bias. If our portfolios are large enough, we may wish to gain exposure to both types of managers. However, international managers can also be classified as "top-down" or "bottom-up" in their approach, and this taxonomy is likely to prove more useful to us in diversifying our international exposure.

A "top-down" manager tends to observe conditions in global regions and countries and to decide which of those locations are likely to offer the most attractive investment prospects. Only then does the manager begin to look for individual companies in those regions. A "bottom-up" manager tends to look for the best companies regardless of where they may be domesticated, and then only secondarily will the manager make sure it is diversified regionally and by country. While the long-term results of these two types of managers will be similar, over intermediate periods of time top-down and bottom-up managers will exhibit quite different return patterns, justifying diversification between those two approaches when possible.

Fixed Income

Fixed income markets—bond markets—tend to be efficient, meaning that it is difficult for any manager to produce sustained outperformance. They tend to be low-returning, net of inflation, meaning that there is little wealth-creation potential to be had in the sector. Finally, they tend to be "boring," with little in the way of the spectacular peaks and valleys that characterize equity markets. Instead, fixed income markets tend to follow broad secular trends as interest rates rise over the course of many years (the 1970s, for example), then decline slowly over the course of many more years (the 1980s and 1990s, for example). As a result, we might expect to find that investors have such markets well in hand and that we can safely focus our advisory attention on the gamier equity side of client portfolios.

In fact, however, my experience is that investors tend to make more mistakes on the bond side of their portfolios than on the equity side, probably because, for the reasons just mentioned, investors don't pay enough attention to fixed income. Granted, mistakes in bond portfolios tend to be less disastrous for investors than mistakes elsewhere, but foolish deployment of our capital is always harmful to our wealth, whether the harm occurs in brief, spectacular fashion (as with equity mistakes) or slowly and largely invisibly (as with bond mistakes). Let's examine some of the typical mistakes we make in our fixed income portfolios, and then turn to best practices in this sector.

Employing managers who "cheat." Given the extraordinary efficiency of the bond markets, especially on the taxable side, it is surprising to observe how many bond managers claim to have outperformed the indices. Closer examination almost always discloses, however, that the managers have exposed their clients to significantly more risk than was embedded in the index, and it was that added risk that explains the outperformance, not the managers' skill. Let's look at how a typical taxable bond manager "outperforms."

> *Wily Bond Management, Inc.* Wily manages taxable bond accounts for institutional investors and for families who have private foundations or large IRA accounts. Its typical benchmark is the Lehman Brothers Aggregate Bond Index, a very broad long-intermediate index. Over the past ten years, Wily has outperformed the Lehman Aggregate, and this fact is naturally trumpeted in its marketing materials. Looking at this record, many investors have hired Wily and Wily's business is growing and profitable. But a closer look at Wily's performance discloses what is not disclosed by the firm's sales staff: Wily has subjected its client accounts to very considerably more risk than is contained in the Lehman Aggregate Index, and it is that increased risk, pure and simple, that accounts for Wily's so-called outperformance. In fact, controlling for the risk it has taken, Wily has actually under-performed the Index by a considerable margin.
>
> How does Wily take on more risk than the Index? In at least three or four ways. First, Wily has exposed its clients to greater *duration*[269] risk. Over the past ten years the average duration of the Lehman Aggregate Index has been about 3.8 years, while the average duration of the Wily portfolios has been about 4.1 years. Over time, longer duration portfolios will outperform shorter duration portfolios, albeit

---

[269] Duration is a more accurate measure of the interest rate sensitivity of a bond portfolio than the more commonly used "maturity," since duration includes all cash flows coming in from the bond, including interest payments and principal repayments. Thus, a bond with a ten-year maturity and a 5% yield will have a much shorter duration (and hence will be much less susceptible to interest rate changes) than a bond with a ten year maturity and a 3% yield.

with far greater price volatility along the way. This is what has happened to the Wily accounts.

Second, Wily has exposed its clients to greater *credit* risk. The average credit quality of the Lehman Aggregate Index is AA, but the average credit quality of the Wily portfolios is A-. While this may not seem to be a big deal, lower credit quality bond portfolios naturally tend to return more than higher quality portfolios for the simple reason that investors demand more return to take on the increased risk of default.

Third, Wily has exposed its clients to greater *optionality* risk. Many corporate bonds are callable, that is, under certain conditions the issuer can redeem the bonds long before they are scheduled to mature. Naturally enough, companies tend to call their bonds when they can replace them by issuing new bonds at lower interest rates. For the unhappy investors, this means that we have received our money back exactly at a time when we don't *want* it back—because we will have to reinvest it at lower yields. Issuers of callable bonds pay a very small premium yield for the privilege of being able to call those bonds, and Wily has taken advantage of that by buying a far higher percentage of callable bonds than is represented in the Index.

Finally, Wily has exposed its clients to benchmark risk in other ways—by owning more structured products (mortgage-backed and asset-backed instruments, for example) than are present in the Index, by over-weighting certain sectors of the Index, and so on.

There is nothing inherently wrong with anything Wily has done with its client portfolios, *except for the singular omission that none of it was disclosed to the clients.* Thus, Wily has achieved outperformance against the Index, but it has not achieved something far more important—risk-adjusted outperformance. Nor is this a hypothetical problem for investors. If we look at Wily's aggregate performance over the past ten years, we do, indeed, see long-term outperformance against the Lehman Aggregate (though not risk-adjusted outperformance, of course). But if we look, instead, at each individual account Wily has managed over that time period, we observe problem after problem. Investors look at Wily's aggregate performance and hire the firm, looking no further. Things go along well enough for a period of time, but then suddenly the risk embedded in the Wily portfolios jumps out and bites us.

Perhaps it is an unexpected jump in interest rates that harms the Wily portfolios much more than we expected (and much more than the Index was harmed, as a result of its shorter duration). Perhaps slowing economic conditions have caused several of the weaker credits in the Wiley portfolios to be downgraded or—horror of horrors!—to default. (The Index will experience downgrades, too, but at a less frequent pace as a result of its higher average credit quality.) Perhaps rates have fallen and many issuers have called their high-yielding bonds, forcing us to go out and buy lower-yielding bonds to replace them (the Index will also have experienced calls, but fewer of them due to its lower optionality).

Yes, investors who stayed the course with Wily for the entire ten-year period will actually have beaten the Index, albeit with many unhappy surprises along the way. But there will actually be few such investors. Many more investors hired Wily, were unhappily surprised by the risks that bit them, then fired Wily, poorer but wiser. We don't want to be one of those investors, and so we need to look much deeper before we hire bond managers who claim "outperformance."

Using stockbrokers to build bond portfolios. All-too-many investors, believing that bonds don't generate enough in the way of returns to justify hiring a professional manager, turn to stockbrokers[270] to build bond portfolios for them. Except perhaps for trying to buy bonds on our own, this is probably the worst way to build a fixed income portfolios. There are many reasons for this, but the primary reason is that brokers are salespeople, not objective advisors. They only make money by selling bonds to us, whether we need them or not, and whether they are the right bonds or not. And how many investors are in a position to know whether our brokers are telling us the honest truth about a new bond or are just blowing smoke?

Unlike most stocks, which are listed on a stock exchange or otherwise traded in a manner that is largely transparent, the pricing of bonds is devilishly difficult to discern. Brokers sell us bonds and charge commissions that are difficult to puzzle out. Worse, they often sell us bonds out of their own firm's inventory, charging a "markup" rather than a commission—and if you think commissions are difficult to calculate, try figuring out what your broker is charging you through markups. When a broker is selling bonds to us he or she is in a position antagonistic to us and our interests, exactly what we want to avoid in managing our money—we want our advisors interests to be aligned with, not opposed to, our own interests.

---

270 We easily recognize stockbrokers when we encounter them at firms like Merrill Lynch, Salomon Smith Barney, or Dean Witter. But we seem to become brain-dead when we engage client relationship personnel at firms like Goldman Sachs or Morgan Stanley. These folks are brokers in every sense of the word, and the cautions expressed above apply to them every bit as much as they apply to "retail" brokers. A firm can be, and frequently is, a first rate investment banking outfit and a third rate investment advisory outfit.

Finally, brokers tend to be in no position to monitor the bond portfolios they have built for us. If a bond was bought when it was rated AA, will the broker recognize that the issuer's prospects are dimming and that there is a danger of a downgrade? Far more likely, the broker will contact us *after* the issue has been downgraded, to suggest that we sell the dog and buy a better bond (allowing the broker to make money both ways).

Paying too much for bond management. While some investors are being pennywise and pound-foolish (by hiring brokers to build their bond portfolios or by doing it themselves), other investors are simply paying way too much to have their fixed income portfolios managed. Keep in mind that the long-term expected return on an intermediate bond portfolio, net of tax (or using tax-exempt bonds) is going to be on the order of 5%. Yet, according to Morningstar, the average intermediate bond fund has an expense ratio of 1% and charges an average load of 0.83%. That's nearly 2% in the first year, or roughly *40% of the long-term expected return*! Bill Gross's vaunted PIMCO Total Return C Shares boast an astonishing annual expense ratio of 1.65% and they tack on a 1% deferred load just for good measure.[271] On the other hand, the Vanguard Total Bond Market Index Institutional Shares (minimum account size = $10 million) carries an expense ratio of a piddling 10 basis points, or 1/10 of 1%. Now, Bill Gross is undoubtedly a bond genius, but here is how the Vanguard, PIMCO and average bond funds stack up over the past five years:

	5-Year Return thru 3/31/03
Vanguard Total Bond Market	7.16%
PIMCO Total Return	6.95%
Average intermediate bond fund	6.23%

Employing best practices in building bond portfolios. The world of bonds may seem like a simple place, compared to equities and alternative assets, but it is actually a very complicated asset class. Consider that it includes government bonds, corporate bonds, municipal bonds, high yield bonds (corporate *and* municipal), and cash management, as well as the whole other world of foreign

271 Affluent investors will presumably have the good sense to buy the PIMCO Total Return Administrative Shares, which have no loads and an expense ratio of 0.68%. This fund has a minimum investment of $5 million, but the clients of some investment firms are able to buy into the fund at much lower minimums.

sovereign and corporate bonds and Yankee bonds. Let's look at some of the best practices associated with successfully navigating the world of fixed income securities.

Building laddered bond portfolios. Since bonds deliver relatively little in the way of return, and are used by investors mainly to produce income and to control portfolio risk, one way to keep bond management costs down is to ladder our fixed income portfolios. If, for example, we want to build a $1 million bond portfolio with an average maturity of five years, we might simply buy the following bonds:

	Dollar Amount	*Maturity*
Bond #1	$100,000	2004
Bond #2	$100,000	2005
Bond #3	$100,000	2006
Bond #4	$100,000	2007
Bond #5	$100,000	2008
Bond #6	$100,000	2009
Bond #7	$100,000	2010
Bond #8	$100,000	2011
Bond #9	$100,000	2012
Bond #10	$100,000	2013

This gives us a $1 million bond portfolio with an average maturity of five years. Each year, one of our bonds will mature and we will use those proceeds to buy the longest maturity needed to maintain our five-year average maturity. (In 2004, for example, we will use the proceeds of Bond #1 to buy a $100,000 bond maturing in 2015.) The advantages of this laddered approach are considerable. First, the cost is minuscule, particularly if, as we should, we are using US Treasury notes and bonds.[272] Second, because a bond matures every year, we have fairly short liquidity if we should need it. Third, since we are buying bonds over a long period of years, we are averaging into interest rate changes. Finally, since we are planning to hold each bond until it matures, we can't experience a capital loss in our bond portfolio.

272 Commissions on the purchase of US Treasury securities are very small, and can be avoided altogether by using the Treasury Direct program. Since we are planning to hold all our bonds until they mature, there will be no commissions on sales.

But laddered bond portfolios are not entirely without their complications. In the first place, they should only be used in circumstances where the use of US Treasury securities is appropriate. These securities are the safest paper available and they are not callable. (The US Treasury does, from time to time, attempt to repurchase its notes and bonds on the open market.) Some investors build laddered bond portfolios out of corporate or municipal bonds, but this is dangerous, since many of these securities are callable—defeating the purpose of holding them until maturity and reinvesting at the then-prevailing interest rates—and since nobody is watching the credits of the issuers. (Ah, you say, you plan to confine your fixed income ladder to the best investment grade bonds. Well, the next time you find yourself thinking along these lines, here is a useful corrective. Repeat to yourself this phrase: "Enron, WorldCom, Global Crossing; Enron, WorldCom, Global Crossing....")

In the second place, owning a laddered bond portfolio requires iron discipline in not abandoning the ladder in the face of disquieting conditions. In a rising interest rate environment, for example, there will be paper losses in the laddered portfolio and we may be tempted to sell out of some of the bonds and replace them with higher yielding securities. This will almost surely prove to be a double mistake: we will lock in our loss on the sold bonds and rates will continue to rise on us, causing us to lose money even on our newly purchased bonds. Similarly, in a declining rate environment our bonds will show gains and we may be tempted to capture those gains before rates rise and they disappear. Again, this is almost certain to prove a foolish strategy: rates will continue to decline and we will simply be destroying our income stream. In short, the whole thesis underlying laddered fixed income portfolios is the impossibility of foreseeing the direction or rapidity of interest rate changes or the shape of the yield curve.

Owning only high-grade, non-callable, long-term bonds. Many investors believe that the only fully justifiable excuse for owning bonds—which, after all, impose very substantial opportunity costs on portfolios as a result of their low real returns—is as a hedge against the outbreak of deflation. Deflation is a very serious economic condition in which prices actually decline in real terms.[273] About the only investment assets that will perform well in a deflationary environment are long-term, high grade, non-callable bonds: i.e., 30-year US Treasury bonds. My own view is that the likelihood of deflation is, in general, so remote that the costs associated with holding only 30-year Treasuries makes the game unworthy of the candle for taxable investors.

---

[273] Deflation is not to be confused with disinflation, a propitious condition in which the rate of inflation is declining.

Actively managing municipal bonds. Unlike Treasury securities and corporate bonds, the municipal bond sector is complex and inefficient, and fairly cries out for competent active management. That said, we have to keep firmly in mind that the municipal sector embraces a particularly unattractive set of issues: it is complex and difficult to succeed in the sector, it is essentially impossible to add wealth to our portfolios no matter how well we do in the sector, and yet the sector represents an essential asset class for most families.

Regarding complexity, consider that the municipal sector includes general obligation (GO) issues floated by all fifty states, issues floated by thousands of cities and towns, issues floated by tens of thousands of special purpose districts, hospitals and airports, issues floated by water authorities, pre-funding issues, etc., etc. The creditworthiness of these many entities is always suspect and is always changing. There are also odd seasonal issues associated with the municipal sector that must be dealt with, as certain issuers tend to come to market at certain times and as certain large holders of munis tend to liquidate those holdings at certain times. Finally, munis are susceptible to all the interest rate dynamics that bedevil other sectors of the bond markets. In short, individual investors who imagine that they can intelligently assess this world, and then continue to monitor it, are simply kidding themselves.

The best way to manage a substantial municipal bond portfolio is not to give our money to a muni bond manager and hope they do well. Instead, we (and our advisors) should develop a detailed set of objectives and guidelines and insist that our muni bond manager abide strictly by them. The objectives will typically address the relative priority among capital preservation, liquidity and income. The guidelines will have to do with a target average duration for the bond portfolio (either an absolute target or, more commonly, a target set in relation to the municipal bond index we wish to have our money managed against); maximum and minimum durations for individual securities in the portfolios; minimum average credit quality for the overall portfolio; minimum credit quality for individual issues in the portfolio; maximum exposure to individual issuers (allowable exposures will differ depending on the perceived creditworthiness of the issuer types); use of leverage in the portfolio; employment of derivative securities; the amount of cash permitted to be held; and how the performance of the portfolio will be monitored and evaluated.[274]

---

274 The guidelines will also give tax information about the investor. While most municipal bond investors will be in the highest Federal and state tax brackets, family investors increasingly fall under the provisions of the Alternative Minimum Tax. AMT taxpayers will sometimes find that tax-exempt bonds

In other words, in looking for competent municipal bond management firms what we are really looking for is sophistication in the sector, intense tax awareness, sufficient volume to keep trading costs down, willingness to work as our agent,[275] and strong internal control and management systems that will give us confidence that the manager can actually comply with sophisticated guidelines. Simply looking at past investment performance is a very low priority.

One final issue associated with municipal bond investing has to do with whether we should insist that all bonds in our portfolios be tax-exempt in the state where we pay income taxes. The tradeoff here is higher after-tax income versus the increased risk that arises from having all our bonds concentrated in one state. Tax rates in some states are so high that most investors in those states will find it prudent to accept the concentration risk (California, Massachusetts and New York, for example). Even in these states, however, it will sometimes pay to buy out-of-state bonds, and hence that flexibility should be given to our municipal bond manager.

In most other states, however, it will generally pay us to accept slightly reduced after-tax income in order to avoid highly concentrated bond portfolios. Assume, for example, that our muni bond portfolio is yielding, on average, 4%. Assume that the state income tax is 6%. If all our bonds were exempt from tax in that state, our net after-tax yield would be 4%. If *none* of our bonds were exempt from tax in that state (but were only exempt from Federal tax) our after-tax yield would be 3.76%. Given that we can buy many in-state bonds that are fully tax-exempt and still build a nationally diversified bond portfolio, our actual after-tax yield is likely to be much closer to the 4% that is maximally possible. And given the damage that can happen to our portfolio as the result of a series of downgrades (or, horrors, defaults) resulting from negative regional economic factors, we will generally be better off with a nationally diversified portfolio that has, perhaps, a state-of-residence focus.

Actively managing corporate bonds. Most everything I have said, above, about managing municipal bond portfolios can also be said about managing corporate bond portfolios. The main difference is that the corporate bond sector is more efficient and hence fees should be lower. Aside from that, however, most of us will be better off either indexing in this sector or insisting that

---

will be appropriate and that sometimes taxable bonds will be appropriate. Our municipal bond manager must therefore possess capabilities in both taxable and municipal securities.

275 In other words, buying and selling bonds through dealers on our behalf, not selling bonds to us as a broker would do.

our corporate bond manager manage our account to our exact specified guidelines.

Indexing can be accomplished via, for example, the Vanguard Total Bond Market Index Fund. For bond portfolios over $250,000, Vanguard charges only 17 basis points (17/100 of 1%) per year. Larger portfolios can use the Vanguard Institutional version of the fund, which charges only 10 basis points, or can have their bond portfolios custom indexed by a large financial institution. There are also exchange-traded funds that offer indexed corporate bond management.

Bond accounts managed according to our own guidelines should be handled by bond managers who possess the systems and controls required to ensure that those guidelines are adhered to, and who manage sufficient bond assets to ensure reasonable trading costs. As emphasized above, we will want to work with a bond manager who is buying and selling bonds as our agent using other dealers, not with a brokerage firm selling bonds to us out of their own inventory.

High yield bonds. I have put the discussion of high yield bonds under *Fixed Income* because, legally speaking, high yield bonds are in fact bonds—they pay a fixed coupon. But in virtually every other way, high yield bonds are far more analogous to equity securities. For example, high yield bonds experience price volatility that is more akin to that of stocks than to that of bonds. In addition, the use of the proceeds raised by issuers of high yield bonds is typically for longer term corporate activities that would normally be funded by issuing equities, except that the company is not strong enough to be of interest to the equity market. Finally, astute investors treat high yield bonds more like stocks in terms of how they spend, or don't spend, the return. Most bond investors spend most of the return their bonds generate—the coupon payments—but most stock investors spend, if anything, only dividends paid on their stocks and often not even that. Since virtually all the return on high yield bonds comes from their unusually high yields, investors who spend the entire yield will achieve a zero return (a negative real return) on their high yield holdings. Hence, smart investors will tend to spend only a small portion of the yield on high yields, or spend none at all.

The term "high yield" is, of course, a euphemism. The traditional term for bonds issued by non-creditworthy companies is "junk." The term was not changed in an effort to be Politically Correct—a disease happily almost completely absent from the financial services world—but for sales reasons. Investors who wouldn't touch a "junk" bond will snap up a bond that is described as having a "high yield." It is, however, a useful corrective to keep in mind that, while bonds in this sector do indeed have high yields, they are in fact junk bonds.[276]

Bond ratings were created by credit rating agencies to assist investors in evaluating the credit quality of the issuers of bonds. The highest credit rating, AAA, is enjoyed only by the most creditworthy firms. As a result of their high standing, these firms have to pay interest on their bonds that is only slightly higher than the interest paid on US Treasury securities with similar maturities. This difference between Treasury yields and yields on other bonds is referred to as the "yield spread." Junk bonds—those bonds rated below BBB—are considered "speculative grade" by the ratings agencies and must pay much higher rates of interest in order to have any chance of selling their bonds. Hence, their "spreads" are much wider.[277] (Bonds rated D are already in default.)

Junk bonds entered center stage in the capital markets with Michael Milken and Drexel Burnham Lambert in the 1980s. That episode ended in scandal and in the collapse of many of the lower-rated companies Milken had championed. Nonetheless, the notion that weaker firms should have access to capital was an attractive one, and many of the innovations launched by Milken survived his own troubles. Today, the junk bond market is thriving, and many firms that simply would not have survived in the capital-starved pre-Milken world have grown into pillars of the corporate community.

Junk bond managers range all over the lot, from managers who dip only slightly below investment grade (their portfolios will have average ratings of BB or BB-) to managers who deal in the true heart of junk bond land—the C credits—to managers (many of them organized as hedge funds) who deal in seriously distressed securities, many of which are already mired in bankruptcy proceedings.

Because the junk bond sector is highly cyclical, there are only two intelligent ways to play the junk bond game for most family investors. The first is to create a permanent allocation to junk (say, 10%) and to rebalance religiously back

---

276 Ok, ok, some companies that technically fall into the junk bond category, especially the upper echelons of junk (BB rated bonds, let's say) are hardly "junk companies." Some simply happen to be in an industry that is powerfully out of favor (telecoms in 2002, for example), while others are going through a rough period financially but are fundamentally sound. Most issuers of junk bonds, however, are highly speculative investments.

277 In the fall of 2002, spreads between Treasuries and junk bonds reached their widest gaps in history. This was, to say the least, a propitious time to buy junk bonds.

to that allocation whenever it is exceeded or whenever the actual allocation falls below the target. This disciplined rebalancing will introduce a countercyclical effect into the junk bond portfolio, causing us to sell junk when the bonds are outperforming and to buy junk when the bonds are under-performing. Over time, this will provide a nicely enhanced return to our portfolios and will inject considerable diversification.

A more sophisticated approach is to buy junk on an opportunistic basis, that is, whenever spreads significantly exceed their long-term norms, and to sell junk when spreads return to their long-term norms. This approach will provide higher returns, but it is difficult, both technically and emotionally, to implement.

Managing Cash

Managing cash may appear to be simplicity itself, but in fact managing very large amounts of cash—as in very large family portfolios or where cash has been received following a liquidity event—can be complex and, indeed, agonizing. True, the returns that are possible on cash investments, especially net of tax, are piddling. Yet, we are reminded of Henry Kissinger's remark about faculty disputes being so bitter precisely because the stakes are so small: mismanaging cash investments rarely proves to be a complete disaster, but the failure to eke out a tiny increment of return above some benchmark can cause investors to suffer agonies wholly disproportionate to the actual harm.

Middle income investors have a simple answer to the problem of investing cash—send it to a money market fund. But if the amounts are very substantial, that is unlikely to be the optimal strategy. In the first place, most money market funds are uninterested in receiving gigantic sums of new money from wealthy investors, especially in a declining rate environment. The problem of investing all the money can reduce the already-low rates of return on the fund, and the money market fund market is intensely competitive. Taking $1 billion in cash from one investor can cost the fund many more billions of dollars as other investors flee the resulting depressed returns: in a declining rate environment the new money must be invested at current interest rates, which are, by definition, lower than past rates; this brings down the average return of the fund. Finally, while money market funds are used to dealing with "hot money"—investors who are constantly moving from fund to fund to get the highest interest—they are unwilling to take in very large sums from one investor who is likely to pull it out soon. In other words, it is much more difficult for a large cash investor to "roll down the yield curve"[278] than it is for smaller investors.

Investors deploying large sums of cash will typically be better off creating their own "money market fund" by engaging one or more managers who will purchase and sell individual financial instruments that comply with precise guidelines covering such issues as the following:

- The tax status of the investor. This can be especially important for investors in high tax jurisdictions (such as New York City) and for investors who may be subject to the Alternative Minimum Tax. (Note that some states have their own AMT categories.)
- The investor's risk tolerance.
- A description of which securities will be allowable in the portfolio (e.g., dollar-denominated securities issued by the United States, agencies thereof, money market funds, municipal securities, asset- and mortgage-backed securities and non-dollar denominated government bonds that are currency hedged).
- Whether derivatives may be used (usually not).
- Any restrictions that may be placed on the use of money market funds (e.g., minimum fund assets, maximum amount of the portfolio that may be placed with any one fund, etc.)
- Diversification and credit quality constraints. Typical constraints might include the following:
    - The portfolio shall contain no security with a maturity longer than 36 months.
    - At least 90% of the fund shall consist of securities with ratings at or above A1/P1 or A (defined as A+, A, A-, or A1, A2 or A3). The balance shall contain no security rated below BBB/Baa3.
    - The portfolio shall maintain a modified duration of not more than 180 days.
    - The maximum percentage of the fund in any one non-governmental issuer shall be 10%.

---

[278] This phrase refers to the phenomenon just noted: a money market fund that purchased many of its investments when rates were higher will still own those investments until they gradually mature. Thus, the interest rate offered by the fund will be higher than the interest rate investors could get by buying similar investments today. The fund's yield will gradually decline, of course.

- The maximum in non-dollar denominated securities (currency hedged) shall be 10%.
- The maximum in US Government securities shall be 100%.
- The maximum in agency securities shall be 100%.
- The maximum in money market funds shall be 100% (subject to the constraints specified above).
- The maximum in NAV fixed income funds shall be 100%, provided that the fund shall have at least $1 billion in assets at all times and that the client shall represent no more than 10% of the assets in any one fund without the client's prior consent.
- The maximum in municipal GO securities shall be 100%.
- The maximum in other municipals shall be 75%.
- The maximum in asset-backed securities shall be 60%, with no security rated below AAA.
- The maximum in non-agency mortgage-backeds shall be 30%.
- The maximum in privately placed municipal securities shall be 30%.

♦ Explicit use of leverage in the portfolio. (Typically, leverage will not be undertaken without the prior written consent of the client. Leverage is defined as a situation in which the portfolio as a whole is more than 100% invested in the securities permitted by these guidelines.)

♦ Third party payments. The guidelines should specify that the client has entered into a cash management relationship with the manager based on the assumption that the manager is receiving no payments from any person other than the fee paid by the client. This prohibition would include commissions, spreads, markups, concessions and any other payments.

♦ Contributions and Withdrawals. For example:

- 1. Cash flows generated by the portfolio will remain in the portfolio for reinvestment unless otherwise directed by the client
- 2. Additional contributions or withdrawals will be directed from time to time at the discretion of the client. No withdrawals can be made from the account unless authorized in writing by the client.

♦ Performance Measurement, Benchmark and Reporting. For example:

- 1. The account's total return will be reported by the manager on a time-weighted linked basis by combining capital gains and income, adjusting for inflows and outflows, and compounding on a monthly basis.

- 2. The total portfolio return will be measured, net of fees, at the end of each month and the resulting performance will be compared to the higher of the return of the MFR All Taxable Money Fund Index (tax-adjusted) or the MFR Tax-Free Money Fund Index.
- 3. Unless directed by the client, the manager will act as custodian and will provide a monthly statement detailing portfolio holdings and transactions to the client. In the event that the manager cannot act as custodian,[279] any additional custody fees incurred by the client will be assessed against the account for performance measurement purposes.
- 4. The manager will initiate oral communication with the client whenever unusual events occur in the cash and fixed income markets that have the potential to significantly affect the portfolio.

♦ Review and Modification. For example:

- 1. These guidelines shall be reviewed periodically and revised or confirmed as appropriate.
- 2. Any changes deemed necessary by either the manager or the client will be agreed upon by both parties and confirmed in writing.

In short, while managing cash may seem simple, it can actually be quite complex and surprisingly emotional. By structuring a separate account arrangement with strict guidelines, investors are likely both to fare better and to sleep better.

[279] Some firms can (or will) act as custodian only for their own money market funds, not for "money market funds" that are operated as separate accounts, as we are discussing here.

Three

Chapter 12

Asset Class Strategies—Alternative Investments

Buying stocks long is to selling stocks short what touch football is to Iwo Jima.[280]

Chapter 11 discussed asset class strategies for the traditional asset classes. I have chosen to discuss strategies for non-traditional assets—so-called "alternative" assets—in a separate chapter, for several reasons. The main reason is that the approaches to alternative assets are typically quite different from the approaches to traditional asset classes. In addition, some "alternative" assets are not really separate asset classes at all in the usual sense of the term, even though they do require special techniques to be successful. Finally, investors are still struggling with the role alternative assets should play in their portfolios.

Although many kinds of investment assets could be considered "alternative" assets, this chapter will focus on the three kinds of alternative assets that are most commonly of interest to taxable investors: hedge funds, private equity (including venture capital) and "real" assets: real estate, timber, oil and gas, commodities, etc.

Hedge Fund Investing

Because most taxable investors have a strong capital preservation orientation, and because many hedge funds also have a capital preservation aspect to their activities, it is hardly surprising that hedge fund investing has become extremely popular among affluent families. In the past ten years, hedge fund

---

280 With thanks to Dave Barry for this lovely analogy, employed by him, of course, in a very different context.

investing has gone from a fringe activity practiced by obscure gnomes to the most rapidly growing of all investment opportunities.[281] There are at least 6,000 hedge funds in existence today, far more than there are stocks on the NYSE. There are so many hedge funds around that, if we don't count money market funds, they are challenging mutual funds as the single most popular investment vehicles in the world. Indeed, in an average year, hedge fund managers generate more income than will all the mutual funds registered in the U.S. Indeed, what used to be exclusively the province of wealthy and institutional investors is now hot retail territory. "Retail" hedge funds of funds offered by large financial institutions and requiring very low minimum investments are sprouting everywhere.

Why are hedge funds so hot? One reason is that, as a group, hedge funds have produced extraordinary risk-adjusted performance over the past decade. Exhibiting roughly bond-like price volatility, hedge funds nonetheless clobbered the major equity indices between 1990 and the end of 2001:

Long/short equity hedge funds..........................20.3%
S&P 500 ....12.9%
MSCI EAFE..2.7%[282]

$1 million invested in hedge funds would have grown over that period to nearly $7.5 million, versus $3.6 million for the S&P and a mere $1.3 million for the EAFE.

In addition, while hedge fund returns declined significantly in 2002—as a group they showed flat-to-slightly-negative performance—the stock markets remained mired in their worst showing in thirty years, private equity returns fell off the edge of the earth, and even bonds began to look vulnerable in the face of rising interest rates. So why not hedge funds?

Why not, indeed. The point of this chapter is not to suggest that family investors avoid hedge funds. The point I wish to make is that the game has changed: the easy money has been made in hedge funds, the future will differ significantly from the past, and hedge fund investors will have to proceed with

---

281 *From Infamy to Fame—The Rapidly Changing Landscape of the Hedge Fund Industry, Advent Client News* (Advent Software, Inc., 2nd Quarter 2002), p. 1.

282 Source: Hedge Fund Research, Inc., Bloomberg L.P., Morgan Stanley Capital International, Inc. Cited in Jonathan Lach, "Investing with Wolves: Classic Hedge Funds—Better than Equities," *The Journal of Wealth Management* (Fall 2002), p. 75.

far greater caution going forward. In short, we have seen the end of the beginning for hedge fund investing: it's now a whole new world.

What Is a Hedge Fund?

Before we examine some of the reasons for proceeding carefully in this sector, let's define what it is we're talking about: what, exactly, is a hedge fund? The President's Working Group on Financial Markets, which looked into the causes of the failure of Long Term Capital Management, defined a hedge fund as "a pooled investment vehicle that is privately organized, administered by professional investment managers, and not widely available."[283] This is about as unhelpful a definition as one could wish for, aside from being hopelessly outdated. But it makes the point that hedge funds are very hard to define. Many hedge funds don't hedge at all, for example, and some are quite widely available.

The first hedge fund, so far as we know, was established half a century ago by Alfred Winslow Jones, a former financial reporter. If Jones had $100 to invest he would invest it all in the stock market. He would then borrow another $30 and invest that as well. Then, in order to "hedge" the risk of the leveraged $30, Jones would sell $30 worth of stocks short. His idea was that if his stock picks were very good he would make far more money than a typical long-only investor: he would make money on his long positions, of course, but he would also make money on both his leveraged positions and his shorts. If his picks were only "good," he might lose money on his short positions but make it up on his long and leveraged positions. His only real danger, aside from incompetent stock-picking, was a very bad down market, in which his long and leveraged positions would overwhelm his short positions. (This actually happened to Jones in 1969–70.)[284]

Today a "hedge fund" can be defined as any investment vehicle organized as a partnership in which the manager shares in the profits and in which (speaking very generally) the manager invests in marketable securities.[285] (In other words, private equity funds don't count.) The manager may or may not sell

---

283 *Hedge Funds, Leverage, and the Lessons of Long Term Capital Management*, The President's Working Group on Financial Markets (1999).

284 I am indebted to James Grant, an infinitely provocative financial writer and investor, for this description of Jones' hedge fund, A.W. Jones & Co. James Grant, "Yes, But," *Forbes* (June 10, 2002), p. 220.

285 Of course, many of the securities purchased by hedge funds are highly illiquid. Because a hedge fund manager deals in marketable securities, that doesn't mean that his portfolio can be accurately marked-to-market every day.

short; he may or may not employ leverage; he may specialize in a specific niche or market sector or he may migrate from niche to niche and sector to sector. The only way to know what a hedge fund is doing is to speak at length with the manager and to check everything he or she says.

Types of Hedge Funds

Speaking very generally, hedge funds can be categorized as "directional" funds (so-called macro funds and most long/short funds) and absolute return-oriented or ARO funds (sometimes called non-directional funds or market neutral; hedge funds, however, are *not* "non-directional" or "market neutral"). Directional macro funds employ little or no hedging strategies but simply make bets on their specific ideas, while long/short funds are mainly similar to long-only managers except that they also sell stocks short, thus reducing (but not eliminating) their exposure to broad market trends. Many hedge funds fall easily into these broad categories, but some do not.

Hedge funds can also be categorized according to the kinds of investment strategies they follow. Following are some examples of strategies a hedge fund might focus on:

Convertible security arbitrage. Many companies issue convertible securities—a security that is convertible into another company security at a stated price. Depending on the characteristics of the company, the price volatility of the securities, the relative price level of the securities, the level of interest rates, and other factors, the two securities will tend to trade in a price relationship with each other that can be ascertained. If the securities are trading outside this range the difference can sometimes be arbitraged at a profit. Since convertible securities rarely trade wildly outside their traditional range, profit opportunities tend to be frequent-but-modest. As a result, most convertible arb managers leverage their bets. Since the risks associated with betting that pricing anomalies will return to their traditional ranges are small, leverage typically improves returns without incurring significant risk. Occasionally, however, economic events will conspire to blindside leveraged managers.

Distressed debt. Most investors are familiar with high yield bonds—lower rated bonds that must provide a much higher yield than traditional bonds. Hedge funds tend to work even lower down in High Yield Land, buying all or parts of bond issues that have already defaulted and that are mired in bankruptcy proceedings. This sector of the distressed debt market is, or was, highly inefficient. Not only must the hedge fund accurately estimate the issuer's ability to reorganize and make good on the bonds (or at least pay more for them than the hedge fund paid), but the hedge fund must assess the complex legal rights of the parties to the bankruptcy proceeding and estimate when (if ever!) the company will emerge from bankruptcy. Very often, distressed debt investors find that they must get proactively involved in the bankruptcy proceedings or even in the management of the company in an attempt to realize value.

Event-driven. These are mainly[286] merger arbitrage hedge funds. When a merger is announced there will always be at least some degree of doubt about whether the transaction will actually close. As a result, if the buyer is offering $27 a share, the seller's stock price will remain somewhat below $27 until the transaction actually closes. Arbitrageurs who study the potential acquisition carefully can buy the seller's stock long, sell the buyer's stock short, and make a profit when the transaction closes—a profit that is largely independent of the direction of the market (since the arbitrageur has hedged his position).

Long/short equity. This is the classic hedge fund, buying stocks long that the manager believes will rise in value and selling stocks short that the manager believes will decline in value. As noted elsewhere, this promising-looking strategy is much more difficult to implement successfully than it looks—especially on the short side.

Short-selling. Short sellers are increasingly rare for a good reason: when a long only or long/short manager performs poorly, he simply underperforms; when a short seller underperforms he goes bust. When we buy a stock long we limit our risk to the price of the stock—it can only go to zero. But when we sell a stock short our risk is theoretically unlimited.

Global macro. These hedge funds scour the investable universe for compelling opportunities, then make (often staggering) bets on them. The manager might be shorting the kroner or trying to dominate the silver market, and might be leveraging those bets as well. Not for the faint of heart.

Multi-strategy. As the name implies, multi-strategy hedge funds move their capital around among strategies depending on where they are finding value and opportunity. If opportunities in event arb have

---

[286] Event-driven hedge funds also invest in other special situations that are expected to dramatically change the financial or operating conditions of a firm.

dried up, a multi-strategy manager might move capital to distressed debt or convertible arb. Given the level of difficulty involved in outperforming in any single strategy, imagine the difficulties posed by performing well in many different strategies. Multi-strategy funds are therefore relatively rare and tend to be very large—large enough to employ specialist managers in several different disciplines.

Hedge funds, especially directional funds, are not, strictly speaking, a separate asset class. Hedge fund managers are buying and selling the same kinds of investment assets as long only managers—they are just employing different techniques. It is true, to be sure, that the risk-return profile of a well-diversified group of long/short hedge funds will be quite different from that of a well-diversified long-only portfolio, and therefore it is important to evaluate directional hedge exposure independently. But this doesn't make directional hedge a separate asset class: a leveraged exposure to the NASDAQ will have a very different risk-return profile from a long-only exposure to the NASDAQ, but no one would consider it a separate asset class. It is better to think of most hedge funds—the so-called long/short, or directional funds—as alpha strategies[287] that can complement the long-only strategies in our portfolios.

Non-directional hedge funds—more properly called absolute return-oriented funds, or "ARO" funds—on the other hand, do tend to exhibit more of the characteristics of a separate asset class, at least when we invest in a diversified portfolio of ARO strategies. These strategies tend to be uncorrelated—or loosely correlated—to the broad markets.

Challenges for Hedge Fund Investors

A few years ago advisory firms faced an uphill battle trying to convince investors to add hedge fund exposure to their portfolios. Today the problem is almost the opposite—when an advisor first encounters new clients they are as likely to have too much hedge fund exposure (or the wrong kind of exposure) as to have not enough. Whether investors are drawn to hedge funds for their return potential, whether they are fleeing debacles in other capital markets, or whether they are simply seeking prudent diversification, the problems today are too much haste, too little caution, diligence that is too superficial.

Probably the main challenge for investors in hedge funds going forward is the one just mentioned: the popularity of hedge fund investing. The more money that pours into a sector, the more difficult it will be for managers to add value. Vendors in the hedge fund business will argue that, while some strategies

---

287 "Alpha" is simply a measure of risk-adjusted return.

are naturally capacity-constrained—merger arbitrage, for example—others are not.[288] Long/short equity managers and fixed income arbitrage managers play in markets that are measured in the trillions of dollars. Hence, so the argument goes, even a manager with several billion dollars under management will represent only a tiny drop in the vast ocean of opportunities.

But this is the wrong measure. In US large caps, the question isn't whether or not any individual manager has a lot or a little money to work with. The question is how much money, and how many players, are at work in the sector. As more and more managers engage in long/short equity or fixed income arbitrage, the information available to everyone in those sectors will expand, leaving even talented managers with little room to run.

More broadly, we should assume that all alpha-based strategies are inherently capacity-constrained. The most talented managers may develop many more good ideas than less talented managers, but less talented managers are exceptionally good at copying successful strategies. Hence, as more and more players enter a field, the half-life of good ideas declines precipitously. In addition, while there may be trillions of dollars invested in global equities and fixed income, the subset of those markets that have value to be exploited is far, far smaller. Managers who identify value and act on it will find that their activities are much more conspicuous than we would imagine if we think only about the aggregate size of the equity and bond markets.

Let's examine some other challenges faced by prospective investors in hedge funds.[289]

Survivorship bias. Earlier, I cited the extraordinary returns achieved by hedge funds over the past ten years. But that data is highly suspicious, not least of all[290] because of the phenomenon of survivorship bias. This phrase refers to

---

288 "While one must admit there are capacity issues in some sectors, a careful strategy-by-strategy review suggests this is not a concern for the bulk of the hedge fund industry." R. McFall Lamm, Jr. and Tanya E. Ghaleb-Harter, *An Update on Hedge Fund Performance: Is a Bubble Developing?*, Deutsche Asset Management research monograph (September 1, 2001), p. 3.

289 Interested investors may also wish to look into Daniel Quinn Mills, *Wheel, Deal, and Steal* (Pearson Education Inc., 2003). Mills, a professor at Harvard Business School, levels very broad charges at the hedge fund and funds of funds industry, and suggests that hedge fund investors may face losses similar to those suffered during the dot.com bubble of the late 1990s.

290 Hedge funds are unregulated, do not have to report AIMR-compliant numbers, and often buy illiquid securities with respect to which mark-to-market pricing is unavailable. Hence, manager returns are also inflated by suspect numbers and, especially, managed or stale pricing.

the fact that only the most successful hedge fund managers have survived for the ten-year period we are measuring. Less successful managers long ago went out of business, and their demise has imposed a kind of double-whammy on reported returns. First, because they are no longer in business and reporting their results, the (poor) performance of failed managers has been removed from the historical record, dramatically raising the reported performance of "all" managers. Second, because they are no longer managing money, failed managers are no longer turning in those lousy returns, which would continue to bring down the averages.[291] In other words, the actual returns achieved by *investors* in hedge funds over the past ten years are far lower than the actual returns achieved by the surviving managers over that period. In the Lake Wobegon world of hedge funds, all managers are above average.

Volatility and risk. When investors and their advisors design portfolios, they tend to use volatility as a proxy for risk. But in the hedge fund world price volatility does not capture anything like all the risks embedded in the sector. Specifically, volatility ignores the liquidity risk inherent in hedge fund investing, as well as the risk of fraud or other misconduct. Most hedge funds offer only quarterly liquidity, while some impose one-year lockups or even longer. For an investor who needs or wants cash, even a quarter can be an eternity. Fraud, while rare, is hardly unknown among hedge fund managers, and when it happens the consequences for investors in the affected funds can be truly disastrous. The long and short of this is that investors who look only at hedge fund volatility in designing their portfolios will almost certainly end up with an over-exposure to the sector: the apparently attractive combination of low risk (volatility) and high returns will cause hedge funds to dominate the optimizer, resulting in "optimal" hedge fund exposures of 60% or more.

Skewness and kurtosis. As noted above, most hedge funds do not constitute a separate asset class—they simply represent an alpha strategy. Hence, the use of traditional modern portfolio theory tools to design hedge fund portfolios (Standard Deviation, correlation, expected return) simply will not work. The problem in technical terms, is that the hedge fund world is characterized by skewness and kurtosis. Translated into English, this means that (a) hedge fund returns don't occur in a normal, bell-shaped distribution the way returns occur in equity markets, and (b) the likelihood of very bad outcomes is very high. Among other things, hedge funds occasionally blow up for all sorts of reasons, resulting in the loss of all or most of the fund investors' capital. But it is also important to keep in mind that, while adding hedge funds to

---

[291] Jonathan Lach refers to "the tailwind of survivorship bias," op. cit., note 282, p. 75.

a traditional portfolio will typically reduce the dispersion of outcomes, it will also increase the likelihood of a negative outcome.[292]

A diluted manager talent pool. Ten years ago only the most talented managers could hope to be successful in raising money for a hedge fund. These days, however, there is so much demand for hedge fund exposure that it seems as though anyone with a high school diploma can successfully set up a hedge fund. Many newer hedge fund managers do not even have investment track records—they may have been financial analysts, for example. Even those with direct investment experience often have no experience selling stocks short or employing other hedging strategies. Short selling is a nerve-wracking activity in which potential losses are unlimited and potential gains limited. Other problems with new managers include inexperience managing people and complex back-office challenges.

Too much capital coming into the business. Very few investment strategies can preserve returns when massive amounts of capital pour into the business, and hedge fund investing is no exception. Some of the new capital in the hedge fund world emanates from investors who are thoughtful and experienced, but who must invest so much capital (in order to have any impact on the returns in their gigantic portfolios) that they simply cannot do a good job of putting the money to work.[293] Other capital is coming from sources that have precious little experience investing in hedge funds and who are proceeding with such undue haste that it is clear they are simply exploiting the public's sudden appetite for hedge exposure. A particularly worrisome development involves the advent of so-called "capital guaranteed" products. Many European banks (and, recently, some American banks) have raised massive amounts of capital from inexperienced investors via this tactic, under which the financial institution guarantees investors that they will not lose money in hedge funds if they keep their money

---

292 See, for example, "10 Things That Investors Should Know about Hedge Funds" *The CFA Digest*, v. 33, no. 3 (August 2003); Gaurav S. Amin and Harry M. Kat, "Hedge Fund Performance 1990–2000: Do the 'Money Machines' Really Add Value?", *Journal of Financial and Quantitative Analysis*, v.38, no.2 (June, 2003). Professor Kat has been a vocal opponent of the mindless use of hedge funds and his many writings on the subject, though somewhat technical, are well worth looking into. Kat is the Director of the Alternative Research Centre at the Cass Business School in London.

293 Some large pension plans are reportedly planning to invest $1 billion a year in hedge funds for the next five or ten years.

invested for some minimum period of time, usually five or six years.[294] Other structured products—typically levered—are also being offered, as well as the retail products described above.[295]

Tax inefficiency. For taxable investors, the gross returns of hedge funds have to be adjusted for their tax inefficiency. And this inefficiency can be huge, since, for most funds, almost all the return is generated in the form of short-term capital gains and ordinary income.[296] There are techniques that can be used to shelter hedge fund gains, or to convert them into long-term gains, but these techniques bring their own complex challenges.[297]

Lack of transparency. For investors who are used to tracking their portfolios every day (or every hour!), the lack of transparency that characterizes hedge fund portfolios is likely to provide a whole new experience. What is transparency all about?[298] Transparency refers to the ability of an investor in a hedge fund to understand what the manager plans to do,[299] how he plans to

---

294 See Erik Portanger and Alistair McDonald, "Hedged Hedge Funds Get Popular in Europe," *Wall Street Journal* (September 10, 2002), p. C13. Because in many cases the financial institutions haven't hedged their own obligations to the investors, these institutions are extremely skittish and pull out of funds very quickly following negative performance, wreaking havoc with manager strategies.

295 "Democratize the hedge fund business? Sure, and as long as we're at it, let's democratize the New York Philharmonic. We'll all play first horn." James Grant, op. cit., note 284.

296 See, for example, Cohen, James R., Jeffrey S. Bortnick, and Nancy L. Jacob, "Tax-Efficient Investing Using Private Placement Variable Life Insurance and Annuities." *The Journal of Private Portfolio Management* (Winter, 1999); Muhtaseb, Majed R., "To Outperform the Market: Get Out of It!" *The Journal of Wealth Management* (Fall, 2002). These authors suggest that roughly 80% to 90% of hedge fund returns are generated in the form of dividends, interest, and short-term capital gains.

297 For example, hedge funds can be placed in tax-exempt accounts, such as IRAs or charitable foundations. Hedge funds can also be wrapped in on-shore or offshore insurance products.

298 "Hedge fund transparency is like pornography—it is hard to describe, but you know it when you see it." Mark Anson, "Hedge Fund Transparency," *The Journal of Wealth Management* (Fall, 2002), p. 79.

299 Try reading a hedge fund offering memorandum and figuring out what the hell the manager plans to do with your money.

do it,[300] and whether he is actually doing it.[301] Without transparency, investors can't understand the nature of the risks they are taking, and hence cannot, for example, hedge those risks by investing with managers using other strategies.[302]

Conflicted prime brokers. In a typical separate account money management arrangement cash and securities are held by a bank acting as custodian. The manager has only a limited power of attorney to direct the investments in the account, but cannot remove cash or securities. The investor is the bank's customer, not the manager. If anything even remotely fishy is going on in the account the bank will notify the investor immediately. Hedge fund accounts, however, are not custodied in the usual sense. Instead, the funds reside with a "prime broker," typically an investment banking/brokerage firm that serves as global custodian, broker, lender (via margin loans), vendor of derivative transactions and even fund raiser for the hedge fund. The customer is the hedge fund, not the investor. Prime brokers play so many roles, have so many conflicts of interest, and earn such large profits for their firms that they cannot be counted on to blow the whistle on shenanigans committed by hedge fund managers with whom they work.

Advantages are also disadvantages. In the upside-down world of hedge funds, virtually every advantage claimed by the industry also represents a potential disadvantage for investors. For example, Jonathan Lach lists the following "burdens" hedge fund managers are able to avoid (relative to other money managers): "excessive capital under management, benchmark objectives, diversification requirements, daily liquidity, and significant organizational

---

300 See the preceding footnote.

301 In their inquiry into the failure of Long Term Capital Management, the President's Working Group on Financial Markets wrote: "An issue here is whether the LTCM Fund's investors...were aware of the nature of the exposures and risks the hedge fund had accumulated. * * * They almost certainly were not adequately aware since, by most accounts, they exercised minimal scrutiny of the Fund's risk-management practices and risk profile." Quoted in Mark Anson, op. cit., note 298, pp. 81-82. One important reason why LTCM's investors "exercised minimal scrutiny" was that LTCM wouldn't stand for it.

302 I don't mean to suggest that hedge fund investors need to have full position transparency on a regular basis. I do suggest that many hedge fund managers offer so little in the way of tactical and risk transparency that investors would be better off avoiding such managers altogether.

time demands."[303] Lach is right, and these are in fact important advantages of hedge funds. But many investors will view all but the first and last[304] of these not so much as "burdens" but as important risk controls. Or consider the "advantage" that many hedge fund managers have much of their own money invested in their funds. This is certainly an advantage in the sense that such a manager is likely to pay close attention to the business. But that is a different issue from the question whether the manager's interests are aligned with the investors—they typically aren't. If a manager has much of his net worth invested in his fund while a typical investor has only a modest portion of his net worth invested in the fund, the interests of manager and investor are structurally misaligned from the beginning. Moreover, manager and investor may have different time horizons and may have very different feelings about leverage, downside risk, long and short exposures, and so on.

High fees. Hedge fund managers charge annual fees of 1% to 2%, plus 20% of any profits. Some managers are worth every penny of this, but they are rare, indeed. In other words, there is nothing inherent in the hedge fund format[305] to justify such fees—only talent justifies them. Investors who don't aggressively seek out talent are likely to be disappointed in their hedge fund returns in part because too much of the return is going to the manager.

Mischievous fee structures. Hedge funds often have both a "hurdle rate" and a "high water mark." The hurdle rate means that the manager cannot get any part of his 20% share of the profits until the fund has exceeded some pre-set annual rate of return—8%, for example. The high water mark simply ensures

---

[303] Lach, op. cit., note 282, p. 77.

[304] Even these characteristics can be viewed as disadvantages. Hedge funds can avoid having excessive capital under management by closing to new investors. But this means that, just about the time a sensible investor has concluded that the manager knows what he is doing, it's too late to get in. Organizational time demands are certainly a bugaboo for long-only managers associated with large institutions, but organizational supervision also tends to reduce the kind of fraud and mismanagement that occurs in the hedge fund industry.

[305] Some would argue with this view. R. McFall Lamm, Jr., for example, argues that, "Conceptually, the long-only manager faces a constrained optimization problem [that is, he can only buy long; he can't sell short], while the equity hedge manager is unconstrained." R. McFall Lamm, Jr., "How Good Are Equity Hedge Fund Managers," *Alternative Investment Quarterly* (January, 2002), p. 21. Conceptually, yes, but the execution challenges facing the unconstrained manager make it likely that only the most talented managers will be able to use the unconstrained vehicle to full advantage.

that, once a loss is incurred in a fund, the manager cannot receive his 20% share of the profits until the loss has been recovered. Both elements of the fee structure are perfectly fair, but they can easily combine to produce odd incentives. Consider a fund with a 1% annual fee, an 8% hurdle rate and a high water mark provision. The fund starts with $100 million in year one, rises to $200 million in year two (a hell of a year, to be sure), declines to $150 million in year three, and rises to $175 million in year four. In year four, the fund is not yet back to its "high water mark" of $200 million. In addition, the manager has failed, over years two and three, to earn the 8% hurdle rate. Moreover, as the hurdle rate piles up and the high water mark looks more and more unattainable, the manager is faced with receiving nothing but his 1% annual fee for many years. He didn't go into the hedge fund business to earn a 1% fee, so what does he do? As Roland Lochoff puts it, "It is not uncommon for a fund to fall so far underwater that the chance of ever reaching the high water mark is improbable. It simply pays the hedge fund manager to go out of business and start afresh with a new name."[306] In other words, heads he wins, tails we lose.

High tracking error. Investors who have traditionally focused on tracking error to monitor their managers will be sorely disappointed with hedge funds. It is virtually impossible to create a benchmark that will be useful for monitoring a hedge fund portfolio. As a result, whatever benchmark is used, tracking error will be impossibly high—so high as to be largely useless as a manager monitoring tool.[307]

Correlations increase just when you need them not to. Over long periods of time hedge funds have demonstrated low correlations to the equity and fixed income markets. Unfortunately, during liquidity crises (August 1998 and the summer of 2002, for example), the correlations between hedge funds and marketable securities increase dramatically—just when you most need the diversification. In other words, hedge funds provide diversification over the long run but not over the short run.

Selling beta as alpha. Investors can buy beta cheaply—via index funds, exchange-traded funds, and so on. Alpha is expensive, and properly so, since it is so rare. Hedge funds charge very high fees because they claim to be delivering alpha. Some, surely, are doing so, but most are simply expensive beta shops. Bridgewater Associates recently measured the performance of managers in seven popular hedge fund strategies against the performance that would have been obtained by naively replicating the systematic risks taken by the managers.

---

306 Roland Lochoff, "Hedge Funds and Hope," *The Journal of Portfolio Management* (Summer, 2002), p. 92.

307 See R. McFall Lamm, Jr., op cit., note 305, p. 23.

They found that the naïve strategies typically outperformed the average hedge fund manager.[308] To take a simple example, instead of investing with merger arbitrage hedge funds, an investor could simply have bought the top ten acquirees during 2003 and sold the top ten acquirors short. That investor would have achieved a 10% return, versus 9% for the average merger arb hedge fund.[309]

Investor expectations may be irrational. Looking at the high relative returns generated by hedge funds over the past ten years, many hedge fund investors may be expecting the impossible, namely, that hedge fund returns will remain high even in the face of sustained bear market conditions. But, as Barry Colvin puts it, "Hedge funds attempt to produce returns that are independent of the overall market, but not *despite* the market."[310] For a hedge fund that produced returns of 15% to 20% during the bull market to produce essentially flat returns during the worst bear market in a generation is a very strong performance. Yet, many hedge fund investors were very unpleasantly surprised by that kind of performance in 2001–02.

The difficulty of ongoing monitoring. It is difficult enough to perform enough diligence on a hedge fund to justify investing in it. Unfortunately, that is far less than half the battle. Investors in hedge funds find themselves in hot water not so much because of the lack of up-front diligence—though there is a lot of that going around—but because of the almost complete lack of ongoing diligence. It is hardly an exaggeration to say that most investors' ongoing diligence is limited to checking their returns. But an ongoing understanding of exactly what our hedge fund managers are doing, why they are doing it, and how well they are doing it, is critical to avoiding disasters. It is exceptionally rare for a hedge fund manager simply to blow up with no warning whatever. More typically, there were alarming red flags flying for months or years before the blowup, but most investors weren't paying attention. Some of those red flags should have been identified in upfront diligence—a checkered regulatory or personal history, for example. Others show up only months or years later. An example would be suspiciously good or consistent performance versus other similar hedge fund managers. Another would be an increase in leverage or other kinds of risky behavior. Ongoing diligence conducted at a level of detail that matters virtually requires (a) spot-checking position-level detail for each manager (though not necessarily in real time), and (b) a staff with the

---

[308] *Bridgewater Daily Observations* (February 17, 2004).

[309] Ibid., p. 4.

[310] Barry H. Colvin, "Hedge Fund Expectations Require Trimming," *Investment News* (September 30, 2002), p. 13. (Emphasis in the original.)

trading sophistication to understand what the trades mean. The group of investors who can't perform this sort of diligence includes virtually all private families and family offices, virtually all investment consulting firms, and, alas, most hedge funds of funds.

In the face of all these challenges, it is inevitable that, as has always been the case with private equity funds, performance dispersion among hedge funds will widen until, unless we are invested with top quartile funds, we should, like Yogi Berra, have stood in bed.

Examining Various Hedge Fund Strategies

Designing a separate hedge fund portfolio. A great many investors have built what they think of as separate hedge fund portfolios that are designed to improve their overall returns, but that aren't thought of as playing a particular role in the overall investment portfolio. The trouble with this approach is that, if we don't have an expectation for exactly how the hedge fund portfolio is supposed to behave, how can we know whether it is working for us or not? The notion that it doesn't really matter as long as the hedge fund portfolio is performing well is naïve. No hedge fund portfolio, however well designed, will always perform well. Thus the question is always before us: when the hedge fund portfolio isn't performing well, is it still playing a worthwhile role in our overall portfolio?

Mean variance optimization and hedge fund portfolios. We are so used to thinking of investment portfolios in the context of mean variance optimization that we naturally tend to apply that logic to the design of our hedge fund portfolios. This is, unfortunately, a big mistake. The investment returns associated with traditional asset classes do in fact tend to cluster around a long-term mean return, forming the familiar bell-shaped curve. Events close to the mean return tend to be very common, while events out toward the "tails" of the bell curve are very uncommon. We can calculate Standard Deviations of the returns, so that we can estimate what range of returns to expect 67% of the time (1 S.D.), 95% of the time (2 S.D.) and so on. Hedge fund returns, alas, occur in non-normal distributions characterized by what modern portfolio theory gurus would call "skewness" and "kurtosis." As noted above, this means that (a) hedge fund returns don't occur in a normal, bell-shaped distribution, and (b) the likelihood of very bad outcomes is very high. Thus, investors (and hedge funds of funds) that design hedge fund exposures using traditional mean variance optimization procedures will be sorely disappointed.

Using long/short hedge funds as the high-alpha component of an asset class strategy. One of the best uses of hedge funds, especially directional funds, is as the high-alpha portion of an equity strategy. We could decide to index a core position in US equities, then build a satellite position using long/short hedge funds. The trouble is that hedge fund managers tend not to keep doing what they were doing when we hired them, with the result that our overall US equity exposure will tend to behave in quixotic ways. A better idea would be to use one or more long/short hedge funds of funds, which will tend to have performance characteristics that are more consistent over time.

Using hedge funds of funds. All but the very largest families will likely find that the safest strategy in the hedge fund space is to build a core hedge fund exposure by investing in a hedge funds of funds. Yes, this adds yet another (often substantial) layer of fees to the already burdensome fee structure. But a best-in-class hedge fund of fund will perform at least the following services for investors:

- The fund of fund will offer instant diversification among hedge fund styles, hedge fund managers and different levels of risk.
- The fund of fund will, one hopes, have designed its risk-return profile in the context of the issues of skewness and kurtosis mentioned above (but see the discussion above).
- The fund of fund will have conducted extensive diligence on hedge funds and their professional staffs, including intensive background tests.
- Perhaps most important of all, the fund of fund will conduct serious, thorough, ongoing monitoring of every hedge fund in the portfolio (as well as any hedge funds the fund of fund is considering investing in). Given the lack of transparency and forthcomingness of many hedge fund managers, this ongoing diligence process is extremely expensive and time-consuming.

Alas, it is also true that the great majority of hedge funds of funds either can't or don't provide high quality ongoing monitoring of their managers. Of the more than 1,000 hedge funds of funds available to investors, no more than a few score are worth their fees. It is, in other words, nearly as difficult, though perhaps not as dangerous, to identify best-in-class hedge funds of funds as it is to identify individual hedge funds. Intense diligence will be required before engaging such a fund of fund.

Using directional hedge funds. Most family investors are invested with long/short or macro hedge funds. As noted above, these funds don't really constitute a separate asset class. Hence, the optimal strategy in this sector of the hedge fund market will usually be to use long/short managers[311] as the "satellites" around a core position. In the US large cap space, for example, I have suggested (see Chapter 11) that families might consider creating a passive, tax-aware core position, surrounded by smaller positions with managers who have a real chance to add net alpha. Best-in-class long/short hedge funds are an ideal example of this class of managers. Note that even if our directional hedge fund exposure produces no true alpha (an all-too-likely scenario), the lower volatility associated with that sector of the portfolio, and especially the downside protection it offers, may well prove nearly as valuable.

Using non-directional hedge funds. Non-directional hedge funds—more accurately referred to as absolute return-oriented hedge funds, or ARO funds—exhibit more of the characteristics of a separate asset class, at least when combined into numerous ARO strategies. Typically, then, the best practice with ARO funds is to create a separate allocation to these strategies. A well-balanced group of ARO funds (accessed in most cases via an ARO hedge fund of fund) should exhibit volatility roughly similar to that of bonds but should generate returns more similar to those of stocks. But don't be fooled by the low volatility. ARO hedge funds pack plenty of risks, even though volatility measures don't necessarily pick up those risks.

Using multi-strategy hedge funds. Most individual hedge funds focus on one investment strategy, or perhaps two related strategies. Some funds, however, are so-called "multi-strategy" hedge funds. These funds tend to engage in a variety of strategies, many of them unrelated to each other. The senior professionals overseeing the multi-strategy fund will allocate capital among the various strategies depending on where they see value in the marketplace. Thus, if spreads have tightened in the distressed debt markets, the multi-strategy fund might reduce the capital employed in that strategy and move it to, say, convertible arbitrage. In a sense, then, multi-strategy funds can sometimes stand in for funds of funds, offering strategy diversification within one investment partnership. Investors should keep in mind, however, that executing many different strategies successfully will severely tax all but the very best multi-strategy funds—and many of those will be closed or will demand very high minimum investments.

Using tax-efficient strategies. High-taxed short-term capital gains and high fees (especially at the fund of funds level) have led some sophisticated families to re-think hedge fund investing from the bottom up. Rather then viewing

---

311 So-called "macro" managers are best avoided, although they should not be confused with the multi-strategy managers discussed later.

hedge funds as an alpha opportunity, these investors have consciously decided to forego potential alpha in favor of certain tax savings. These strategies involve gaining derivative exposure to a hedge fund index, typically via a structured note whose value is linked directly to the performance of the index. These linked notes should be treated for tax purposes as a forward purchase contract, with all profits deferred and converted to long-term capital gain once the one-year holding period has been met. Linked notes usually have weekly liquidity and can be purchased in lots as small as $50,000. No K-1s or 1099s are issued and the notes are DTC eligible, which means they can be custodied along with the client's other assets. As an extra bonus, investors in the notes need not meet the super-qualified investor standards required by many funds of funds. While this will not be an issue for most family investors themselves (the requirement is $5 million in investable assets), many substantial families will have family foundations that do not meet the $25 million (assets) standard for a "qualified purchaser," and hence will be frozen out of most better hedge funds of funds. It is important to remember that, as with any structured product, there is counterparty risk (that is, the party selling the structured note—usually a large bank or other financial institution—could possibly go bankrupt before paying us off).

A Process-Based Approach to Hedge Fund Investing

As we build our hedge fund portfolios, we are typically looking for a hedge exposure that (a) meets our risk/return objectives, (b) plays a propitious role in our portfolio relative to the other asset classes we are invested in, (c) will outperform other similarly structured hedge fund portfolios, and (d) will avoid blowups and meltdowns (i.e., very serious individual manager underperformance). But, as noted, what we are looking for and what we get are all-too-often very different.

For this reason, and many others, most of us seek advice in building out our hedge fund exposure. But in doing so, and whether we are aware of it or not, most of us are following an *outcome-oriented* approach to designing, implementing and maintaining our hedge fund portfolios. We are saying, in effect, "Here's my money. Get me 15% per year with bond-like volatility." The inevitable outcome of this approach is that the very activities that might actually lead to something like that outcome are hopelessly compromised. We compromise by accepting systemic conflicts of interest. We compromise by paying high fees. We compromise by taking it on faith that our fund of fund is performing necessary upfront and ongoing diligence, even though we know that all the incentives point the other way. Small wonder that outcome-oriented approaches tend to fail. Let's examine, in more detail, why this is the case.

Hedge funds of funds: pros and cons. The main outcome-oriented approach to building a hedge fund exposure is to invest in one or more hedge funds of funds. The fund of fund approach has been a lifesaver for many investors who simply could not have gained intelligent access to the hedge sector on their own. No doubt this accounts for the proliferation of hedge funds of funds. (You heard it here first: soon there will be more hedge funds of funds than there are individual hedge funds, just as there are already more mutual funds than there are listed stocks.)

Hedge funds of funds certainly offer a number of advantages, especially to smaller or unsophisticated investors. The most important of these advantages is diversification: by investing in many different hedge funds, a fund of fund ensures that a disaster associated with one, or even two, individual hedge fund managers won't decimate investor capital. Close behind the diversification advantage is the diligence advantage—hedge funds of funds can afford to perform the kind of intensive diligence on managers that individual investors cannot hope to replicate. In distant third place is the fact that some hedge funds of funds offer access to managers who are otherwise closed to new investors.[312]

But hedge funds of funds also come with a dispiriting list of disadvantages. Let's examine some of them.

Expense. Most hedge funds of funds are expensive. Hedge fund managers themselves typically charge "1 and 20," that is, a 1% annual management fee plus 20% of all profits, sometimes above a hurdle rate. We've seen much worse, however: "1.5 and 25," even "2.5 and 30!" It seems like world-class chutzpah to add additional fees on top of this, but the typical hedge fund of fund adds another "1.5 and 10," that is, an additional 1.5% annual management fee and an additional 10% of the profits. It will be a rare hedge fund of fund, indeed, that can add enough value to justify all these fees.

Conflicts of interest. While some hedge funds of funds are completely open architecture in their approach, many, many others are chock full of conflicts of interest. A fund of fund that is a unit of a large bank or investment bank, for example, will typically use hedge funds for which an affiliate acts as prime broker.

---

312 There is almost always less to this advantage than meets the eye. If hedge fund managers continue to accept new capital from some hedge funds of funds, those managers will quickly outgrow their ability to produce alpha. If they constrain new money from hedge funds of funds, then the funds of funds won't have enough access to them to matter, given the large number of managers included in most funds of funds portfolios.

The parent firm may also invest directly in recommended hedge funds, seeding the fund with capital in return for a share of fees and profits. We should keep these conflicts firmly in mind when we evaluate funds of funds that are associated with larger financial firms.

Diversification. The diversification offered by hedge funds of funds is often illusory. Sure, owning pieces of thirty underlying hedge funds will ensure that our capital isn't devastated by an occasional blowup, but those occasional blowups will still dramatically reduce our returns. Besides, we could get the diversification advantage ourselves by simply investing in any random thirty hedge funds and putting 3.3% of our hedge allocation in each of them. A hedge fund of fund must offer a great deal besides diversification to justify its fees.

Up front diligence. The upfront diligence performed by hedge funds of funds is often less than meets the eye. The main reason for this is that the temptation to skimp on diligence is enormous. Hedge funds of funds can be very profitable products, but there are only three ways to generate or improve that profitability: (1) Produce outstanding returns and share in those returns to the tune of the 5% carry. This is very, very difficult, however. Over time, very few hedge funds of funds will earn much from their second layer of profits interest. (We, the investor, have the third layer of profits, alas.) (2) Build a huge asset base and get rich on the annual management fee, regardless of lousy performance. If there is one thing we can count on for the financial services industry to be good at, it's sales and marketing. Hence, many hedge funds of funds that are associated with larger financial firms are exceedingly good at building their asset bases. Unfortunately, as investors we don't share in the annual management fees and our returns come only after that and the fund of fund's profits interest. (3) Skimp on diligence and watch happily as the "1 and 5" fees fall directly to the bottom line. Since generating great performance is excessively difficult, and since many *independent* hedge funds of funds aren't all that good at marketing themselves, skimping on diligence is the only way to make or improve profits for many hedge funds of funds.

Ongoing diligence. Even funds of funds that perform an acceptable amount of upfront diligence tend to skimp on the ongoing diligence that spells the difference between good and mediocre returns, or between blowups and no blowups. Ongoing diligence can be exceptionally time-consuming and it lacks the sex appeal of going out to meet new managers. As a result, all-too-many hedge funds of funds substitute manager diversification for the ongoing monitoring they should be doing. But the fact of the matter is that careful ongoing diligence performed on managers already engaged is one of those minimum types of diligence that simply must be performed.

Access. The claim made by many funds of funds that they have access to great-but-closed managers is sometimes true, but it is always ephemeral and usually inconsequential. It is inconsequential because, no matter how good the "closed" manager is, the fund of fund is not going to put much of our money with him. Hence, his impact on our overall returns is likely to be marginal at best. The claim is ephemeral for this reason: either the great-but-closed hedge fund manager is serious about continuing to produce good returns, in which case he will eventually close to everyone, including the hedge fund of fund, or he isn't worth gaining access to in the first place.

Impenetrability. Most individual hedge fund managers guard their strategies and tactics and, especially, their individual positions very closely. If other managers knew what one hedge fund was doing, the opportunity would soon disappear. Worse, other managers could attempt to "squeeze" the hedge fund, turning a small loss into a very big loss. For these and other reasons, most individual hedge funds offer limited transparency to their investors. That is bad enough, but when we invest through hedge funds of funds we must endure yet another layer of non-transparency: most funds of funds won't even tell their investors which managers they are using, much less share any transparency they have received from those managers. Thus, at the funds of funds level, most investors are dealing not with limited transparency but with true impenetrability. Too many hedge funds of funds investors are taking a very big leap of faith.

Illiquidity. Most substantial investors should be willing to trade liquidity for return. But the illiquidity associated with investing in hedge funds—limited redemption windows, long initial lockups, and the discretion of hedge fund managers to refuse or limit redemption requests—is a real risk and one that is difficult to model and manage. If we wake up some morning and realize that there is something fishy about a long-only manager, we can suspend trading authority on the account immediately. If necessary, we can close the account and transfer the securities elsewhere. But if we wake up some morning and find something fishy at a hedge fund, we will have the pleasure of waiting helplessly while a series of unfortunate events play themselves out. At the funds of funds level, investors face a new set of liquidity constraints layered on top of the constraints that exist at the individual hedge fund level. These fund of fund-level constraints relate both to the timing of redemption opportunities and to the all-or-nothing nature of the available redemptions. Thus, not only may the fund of fund not be able to exit a manager that is blowing up, but even if we are deeply concerned about an underlying manager the only way we can avoid him (if at all) is to redeem our entire account from the fund of fund—in effect, throwing out the baby with the bath water.

Compounded tax inefficiency. As noted above, hedge fund investing almost inevitably results in high-taxed short-term capital gains, rather than low-taxed long-term capital gains. But when we invest in a fund of funds, we face another tax inefficiency: we pay taxes on gains we never receive. On the K-1 we receive from our hedge fund of funds, the fund's total return is shown, with the fund of fund's fees (management fee plus performance fee) shown as miscellaneous deductions. But most of us—the vast majority of investors—can't deduct miscellaneous itemized deductions because to be deductible they must exceed 2% (or 3%) of our adjusted gross income.

Funds of funds design and investor needs. Each hedge fund of fund is designed differently from each other hedge fund of fund. Some pursue pure long/short, highly directional strategies. Some pursue pure long/short, modestly directional strategies. Some are absolute return-oriented, with no macro managers and few, if any, long/short managers. Some employ nothing but multi-strategy managers. Given that there are more than 1,000 hedge funds of funds available, surely we ought to be able to find several that are pursuing exactly the strategies we are looking for.

In fact, this is unlikely to be the case, for two reasons. The first is that the immediate need most of us have in gaining hedge fund exposure is the very design of that exposure. No hedge fund of fund is going to help us with that key problem. They do what they do and that's all that they do, as Popeye might say. Hence, the first reason we won't be able to find hedge funds of funds that are pursuing the strategies we need is because we don't know what those strategies are.

The second reason has to do with the very poor quality of most hedge funds of funds. Yes, there are 1,000 hedge funds of funds in existence, but there are probably no more than 100 that deserve even a second look. Among those 100, it might be possible to cobble together a piece of this one and a piece of that one to get the exact exposure we want, but more likely we will end up settling for something that gets us—maybe—75% of the way home. What we really need is a selection of hedge funds that meets our particular needs in precisely the way our selection of long-only managers meets our particular needs.

An outcome-oriented solution that doesn't have the right outcome. Given all the disadvantages burdening hedge funds of funds, it should come as no surprise to anyone to learn that hedge funds of funds have substantially underperformed hedge funds. The main problem of course, is the huge fees hedge funds of funds charge, but all the issues set out above have contributed to this dismal result.

The crux of the matter is this: hedge funds of funds are outcome-oriented investment products, when what we really need is *process-oriented* advice:

advice about what the characteristics of our hedge fund portfolio should be, advice about which hedge fund managers to invest with, advice about how much money to put with each manager, and ongoing advice about whether to remain invested with each manager and when to add new managers.

Hedge funds of funds exist because the financial industry created them and they turned out to be highly profitable. They have, as a consequence, multiplied like rabbits on Viagra. Investors turned to hedge funds of funds because we were anxious to gain diversified hedge fund exposure and were unable to accomplish it intelligently on our own. Perhaps because our aspirations for our hedge fund exposure are so high, we have been willing to take an outcome-oriented approach and to pay through the nose for it. As noted, that approach has failed when we look at the entire group of hedge funds of funds. Even in cases where we have selected funds of funds whose performance has justified their fees, we have often found that our hedge allocation has played a negative role in our overall portfolio—because it was inappropriately sized and/or inappropriately designed relative to the balance of the portfolio.

Evaluating a Process-Oriented Solution

But another reason we turned to hedge funds of funds is because there was no other solution. We weren't actively looking for an outcome-oriented solution, but that's the one that happened to be available. Our only choices were to build our own hedge portfolios or to invest via hedge funds of funds. But let's think outside the box about this problem. We'll engage in a modest thought experiment in which we will assume that hedge funds of funds don't exist. Instead of approaching the challenge of obtaining sound hedge exposure from the outcome-oriented perspective of the financial services industry ("Let's create a wildly profitable (for us) product everyone will have to buy"), we'll approach the problem from an investor-friendly point of view.

> ***Bespoke Hedge Fund Advisors, Inc.***[313] Bespoke is a unit of an existing open architecture firm, or perhaps it's a newly formed unit of a larger financial firm but is operated in an open architecture manner. (Meaning, most especially, that it won't invest in hedge funds for which an affiliate serves as prime broker or in which an affiliate has invested or has a fee or profits interest.) According to Bespoke's marketing brochure, the firm does not build hedge funds of funds, but instead offers advice—that is, it works as a consultant to build hedge

[313] Bespoke is a fictional firm.

exposure for its clients. Specifically, Bespoke offers the following services (we are quoting from the Bespoke brochure):

- We review the strategies employed in your current portfolio, then discuss with you the appropriate design characteristics of your hedge fund exposure, having in mind both the importance of adding value to the existing portfolio and the need to accommodate your own risk and return preferences. The outcome of this process is a recommended design for your hedge fund exposure in terms of style, strategy, sector and directional exposure, and in terms of expected risk and return.
- Next, we identify the smallest number of hedge fund managers that will accomplish the hedge fund strategy as designed. (Using too many managers merely adds costs and dilutes the strategy via over-diversification.) Managers are identified using Bespoke's due diligence template and our three-level hedge fund manager review and recommendation program. If you are already invested with hedge fund managers, we will evaluate those managers using the same diligence template and manager recommendation program.
- Next, we structure an implementation plan for funding the managers we have identified.
- As the hedge fund portfolio is built out, and thereafter, we conduct ongoing diligence on the funded managers.
- On a quarterly basis we supply individual and consolidated performance reports on the hedge funds in your portfolio. Based on the performance of individual managers, we may recommend that funds be reallocated among the hedge fund managers or that individual managers be terminated and replaced by other managers. (Terminations are typically subject to liquidity constraints.)
- On an ongoing basis, we continually monitor other hedge fund managers in an effort to maintain the representative nature of our recommended and monitored hedge fund manager universe.
- All our activities and recommendations are made from an open architecture platform. Bespoke has no interests in prime brokers, hedge funds or otherwise which could compromise the integrity of our advice.

Gosh, we're thinking, this sounds too good to be true. Being naturally skeptical, we inquire of Bespoke about its fees for all this. To our astonishment, the fees are far lower than the fees charged by hedge funds of funds. Specifically, Bespoke charges a first year fee of 100 basis points (1%) on the value of the proposed hedge fund exposure. Subsequent year fees are 75 basis points (3/4 of 1%)

Flaws in the Bespoke approach: no performance representations. The main "flaw" in Bespoke's approach arises out of the very reason for its existence: it isn't an outcome-oriented approach. Bespoke is very careful to state what it is doing and what it is not doing. What it is doing is taking a disciplined, process-oriented approach to building a hedge fund exposure for its clients, conducting specified diligence that Bespoke believes to be best-in-class. What it is not doing is taking an outcome-oriented approach. Bespoke believes that its process-intensive approach will in fact produce performance results that are superior to outcome-oriented solutions (such as hedge funds of funds), but all it is representing is that it will in fact conduct the process it lays out in a professional and competent manner. It's possible that some of Bespoke's clients will not be pleased with their hedge exposure. Market conditions might be more difficult than Bespoke anticipated. Bespoke might have designed a hedge exposure that in fact didn't meet the client's needs. Bespoke might have recommended managers who under-performed. But because Bespoke focuses on process—on doing the things that tend to lead to acceptable results—the great likelihood is that Bespoke's clients will do better than hedge funds of funds clients.

Flaws in the Bespoke approach: potential conflicts in the hedge-non-hedge allocation. Most of Bespoke's clients have engaged it solely to advise on hedge fund investing. But some clients have engaged Bespoke to advise generally on their portfolios. Since Bespoke's fee on the hedge fund component of the clients' portfolios is higher than its fee on the long-only component, Bespoke may be tempted to recommend a hedge exposure that is larger than is appropriate. There is no escaping the potential for this conflict, but Bespoke can take steps to minimize it. For example:

- It may be that even though Bespoke's hedge fund fee is higher than its long-only fee, the actual profit margin might be fairly similar, largely eliminating any incentive for Bespoke to lean one way or the other.
- Bespoke can take steps to ensure that the procedures used to determine the size of a client's hedge fund exposure are consistent (from client to client) and transparent, so that the clients can see for themselves that the hedge exposure is designed straight-up.
- Bespoke could offer to its general-engagement clients a discount on the hedge fund work relative to what Bespoke charges hedge fund-only clients.

The point is that Bespoke's approach to designing and building a hedge fund exposure for its clients is process-oriented and investor-friendly. It avoids the alarming fees of hedge funds of funds and it proceeds in a manner that is quite similar to the way investors find managers for their long-only portfolio. The only problem is that Bespoke doesn't exist.[314]

The Future of Hedge Fund Investing

As the hedge fund industry matures, and as family investors gain more and more experience investing in hedge funds, it is interesting to speculate about what the future of hedge fund investing might look like. Already it seems clear that sophisticated investors are increasing their exposures to hedge fund strategies, developing thorough techniques for evaluating hedge fund managers and monitoring their ongoing performance, and gaining a fuller understanding of hedge fund risks and hedge fund portfolio design. Some investors are clearly separating alpha and beta strategies, by gaining access to individual asset classes (the beta strategy) as inexpensively as possible,[315] then focusing intensely on generating alpha[316] by employing the most talented managers available in the manager habitat most likely to encourage relative outperformance. These so-called "portable alpha" strategies are currently employed only by the largest and most sophisticated investors, such as gigantic pension plans and huge university endowments.[317]

Investing in Private Equity

The most important strategy associated with private equity investing can be stated simply: access, access, access. The average PE partnership produces returns that are roughly in line with those of long-only equity managers, dramatically under-compensating investors for the risks, illiquidity and non-transparency of their PE investments. According to FLAG Capital Management, one of the best PE funds of funds operators, top quartile PE partnerships—that is, those whose investment results place them in the top 25% of all partnerships—outperform average PE funds by an astonishing 1,500 basis points per year.

---

[314] For very large investors, Albourne America, LLC comes closest. See www.albourne.com.

[315] Via indexing, S&P 500 futures, passive tax-aware overlays, etc.

[316] Hedge funds typically exhibit little beta because they are hedged, and they attempt to magnify alpha through the use of leverage. This is, of course, a two-way street.

[317] Portable alpha strategies are discussed in Chapter 17.

Compounding capital at such high relative rates can create very substantial wealth over time. But getting into those top quartile funds is an impossible challenge for most family investors. Thus, the first rule of PE investing for most family investors is to launch their PE exposure via a best-in-class PE fund of funds. The fund of funds will bring many benefits to justify its extra layer of fees, but the principal benefit is the one just mentioned: access to the best PE partnerships, a benefit that PE investors simply cannot do without.

For a variety of reasons, PE partnerships that develop excellent track records tend to persist in the top quartile for many years—generations, in some cases. One obvious explanation for this persistence—which is rare among long-only managers—has to do with deal flow. Once a PE firm establishes itself as superior to most of its peers, entrepreneurs will seek it out, and they will often be well-advised to accept a slightly lower-priced deal from a top firm rather than taking top dollar from a lesser firm. Top quartile PE firms offer entrepreneurs more than capital—they offer advice based on their own vast experience with smaller firms, they have extensive contacts that can be called upon as necessary, and the uniformity of their talent ensures that the entrepreneur won't have to settle for the second team when, as it always will, the going gets tough.

The issue of talent is another reason top PE firms tend to stay at the top. Among long-only managers and hedge fund managers, talent is very much a person-specific issue. Excellent managers are more like artists than engineers—a less talented manager can study at the feet of Warren Buffett for many years without having the magic rub off. In the PE world, however, younger professionals can more easily be mentored by more seasoned people. Qualities like hard work, learning the ropes, and developing an extensive web of contacts mean a great deal in the private equity world, and these characteristics can be learned.

Assuming that a family can gain access to top quartile private equity funds, either via funds of funds, via the sheer size of its PE portfolio or via extraordinarily hard work, there are other important aspects of successful PE investing, and most of them have to do with diversifying PE exposure among various dimensions. For example, investors will want to diversify their PE exposure by:

- Type, i.e., venture, buyouts, mezzanine.
- Stage, i.e., early, mid, and late-stage venture capital investments.
- Industry, i.e., technology (and various sectors of the tech industry), healthcare, manufacturing, etc.
- Geography, *i.e.*, not just Silicon Valley or any geographical space that may be susceptible to simultaneous economic swoons.

- Deal size, i.e., large, middle market, etc.
- Vintage year. I mention this issue last, but in some ways it is the most important. PE returns are cyclical, and it is virtually impossible to anticipate those cycles. The only way an investor can ride out the bad vintage years is to be sure to be invested during the good vintage years. And the only way to do that is to invest consistently year after year.

The due diligence process to be used in selecting specific private equity funds of funds is discussed in Chapter 13.

Investing in "Real" Assets

"Real" assets are those that, in contrast to "financial" assets, are actually tangible. But more important than their tangibility is the pattern of their typical returns. Real assets tend to perform well at crucial periods of time—periods of rapid, unanticipated inflation—when virtually all other investment assets tend to perform very poorly. Since high inflation—and even moderate inflation—is the principal enemy of families wishing to preserve their wealth, it will be a rare family that should not have at least some exposure to real assets.

Real Estate

The most common real asset is real estate; indeed, real estate is the largest single asset class in the world. Properly structured real estate portfolios will exhibit low correlations to equity and fixed income assets, will provide a strong ongoing yield, will appreciate slowly but consistently, and will perform well during the periods of unanticipated inflation referred to above. It's a pretty compelling portrait, marred only by the fact that, over long periods of time, real estate will tend to under-perform stocks, and therefore there are modest-but-real opportunity costs associated with allocating too much money to real estate.

Assuming that an allocation is going to be made to real estate, families will have many possible strategies available to them. Among the more prominent are:

REITs. Public, open-end real estate investment trusts operate much like mutual funds. Investors buy shares in the REIT, which in turn uses the money to invest in actual properties, mortgages (or mortgage-backed securities), operating real estate companies, or other REITs.[318] The advantages of REITs

---

318 Vanguard offers a mutual fund that is a REIT index fund. Other mutual funds also specialize in investing in real estate-related companies—the Third Avenue Real Estate Value Fund, for example.

are their liquidity and their frequent high yields. Disadvantages include REITs' higher correlations with equities (especially small cap value stocks). In addition, the liquidity offered by REITs is somewhat misleading. Yes, it's easy to get in and out of REITs, which offer daily liquidity, but real estate is a cyclical, long-term investment. Attempting to time the real estate markets—an almost overwhelming temptation when investing via REITs—is a loser's game, and hence even investors who plan to gain all their real estate exposure through REITs should consider those REITs to be long-term investments, notwithstanding their liquidity.

Open-end funds. Many firms offer open-end real estate funds, that is partnerships or LLCs that are always open to new investors (though sometimes with quarterly windows) and that usually offer some form of liquidity after an initial lockup period. These funds can be "core" in nature, that is, they invest in a very broad range of real estate assets, including direct properties, REITs, closed-end funds, collateralized mortgage obligations (CMOs), and even other open-end funds. Other open-end funds may be focused on a specific sector of the real estate market: multi-family residences in the Southeast, for example. Open-end funds can provide attractive opportunities for families seeking to establish a core position in real estate.

Closed-end funds. Closed-end funds are similar to open-end funds in that they raise capital from investors and then redeploy that capital in broad or narrow real estate investments. Unlike open-end funds, however, closed-end funds do not continue to accept new capital from investors. Once the fund is raised it closes and thereafter focuses on managing the portfolio. An advantage of closed-end funds is that the partners are not constantly distracted by the need to raise funds—they can focus on making money for their investors. A disadvantage is that, because all the capital is raised at once, the fund may find that it has bought into the market at a bad time. Investors may find, therefore, that closed-end funds make more sense for targeted investments in specific sectors of the real estate market that are believed to be currently undervalued.

Direct properties. Probably the most common way to gain real estate exposure is simply to buy properties directly. More American families have created their wealth through direct real estate investing than in any other way. On the other hand, this is also the most difficult and most dangerous strategy. Buying individual properties puts an investor directly into the real estate business, which is a competitive enterprise like any other. Families that buy individual properties but who don't staff up to manage them professionally will likely be sorely disappointed in the outcome. One exception to this generalization involves families who act as equity providers to real estate developers through partnerships structured in such a way as to align the developer's interests with the family's interests. These kinds of deals typically make sense mainly for large families who plan to commit a sizeable sum to real estate, who plan to invest year-after-year, and who are willing to staff up at least to some extent.

Other Real Assets

Oil and gas. Whether a family will have a significant allocation to oil and gas tends to depend on where the family is located. Wealthy families in Texas and Oklahoma, for example, are more likely to own oil and gas than to own real estate. Similar families in New York or Florida may well have no oil and gas exposure at all. Even more than with real estate, managing a successful oil and gas portfolio requires that a family be willing to "be in the business," to learn the arcane jargon and (often) slippery practices in the industry that can lead amateur investors astray. Once a family decides to make a commit to the asset, there are many strategies available: buying royalty interests, buying pieces of producing wells, investing in low-risk, low-return drilling partnerships, investing (speculating?) in wildcat drilling, buying up leases, investing in operating companies, and so on.

TIPS. TIPS are Treasury Inflation-Protected Securities issued by the US government,[319] as well as a few other nations.[320] TIPS offer a "real," that is, net of inflation, return to investors, and therefore they can play a highly useful role in portfolios. TIPS provide a periodic coupon payment at a fixed rate, plus an inflation adjustment to the bonds' principal balance, paid at maturity. Our investment therefore keeps pace with inflation, unlike investments in traditional bonds. The trouble with this lovely world is that both the coupon payment and the inflation increment on the bonds—the increase in its principal value—are taxed currently, at ordinary income rates, even though the inflation increment will not be received until the bonds mature many years in the future. While it seems unlikely that the coupon payment on TIPS would not be large enough to cover the taxes—i.e., there should be no cash flow problem—most families who buy TIPS have tended to place them in tax-exempt structures (IRAs, foundations, etc.)

Commodities. Perhaps the purest form of "real assets" is commodities—industrial and agricultural stock whose prices fluctuate directly with economic conditions and inflation. These assets are "commodities" because there is no

---

319 The US Treasury first issued TIPS in 1997. Current maturities range from 3 years to 28 years.

320 The United Kingdom, France, Sweden, Canada, Italy, and Australia (listed in order of the volume of outstanding inflation-linked bonds, or ILBs). The US accounts for 43% of all outstanding ILBs.

way to differentiate among the products themselves, which are identical. Over long periods of time commodity returns tend to be low and their price volatility tends to be high—a particularly unhappy combination that may make a sensible investor wonder why anyone would ever invest in them. The reason has to do with the extremely low correlation commodity prices have with the returns on other assets. As a result of this low correlation, a small exposure to commodities will improve the risk-return profile of almost all portfolios. The challenge, however, is to avoid focusing on the risk-return characteristics of the commodities allocation itself.

Three

Chapter 13

Working with Money Managers[321]

I'm more interested in the return of *my money*
than in the return on *my money.*
—Mark Twain

Working with money managers is the aspect of the investment process that is usually the most interesting for investors but that all too often adds least to the growth of investor wealth. In fact, one of the principal methods of identifying investors who will encounter little success over time is to observe those who are most obsessed with money managers. The reason that money managers typically subtract value from, rather than add value to, the investment process is not that money managers are incompetent but that their services are, on the whole, overpriced relative to the value they bring to their customers. In the asset classes that matter most to investors—US large and mid-cap stocks and bonds—most managers will under-perform over time by at least an amount equal to their fees and trading costs, to say nothing of taxes. In the more complex and obscure asset classes, where useful information is difficult to come by, talented and hardworking managers may modestly add value net of all costs.

The main reason investors spend so much time and emotional energy on working with managers, despite the modest-to-negative return we are likely to receive for our efforts, is that money managers are actual human beings, while almost all other aspects of the investment process are purely intellectual. It's a lot more fun and a lot more interesting to spend time talking with an intelligent

---

321 Parts of this chapter were originally published as a Greycourt white paper and were co-written with Gregory R. Friedman, Chief Investment Officer at Greycourt & Co., Inc.

money manager than it is to run mean variance optimization algorithms or participate in long conference calls with accountants about tax managing our portfolios.

In this chapter I try to address a couple of the principal issues associated with money managers. Specifically:

- Why it is so difficult to identify best-in-class managers in time to profit by investing with them?
- Why it is that good past performance can be completely meaningless.
- I identify the (mainly qualitative) characteristics of best-in-class managers.
- I describe how my own firm, Greycourt & Co., Inc., goes about the process of identifying best-in-class managers.
- I discuss, briefly, some approaches to optimizing the mix of managers in our portfolios.

The issue of selecting money managers is very closely associated with the challenge of identifying optimal strategies for each asset class that will be included in our portfolios. Hence, this chapter should be read in conjunction with Chapters 11 and 12. Some information is duplicated in these two chapters for clarity of the presentation.

The Business of Money Management

But before we look at traditional and alternative managers in depth, let's take an overall look at some of the challenges active managers face. We'll start by following a new US large cap management firm to see how it operates.

> **Hapless Asset Management.** The principals of Hapless Asset Management, having worked extensively in the money management industry, understand all-too-well the dynamics of the business. They know, for example, that attracting new clients—especially private investors—is a difficult, time-consuming and expensive activity. But they also know that once a client has signed on, the marginal cost of servicing that client's account will be negligible. After all, Hapless will buy and sell pretty much the same stocks for every client, so it can manage $10 billion almost as easily as it can manage $100 million. Sure, new clients sometimes want to meet with Hapless too often (from Hapless's perspective), but most clients soon settle into a routine that is highly cost-effective for Hapless. After all, clients are busy people, too.

Thus, the main challenge for Hapless is to keep the clients it gets. Those clients provide an annuity income for Hapless, and given the cost of obtaining new clients, Hapless wants to do everything it can to avoid losing accounts. The main way Hapless is likely to lose accounts is for the firm to generate truly dismal performance numbers. If the numbers are really awful, clients will defect after one year of bad performance. If the numbers are merely bad, clients may wait two years to dump Hapless. But dump they will. Hapless, therefore, wants to avoid really bad performance at any cost.

How does Hapless ensure that it will never experience terrible investment performance relative to the benchmark its clients are measuring it by (in this case, the S&P 500)? The answer is surprisingly simple: Hapless will manage its portfolios as "closet index funds." Here's how this works. Let's suppose that Microsoft and General Electric both represent 3% of the S&P 500 Index (which is roughly the case). Let's suppose, further, that Hapless believes that Microsoft's price will rise and that GE's price will fall. We might imagine that Hapless would load up on Microsoft and own no GE at all—but that's because we don't understand how money management actually works.

What Hapless actually does is to modestly overweight Microsoft in its portfolio and modestly underweight GE. If we examine Hapless's portfolio, we might find that it consists of a 3.3% exposure to Microsoft and a 2.7% exposure to GE. Other stocks that appear in the S&P 500 might also be modestly over- or under-weighted, and the rest will be held exactly at their index weighting. If Hapless is right about both its over- and under-weightings, Hapless will generate a nice-but-modest outperformance versus the S&P 500. If Hapless is right about some weightings but wrong about others (the most likely case), Hapless will generate modest underperformance roughly equal to its fees and costs.[322] If Hapless is more often wrong than right, it will generate negative-but-modest underperformance versus the S&P 500.

In other words, while Hapless may, in an occasional year, outperform its benchmark, in most years Hapless will experience underperformance, but only modest underperformance. Hapless knows that

---

[322] Management fees are usually transparent to Hapless's separate account clients, but they are hidden for its mutual fund accounts (that is, they come out of Hapless's return, rather than being paid separately). But all the other costs—commissions, spreads, market impact and opportunity costs—are hidden from all its clients.

> the same clients who would dump it in a second following really bad performance will stick around for years if Hapless can generate occasional outperformance but overall underperformance. In other words, just when the client's patience has about been exhausted by several years of underperformance, Hapless will have a good year, and the client will stick around. From the client's point of view, this behavior is perfectly rational. After all, it is expensive to terminate a manager (see Chapter 14), and there is no guarantee that a new manager will do any better than Hapless.
>
> The net result of all this is that Hapless will build a growing and highly profitable money management business even though it is a fairly poor money manager, and even though it is imposing significant opportunity costs on its clients. In other words, if Hapless's clients had simply earned the return on the S&P 500 Index, they would be wealthier. If those clients had been with a best-in-class manager, they would be a lot wealthier.

What is going on at Hapless, and what goes on at most long-only money management firms, is the creation of what is known as portfolio "deadweight:" most of Hapless's portfolio looks suspiciously like the S&P 500 Index. Hapless is making only modest bets on the stocks it likes and against the stocks it doesn't like. Hapless lacks the courage of its convictions because it can't afford, from a business point of view, to be wildly wrong in any year (and, God help it, in any two consecutive years). Therefore, no matter how confident Hapless may be that Microsoft is going up and GE is going down, Hapless will back that confidence with only modest over- and under-weightings in those securities.

In the example cited above, the Hapless portfolio is about 90% an index fund and is only 10% actively managed. *Yet Hapless is charging a full active management fee on the entire portfolio.*

This phenomenon of portfolio deadweight imposes huge costs on the investing public. In a fairer world, investors would demand that Hapless charge an index fund-like fee (i.e., a few basis points) on the 90% of the portfolio that is indexed, and charge an active management fee only on the 10% that is, in fact, being actively managed. Unfortunately, most investors don't understand how damaging deadweight is, and very few managers would ever consider such a bifurcated fee arrangement. In a moment, however, we will examine strategies that are designed to replicate bifurcated fees.

Style and cap size diversification. It is largely true that most money managers tend to favor either "growth" or "value" investment styles and tend to work largely in a particular capitalization sector (mega-cap, large cap, mid-cap, etc.). It is also largely true that investors who diversify their portfolios by investment style and cap size will tend to reduce the price volatility of their portfolios[323] without necessarily reducing their returns. It is also true, however, that style and cap size labels are largely contrivances of investment consulting firms working with institutional investors. (Institutional investors will be very familiar with consultant "style boxes," charts used to categorize managers by their growth or value approach and, usually, to punish or avoid managers who don't fit neatly into a particular style box.) In this discussion I will focus mainly on the issue of style diversification, but my comments apply equally to cap size diversification.

Given the institutional origin of style diversification, it is worth posing the question whether such diversification is actually appropriate for taxable investors. There are four main problems with imposing style criteria on managers. The first is that it tends to convert managers from skill-based entities seeking alpha (risk-adjusted return) into humdrum entities content largely to replicate a style benchmark. The second is that it is expensive, since it forces turnover whenever a stock changes from being a growth stock to being a value stock (or outgrows the cap size constraint). The third is the arbitrariness of the style classifications: the 250 stocks in the S&P 500 with the highest price/earnings ratios are defined as "growth" stocks, while the other 250 stocks are classified as "value" stocks. Finally, even private investors who aren't motivated by the day-to-day price volatility inherent in owning portfolios with style biases will find that there are less expensive ways to avoid those biases.

Given all these issues, many families will want to abandon the notion of style (and cap size) diversification altogether. And even families who want to preserve active style diversification[324] may find that it will improve performance if

---

323 This occurs because value and growth stocks tend to perform well or badly at different times and under different conditions. Stocks of different capitalization sizes also tend to perform well or badly at different times and under different conditions. As a result, if an investor's portfolio has all its US large cap exposure in mega-cap growth stocks, that portfolio will tend to perform extremely well at times and extremely poorly at other times In other words, the portfolio will exhibit significantly greater price volatility than if the portfolio also had some value exposure and some large and mid-cap exposure.

324 One advantage of preserving active style diversification is that it makes it possible to engage in tactical bets when either growth or value seems seriously under-valued. See the discussion of tactical bets versus market timing in Chapter Sixteen.

they don't construct their entire US large and mid-cap exposure in this manner, but instead build style diversification around a core position.

Survivorship bias. Virtually every study of active management in the US large cap space shows that 70% to 75% of all managers will under-perform the S&P 500 Index over longer periods of time.[325] But the truth is that the dismal performance of active management is actually far worse than it appears. If we were to conduct a study today of 1,000 randomly selected managers, we would, indeed, discover that roughly 75% of them have under-performed the S&P 500 over the past twenty years. But our study would have missed many managers, most of which had truly dismal records. We would miss them because they are no longer in business, having been liquidated or absorbed into other management firms that dropped their losing track records. But while those managers were in business they managed billions of dollars of client money, and managed it badly. They are part of the miserable track record of active management, whether their contribution can be measured or not. Thus, the challenge of finding managers who will outperform is even worse than it appears.

Survivorship bias shows up in another way as well. Investors often proudly show me that their portfolios are employing only, or mainly, managers who show long-term outperformance. Indeed, a snapshot of many family portfolios will show such a phenomenon. But if we viewed not the snapshot version of the portfolio, but the full-length movie version, we would see a very different story, namely, manager after manager who is hired after a few good years of performance but who then under-performs, is fired and thus disappears from the current snapshot. But those managers held those investors' money and the under-performance they generated has had a permanent negative effect on the investors' wealth.

Fees and costs. Active managers, especially in the large and mid-cap sector, but elsewhere as well, are working against a powerful headwind of fees and expenses. Managers charge fees that are stunningly high considering the little value they add to—and more often subtract from—investment portfolios. Most manager fee schedules start at 1%, then decline as the size of the account increases. But even very large family accounts are often charged 50 to 75 basis points. (There are 100 basis points in 1%.) According to Morningstar, the average US large cap

---

325 Active managers can outperform during bear markets, not because they are skilled but because they tend to hold cash (there is no cash in the benchmark). The modestly positive return on that cash gives the managers an advantage against an index when the index is declining.

mutual fund has an expense ratio (management fees plus 12b-1 fees[326]) of about 150 basis points (1.5%).

But to these costs we must add on the roundtrip costs of brokerage commissions (roughly 10-11 cents per share for large managers), the spread between bid and ask prices (slightly higher), the cost of market impact (roughly 25 cents) and opportunity costs (10-12 cents). Given that the average share price of a US large cap stock is about $27 (mid-2003), this means that, in addition to the manager's fee, we must add more than 2% for trading costs. In other words, merely to match the performance of the index, a manager must outperform it by roughly 3% per year—a truly Herculean achievement.

As noted, virtually all long-only managers charge asset based fees. The idea behind this approach—which would be odd, indeed, in most other industries[327]—is that the manager is adding more value in absolute terms to larger accounts than it is adding to smaller accounts. If Hapless Asset Management outperforms the S&P 500 index by 1% in any year, it has added $1 million to a $100 million account, but only $10,000 to a $1 million account.

But there are several problems with this justification. The first problem is that the asset-based fee has nothing to do with the actual cost of managing money. It doesn't cost Hapless Asset Management 100 times as much to service its big client as it does to service its small client, even though the big client is 100 times larger. Sure, sensible businesses don't typically price their services on a cost-plus basis, but competition in most industries eventually drives prices down quite close to cost, so that only the most efficient firms can survive. In the money management industry, however, we are such lousy consumers that this hasn't happened.

But it gets worse. Hapless Asset Management, along with most other money managers, is far more likely to *subtract* value than to add it. Let's say that Hapless *under*-performs the S&P 500 by 1%—a far more likely scenario. If Hapless charges our hypothetical $100 million client 50 basis points (½ of 1%) and charges our $1 million client 1%, Hapless has earned $500,000 on the big

---

[326] So-called 12b-1 fees are fees added to mutual fund accounts to cover the cost of advertising and paying trailing commissions to brokers and financial planners who sell load mutual funds. The SEC approved charging these fees to mutual fund shareholders, but the SEC was wrong and the decision should be reversed.

[327] Money management fees are more akin to those charged by plaintiffs' attorneys than to any other advisor typically used by families, such as estate planning attorneys, tax accountants, intergenerational consultants, and so on.

client and $10,000 on the small client. But the big client has *lost* $1 million and the small client has *lost* $10,000. What sort of alignment of interests is this? As noted above, Hapless Asset Management, along with most other asset management firms, has created a very successful and profitable business by subtracting gigantic amounts of money from client portfolios.

What's to be done? Unfortunately, most family investors are too small to wield the clout that would be required to change pricing practices in the money management business. Even investors that one would think of as being large enough to wield such clout—huge endowed institutions and pension plans—have had little success in forcing through radical changes in pricing. However, it is sometimes possible to negotiate incentive fees with managers who are very confident in their ability to add value to client portfolios. Even here, however, we need to proceed with caution, as poorly designed incentive fees can create counterproductive motivations.

Perhaps the most sensible form of incentive fee for a long-only manager takes the form of a "fulcrum" fee. In such a fee arrangement, we ask the manager how much outperformance he expects to deliver to our portfolio. Let's say that the manager claims to be able to deliver 80 basis points per annum above the benchmark on average. Let's say, further, that *we* expect the manager to deliver about 30 basis points above the benchmark. We will then create a fee structure that (a) will give the manager approximately his standard fee if he outperforms by 30 basis points, (b) will give him a much higher fee if he outperforms by 80 basis points, and (c) will give him a fee much lower than his standard fee of he delivers less than 30 basis points of outperformance.

Fulcrum fees should have both caps above them and floors under them. The purpose of the floor—which we set at about the manager's breakeven operating cost—is to ensure that the manager pays attention to the account. Even during a period when the manager's style is out of favor and its performance is weak, we don't want the manager to ignore us or to terminate our account. (We want the account to be terminated only when *we* want it to be terminated.) The purpose of the cap is to eliminate any incentive on the part of the manager to take extravagant risks with our money in an attempt to earn a higher fee.

It's not enough just to be right. Suppose that back in the 1970s Hapless (or, more likely, a predecessor firm, since most money management firms don't survive that long) had had the foresight to anticipate the technology boom of the past thirty years and had loaded up on tech stocks. Hapless would have made a killing, right? Wrong. Hapless would have underperformed the broad market by roughly 130 basis points *per year* (1.3%).[328] The reason is that lots

[328] *Bridgewater Daily Observations*, Bridge Water Associates, Inc. (July 8, 2004).

and lots of investors anticipated a technology boom and as a result much of the future appreciation in that sector had already been priced in. For Hapless to make a killing, it would have had to anticipate a development that very few others anticipated.

With all this background information in mind, let's look at why it is so difficult to identify managers who will outperform in the future—that is, while they have our capital under management—as opposed to in the past—when they didn't.

Traditional Managers

Investing is easy. I just buy a stock and hold it 'til it goes up.
If it don't go up, I don't buy it.
—Will Rogers

The Challenge of Identifying Best-in-Class Managers

It is almost impossible to express how difficult it is to identify truly outstanding portfolio managers in time to profit by investing with them. By "truly outstanding," I mean managers whose outperformance relative to the broad markets and to other managers will be so great as to result in significant wealth creation for their investors. Consider that since 1970 several thousand Americans have won large lotteries—lotteries large enough to result in significant wealth for their winners. But since 1970 how many Warren Buffetts have there been? More than one, to be sure. But not thousands. Not hundreds. Not even dozens. Statisticians will tell us that playing the lottery is a fool's game,[329] that in the aggregate lottery players lose far, far more money than they win, and that even the remote possibility of gaining great winnings doesn't begin to justify the cost of playing. What would statisticians tell us about the challenge of finding outstanding money managers?

Periodically, my firm, Greycourt & Co., Inc., takes a look at manager out- or under-performance over longer periods of time. Recently, we took a look at the percentage of US large cap mutual funds that have outperformed the Vanguard S&P 500 Index Fund (Institutional) over the past ten years (through 12/31/02). Of the 3,724 US large cap stock managers in the Morningstar database, only 500 had a ten-year track record,[330] only 98 outperformed on a pre-tax basis, only 79

329 Voltaire supposedly remarked that a lottery is simply a tax on stupidity.

330 Which tells us something important about survivorship bias.

outperformed on a pre-tax, risk-adjusted basis, and only 40 (forty!) outperformed on an after-tax, risk-adjusted basis.[331] Now if you believe that, back in 1991, you could have picked those forty mutual fund needles out of the huge Morningstar haystack, you are a very confident investor!

And if identifying great managers weren't difficult enough, *timing* in the enterprise is everything. People who invested with the legendary hedge fund manager, Julian Robertson, early in the game had little idea how much money they were about to make. But people who invested with Robertson late in the game had little idea how much money they were about to lose. Same great manager, very different outcomes.

And the same phenomenon is commonly encountered on a mass basis. Consider that between 1984 and 2000, while the S&P 500 was producing an annualized total return of 16.3%, the average mutual fund equity investor realized an annual return of only 5.3%.[332] Those investors could have achieved an annual return of 5.8% by simply investing in risk-free Treasury bills. True, equity mutual funds substantially underperformed the market during that period, but the worse culprit was extremely poor market timing by investors—retail investors chased performance, constantly selling out of funds that had underperformed (just as they were about to outperform) and buying funds that had outperformed (just as they were about to underperform).

Finally, outperformance among managers tends to show little persistence over time, at least if we define outperformance to mean "consistently landing in the top quartile of all similar managers." Not long ago Greycourt looked at persistence even among managers in a sector of the market that is generally considered to be inefficient, and where talented managers should have room to run—namely, small cap managers.

We prepared an analysis using a group of 57 small cap growth managers and compared relative performance over time.[333] Most investors believe that capable managers should be able to add value in inefficient sectors with reasonable consistency over time. Hence, the purpose of the exercise was to determine how often managers remained outstanding performers over time. Our analysis illustrates the difficulty managers face in maintaining their top performance rating over even relatively short periods of time. Of the top fifteen managers in 1995, only two remained in the top fifteen by 2002. On the other hand, the manager who finished dead last (57th) in 1995, was the eleventh

---

[331] This work was performed by Gregory R. Friedman, Greycourt's Chief Investment Officer.

[332] *Quantitative Analysis of Investor Behavior* (DALBAR, 2001 Update).

[333] This study was performed by Claude R. Perrier and Patrick M. Parisi.

rated manager by 2002. In other words, investors hiring any of the top performers in 1995 would have been sorely disappointed by 2002.

In our analysis of the small cap growth managers, "adding value" was determined by the extent of wealth accumulation. To illustrate this point, we assumed that each of the 57 managers was given $1 million at the beginning of 1996 and we then calculated the wealth accumulation through 2002 based on each manager's returns over that period. The best performing manager at the end of 2002 had accumulated $3.3 million. Unfortunately, that manager had been ranked number 48 of the 57 managers in 1995, and hence was highly unlikely to have been hired in 1996. The worst performing manager at the end of 2002 had reduced client wealth to $700,000 over the period. It will not surprise you, I hope, to learn that the worst-performing manager had been ranked number 1 of 57 in 1995. That manager was highly likely to have been hired by investors in 1996.

The non-persistence of manager outperformance wasn't limited to these unhappy examples—non-persistence was characteristic of the entire group. As noted, only two of the top fifteen managers in 1995 appeared in the top fifteen based on accumulated wealth through 2002, and a full *two-thirds of the original top performers in 1995 had fallen below the median manager* in wealth accumulation by the end of 2002.

The Main Problem: Recent Good Performance Is Almost Irrelevant

The main mistake investors make in engaging managers is hiring a firm that has experienced good recent performance—say, a better-than-average five-year track record. The reason this is a mistake is that, more often than not, a good five-year track record says virtually nothing about how the manager is likely to perform over the next five years. That track record *might* indicate that the manager will continue its outperformance, but it is far more likely that the track record indicates one of the following:[334]

The good track record is simply the result of "the law of small numbers." In his endlessly amusing book, *A Mathematician Plays the Stock Market,*[335] John

---

[334] I list these possibilities merely as examples; there are many other ways in which "a good five-year track record" can prove to be meaningless to future clients of the manager.

[335] (Basic Books, 2003). Paulos's other books are also well worth looking into, especially *Innumeracy: Mathematical Illiteracy and Its Consequences* (1988), and *A Mathematician Reads the Newspaper* (1995). On the subject of innumeracy, see Chapter 3.

Allen Paulos points out that we tend to misunderstand the role chance plays in the outcomes of apparently even games. Imagine that two people—I will call them George Soros and George Bozos—flip a fair coin 1,000 times each, competing to see who can come up with the most heads. We tend to imagine that, after that many flips, the outcome would almost always come out very even, with Soros and Bozos each getting about 500 heads and 500 tails. We infer from that conclusion that if one of the players actually ends up well ahead of the other, that outcome must be due either to an unfair coin or to the special skill of one of the players.

In fact, as Paulos points out, there is a far greater probability that after 1,000 fair coin flips, Soros or Bozos would be well ahead of the other, having flipped 525 heads to, say, 475 heads. We might call this "the law of small numbers," that is, 1,000 flips may seem like a lot, but actually it's not enough observations to ensure that Soros and Bozos will come out even. Thus, if 10,000 people all flipped a fair coin 1,000 times, the aggregate results would tend to be that a goodly number would end up with pretty darn good records and an equal number would end up with pretty sorry records. A very few would have spectacular records and a very few would have abysmal records. Far fewer than we might expect would have "even" records.

This outcome looks alarmingly like the outcome of money manager five-year track records (which are based, after all, on only sixty monthly observations, or in some cases on only twenty quarterly observations): a tiny number have spectacular records, a tiny number have abysmal records, a goodly number have pretty darn good or pretty darn bad records, and only a few have average track records. None of this, however, means anything. Investors who engage managers purely on the basis of good five-year track records are likely to fall victim to "the law of small numbers."

The good track record is simply the result of fortunate timing. Imagine a money manager who has been in business for fifteen years and who, for thirteen of those years, has reliably turned in undistinguished performance. But during the past two years, for reasons unknown to us or the manager, performance has been quite good. These two "lucky" years of performance pulled the manager's five-year track record up to the point where it is now quite creditable. As a result, many unfortunate investors, impressed with that record, will engage a manager who is clearly undistinguished and who can be relied upon to continue in that vein.

The good track record is simply a result of style rotation. Let's consider two managers. We'll call them Value Capital Investors (VCI) and Capital Value Investors (CVI). Both are deep value managers who do well, naturally enough, when value stocks are in vogue and less well when growth stocks are in vogue.

Both have been in business for many years and have built their businesses in the same way. Just after periods of value outperformance, when their track records are strong, VCI and CVI both aggressively market their records, building their asset bases. After periods of value under-performance, when their track records are weak, VCI and CVI both work hard to keep their clients from defecting. The result of all this is a repeating pattern of strong asset growth followed by weak asset growth or even asset contraction, followed by strong asset growth, etc.

But there two things wrong with this picture. The first is that investors are constantly making the wrong decisions about VCI and CVI: engaging them just when they are about to enter a period of weak performance and terminating them just when they are about to enter a period of strong performance. Investors are, in effect, buying high and selling low.[336]

The second problem is that VCI turns out to be a very competent manager, while CVI is well below average: investors should be engaging VCI and should be avoiding CVI. But investors don't do this because the differences in aggregate performance between the firms are overwhelmed by the sector rotation effect: being a deep value manager had more impact on a manager's performance than did being a good manager.

The manager's performance has been "managed." As I noted back in Chapter 6, corporate executives have become adept at "managing earnings," ensuring that investor expectations for quarterly per share earnings are met, but in the process giving a misleading picture of the consistency of the company's operations. Money managers can also be quite adept at "managing performance," i.e., putting the best possible spin on a checkered track record. Recently, for example, a well-known—and well-regarded—aggressive growth manager touted its excellent 2003 record (+60%) and its excellent ten-year record (+16.9%). What the manager failed to note was that in the years 2000, 2001 and 2002 it ranked in the 95th percentile among all mid-cap equity managers. In other words, for three years running the manager was among the worst 5% of all its competitors. So which picture was truer—the good long-term performance or the disastrous recent three-year performance? The

---

[336] This is usually a measurement problem: investors are measuring both managers against something other than the appropriate benchmark (in this case it would be something like the Russell 1000 Value Index). Over very long periods, it's appropriate to measure deep value managers (and aggressive growth managers, etc.) against the S&P 500. But if we do that over shorter periods we will find ourselves constantly buying high and selling low.

answer is both. But the manager "managed" its performance claims to make it look far better—far more consistent—than it really was.

The good track record is genuine, but the manager is a changed firm. Finally, the manager's good five-year track record may be unimpeachable, but investors who engage the manager will find that they have hired a very different firm from the one that produced the good performance. The firm may have changed, for example, because the asset base of the firm has grown dramatically and the founding professionals can no longer both manage the business and pick good stocks. (There is no necessary correlation between people's ability to pick stocks and their ability to manage a business.) Or the firm may have changed because the investment professionals who produced the track record are no longer with the firm. Or the firm may have been sold, and the original owners are now rich and lazy or, worse, reporting to some bureaucrat in Duluth.

In other words, in addition to the track record being real, it is always useful for investors to be sure that the firm that built the track record is the firm we are hiring.

Characteristics of Best-in-Class Managers

It is, alas, not possible to define the characteristics of best-in-class managers in a way that is detailed enough to enable investors to apply a simple template and see if the manager fits it or not. Too much judgment and experience are involved. Nonetheless, the main characteristics of best-in-class managers are simple enough to state. They are as follows:

- *Investment philosophy.* The quality of a portfolio manager's investment philosophy is perhaps the single most critical element in judging whether the manager is likely to be capable of sustained outperformance. Unfortunately, this issue is also likely to be of little help to individual investors in identifying best-in-class managers. The reason is that there is no such thing as a money manager who can't articulate an investment philosophy that sounds good. The only way to know whether or not what sounds good actually holds any water is to put the manager through a thorough, multi-level scrutiny, ending with an intensive on-site grilling of the manager and its senior team by an investment professional who has had vast experience interviewing and working with managers.
- *Discipline.* Even the most solid investment philosophy won't create wealth unless it is implemented in a disciplined manner. To determine whether the manager is a disciplined investor and is sticking to its philosophy in

good times and bad, it is necessary to conduct a detailed review of the manager's performance during periods when the wind has been at its back and when the wind has been in its face. Attribution analysis and a close examination of investment decisions that turned out badly can shed important light on these questions. In particular, "sell discipline"—strict rules that determine when a security is to be sold—is important. As noted above, sell discipline tended to disappear during the bull market of the 1980s and 1990s. Under more normal market conditions, however, sell discipline is crucial. Otherwise, managers will tend to hold appreciated securities far too long and to believe that they are "smarter than the market," therefore holding on to under-performing securities that should be sold.

- *Experience.* Any manager can outperform over a short period of time, and investors who hire such managers after that period of outperformance will almost always—*almost always*—be disappointed. The five-year rule is intended to enable investors to observe a manager's performance over a full market cycle, that is, a period of time during which the manager's investment style and philosophy are in vogue as well as a period of time when they are out of fashion. Hence, five years might be too short a period of time or, in a few cases, it might be more time than we need.
- *Asset base.* Some investment philosophies and styles can be carried on at huge scale, but others will be successful only if they remain niche businesses. Bond managers can oversee tens of billions of dollars with relative ease. Indeed, scale matters in bond management because trading costs, especially the costs of trading municipal bonds, can eat up a large fraction of the potential returns. But small cap managers face the opposite problem: the float[337] of most small cap stocks can be very thin, making the management of even a few hundreds of millions of dollars problematic. Many professionals believe that trading costs are so high with smaller stocks that any return advantage is completely negated. Thus, with small cap stocks smaller really is better all around.
- *Alignment of interests.* Money management is a business, and like any business operator, money managers will attempt to maximize their profits. If those profits can only be maximized by acting in the interests of clients, the manager-client relationship is likely to be satisfactory to both

[337] "Float" is simply a measure of trading volume. It is the total number of outstanding shares less the number of restricted shares.

parties. Unfortunately, there are many ways in which money managers can increase their profits at the expense of client investment returns. One obvious example is for the manager to emphasize asset gathering over alpha generation.[338] It is far easier for a manager to increase its fee revenue by focusing on proven sales techniques than by focusing on the complex challenges associated with investment outperformance. As a result, most money management firms are really sales organizations, not money management organizations, and are to be avoided on that ground alone.[339] The general practice of charging asset-based fees is also problematic. If the manager's results are poor, the manager's fee declines but he still gets paid; the client, on the other hand, has lost real money.

- *Organizational stability.* A sound investment philosophy can only be implemented by an investment team that has worked together for years and that has experienced little, if any, turnover. Even among managers who have produced outstanding long-term track records, organizational instability is an excellent early warning sign that performance is likely to deteriorate. The same is true of asset management firms that have recently been purchased—this is almost always a sure sign of bad things to come.
- *Quality of the client base.* This may seem an odd characteristic to focus on, but in fact the quality of a manager's client base can make an important difference in the manager's ability to function with minimal interference and maximum stability. Typically, managers who have performed competently over the course of many years, but who are never (or rarely) the best-performing managers in any year, will wind up with a stable, sophisticated client base that understands what the manager is doing and that will be patient with periods of underperformance. Managers who have shot the lights out now and then, followed by periods of very poor performance, will tend to wind up with a client base consisting mainly of unsophisticated, "hot money" clients. It is virtually

---

338 "Alpha" is a measure of risk-adjusted outperformance.

339 Looking at the manager-client relationship in terms of principal-agent theory, David Swensen (CIO at Yale) has acutely analyzed the problems investors face in trying to align manager interests with their own. See David Swensen, *Pioneering Portfolio Management: An Unconventional Approach to Institutional Investment* (The Free Press, 2000), pp. 4-6, 197, 248-292.

impossible for a manager to operate sensibly if clients are constantly pouring money into the firm and then pulling it out again.

- *Personal integrity*. This should go without saying. While it may seem harsh, any blemishes on a manager's record should disqualify the firm from serious consideration. This includes regulatory problems at the firm level and also personal problems at the individual professional level and even, on occasion, at the individual personal level.

President Reagan, during the SALT[340] negotiations, was fond of saying, "Trust—but verify." The same is true of managers. It is always interesting to hear a manager talk about its style, but a returns-based style attribution analysis rarely exaggerates. The professionals at a firm may appear to be the very soul of rectitude, but a background check will result in far fewer sleepless nights for investors. Broadly speaking, substantial families have no choice but to place their capital at risk. But narrowly speaking, substantial families never have to place their capital with any particular manager. Before we entrust our capital to a manager, we should always "trust—but verify."

Objectionable Characteristics

In addition to the useful characteristics of managers just discussed, it is also important to look for the presence or absence of objectionable characteristics in asset management firms, such as a focus on asset gathering, a weak trading or back office operation, a predominance of inexperienced personnel, a bureaucratic organizational framework, a history of regulatory problems, an organization that is primarily engaged in activities other than money management, and so on. The presence of even one of these objectionable characteristics should raise an immediate alarm, requiring further investigation, and the presence of two or more should send investors running in the other direction.[341]

Manager Habitat

Several of the positive and negative characteristics of managers discussed above are closely associated with the kind of organization in which a manager works. These organizations range from gigantic global banks that are involved

---

340 Strategic Arms Limitation Talks.

341 One of the best summaries of desirable and undesirable manager characteristics was produced by The Investment Fund for Foundations. See TIFF's Web site at www.tiff.org.

in asset management activities only to help smooth out their earnings streams, to tiny boutique firms consisting of a manager, a trader and an administrative person. Managers can be paid salaries, can be paid salaries plus a bonus for performance or asset gathering, or can own the revenue stream of their firms.

Generally speaking, the closer a manager's working habitat is to the "boutique" end of the spectrum, the more likely the manager is to produce sustained outperformance. Managers who work in large organizations that are mainly engaged in activities other than asset management are really middle managers in a gigantic bureaucracy that doesn't much care about the work they do. The parent firm will blow hot and cold on asset management as a business depending on its short-term profitability. Managers with very modest talents can survive, and even thrive, in such firms because there are many career paths open to them. Managers with talent, and who are uninterested in other kinds of work, tend to migrate away from large organizations and toward smaller organizations that exist only to manage money and which will sink or swim according to the quality of their performance. Hence, investors looking for talented managers will do well to focus on smaller management firms.

In particular, hedge funds would appear, at least on the surface, to represent the ideal habitat for a talented manager. In a hedge fund the investment professionals own the firm and make their money mainly by generating good absolute performance. In addition, many hedge fund managers have much of their own money invested in their firms. Because most hedge funds are small, the annual asset-based fee will be relatively unattractive. In other words, most of hedge fund managers' compensation is expected to come from their share of the profits, plus their increase in wealth that results from the sound management of their own capital. As a result, untalented managers simply can't survive in the hedge fund world, or can't survive as well as they could if they were buried in a large, bureaucratic firm where good behavior and sucking up to senior management will count for more than alpha generation.

But there are exceptions to every general rule and this one is no exception. Hedge funds, for example, have characteristics that make them problematic for many investors (including illiquidity and lack of transparency). But even among traditional, long-only managers, some asset classes and management styles tend to work better in larger, rather than smaller, institutions. As noted above, for example, bond management lends itself to large scale, and hence we find many talented fixed income managers who are happily working in very large organizations where scale results in much lower trading costs and where the cost of technology can be readily borne. The same is true of cash management and of certain complex derivative transactions that can only be conducted by firms with serious capital bases.

Ongoing Monitoring of Managers

This topic is beyond the scope of the chapter,[342] but it is important to point out that engaging a manager, even a very good one, is only half the battle. We must also monitor the manager closely to ensure that it is performing as advertised. The peculiar difficulty with this task is that we must balance monitoring that is strict enough to uncover early danger signals with the patience and perspective not to terminate the manager at the first sign of trouble. Every manager experiences periods of under-performance, markets when its investment style is out of fashion, quarters or even years during which it seems to have lost its way. The main mistake investors make, it should be remembered, is firing high quality managers just after a period of under-performance and hiring another manager who, over the next market cycle, under-performs the terminated manager. Roughly 75% of all manager terminations are mistakes in exactly that sense.[343]

Finding Best-in-Class Managers

I don't know how other advisory firms go about the process of identifying managers who are likely to outperform,[344] but I know how we do it at Greycourt & Co., Inc. And while our processes and procedures—to say nothing of our judgment—could perhaps bear tweaking from time to time, I think the Greycourt system works pretty well. It's a three-level analysis, and it works generally like this.

The early phases of this process rely largely on quantitative screening and evaluation criteria while later stages are almost entirely qualitative in nature. Our ultimate goal is not to identify which managers have outperformed in the past—any fool with a computer can do that! Rather, our objective is to identify the reasons *why* selected managers have outperformed in the past and to judge whether those reasons are likely to persist into the future.

The first step ("Level I") in our due diligence process requires managers to be measured against a series of six objective criteria. These criteria vary somewhat from asset class to asset class but generally are as follows:

- Criteria #1: Appropriate R^2 to the relevant benchmark.

---

[342] See Chapter 13, which contains a sample form of manager guidelines, which are essential to the successful monitoring of manager performance.

[343] Note that this mistake is the flipside of the mistake of hiring a manager who has recently shot the lights out.

[344] Well, ok, I do know how other firms do it; I'm just too polite to rat them out.

- Criteria #2: Product return rank was in the top third of the peer universe.
- Criteria #3: Product return rank was not in the bottom quartile of the peer universe in any of the most recent 5 calendar years.
- Criteria #4: Product risk adjusted return rank was in the top third of the peer universe.
- Criteria #5: Product upside capture was at least 100%.
- Criteria #6: Product downside capture was close to the benchmark.

Greycourt uses these screening criteria in two ways. First, the Level I screen allows us to quickly determine if we should spend our limited time meeting with salespeople seeking to introduce us to their products. Second, The Level I screen allows us to efficiently comb through publicly available manager databases such as Morningstar, PSN and HFR to see if there are potentially interesting managers that we may not yet have knowledge of. It is important to note, however, that many of the managers we use or are interested in do not always pass all six of our Level I criteria. For example, we are often interested in concentrated equity managers who have low R^2 statistics but who otherwise are excellent. Greycourt Managing Directors have the discretion (which they use often) to pursue further research on any manager whether or not they pass all six Level I criteria. Finally, while the Level I screening process works well for most long-only asset classes, it is somewhat less useful in evaluating alternative asset classes such as private equity, real estate, hedge funds, etc.

The next step (Level II) in our manager process involves gathering as much information as possible about a potentially interesting manager. Initially, our information-gathering focuses on further screening-out inappropriate managers. For example, we seek to determine if a manager is closed to new assets, whether they have reasonable minimum account sizes, whether their fees are competitive, what kinds of investment vehicles they offer (e.g., separate accounts, limited partnerships, mutual funds, etc.), or whether they have unusually high turnover which may cause them to be tax inefficient. These additional early Level II questions do not take much time to complete and often weed out another 25% to 50% of the managers who made it past the Level I process.

Once the list of qualified manager candidates has been narrowed, we seek to gather a broad array of information about each manager in order to formulate an opinion as to how they were able to generate attractive results in the past. The types of information typically acquired includes:

- Obtaining manager pitch books
- Arranging for a live manager presentation

- Completing a Greycourt Manager Questionnaire
- Reviewing SEC Form ADV
- Conducting web searches for relevant news and articles on the manager
- Preparing comprehensive style-based return attribution analysis

All information gathered is immediately recorded in Greycourt's proprietary manager database so that it becomes instantly available to each of our investment professionals. We view our ability to access all manager information on a timely basis as critical to our ability to deliver high quality and consistent advice to our clients. As a result, we are constantly trying to improve the quality of available data. For example, one of the most recent enhancements to the Greycourt database has been to deploy WebEx technology, enabling us to record live manager presentations for later review.

Once we have evaluated all of a manager's information, a Greycourt investment analyst will prepare a brief two-page profile summarizing the manager's key attributes. At the same time, a Greycourt Managing Director will begin to formulate an initial opinion (referred to internally as our "Investment Thesis") seeking to articulate concisely why we believe the manager in question has succeeded in generating superior results in the past.

The third phase of our evaluation (Level III) is the most important and also the most qualitative. The objective of our Level III analysis is to attempt to validate the preliminary Investment Thesis established during the earlier Level II review. During this final phase, one or more of Greycourt's Managing Directors will meet with the senior members of the candidate manager's firm usually in their offices. At these meetings we seek to better understand the manager's investment philosophy, risk controls, tax sensitivity, organizational structure, incentive compensation plans, operating infrastructure, compliance efforts and interpersonal dynamics.

Our Level III efforts culminate in a peer review in which the sponsoring Managing Director articulates, in writing, his or her view of the candidate manager's differential advantages, comments on the sustainability of those advantages, and identifies potential risk factors that might invalidate the perceived sustainable advantage. Managing Director-wide conference calls are held approximately twice each month to discuss candidate managers who have completed all three levels of review. Very often the Level III peer review call results in additional questions being raised or further information being requested. Assuming that all additional questions are satisfactorily addressed, a formal vote is conducted in which all Managing Directors either approve or reject the candidate manager for inclusion on Greycourt's recommended list.

Once approved, we seek to monitor approved managers' continuing quality in several ways. First, Greycourt generates a report that measures the difference between each manager's monthly return and its relevant benchmark (this difference is referred to as "tracking error"). We then compare that month's tracking error to the manager's 5-year historical tracking error. To the extent that a manager's tracking error in any given month is +/- 1 standard deviation away from its historical tracking error, we initiate a call to the manager. During these calls we will ask them to describe what factor(s) caused them to perform unusually well or unusually poorly that month. Their responses are recorded in our database. Simply as a result of this monthly review process, we will, on average, speak to our managers three times per year. Our second form of review is to formally re-evaluate each approved manager on an annual basis in order to re-affirm our belief in our stated Investment Thesis.

When one of our managers experiences a change of control, acquires another firm or suffers the loss of a key portfolio manager, we immediately seek to understand how these changes may affect our stated Investment Thesis. The urgency with which we re-examine a manager undergoing a change depends on that manager's inherent volatility. For example, the departure of a key professional at a municipal bond manager is less alarming than the departure of a key professional in a small cap growth firm. We seek to quantify our view of each manager's inherent risk by developing a numerical risk measure on each manager used. Developing this numerical assessment of manager risk is a regular part of our Level III analysis. Also, as noted earlier, part of our Level III review is to articulate specific risk factors that may invalidate our Investment Thesis. If one of those identified risks becomes a reality (such as a key professional's departure) we will fully re-examine the manager.

Managers are rarely terminated for poor performance alone. Greycourt terminates managers when it is deemed that they no longer maintain the differential advantages that caused us to hire them in the first place. Examples of reasons that have prompted us to terminate managers in the past include:

- Departure of a critical investment professional(s)
- Significant style drift
- Failure to limit asset growth to levels promised
- Failure to communicate or be responsive to requests for information

It is the responsibility of the Greycourt Managing Director assigned to track a particular manager to identify and research potential problems and to recommend a course of action.

Obviously, this approach to identifying best-in-class managers will be far beyond the capabilities of most individual families. And there is nothing sacrosanct about the way Greycourt goes about the process. However, if our financial advisors aren't following something like the process as described above, perhaps we're working with the wrong advisors.

Optimizing Manager Selection

In some ways, building a portfolio of money managers is analogous to designing an overall investment portfolio. Let's examine several ways in which manager selection is similar to selecting assets classes.[345]

The problem of variance drain. Most investors understand that riskier portfolios must significantly outperform less risky portfolios because of the headwind of variance drain: a high return doesn't generate wealth very quickly if it is associated with high volatility, simply as a result of the mathematics.[346] The same principle holds with high-returning managers, but here the problem is even more insidious. Investors looking for talented managers understand intuitively that managers who hug their benchmarks are unlikely to outperform (thanks to their fees and trading costs), and that such managers are especially unlikely to outperform significantly (by definition, since they are benchmark huggers).

Hence, many investors focus their search for talented managers on firms that own highly concentrated positions—often no more than 10 to 20 stocks. Presumably, each of these positions represents an idea of great conviction on the part of the manager, and since the manager's portfolio is quite different from that of the index it is managing against, the possibility of outperforming that index—and even of outperforming it significantly—is considerable.

---

345 An excellent discussion of this issue, from a slightly different perspective, appears in *Finding Consistent Alpha*, by Seth J. Masters and Drew W. Demakis (Alliance Capital Management LP, July 2003).

346 To adjust wealth calculations for the variability of the returns, investors can use the approximation: C = R—σ2/2, where R is the mean return and σ is the variance in the return. See Tom Messmore, "Variance Drain," *Journal of Portfolio Management* (Summer 1995), p. 106. But there is an even simpler way to understand the point: portfolios that decline by any amount must appreciate by a greater amount just to break even. A portfolio that declines by 50% in year one must appreciate 100% in year two to get even. And it works the other way: a portfolio that appreciates 100% in year one, then declines only 50% in year two, is back to breakeven.

Alas, this is the beginning of the inquiry, not the end. Like portfolios, managers face the headwind of variance drain. Our concentrated manager may outperform all right, but unless that outperformance is very considerable, it may not add as much to our wealth as the more modest outperformance of the benchmark-hugger we so easily disdained a few paragraphs ago. The problem is that risk drag rises faster than alpha, so that high-alpha managers must not simply outperform to grow our wealth—they must outperform very substantially. Let's examine briefly how this phenomenon works.

We measure the volatility of investment portfolios absolutely (the Standard Deviation of the portfolio around its mean return), but the volatility of managers is typically measured relatively—relative to the benchmark the manager is being measured against. The measuring rod is "tracking error," the average deviation of the manager's performance from the performance of the benchmark. Managers can only add value to a benchmark's return by deviating from the benchmark, of course. They may own fewer stocks, they may buy and sell those stocks at different times, they may own stocks in weights that differ from the index weightings, and so on.

As noted above, many investors look for managers who hold fewer, higher-conviction positions. Unfortunately, these managers virtually always exhibit significant tracking error, and the larger that tracking error is the greater the manager's outperformance must be to grow wealth rapidly. A manager with low tracking error (our despised benchmark-hugger, for example) can grow wealth nicely by producing modest outperformance. But our venerated manager with the concentrated portfolio will have to outperform very substantially to produce as much wealth for us.[347]

Having our cake and eating it, too. Let's stare our dilemma straight in the face. As investors, we have three choices in our search for outperforming managers who will grow our wealth rapidly:

- We can throw in the towel and index our exposure. This will give us the market return—the risk premium we obtain simply by investing in

[347] We can handicap managers by combining tracking error with outperformance to determine a manager's "information ratio." Nobel laureate William Sharpe developed this concept, dividing the value added by a manager by the manager's tracking error. Obviously, managers who can deliver the same value-added with lower tracking error will have higher information ratios, and therefore be more desirable. Unfortunately, the time period required for an information ratio to be meaningful is huge: it requires 16 years to identify a top-quartile manager with 95 percent confidence. Masters and Demakis, op. cit., note 344, p. 3.

stocks rather than T-bills—but our search for alpha will be over before it began.

- We can engage benchmark-hugging managers—firms that, in the large cap sector, may own 250 stocks. We might do this because we are fearful that more concentrated managers might dramatically *underperform*. Or we might do it because we recognize that the low tracking errors of benchmark-hugging managers mean that even modest outperformance will grow our wealth nicely: such managers face only very modest variance drain. But this choice is fraught with danger. If our benchmark-hugging manager has an information ratio of +0.1, it would require an astonishing 271 years for us to be 95% confident that the manager's performance wasn't just lucky.[348]
- Finally, if we are really serious about finding alpha, we can engage managers who hold only a few positions, in each of which they have great conviction. We are getting, we hope, only the managers' best ideas. If these managers have information ratios of +0.5, we could have 95% confidence in their skill after "only" 11 years. The problem, as noted above, is that risk drag grows faster than manager alpha, with the result that only the most extraordinarily talented managers will outperform sufficiently to grow our wealth faster than the index fund or the benchmark-hugger.

What to do? One approach is to treat managers like asset classes. When we design our overall investment portfolios, we mix and match asset classes that have less than perfect return correlations in an attempt to achieve "the only free lunch available in the investment world," as someone has said. If we design our portfolios correctly, we will achieve both higher expected returns and lower expected risks than naively designed portfolios. Why not adopt the same approach with our money managers?

Like asset classes, the investment performance of any two or more managers can be highly correlated, can exhibit low correlation, or could even be negatively correlated. And while negatively correlated asset classes are hard to come by, it is relatively easy to find managers whose performance is negatively correlated.

Imagine that we are building out our US large cap portfolio. Rather than indexing or engaging a benchmark-hugger, we identify two highly concentrated managers in whom we have great confidence. Importantly, these managers are very different: a deep value manager and an aggressive growth manager. The likelihood that these two managers would own any securities in

---

[348] Masters and Demakis, op. cit., note 344, p. 3.

common would be remote, and it is nearly as unlikely that they will be invested in the same industries or sectors. While it is true that each of our managers would have a high tracking error, *the combination of the two managers would have a much lower tracking error*. Our US large cap portfolio would track the S&P 500 Index pretty closely, and yet we would be receiving most of the benefit of the high alpha we expect each manager to deliver. We have succeeded in capturing the Holy Grail of high outperformance and low tracking error, and our wealth will grow rapidly.

Alternative Managers—Hedge Funds

Prophesy as much as you like,
but always hedge.
—Oliver Wendell Holmes

As Gertrude Stein might say, a manager is a manager is a manager. But a hedge fund manager is a manager only more so—a manager on steroids, if you will. Everything said above about managers in general goes for hedge fund managers, but they are all even more critical. Long-only managers can underperform, sometimes substantially, but they rarely blow up and lose all an investor's capital. Hedge funds do this quite regularly.

The fundamental concern about hedge funds is that the assets managed by hedge fund managers are not held in custody in the usual sense of the word. Custody issues are discussed in Chapter 17, but in brief, when an investor engages a long-only manager, the manager never actually gains control of the investor's cash or securities. Cash and securities remain in the hands of a bank or brokerage firm that is acting as the asset custodian for the investor. The portfolio manager has, in reality or in effect, a limited power of attorney to direct the investments in the account. The manager can cause the account to sell GE and buy Microsoft. But the GE stock doesn't leave the custodian's hands until the proceeds from its sale arrive, and the funds required to buy Microsoft don't leave the custodian's hands until the Microsoft stock arrives. (All this occurs electronically, of course, and is subject to the prevailing settlement rules.)

But when an investor engages a hedge fund manager, the cash and securities are held in accounts controlled by the hedge fund, not the investor. Typically, the cash and securities are held by a so-called "prime broker" for the hedge fund. But whereas in a traditional custody arrangement the investor is the custodian's client, in a prime brokerage arrangement the hedge fund is the broker's customer. The prime broker's loyalties—to say nothing of his lucrative business dealings—lie exclusively with the hedge fund. If the hedge fund manager wakes up some morning with a hankering to go to Brazil, he can simply wire all the funds in the hedge fund account to his private account in Sao Paulo and hop on the next plane. (He or she will have more trouble passing through security at Kennedy Airport than stealing our money.) The same is true if the manager wakes up in the morning with a hankering to buy his girlfriend a new Jaguar or to bet the house shorting an obscure tech stock whose price is about to go through the roof.

In short, when looking for a hedge fund manager to engage, we will want to keep in mind all the challenges discussed above about long-only managers, then perhaps square them. And after we have finished all that diligence, we will want to add a whole new level of inquiry, namely, thorough background checks (civil and criminal) on the principals in each hedge fund we are considering. Background checks won't necessarily identify hedge fund managers who will turn out to be incompetent or foolish, but they will identify managers who have checkered pasts and who are therefore exponentially more likely to keep checkering away—this time with our money.

Issues to Focus On

The issues we should focus on in identifying hedge funds that are likely to outperform in the future, and to avoid hedge funds that (a) won't, or (b) will blow up, are those discussed in Chapter 12. Before looking for hedge fund managers, investors should review Chapter 12 carefully, but here is a summary of the challenges associated with investing in hedge funds:

- Although many of the most talented money managers have migrated to the hedge fund platform, many more incompetent or venal managers have also taken refuge there.
- As large pension plans try to gain exposure to hedge funds, vastly too much money is coming into the business, driving down returns.
- Hedge fund returns often come in the form of short-term gains, which are highly taxed.
- The lack of transparency that characterizes hedge fund portfolios presents a kind of risk that ought to be unacceptable to most investors.
- Rather than using traditional bank custodians, hedge fund managers use prime brokers. The prime brokers have gigantic conflicts of interest, and in any event their interests are far more aligned with the hedge funds than with the investors.

- ♦ In the upside-down world of hedge funds, virtually every advantage claimed by the industry also represents a potential disadvantage for investors. The absence of excessive capital under management, benchmark objectives, diversification requirements, daily liquidity, and significant organizational time demands are plusses, to be sure, but they are also gigantic minuses.
- ♦ The high fees charged by hedge fund managers is not justified by anything inherent in the hedge fund format; only talent justifies them.
- ♦ Hedge fund fee structures have features that can prove to be mischievous, especially high water marks.
- ♦ Investors who have traditionally focused on tracking error to monitor their managers will be sorely disappointed with hedge funds, as it is virtually impossible to create a benchmark that will be useful for monitoring a hedge fund portfolio.
- ♦ Investors will find that the correlations between hedge funds, on the one hand, and the equity and fixed income markets, on the other, will tend to increase dramatically just when investors most need diversification.
- ♦ Many hedge fund investors may be expecting the impossible, namely, that hedge fund returns will remain high even in the face of sustained bear market conditions.
- ♦ It is extraordinarily difficult to monitor hedge funds on an ongoing basis. Yet, they require far more in the way of monitoring than do long-only managers.

Alternative Managers—Private Equity Funds

Private equity, broadly speaking, encompasses venture capital, management or leveraged buyouts, and mezzanine financings. These strategies can be executed directly, by investing in individual deals; indirectly, by investing in venture, buyout, or mezzanine limited partnerships (which then invest in direct deals); or very indirectly, by investing in funds of funds which invest in limited partnerships which then invest in direct deals.

Investing Directly (Angel Investing)

A very large percentage of wealthy families invest in direct deals—venture capital startups and slightly more advanced companies, mainly—acting as "angel" investors. Sometimes these investments work out very well, especially when the family has expertise in the field they have invested in. Far, far more often, however, the word "angel" is all too appropriate—the families are providing capital to hopelessly doomed enterprises in precisely the same way that the residents of heaven provide salvation to hopelessly fallen sinners. Investing successfully in individual deals requires a special skill set as complex as, or more complex than, successfully buying and selling individual securities. It also requires a huge commitment of time—100-hour weeks are routine for successful venture capitalists. Finally, it requires access to a strong and diversified deal flow. Unless family members have the skills of professional venture capitalists, are willing to commit the necessary time, and have the required deal flow, the results of angel investing are likely to be more or less precisely proportional to the constrained capabilities.

Of course, there is another way to look at angel investing. In Chapter 2, I point out that the results to American society of angel investing are profoundly greater than the results to the angel investors themselves. In addition, many members of wealthy families hugely enjoy working with young entrepreneurs. From these perspectives, angel investing can be seen as a civic project of some importance, and the (usually dim) financial outcomes to be a minor consideration. Thus, viewed from the perspective of the greater good, we can applaud angel investors and only wish there were even more of them. At the same time, when we are counseling individual families we have to point out that these are low percentage activities and that they come with at least modest opportunity costs.

Investing Indirectly via Individual Partnerships

If investing directly in deals as angel investors is likely to prove unproductive, the obvious solution would seem to be to engage professionals to do our investing for us, by investing in private equity limited partnerships. Alas, as with so much in the investment world, the obvious solution would likely be wrong. I pointed out above that successful investing in private equity requires a special skill set, a huge commitment of time, and a strong deal flow. It doesn't seem impossible to believe that many dozens of partnerships, perhaps hundreds, could amass this human and business capital and achieve results far superior to those of amateur angels. Indeed, this is precisely the actual outcome—the average PE fund significantly outperforms the average angel investor.

Unfortunately, however, this is not enough. Committing capital to private equity funds carries with it very significant risks, including long-term illiquidity and the possibility that all or most of the capital will be destroyed. These risks require a return that is not merely better than that of angel investors, but a return that is exceptional in absolute terms. The track record of private equity partnerships is reasonably good, but unfortunately it is not good enough: the average private equity partnership performs over time barely better than an indexed position in the US equity markets. Since those equity markets offer us almost instant liquidity and the virtual assurance that our capital losses over time will be modest at worst, we will have to do not just a bit better to justify investing in private equity—we need to do a whole lot better.

Looking at the actual investment performance results, what we find is that only a small group of the very best private equity partnerships can be relied upon to produce superior returns over longer periods of time. By "superior" returns I mean roughly a 3X return cash-on-cash. Given the time period over which the cash goes out and comes back, this typically equates to IRRs of 15% in the worst vintage years, and 20% plus in decent years.[349] Of the hundreds of PE partnerships in existence, only a few dozen will consistently achieve these results, and the chance that our local venture capital fund will be one of those tiny few is extremely remote.[350]

Investing Indirectly via Private Equity Funds of Funds

In PE investing then, the name of the game is access, access, access. If we can have our capital managed mainly by the very top partnerships in the business, and if we can have the discipline to invest regularly year-in and year-out,[351] PE investing will prove invaluable to us. The only reasonably sure way to achieve this result for most families is to invest through a fund of funds.

Private equity funds of funds aggregate investor capital, then select a group of individual partnerships in which to invest. Some funds of funds focus on

---

349 Long-only manager performance is typically calculated using time-weighted returns, but this approach doesn't work well with private equity. IRRs and cash-on-cash will give a better idea of the true value of a fund of funds.

350 According to FLAG Capital Management, one of the best PE funds of funds, top-tier venture capital funds have outperformed the median fund by 15% per year (per year!), and top-tier buyouts funds have outperformed the median fund by 10% per year. *Venture Insights*, FLAG Capital Management (2nd Quarter, 2001).

351 In addition to diversifying our PE exposure by stage and type (venture, buyouts, etc.), by industry (tech, biotech, software, etc.), and by partnerships, it is very important to diversify by vintage year. The year in which we commit our capital will have a profound effect on our return. This is because PE returns are cyclical—but, unfortunately, not predictably cyclical. We must therefore invest regularly.

one sector of the private equity market—buyouts, let's say, or venture capital—while others offer blended exposures to several sectors. The key to identifying a good fund of funds is to look at the quality of the underlying partnerships. Simply using funds of funds to achieve diversification isn't good enough—we just discussed the fact that the average private equity fund doesn't generate enough of a return to justify its risk. Unfortunately there are now well over 100 PE funds of funds in existence, which means that most of them are investing in ordinary partnerships. And, unfortunately, most investors can't distinguish top-tier partnerships from run-of-the-mill partnerships (which is what enables so many funds of funds to exist). If we can't identify top-tier funds ourselves, we will need to engage an advisor who knows the PE fund of funds space and can help guide us through the wilderness.

In brief, however, here are some of the things we should be looking for in a private equity fund of funds:

- *Access.* Enough said.
- *Fund size.* There are two ways to make money in the fund of funds business. One way is to raise one gigantic fund after another, using not terrific past returns to gather capital, but terrific marketing teams. The annual fees on huge funds will make everyone at the fund of funds rich, even if the returns to investors are poor. The other way to make money is to raise smaller funds, using the annual fees to cover costs and getting rich, if at all, only from the carry.[352] These are the funds of funds we want to invest with.
- *Investment strategy.* If we are expecting to invest in a buyouts fund of funds, and find that we have instead invested in a venture capital-oriented fund of funds (or vice versa), we are unlikely to be happy about it. It is obviously important to know what the fund of fund's investment strategy is and to make sure it is consistent with our own needs.
- *Track record.* As with individual PE funds, the track records of PE funds of funds tend to be stable: a fund of funds with a good past track record is likely to be a fund of funds with a good future track record. The proliferation of funds of funds means that most of them have very short track records or none at all. Avoid.
- *Experience.* Allied to the last point is the question of how long the fund of funds has been in business, and what level of experience the fund of

352 PE funds of funds charge annual fees plus a carried interest in the profits produced by the underlying partnerships.

fund's managers have. Generally speaking, the longer the fund of funds has been around, the better its track record will be, if only because so many of the newer funds are really asset-gatherers, not investors.

A Note About Holding PE Capital in Reserve

When we commit to a PE fund or fund of funds, all the capital isn't called down immediately. Instead, the manager will call the funds as it finds opportunities to invest it. PE investors are therefore faced with a dilemma. We have committed our capital to a PE fund and we are legally obligated to live up to that commitment. (The penalties for failing to meet a capital call are draconian.) Yet, our PE manager takes no responsibility for the fact that our capital won't be called down for some time—usually, a period of three or four years. If we calculated PE returns from the date of the commitment to the date the fund terminates, our PE returns would look very much worse than they do.

So the question arises: where should committed-but-uncalled capital be invested? Many investors, not wanting to be caught short, keep that capital in a money market fund or some similar low-risk investment. But this creates a very serious opportunity cost for us. Money market fund returns are very low, typically equaling about the rate of inflation. PE returns (we hope) are very high. But when we blend the low returns we get on our money market funds with the high returns we get on our PE funds, the drag of the former on the latter will be substantial.

Instead, investors may wish to invest most of their committed-but-uncalled capital in equities, moving the funds to, perhaps, a short-term bond fund as the likely date of a capital call approaches. Over the long term, this strategy will also reduce the overall return on our committed PE capital, but not by nearly as much as if we kept the total commitment in cash.

Three

Chapter 14

Asset Location, Implementation and Transition

In this chapter we will discuss three issues to which many investors and advisors give short shrift. The first is the asset location issue: how to decide which of the many family investment "pockets" to use for which investment assets. The second issue is the implementation issue: how to move from a fully or mainly liquid portfolio to a fully invested position. (Or how to move from one strategy to a very different strategy, although one hopes this would be a rare event.) Finally, we will discuss the issues associated with transitioning assets from one manager to another. Properly negotiating each of these challenges can have an important impact on a family's wealth.

Asset Location Issues

Because that's where the money is.[353]

If this were a book directed to investment advisors, the examination of asset location issues would require one of the longest and most arcane discussions. "Asset location," as its name implies, refers to the question of where to locate each of the investments expected to be employed in the overall portfolio. Unlike most institutional investors, private investors own their assets in many, many different forms. For example, it is not unusual to encounter, in one large family, assets held in the private accounts of different generations, in the private accounts of many different individuals, in the accounts of different collateral family units, in family investment partnerships and family limited partnerships, in charitable foundations, family trusts, IRAs, closely held corporations, LLCs,

---

353 Willy Sutton, when asked why he robbed banks.

offshore vehicles, intentionally defective grantor trusts, dynasty trusts, and the alphabet soup of tax and charitable vehicles such as GRATs, GRUTs, CRATs, CLATs, CLUTs, CRUTs, NIMCRUTs, cascading GRATs and so on. Each of these vehicles is typically created for a specific, largely non-investment purpose, but each holds assets that must nonetheless be properly invested. The decision about which investments should go into which vehicles is mainly a tax-driven issue, but other issues will also be present and they will sometimes be decisive.

Fortunately, however, this is a book for investors, not advisors, and hence I will only identify the asset location issue as a crucial one and illustrate some of its complexities. We will have to rely on our advisors to possess the knowledge of taxes, trusts, estate planning, prudent investment principles and so on that will be required to make the final decisions about asset location, but it is very important that we recognize the issue and understand its importance. The simple fact is that, all too often, the good work of our tax, trust and estate planning advisors is undone by financial advisors who misunderstand the nature and taxability of complex vehicles.

Asset Location Issues in the Wollason Family

In that spirit, let's examine an asset location issue that appears on the surface to be straightforward, but that will illustrate at least some of the complexities of the process. The Wollason family (a hypothetical family whose circumstances are far too simple to be real!) has only two investment "locations." The first is simply private family assets held in the joint names of the patriarch and matriarch. These assets aggregate about $25 million. The second "location" is the Wollason Family Foundation, a private foundation whose assets are about $15 million—i.e., the foundation assets are significant in relation to the family's overall wealth.

We know, of course, that the private family assets will be taxable in connection with investment activities and that the Wollason Family Foundation is largely a non-taxable entity. (Private foundations, unlike public foundations, do pay a small excise tax.) Given this tax difference, would it make sense to place tax-disadvantaged assets in the Foundation and tax-advantaged assets in the private accounts?

The question is more complex than it appears. We need to keep in mind, first of all, that, legally speaking, the Wollason Family Foundation is an entity entirely separate and distinct from the Wollason family. A private foundation is controlled by its board of directors or trustees (some foundations are organized as non-profit corporations and some are organized as trusts). If the Wollason family should lose control of the Foundation board, say, by appointing directors or trustees who appear to be loyal to the family but who in fact are not, the $15 million in Foundation assets could be placed forever beyond the reach of the family.[354] This consideration tends to argue for entirely separate investment strategies for the family and its Foundation, regardless of the differing tax treatment and the potential advantages that fact offers.

We also need to consider whether the Wollason's income and other liquidity needs are high or low relative to the income produced by their privately held assets. These needs cannot, under any circumstances whatever, be satisfied by resort to the assets of the foundation, due to the strict self-dealing rules imposed by the IRS.[355] In this case, the Wollason's income needs are more than satisfied by their own assets, a consideration that suggests the desirability of taking advantage of the Foundation's tax-exempt status to place tax-disadvantaged investments in its portfolio.

Finally, we need to consider how closely integrated the Family Foundation's activities are with the Wollason family's charitable activities. Imagine a case in which the Foundation is, due to financial constraints, incapable of making a particular grant. Would the family step up to the plate and make that grant? If so, the family's activities and the Foundation's activities are integrated—the Foundation's charitable activities are an extension of the family's charitable activities. This also suggests the possibility of locating tax-disadvantaged assets in the Foundation portfolio. On the other hand, if the Foundation's interests and the family's interests are completely separate, this would argue for separate investment approaches.

In other circumstances, tax considerations may be largely irrelevant. Suppose that the Wollason family had established a dynasty trust—a trust for

---

354 The most notorious examples of families losing control of very substantial foundations—notorious, at least, from the point of view of the families—are the Ford and MacArthur Foundations (Big Mac, not Little Mac). In both cases the families not only allowed control of their foundations to slip away but, to add insult to injury, both foundations promptly began to support causes that were largely anathema to many members of the endowing families.

355 You might be thinking that to the extent the Wollason's liquidity needs relate to charitable commitments, those could in fact be discharged by the Family Foundation. But this is true only in limited circumstances. If the Wollasons make a charitable pledge and that pledge is fulfilled by the Foundation, the directors or trustees have engaged in a self-dealing transaction and can be subjected to large fines. (On the other hand, the Wollasons are free to discharge pledges made by the Foundation.)

the benefit of Wollason family descendants that is exempt from the Rule Against Perpetuities.[356] The main asset location considerations in that case would be (a) the very long investment time horizon of the trust (which argues for locating higher risk, higher return assets there—private equity, for example), and (b) fiduciary and prudence considerations (which argue against going overboard with high risk, high return assets).[357]

Or suppose the Wollasons had established an intentionally defective grantor trust. In these trusts the tax incidence falls on one person (the grantor), while the ultimate appreciation in the assets benefits another person (typically a child of the grantor). The beauty of a grantor trust is that the payment of taxes by the grantor is not considered a gift for purposes of the gift tax. But if care is not taken in locating the correct assets in a defective grantor trust, the grantor may soon tire of paying so many taxes and convert the trust into a non-grantor trust.

Examples of the Investment Implications of Estate Planning Vehicles

In the following paragraphs I give brief examples of estate planning vehicles that are frequently employed by families, along with some of the more obvious investment implications associated with using those vehicles. I want to emphasize that the vehicles are discussed merely as examples of the issues that tend to arise; they are by no means exhaustive.

Asset protection trusts. These offshore vehicles are often used by clients in litigious professions or who fear large legal judgments. They are similar to

---

356 A number of states have enacted statutes exempting certain trusts from the Rule. The Rule Against Perpetuities, first promulgated in England in 1681, generally requires that all assets in a trust vest in a period of time measured by "lives in being plus twenty-one years." If the youngest life in being at the date the trust is established is an infant, and if that infant lives a long life, a trust could persist for more than a century without violating the Rule. At that point, however, its assets would have to be distributed. Long-lasting trusts and the endless litigation they encouraged were hilariously satirized by Charles Dickens in *Bleak House*, published in 1852–53 (it was serialized). In the book, the fictional case of *Jarndice v. Jarndice* came to an end only when the assets of the trusts had been completely depleted via legal fees and court costs and the lawyers had no further incentive to litigate. This book should be required reading for every family contemplating a dynasty trust.

357 This consideration might be overcome in a case where the trustee(s) of the dynasty trust are aware of other assets available to the beneficiaries of the trust.

spendthrift trusts—indeed, they are in effect self-settled spendthrift trusts—except that the trust is established in a foreign jurisdiction with laws that make it difficult for creditors to enforce their rights (often via very short statutes of limitation and very limited discovery rules). A key provision is the presence of a "protector" who will not be subject to US court orders. Unlike true spendthrift trusts, in an APT the presence of the donor as a discretionary beneficiary does not render the gift to the trust incomplete. Hence, APTs can effectively be used to remove assets from the estate of the donor. APTs must be created before a judgment is entered against the donor, and preferably before any claim has been asserted or even arisen. *Investment implications:* All US taxes must be paid on income and gains as they occur, exactly as though the trust were a domestic trust. Consequently, the investment considerations will be similar to those posed by a domestic portfolio. Assets placed in APTs may remain in trust longer, and hence have a longer investment time horizon associated with them, than the same assets may have had when held directly and domestically. On the other hand, many investors who establish APTs see them as an ultimate "anchor to windward" and will wish to see the assets in the trust invested very cautiously.

CLATs—Charitable lead annuity trusts. A CLAT is the opposite of a CRAT, i.e., the trust pays a fixed amount to charity for a period of years, then passes (outright or in trust) to the children or other beneficiaries tax-free. A charitable deduction is available for the expected present value of the charitable payments. A significant amount of property can be removed from the donor's estate at no tax cost using properly structured CLATs. *Investment implications:* Investment implications tend to depend on the charitable intent of the donors. Donors may wish to benefit charity, in which case high-income assets will be placed in the trust. If they wish to benefit the children, on the other hand, low-income, high-growth assets will be placed in the trust. Note that the investment advisor may be representing the donors or the ultimate family beneficiaries, or, in some cases, both.

CLUTs—Charitable lead unitrusts. A CLUT is simply a CLAT that pays to charity a percentage of the fluctuating value of the trust assets, rather than a fixed amount. *Investment implications:* Generally, same as a CLAT. However, the fluctuating value of the payments to charity must be taken into account—the use of very low-yielding assets in CLUTs is usually unwise.

CRATs—Charitable remainder annuity trusts. Assets in a CRAT pay a fixed amount of income to the donor for life or a period of years, then pass outright to charity—which can be a family foundation. Appreciated property is usually placed in a CRAT. The donor receives a charitable deduction for the value of the gift less the value of the income payments. CRAT payments must equal at least 5% of the value of the property. *Investment implications:* Most donors will want to assure the annuity payout to themselves, and may have little interest in how much ultimately passes to charity. However, this is not always the case. Remember that taxes paid by the beneficiary are determined by the nature of the income at the trust level. Highest taxable income must be distributed first.

CRUT—Charitable remainder unitrusts. A CRUT is a CRAT that pays the donor a percentage (not less than 5%) of the fluctuating value of the trust. The donor can make additional contributions to a CRUT, unlike a CRAT. Surprisingly, a CRUT can pay out the lesser of 5% or the "net income" of the trust, making it ideal for appreciating assets that pay little or no income. *Investment implications:* CRUTs are generally used when there is a serious charitable motive. Remember that taxes paid by the beneficiary are determined by the nature of the income at the trust level. Highest taxable income must be distributed first.

Dynasty trusts. This is a term typically applied to any trust that is designed to last for several generations. Dynasty trusts created in states that have abolished the rule against perpetuities (e.g., Alaska, Delaware, Idaho, South Dakota, Wisconsin) can theoretically last forever. *Investment implications:* These vehicles have very long investment time horizons and few income demands. Most donors will want to see the assets in a dynasty trust invested aggressively, consistent with fiduciary principles.

Generation skipping trusts. Gifts that skip a generation are subject to a flat tax of 55%, plus the usual estate tax. There is a $1 million exemption available to each spouse, but those gifts are subject to the gift tax, net of the $600,000 lifetime exemption. The parents create a trust and allocate their GST exemptions to it (or, often, only $1.2 million, rather than the full $2 million, to avoid any gift tax). GST trusts are limited in most states by the rule against perpetuities, but by creating the trust in a state that has repealed the rule (see above) the trust can theoretically last forever. A GST dynasty trust can be leveraged considerably by combining it with a CLUT. *Investment implications:* These vehicles have very long investment time horizons and few income demands. Most donors will want to see the assets in a dynasty trust invested aggressively, consistent with fiduciary principles.

GRATs—Grantor retained annuity trusts. Under a GRAT, the grantor retains the right to receive a fixed dollar amount for a specified number of years. Assuming that the grantor survives the annuity period and that the assets in the trust appreciate rapidly, a considerable amount will pass to the children free of estate and gift taxes. A gift is made upon the creation of the GRAT equal to the initial value of the assets reduced by the value of the annuity payments. Investors can also create zero-gift GRATs by setting the annuity amount so high that no gift is made. Gifts of closely held stock and limited partnerships are especially useful because they are already discounted for lack of marketability. The grantor is taxed on gains in the trust, and these tax payments represent additional tax-free gifts. So-called "cascading GRATs" are often used in situations where it is possible that an investment will appreciate extremely rapidly. If so, a substantial sum is passed tax-free to the children. If not, the GRAT simply expires harmlessly (assuming the grantor survives). *Investment implications:* Investments in GRATs should be as aggressive as is consistent with the need to make the annuity payments (or more aggressively in the case of cascading GRATs).

Insurance wraps. Placing a tax-inefficient asset inside an insurance product (usually a modified endowment contract or a variable annuity contract) causes the tax consequences to pass to the insurance company while the gains remain in the policy as increasing cash value. The insured can access the cash value through low-cost policy loans or simple cash withdrawals. Many insurance wraps are structured through offshore insurance companies to avoid strict state rules on investment options. The ongoing costs of these programs is an important issue, and the IRS is cracking down on perceived abuses. *Investment implications:* These vehicles are useful to shelter the income from growth assets that generate substantial ordinary income or short-term capital gains, e.g., non-directional hedge funds. Keep in mind that the insured cannot select the investments inside the policy.

Intentionally defective trusts. An intentionally "defective" trust is one which will not be includable in the grantor's estate but on which the grantor pays all taxes even though the income or appreciation is going to the children. These taxes represent an additional untaxed gift. A trust can be "defective" by giving the grantor the right to "sprinkle" income or principal among a group of beneficiaries, by retaining the power to reacquire the trust assets by substituting property of equal value, or by providing that the trust income can be distributed to the grantor's spouse. *Investment implications:* Since the donor pays all taxes, his or her tax picture must be kept in mind. It is usually preferable to invest in assets that generate long-term capital gains.

NIMCRUTs. A version of a CRUT containing an income make-up provision that allows more income to be paid out in later years, to the extent that income paid out in earlier years was less than the required percentage amount. Thus, rapidly appreciating property can be placed in a NIMCRUT while the donor is young; later, during retirement, the investments can be switched to high-yield assets paying the donor a very high income. *Investment implications:* Invest in high-growth, low-income assets during the accumulation phase, and high-income assets (e.g., junk bonds) during the payout phase.

Offshore trusts. Offshore trusts offer investors no tax benefits if the donors or beneficiaries are US citizens, but many wealthy clients will have non-US citizens somewhere in their families. This presents the opportunity to site trusts in offshore jurisdictions and avoid all US (and often foreign) taxes. *Investment implications:* These depend entirely on the needs of the beneficiaries.

Private foundations. Foundations can be established as trusts or corporations. Corporations are much simpler to administer and they avoid bizarre state limits on investments. Trusts, however, are better equipped to preserve family control across the generations. A private foundation is a grantmaking organization which must make grants and other payments (or in IRS terms, "qualifying distributions") equal to 5% or more of its average assets each year;[358] pays a 1% or 2% excise tax, depending on the scale of the grantmaking; must file a Form 990-PF with the IRS every year; and must make available to the public either its 990-PF or an annual report. Note that most foundations will likely find themselves the target of unsolicited funding proposals, and failure to respond to these funding requests can harm the family's reputation. Gifts to private foundations are limited to 20% of adjusted gross income, rather than the 50% deduction permitted for gifts to public charities. *Investment implications:* Fearful of not generating enough income to meet the payout requirement, many foundations invest far too conservatively. During extended bear markets (as in the 1970s and early 2000s), the 5% payout requirement, plus the excise tax, can actually amount to a much higher percentage of the current asset base. Even during normal market conditions, overly cautious investment strategies can result in investment returns that are well below those needed to grow the foundations' assets in real terms (payout requirement + excise tax + inflation).

Revocable trusts. Also called revocable inter vivos trusts. These are best viewed as property management vehicles. Revocable trusts have no tax benefits and, in most states, few other benefits (despite the claims of a few unscrupulous lawyers and accountants). Assets placed in a revocable trust must be re-titled in the name of the trust, and if the trustee is anyone other than the grantor, separate tax returns must be filed. In certain states revocable trusts can avoid some of the costs of probate, and such trusts can also, for wealthy families, be useful for complex

[358] As this is written. Congress is considering a proposal to remove a foundation's administrative costs from the 5% calculation, substantially increasing the payout requirement. Since most foundations are already liquidating themselves in real terms, increasing the payout requirement will ultimately significantly reduce the importance of private foundations in the American system of private philanthropy.

asset management situations (where a durable power of attorney might be too simple), and to preserve privacy. In a few states a revocable trust can be used to prevent a spouse from receiving his or her statutory share of the grantor's property at death. *Investment implications:* The only investment issue is the important point that well-drafted revocable inter vivos trusts can be effective asset and property management vehicles with less unwieldiness than a general power of attorney, and therefore assets such as real estate will typically be placed in them.

There are a thousand-and-one other issues associated with the proper location of investment assets in complex family portfolios, but the point is that these issues need to be addressed with care and sensitivity. The most brilliantly conceived investment portfolio and estate plan can be seriously undermined by the failure to locate assets in the right locations.

Implementation Issues

If the future were a repeat of the past,
librarians would be rich.
—Warren Buffett

When a family experiences a major liquidity event, or when an invested portfolio is being substantially restructured, many questions arise about how to proceed. These questions have mainly to do with market timing considerations and risk tolerance issues, but other issues are involved as well, including good old fashioned human emotions.

To examine these issues, let's imagine a family—we'll call them the Goldsmiths—who have just sold their family business for $100 million. The business was built up over four generations, and the current leaders of the family, Mark and Ellen Goldsmith, are acutely aware of their stewardship obligations. They recognize that sitting on $100 million of cash, while certainly reassuring in the short run, is simply a way for the family to become a little poorer every year. Yet they fear that if they deploy assets into the capital markets, those very hard-earned assets could quickly disappear if the markets turn south. Since the family's liquidity event occurred in September of 2002, the third year of a deep bear market, those fears are hardly unfounded. How should the Goldsmiths proceed?

Macro Considerations

We know, from history, that capital markets tend to rise roughly twice as often as they decline. This consideration suggests that the Goldsmiths should invest as quickly as possible, since the long-term odds of the markets going up are in their favor. And, indeed, most financial advisors will suggest that families invest liquidity quite quickly, typically over a few quarters or, at most, a year.[359] While this may be the right course for some families, I suggest that it is far too fast for most families.

For one thing, the long-term odds favoring rising markets disguise some very unhappy short-term possibilities: 1973–74, for example, 1987, and 2000–2002. Thus, the Goldsmiths must ask themselves the question whether getting even richer is as powerful a stimulus for them as getting a lot poorer would be. Since wealthy families are, by definition, already wealthy, and therefore capital preservation-oriented, getting richer is unlikely to provide as much pleasure as getting poorer will provide pain. If the odds of good markets versus bad markets were 10-to-1, perhaps the Goldsmiths would feel comfortable plunging into a fully invested position. But at roughly 2-to-1, the possibility of a bad outcome is simply too high.

Note that this is true not just for wealthy families but for everyone: clever experiments by behavioral scientists have shown that we are more eager to avoid pain than we are eager to experience pleasure. Moreover, we know that for most of us the marginal value of each additional dollar we receive declines the more dollars we have.

Given the dire possibilities the Goldsmiths face, and the relatively little that is to be gained in the short run by getting even wealthier, an interesting default position for Mark and Ellen might be to invest their newly liquid fortune *over an entire market cycle.* In other words, absent a compelling reason to move more quickly or more slowly, they should plan to invest their liquidity over the course of something like twenty quarters.[360]

Note that in the case of the Goldsmiths, this would have meant that they would largely (though not entirely) have missed the market rebound that

---

359 We shouldn't overlook the fact that many advisors won't get paid, or won't get paid much, on the portion of the Goldsmiths' fortune that is invested in cash. We don't want to appear suspicious, but we speculate that it is this consideration, more than anything else, that accounts for the advice to get-invested-quickly. By compensating their advisors equally on the total portfolio, whether the money is invested or uninvested, the Goldsmiths can at least dodge this particular advisory bullet.

360 This default position would not make sense for a family that had only temporarily moved to an uninvested position, perhaps as the result of terminating their investment advisor and moving temporarily to cash. (Note that terminating an advisor can often make sense; moving to cash—as opposed to keeping the invested positions intact—will rarely make sense).

occurred in 2003, when the markets were up powerfully and broadly. But, of course, even if they had invested over the course of one full year they would still have missed much of this appreciation. The point is that while having a few tens of millions of dollars more in paper wealth would have been nice, there was a nearly equal chance that the markets could have gone the other way, and that would have been very unfortunate, indeed. Moreover, the Goldsmiths' money will likely be invested for generations; missing out on a bit of appreciation in the first few years of the portfolio's life will make virtually no long-term difference to the family. On the other hand, if the markets had collapsed with all the family's money fully invested, it could have required decades to make up the loss: a crucial aspect of successful investing is avoiding very bad results.

It is interesting to speculate about what might cause the Goldsmiths to invest their capital more quickly or more slowly. Let's take a look at some of the considerations that might cause the Goldsmiths to depart from the one-market-cycle default position.

Reasons for investing more quickly. Unfortunately, the most common reason for accelerating the investment period would be that stock prices were rising rapidly and the Goldsmiths feared that they were missing a bull market. I say "unfortunately" because it will be a rare case, indeed, in which an investor could jump into a rapidly rising market and emerge unscathed at the very end of the cycle. Short-term bull markets—the only kind the Goldsmiths would miss by investing slowly—have an unhappy tendency to turn very suddenly into bear markets. Consider the bull of the late 1990s and its sudden transformation into the bear of the early 2000s. This is quite different from the period between 1982 and 1998, when stock prices rose consistently over a very long period. Remaining uninvested over that period would have been a true investment disaster, to be sure. But missing a brief and powerful bull ought to be of little concern to the Goldsmiths.

Another common-but-inadequate reason for moving more quickly is simple impatience. The Goldsmiths will naturally be aware that keeping their money in, say, an enhanced cash portfolio (see Chapters 11 and 13), will not only not grow their wealth, but may actually shrink it: net of tax and costs, enhanced cash portfolios sometimes produce less-than-inflation type returns. Inflation is truly a demon enemy of private capital, *but only over longer periods of time*. If the Goldsmiths invest over a five-year market cycle, their average uninvested period will be 2 ½ years. The likelihood that an enhanced cash portfolio would result in any serious loss, even net of inflation, is pretty remote over such a brief period of time.

A better reason for investing more quickly than over an entire market cycle would be if the equity markets were significantly undervalued by historical standards at the time of the Goldsmiths' liquidity event. Market watchers can argue endlessly about what the "fair" value of stocks should be, but periods of serious over- or under-valuation are not difficult to identify, even prospectively. The problem for the Goldsmiths is not concluding that stocks are priced at or near historic low ranges. Their problem is having the courage to invest at such a time. Remember that when an entire equity market is selling cheaply there is likely to be a reason for it.

In late 1974, for example, inflation had spiraled out of control, there were long gas lines everywhere, American preeminence seemed to have been lost to Germany and Japan, and the menace posed by the Soviet Union was very real. Many, many investors bailed out of the markets in 1974. These investors weren't just running from a periodic bear market—they had completely lost faith in the future of the American economy. And yet, late 1974 would turn out to be a terrific time to invest.

In short, *all* serious bear markets are associated with far more than low equity prices. In every case there will be far more to worry about, and it will be those worries that will keep the Goldsmiths from putting capital into the markets at the very time when that capital is likely to be most productive. The one-market-cycle rule can at least help build a little courage in the family.

Reasons for investing more slowly. Reasons to invest more slowly than one market cycle should be very rare. We have just discussed one unfortunate reason: the markets are in a serious bear phase and families will be fearful of putting *any* money to work, just when the return on that money is likely to be at its peak.

Another reason sometimes observed has to do with the difficulty of making the transition from a family that owns and operates a business to a family that owns and operates an investment portfolio. Although in fact it is far more risky to own one business than to own pieces of many of them (that is, both the possible upside and the downside outcomes are far more extreme), it won't necessarily seem that way to the family. In the Goldsmiths' case, the family had owned an operating business for four generations. By definition, it was a successful business, the family was in control, and the family was used to the risks the business posed. Investing in a traditional investment portfolio, while far less risky from an objective point of view, is a new experience for the Goldsmiths and they will naturally worry that they may not be very good at it. They will exaggerate the risks and underestimate the opportunities.

Thus, families new to investing will sometimes go through a very long period of remaining under-invested and of putting money directly into operating businesses, startups and various and sundry other schemes, all because those activities seem more comfortable to them. Only after the family has suffered serious actual losses on its direct investments and serious opportunity costs by being out of the market will they throw in the towel and begin to put money to work in a sensible investment portfolio.

Micro Considerations

Once Mark and Ellen Goldsmith begin to implement their investment portfolio, they will be investing in many different asset classes and, in all probability, in many different investment styles. One strategy the family might follow is simply to average-in to every asset class and style, and this is typically how it is done. Anything else is likely to smack of market timing. A more astute tactic, however, might be to invest more quickly in areas that are believed to be under-valued and less quickly in areas that are believed to be over-valued. This approach will have two salutary consequences. First, it will prevent the Goldsmiths from piling into sectors and styles that are currently "hot" and that are highly likely to collapse at some point. Murphy's Law being what it is ("If something can go wrong, it will"), that collapse will likely occur just after the Goldsmiths have bought in at the top of the market.

A second benefit for the Goldsmiths is that, by investing in out-of-favor categories more quickly, they are at least buying in cheaply. While no one can know when an over- or under-valuation will correct itself,[361] we do know that it will happen and that we will not be nimble enough to get out of the way in time or to jump aboard in time. If we buy into over-valued situations, we can be pretty confident that we will pay handsomely for our folly at some point. If we buy into under-valued situations, we can't know when we will be compensated, but we know that, ultimately, we will be.

Thus, if it appears that value stocks are under-valued relative to growth stocks, the Goldsmiths would be wise to hire their value managers first and to invest more money with them more quickly. Of course, over the full investment period for the Goldsmiths, this valuation differential could easily reverse itself. In that case, the Goldsmith will want to slow down—or even reverse—

---

361 It is surprisingly easy to know intellectually when markets are reaching over-valued levels, since we know a great deal about corporate earnings and about what investors are willing, over longer periods of time, to pay for those earnings. What we can't know is when valuation anomalies will correct themselves. That is because extreme over and under-valuations are caused by investor psychology, not by corporate earnings.

the pace of investment with value managers and to pick up the pace with growth managers. The same principles hold true of large cap versus small cap stocks, of domestic versus foreign stocks, of long versus short bonds, and so on. Over a full market cycle, most asset classes will enter a period of under-valuation, giving the Goldsmiths the opportunity to buy in at rational prices.

Yes, there is an element of market timing to this strategy, but it is market timing that is being done in a thoughtful way and with a conservative bias. In other words, the Goldsmiths aren't going to jump into a hot tech market with the thought that they will be able to time the markets well enough to get out before the collapse. The Goldsmiths are going to invest in *undervalued* assets a bit faster than they will in other assets. Sure, an undervalued asset can always become more undervalued, but the likelihood of a severe collapse in the prices of assets that are already undervalued is slim. On the other hand, the likelihood of a collapse in the prices of assets that are already overvalued is very high. All value investing is, in effect, a form of market timing. We buy undervalued securities not because we believe that our downside risk is modest (though that is an important consideration), but because we believe that at some time in the future the true value of our securities will be recognized and their prices will rise.

Implementing Non-Traditional Asset Classes

One area where valuation anomalies don't apply very well is private equity in general, and venture capital in particular. While the "vintage year" of the investment will be extremely important to the investor's ultimate return, it is essentially impossible to know which vintage years will be good ones and which will be bad ones. Therefore, it will pay the Goldsmiths to invest their PE allocation regularly and systematically year after year.

Hedge fund investing falls somewhere between traditional investing and private equity. Hedge funds do correlate with the markets, though imperfectly, and hence jumping into hedge funds during periods of market over-valuations will likely prove unrewarding. On the other hand, a well-diversified portfolio of hedge funds will likely protect investors on the down side, while still achieving reasonable returns on the upside. As a result of this happy circumstance, investors may wish to move more quickly on the hedge fund side of their portfolio than on the traditional side, all things being equal.

Finally, real estate is an asset class that is subject to periodic booms and busts. Families who will be including real estate in their portfolios will want to take special care not to buy into over-valued real estate markets. Instead, they may wish to postpone gaining real estate exposure or target their initial exposure to sectors of the market that are reasonably priced.

Manager Transition Issues

All investors will find themselves, sooner or later, in the position of having to terminate a manager and replace the firm with another manager.[362] All too often, we are so frustrated with a poor-performing manager that we simply fire the firm, which promptly sells out our portfolio. We then engage another manager, who takes the cash generated by the terminated manager and reinvests it. The round-trip costs of selling the portfolio out, then reinvesting it, can easily cost 3%–5% of the portfolio's value, depending on the asset class. If the sold portfolio contained embedded capital gains, the tax costs can easily rise to shocking levels.

To avoid or minimize these costs, we need to contain our impatience and proceed more deliberately. Thus, before terminating a manager (keeping in mind that roughly two-thirds of all manager terminations are mistakes), we should have identified a replacement firm. We will then show the current portfolio to the new manager and get from it an estimate of how long, and at what cost, it will take for the current portfolio to be restructured to fit the new manager's style and disciplines. Both we and the new manager will need to sort out compromises between the speed of getting to the new portfolio and the tax and trading costs that will be incurred to get there.

Typically, the new manager will be eager to move the portfolio to its style quickly, while we will prefer to minimize costs, even if it means moving more slowly. Considerations in this process will include the scale of any embedded tax liabilities, the trading costs associated with the asset class, the tracking error of the current portfolio to the new manager's portfolio, the tracking error of the current portfolio to the underlying benchmark, and so on. If the portfolio contains sizeable tax liabilities, if trading costs are high, and if tracking errors are relatively small, expense-control should prevail over speed, and we should not allow ourselves to be stampeded by the new manager into moving too quickly.

Indeed, if transition costs are expected to be very substantial relative to the value of the portfolio, it may make sense for us to engage a transitional manager. Such a manager's job would be to transition the portfolio from its current

---

362 Regarding the difficulty of identifying managers who will outperform, see Chapter 13.

profile to a new, specified profile,[363] in the most tax- and cost-efficient manner possible, consistent with our tolerance for higher tracking error. The transitional manager will do this in various ways, but the most prominent way will involve capturing small losses that occur inevitably as prices of our securities rise and fall. These losses accumulate and can be used to sell out-of-profile securities at no tax cost.

Only once we are satisfied with our transition strategy (either as it is expected to play out under the new manager or under a transitional manager), should we notify the current manager of our plans *and immediately suspend the current manager's ability to trade the portfolio*. Once a manager knows that it is to be terminated, its incentive to act in our interests will be almost completely eliminated, and hence we will need to protect ourselves against actions—such as selling out the portfolio—that could be very costly to us.

---

363 If the new manager is to be an index fund, the "specified profile" might be the S&P 500 Index. But if the new manager is to be an aggressive growth manager, the "specified profile" might be quite different

Three

Chapter 15

Managing Investment-Related Taxes

I don't want to achieve immortality through my work.
I want to achieve immortality through not dying.
—Woody Allen

Alas, like death, taxes are one of the few certainties investors face. Indeed, for most family investors, most of the time, taxes will prove to be the single largest drag on investment returns. Uncle Sam is our investment partner, and Governor Bill is also usually along for the ride (and sometimes even Mayor Benny). Thus, while tax avoidance should never be the sole motive for any investment decision, it is crucial that family investors take tax concerns into account.

But before we discuss effective tax management of our portfolios, let's pause a moment to emphasize the point about avoiding tax-motivated decisionmaking. Much of the time, structuring an activity in a way that minimizes taxes will bring with it other "costs." Sometimes these costs may be actual financial costs—as when we select an underperforming tax-aware manager over an outperforming gross-returns manager. More often, the costs are not financial, but are very real nonetheless. Failing to diversify a concentrated stock position because of a reluctance to pay taxes is a tax-motivated decision that could cost us our entire fortune. Setting up strict trusts for our children or grandchildren can save money on taxes, but it can also ruin those people, turning them into trust fund babies even before they are born.

Another problem with managing investment-related taxes is that the tax issue is almost always conflated with risk in such a way that investors are typically faced with choosing between lower-taxes-and-higher-risk or higher-taxes-and-lower-risk. Thus, to obtain capital gains tax treatment we must typically hold our assets for at least one year—i.e., higher risk. We can lower our risk by buying assets that will (or can) be sold in a month, but that will subject us to higher ordinary income or short-term capital gains taxes.

Imagine, for example, that we have owned 60,000 shares of BioTech Strategies, Inc. stock for eight months. We paid $600,000 for our position in the stock and that position has risen in value to $700,000. We are worried that the stock price will decline. If we sell out immediately, our $100,000 gain will be subject to short-term capital gains treatment at the Federal and state levels, roughly cutting our gain in half. If we wait four more months, we can qualify for long-term capital gains treatment and reduce our tax bill very significantly, but we also risk a decline in the price of the stock that might outweigh the tax savings.

Let's assume that, in round dollars, an immediate sale would result in a $50,000 gain net of tax, and that selling in four months would result in an $80,000 gain (net of tax), assuming a constant price. Our best course of action may be to place a stop-loss order on BioTech Strategies at some price that will give us a reasonable risk-return outcome. The exact price we set for the stop-loss order will depend on the expected price volatility of BioTech Strategies and on our own risk tolerance.

Suppose, however, that we set the stop-loss order at $11/share (versus the current price of $11.67/share). If BioTech Strategies declines to $11/share over the next four months, we will be taken out of the stock at a net-of-tax profit of $30,000—lower than what we are showing now, but possibly a risk worth taking. If the stock price declines to only $11.55/share, we will not be taken out, but can sell out at long-term capital gains rates in four months, netting $74,400 after tax. The outcome can't get any worse than a $45,000 after-tax gain, but at any price above $11.55/share the news only gets better.

Designing Portfolios from an After-Tax Perspective[364]

Most financial advisors design client portfolios using expected *gross* returns for each asset class to be included in the portfolio. If we were pension plans, that would be fine. But as family investors, most of our assets are likely to be subject to the complicated regime of investment taxes—short-term gains,

---

[364] The best extended discussion of the tax issues associated with managing family investment portfolios can be found in Jean L.P. Brunel, *Integrated Wealth Management: The New Direction for Portfolio Managers* (Institutional Investor Books, 2002), especially chapters 6 and 14-17.

long-term gains, ordinary income taxes, the Alternative Minimum Tax, plus whatever nightmares our state and city of residence have cooked up for us.

If we think about this for a minute, we will quickly realize that each asset class will be affected somewhat differently by this crazy quilt of taxes. To take two very opposite examples, returns on private equity tend to be extremely tax-advantaged: our money comes back to us taxed at long-term capital gains rates and, in addition, the payment of the tax is delayed, representing an interest-free loan to us from the tax authorities. On the other hand, the return we receive on hedge funds is typically tax *dis*advantaged: these returns are taxed mainly at short-term capital gains rates and we pay the tax right away.

Given the differing impact of taxes on the different asset classes, it is clear that portfolios designed using expected gross returns will be highly inefficient for taxable investors. If a taxable investor wishes to obtain the same expected return as a tax-exempt investor, we will have to accept more risk. If a taxable investor wishes to maintain the same risk level as an institutional investor, we will have to accept lower returns.

We can't level the playing field completely for taxable investors, but we can go a long way toward ensuring that our portfolios will be as realistic and efficient as possible by designing them from an after-tax perspective. This is a more complex process than it might appear, and it is discussed at length in Chapter 10.

Asset Location

As discussed more fully in Chapter 14, families, unlike pension plans and endowment funds, typically have an enormously complex series of entities through which capital must be invested. These entities often exist as part of the family's tax and estate planning strategies, but may exist for other reasons as well. The most obvious of these entities are private trusts, charitable trusts, partnerships, foundations, closely held businesses and the individual portfolios of different family units and generations.

The tax consequences of investing in these different entities can be quite different, and hence it should be obvious that the location of an asset in a family's portfolio will have important implications for the growth of net wealth. A simple example is that sensible investors would not ordinarily put the same kinds of investments in a generation-skipping trust as they would put in a defective grantor trust. Similarly, managers appropriate for the patriarch's personal portfolio may be wholly inappropriate for the family foundation. Yet it is quite rare for a financial advisor to understand these implications and act accordingly.

Asset Class Strategies

The need to develop optimal asset class strategies is discussed at length in Chapters 11 (traditional asset classes) and 12 (alternative assets). For purposes of our present discussion, the important point is that the tax treatment of the various asset classes will significantly affect the selection of strategies that will be optimal for taxable investors. Over time, for example, we know that value strategies have outperformed growth strategies. But much of the return of value investing comes from the high dividend stream typically paid out by "value" companies, and, until recently, that dividend stream was taxed at very high rates. This doesn't mean that taxable investors should have avoided value stocks and value managers, but it does suggest that the relative exposure of a taxable investor to value strategies would have been different—lower—than the typical exposure a tax-exempt investor might seek. (Now that the tax on equity dividends has been reduced, this strategy difference has largely disappeared.)

Similarly, taxable investors should typically hold a lower exposure to most hedge fund strategies than will tax-exempt investors,[365] since the short-term gains produced by most hedge funds are taxed at a very high rate. Placing hedge strategies in an IRA or other tax-sheltered account can help, of course, but most substantial investors will not hold IRAs that are of any significant size relative to their entire asset base.

Similar analyses must be pursued in each asset class to ensure that tax considerations have been taken into account—not, I hasten to add, that tax considerations should always be decisive—in selecting optimal strategies in each category.

Tax-Aware Managers

Institutional managers. The money management business, at least as a professional, thoughtful, disciplined activity, grew up in the institutional world. The overwhelming majority of competent money managers designed their investment strategies and disciplines for, and cut their teeth on, an institutional, non-taxable client base. Since those investors paid no taxes, tax considerations were never incorporated into the investment process. Meanwhile,

[365] In reality, other considerations militate against higher hedge exposure for tax-exempt institutions. The main constraint is the huge asset base managed by many institutions and the fact that hedge strategies are almost always capacity-constrained. Hence, it is quite difficult for a large institutional investor to obtain a significant exposure to hedge funds without seriously compromising the quality of the funds selected.

most family investors were stuck in the trust company and private client backwaters, having their portfolios managed by individuals who were really salesmen or client relations people, not professional portfolio managers.

As families have become more sophisticated over time, they have naturally sought out more professional investment management for their portfolios. Unfortunately, this has taken too many families out of the frying pan and right into the fire. The reason is that the institutional money managers whose thoughtfulness and discipline appeal to sophisticated families are all too often money managers who don't pay the slightest attention to the tax consequences of their investment activities.

As the institutional business has stopped growing and, at the same time, become intensely competitive, many institutional managers have set their sights on wealthy families as a rapidly growing and hugely underserved market. Most, as noted, have simply sold their gross return performance, hoping that family investors will not take the trouble to convert the (often) attractive gross returns into the (usually) unattractive net-of-tax returns.

Some institutional money managers have actually modified their investment disciplines to incorporate tax considerations, but families should be wary of such managers for a whole host of reasons. Imagine, in general, a money management firm that has built up a respectable track record over the years by diligently pursuing a particular investment process. Then, simply because the manager wished to gather assets more rapidly, the firm alters its investment process to incorporate strategies that are currently more popular with investors. Unsophisticated investors might be lured into engaging such a manager, but more experienced investors will look elsewhere. For one thing, the new process is unproven—engaging the manager would be almost like engaging a newly formed firm with no track record. But there is a more serious problem, namely, the cynicism of the change in the investment process. A firm that would engage in such an activity once is a firm that will engage in it again, and we should beware of doing business with such a firm.

Modifying a disciplined investment process to incorporate tax considerations may not seem like a cynical move, but all too often it is. Clearly, for example, the change in the investment process is being made solely to improve the firm's asset gathering capabilities—namely, by appealing to a new market of affluent, taxable investors. More fundamentally, it will be a rare investment process that will work as well considering taxes as it does without considering taxes—simply layering a tax-aware element onto a process that never considered taxes is no different in principle from layering a value element onto a growth discipline.

To take a simple example, let's consider a momentum manager for whom rapid turnover is a fundamental aspect of its style. This firm buys stocks that have risen in price recently and sells them as soon as their price momentum slows down. As a result, some stocks may be held for only a few days or weeks. Virtually all of the gains generated by such a manager will be short-term, taxed at high rates for a family investor. Adding to the process a tax overlay that requires stocks to be held for a full year (to receive long term capital gains treatment) would be absurd. Such a modification of the process would, in fact, destroy it.

With many other investment styles and disciplines, the consequences of adding tax considerations may not be so obvious, but they are almost always serious and corrupting. To ensure that tax considerations will make a meaningful and positive contribution to an investment process requires that tax considerations be an integral part of the process *as it is being designed.* Thus, for a money management firm to enter the market for taxable investors requires far more than simply reducing turnover or trying to harvest losses now and then. It requires the firm to design a new investment process from the ground up. This process will undoubtedly incorporate the disciplines of the firm's tax-exempt product and it will build on the firm's strengths. But the taxable investment product will be quite different from the tax-exempt product and the track record of the tax-exempt product will be largely irrelevant.

The point is that if a money management firm that has historically advised institutional investors wishes to advise taxable investors the firm will have to make a very substantial investment in the project. This investment will include designing the product as a taxable product from the beginning, and will include building a significant track record with the product before it can be marketed widely or successfully to taxable investors.

Identifying tax-aware managers. As noted above, for many years managers—including, unfortunately, banks and brokerage firms whose primary clients were families—paid no attention at all to the tax consequences of their money management activities. More recently, managers have begun to pay lip service to the concept of tax-efficiency, but managers who are truly tax-aware in their disciplines remain rare. As we look for tax-aware managers, some of the characteristics we should focus on would include the following:

- *Managers whose styles include low turnover.* Notice, however, that low turnover is not, in and of itself, conclusive evidence of tax efficiency. For low turnover to translate into tax efficiency, without the employment of other techniques, the turnover must be *extremely* low, typically on the order of 10%. A manager whose turnover is 30% is likely to be no more tax efficient than a manager whose turnover is 100%. Nor is high turnover itself conclusive evidence of tax-inefficiency. Consider a passive, tax-aware manager that is constantly harvesting small capital losses and using those losses to shelter gains elsewhere. Such a manager will exhibit very high turnover, but its activities will in fact be highly tax efficient. Thus, we will want to examine a manager's annual turnover, but we will need to examine it carefully and in context.

- *Managers who are conscious of holding periods and who avoid incurring short-term capital gains whenever possible.* Here the challenge is balancing investment gains against tax losses. Assume a manager buys a security with an anticipated holding period of eighteen months and an anticipated price gain of 40%. If the company's performance falls apart early in the holding period, it will likely make sense for the manager to sell the stock, even if it results in a short-term gain. But if the performance falls apart in the tenth month of the holding period, it may pay the manager to hold on for another two months, since the lower tax may offset the price decline.
- *Managers who aggressively offset losses against gains in an attempt to zero-out the tax liabilities of their buying and selling activity.* Managers naturally tend to be very confident of their skill. But the fact is that few managers will generate enough alpha to offset the taxes they produce.[366] Thus, a manager who is truly tax aware will be willing to take a loss on a stock, rather than stubbornly holding onto it hoping it's price will recover. Such behavior may well hurt the manager's gross-of-tax returns, but it will leave far more money in its clients' pockets.
- *Managers who manage tax lots.* Institutional managers simply accumulate stock positions and then de-accumulate them, in no particular order. But a portfolio manager who works with taxable investors must be aware of the tax lots it holds. For example, as the manager is accumulating a position in Ford Motor, the manager might buy some lots at $51, some at $53.50, some at $56, etc. When it comes time to sell, the manager needs to identify which tax lot he is selling in order to minimize the tax consequence of the sale.

---

[366] The classic journal article on this subject is Robert H. Jeffrey and Robert D. Arnott, "Is Your Alpha Big Enough To Cover Its Taxes?" *The Journal of Portfolio Management* (Spring 1992).

- *Managers who are willing to be flexible in reducing their clients' overall tax burdens.* Imagine a manager who is sitting on significant gains in securities whose prices the manager thinks will continue to rise. The manager has no losses in the portfolio, so it can't shelter the gains if they are realized. However, the manager's client calls and asks the manager to realize the gains on those stocks because the client has losses *elsewhere* in his portfolio that will cover the taxes on the gains. Will the manager sell the stocks? He won't *want* to sell, of course, since he expects the stocks to continue to rise. But if he is truly a tax-aware manager he will indulge the client's wishes, knowing that the client's gain is more important than his own gross returns for the period.[367] The same is true of a manager sitting on unrealized losses, who expects those securities to recover, and who has no offsetting gains in its portfolio. If the client has gains elsewhere in his portfolio, the client may ask the manager to realize the losses.

Of course, some desirable managers are engaged in strategies that are inherently tax-inefficient—absolute return-oriented hedge funds, for example. It would be counter-productive to insist that these managers somehow develop tax-efficient disciplines, since it is the very nature of their strategies to produce short-term gains and ordinary income. But the point is that when we have a choice between a manager who is tax-aware and one who is not, we will almost always want the former, not the latter.

Harvesting Losses

While tax-aware managers can harvest losses that occur in their own portfolios, they will have no idea of the gain and loss positions held elsewhere in our accounts. As investors, however, we (or a financial advisor on our behalf) can carefully monitor activity across the portfolio and coordinate among managers to net out gains and losses, or at least minimize net gains. If Manager A has losses that can be realized and Manager B has gains he cannot offset, we can work with the two managers to net out the tax consequences across the two portfolios.

In this, as in so many other areas, the importance of engaging a qualified master custodian for our investment assets can hardly be over-emphasized. Asset custody is discussed in Chapter 17, but for purposes of this discussion

---

[367] The manager could protect his position in any number of ways. For example, he could buy a security whose price behavior is closely correlated with the sold security. He could buy an ETF in the same industry. He could wait thirty-one days (to avoid the wash sale rule) and buy the security back.

the importance of a master custodian lies in (a) the custodian's role as the keeper-of-record for tax cost basis information on all securities in the portfolio (including identification of tax lots), and (b) the custodian's ability to produce consolidated account statements. These services allow us to observe our tax position across the portfolio, regardless of who is managing our money or how many managers we have engaged. Often, we are able to do so online and in something approaching real time. Absent a central custodian, we are reduced to pouring over paper statements that arrive at different times, or trying to download online information from many different, usually incompatible, sources.

Even among investors who use a custodian and practice tax loss harvesting, a common mistake is waiting until near the end of the year to cross gains and losses. Our managers are buying and selling securities throughout the year. If we wait until November or December to look at our unrealized gain-loss positions, we will have missed many, many opportunities to reduce taxes since most of the tax-realization events will already have occurred. Families will likely find that reviewing tax savings opportunities every quarter will prove optimal, most efficiently balancing investment and tax considerations.

Three

Chapter 16

Monitoring and Rebalancing Taxable Portfolios

All movements go too far.
—Bertrand Russell

The traditional techniques employed in the monitoring of investment performance and in the rebalancing of investment portfolios arose in the institutional world, where such matters are much more clear-cut. The first way in which institutions differ from families is that institutions are typically engaged in a relative performance game. If the S&P 500 is down 28% and the Widget Pension Plan's large cap portfolio is down only 27.5%, Widget is happy and the managers of Widget's pension plan are happy. But under the same circumstances, few families would be happy to be down "only" 27.5%. Families tend to be absolute return investors, as eager to preserve their wealth as to grow it.

In addition, it is generally less expensive for an institutional investor to terminate a manager than it is for a family investor to do so. Institutions pay no taxes, and hence the only costs associated with manager terminations are the transaction costs. When family investors terminate a manager we have to worry about embedded unrealized gains in the manager's portfolio. If those gains are realized during the transition to a new manager, the tax consequences could be very unfortunate, indeed. (This issue is discussed in Chapter 14.)

A third way in which family investors differ from institutions is in the emotional toll that portfolio changes take. Families are made up of human beings and managers are human beings. Firing a manager is, like firing an employee, a traumatic event for both parties. Institutions, on the other hand, are, well, institutions.

Finally, the non-taxability of institutional portfolios means that rebalancing activities, like manager terminations, are simpler and less costly for institutional investors. Long and careful research has shown the importance of rebalancing to achieving the best results from an asset allocation strategy, and hence many institutions automatically rebalance their portfolios when strategic ranges have been exceeded. Unfortunately for family investors, the research on the benefits of rebalancing was conducted on non-taxable portfolios. For families, the rebalancing issue is much more complex, requiring a careful and mainly intuitive weighing of the benefits of rebalancing against the negative tax consequences of doing so.

In short, institutional investors largely live in a world where performance monitoring and portfolio rebalancing is mainly a quantitative activity. Families live in a world where monitoring and rebalancing are far more qualitative than quantitative in nature, and hence they are aspects of the portfolio management process that are far more nuanced, more complex, and more judgment-based.

Performance Monitoring

Family investors may be receiving performance reports from a variety of sources. Money managers send reports to their clients, bank custodians send reports, and if the family has retained an overall advisor, such as an investment consultant, that advisor will also be sending reports. With so many sources of information about performance, we might imagine that most investors do a good job of monitoring investment performance. But nothing could be further from the truth. The source of the failure lies in the complexity of performance reports, in the differing kinds of reports we receive, and in the inability of many of us to interpret the reports appropriately.

Sources of Performance Reports

Money manager reports. All money managers send account reports to their clients, but that's about all that can be said. Some managers send monthly reports, some send quarterly reports, some (especially alternative asset managers) send only annual reports. However frequently or infrequently they send out reports, some managers show only account balances, while others show performance for that period, and some show performance as well for prior periods. Among those managers who show performance, some compare that performance against appropriate benchmarks and some do not. Among those who show performance against benchmarks, some managers use consistent measuring periods and some do not.[368] Finally, managers report only on their own performance, not the performance of other managers, and hence families who rely only on manager reporting will find it difficult—indeed, well-nigh impossible—to produce consolidated reports for the entire portfolio.

As a result of these deficiencies, investors who rely solely on money manager reports to monitor their performance are likely to experience poor results. The only investors who might possibly get by with manager-only reporting are families with very large and sophisticated family offices that can compute—and recompute—manager performance results in ways that are consistent across the portfolio.

Bank custody reports. As discussed in Chapter 17, it will be a rare substantial family investor who should even think about managing a complex investment portfolio without engaging a bank to serve as custodian of the investment assets. The main reason for this is to safeguard the funds, but consolidated reporting is an almost equally important advantage. Unlike money managers, a custodian will send monthly account reports on every account in the our portfolio,[369] as well as a total value for the portfolio as a whole. Typically, these reports show account values, along with cost basis information for each security, statements of income, principal appreciation, a gain/loss report, and so on. Bank custody reports typically do not show manager or account performance, but only the actual values in each account and in the overall portfolio. Some custodians will provide performance reporting for an extra fee. In that case, the bank is acting not simply as a custodian but as an overall advisor, and is producing reports similar to those produced by investment consulting firms, as discussed below.[370]

Investment consultant reports. The main shortcoming of performance reports, from whatever source, is that they tell us in quantitative terms how we

---

368 In other words, the measuring period might be selected to show off the manager's performance in the best possible light. See the discussion of "managing performance" in Chapter 13.

369 Some investment accounts cannot be "custodied" in the normal meaning of the word. Private equity partnerships, hedge funds, real estate, and so on are examples of accounts that are not custodied. The values of these accounts are typically shown by custodians as line item entries. In addition, mutual funds employ their own custodians, so that investors who want to see mutual fund accounts consolidated with their custodied accounts will have to ask their custodians to show them as line item entries as well.

370 There are also firms that provide "performance only" services, although the enthusiasm for this product seems to have waned substantially from the heady dot.com days of myCFO, GreekTrak, etc.

have performed, but they don't tell us whether that performance is acceptable or unacceptable or what, if anything, we should do about it. What we need, in addition to the quantitative reports, is *qualitative* performance reporting.[371]

Families who have engaged investment consulting firms or other overall advisors should be looking to those advisors for a qualitative assessment of their performance. Consultants also provide quantitative reporting, of course—indeed, the better firms will reconcile manager-reported performance with the account values and cash flows shown on the custodian's statements. (But see *Conflicts Between Reports*, below). But the real value added by an overall advisor on the performance reporting side is to give us an informed, objective, *qualitative* report on how we are doing, preferably in simple English prose. (Note that these assessments will be objective only if we have engaged an open architecture advisor. Otherwise, our advisor will have the same temptations to "game" our results as do our money managers.) Performance reports from managers generally start with a description of what happened in the markets during the reporting period. That's fine, of course, but unfortunately the reports stop there. While we might be mildly curious about our managers' takes on what happened in the markets, our attention is actually galvanized by what happened in our own portfolio, and most advisors don't provide that information.

While asking for a qualitative analysis of our own performance seems a simple enough request, in fact the business of supplying investors with qualitative assessments of their performance is extraordinarily difficult to pull off. In the first place, as noted, the advisory firm must have no conflicts of interest that might corrupt the assessment of performance. This eliminates 99% of all the financial advisory firms in the world. Next, the firm must actually employ senior investment professionals who are *able* to assess investment performance. Just to take a simple example, imagine a small cap value manager that has underperformed its benchmark for two consecutive years. Should the manager be terminated, or should the firm be given more of our capital? Either decision could prove to be brilliant or disastrous, and the decision is rarely straightforward.

Finally, the firm must assign to its individual advisors a small enough client load so that the advisors can actually take the time to prepare qualitative

---

371 Earlier in my career, when I was working in a large family office, we received extremely detailed, quantitative performance reports from our advisor every quarter. These reports were so extensive that they formed a pile eleven inches high on the corner of my desk. Somewhere in that pile was something I needed to worry about, but the likelihood that I would find it was extremely remote.

assessments. Brokerage firms typically assign hundreds of accounts to each rep, while bank relationship officers must manage scores of clients. Any advisor who handles more than about two dozen accounts will be way over his or her head when it comes to providing qualitative, customized assessments of performance.

Typical consulting firm performance reports will consist of monthly reports on manager performance and quarterly reports on consolidated account performance. The monthly reports simply take the performance reported by the manager and compare it to an appropriate benchmark for the period and, typically, the year-to-date.[372] The quarterly reports will reconcile manager account statements with the account statements produced by the custodian, will provide performance data on each manager and account, as well as for the consolidated portfolio, will comment specifically on the performance of each account, and will make any recommendations that the client should consider for that period.

Conflicts Between Reports

Family investors who engage money managers and a custodian will find that the statements produced by the manager and the statements produced by the custodian frequently show different balances. While these differences are usually small, they are nonetheless alarming. (Imagine that, at the end of the month, we received a statement from our bank showing that our checking account balance was "somewhere around $52,000"!)

The main culprit in discrepancies between managers and custodians has to do with the differing protocols used by each. When a security trade is made, the pricing of the trade is established by the *trade date*, but the actual proceeds change hands on the *settlement date*. For a money manager, it is the trade date

---

372 The better consulting firms will examine these monthly reports carefully, however. At my own firm, Greycourt & Co., Inc., we embed in each client's report an algorithm that tells us whether the manager's performance dispersion against its benchmark for the month is more than one Standard Deviation greater than its historical tracking error against the benchmark. If this is the case, the manager receives a call to discuss what accounted for the unusual performance. Note, importantly, that this call is placed whether the performance is unusually bad or unusually good. A manager whose performance is consistently above expectation may just be a genius, but it may also be that the firm is fudging its performance results or is engaging in "style drift," that is, moving to an investment style that is currently in favor, rather than the investment style the manager was hired to engage in.

that matters, since that date establishes the price the firm will receive from a sale or will pay on a buy, and it is that price that becomes a part of the firm's permanent track record. Hence, managers tend to prepare account statements using trade dates.

From the perspective of a custodian, however, what matters is whether the proceeds from a trade are successfully received into the account, and what the value of those proceeds is. Until the proceeds from a transaction are actually received into the account, the matter is purely hypothetical. Hence, banks tend to prepare accounts using settlement dates. Managers, in other words, are engaged in a performance game, while custodians are engaged in a money-counting game.

Inevitably, some securities transactions will straddle the closing date for the preparation of account reports. If the trade date for a transaction is September 30, the manager who made the trade will show the proceeds of the trade in its account statements. As far as the bank is concerned, however, no proceeds from the trade have been received into the account. Hence, the bank will not show those proceeds on its account statements for the period ending September 30.

Other discrepancies can arise as the result of decisions about accruing dividends and interest payments, the use of different securities pricing services, and so on.

Unfortunately, when we simply look at differing balances sent to us by managers and banks, it is impossible to know whether the discrepancies are related to harmless protocol-timing issues, or whether the errors may be more serious. Very large family offices will reconcile manager and bank statements, but most families will need to engage someone to handle this chore (and a chore it is!) on their behalf. The usual "someone" is an investment consulting firm that has built a sophisticated back office that downloads account data from the custodian on a daily basis.

Interpreting Performance Reports

As noted above, quantitative performance reports tell us very little. If our three US large cap managers all underperformed the S&P 500 for the month or quarter, should we be alarmed or not? It's impossible to know without knowing a great deal about the nature of the managers and the nature of the markets during that quarter. If our small cap value manager suddenly begins to outperform its peers by substantial margins, should we be moving more capital to the firm or should we be deeply worried about style drift? What sort of benchmark should we be using to measure the performance of our overall portfolio, and should that benchmark be different over shorter and longer periods? If a blowup has occurred at a hedge fund included in our hedge fund of funds, should we be worried or is it inevitable that occasional blowups will occur?

As these questions suggest, interpreting quantitative performance reports is not a game to be played in short pants. The difficulties associated with interpreting performance reports has led family investors to make one of two opposite mistakes. Some families terminate managers or revise their portfolio strategies based on apparent-but-unreal performance deficits, resulting in excessive and expensive manager turnover and in sudden, amateurish changes in investment strategy. Other families, faced with the difficulties of interpreting performance, simply don't do it at all, living for years with underperforming managers and portfolios until some horrible event awakens them from their slumbers.

Unless a family is extremely experienced, or unless it can afford a very sophisticated family office, most private investors will need to engage an advisor to help interpret performance and make recommendations based on those interpretations.

Monitoring Manager Performance

We have touched on this topic before (see Chapter 13). But I would be remiss if I didn't emphasize the important point that most manager terminations are costly mistakes. Mistakes in the simple sense that the terminated manager outperforms the replacement manager over the next market cycle; costly in the sense that we not only give up the superior return produced by the terminated manager, but we must also pay the transaction costs, taxes, time and emotional costs associated with moving from one manager to another.

Most manager terminations occur for what we imagine to be performance reasons. But in fact only a small minority of managers who are terminated really deserved to be terminated—and it is we investors who bear most of the costs associated with unnecessary terminations. Effective manager monitoring requires that we take each of the following steps:

- First, whenever a manager is engaged, we should prepare guidelines[373] for that manager and have those guidelines approved by the manager. The guidelines need not be extensive or elaborate, but they should cover such issues as:
  - The manager's acknowledgement that the account will be managed in accordance with the family's investment policy statement.

373 A sample manager guideline is attached to the end of this chapter.

- Performance expectations, including the benchmark, manager universe and time horizon that will be used to measure the manager's performance.
- The timing and nature of reports the manager will submit.
- An agenda for meetings to be held with the manager, and the frequency of those meetings. Managers are superb at co-opting the agenda of meetings, spending most of the time talking about the state of the markets, the view of the Federal Reserve Bank, the outlook for interest rates and the economy, etc., etc. Everything, that is, except the manager's performance.

♦ If the manager's performance was to be measured over an entire market cycle, it should be a very rare case that the manager would be terminated for performance reasons before that time has expired. Otherwise, we are probably over-reacting to temporary market events or transient underperformance.

♦ We should take care to measure the manager against *appropriate* benchmarks and *appropriate* manager universes. A manager can produce lousy absolute performance and still be someone we want to keep in our portfolio: if the sector in which the manager works has produced dismal results, all managers working in that sector are likely to be doing the same. Trading one manager for another will accomplish nothing.

♦ On the other hand, substantial changes in the management firm itself should be cause for alarm even if performance has not deteriorated. Substantial changes mean that we are no longer dealing with the firm we engaged, but a somewhat different firm. The following changes should be of special concern:

- Very substantial growth or shrinkage in the manager's asset base since the firm was engaged.
- Loss of key professional personnel.
- Sale of the firm or sale of a significant interest in the firm (significant enough to put lots of cash in the senior professionals' pockets).
- Significant personnel turnover or disarray even below the senior professional level.
- Failure of the senior professionals to provide for the continuation of the firm by bringing along younger professionals and sharing equity with them.
- Any (repeat *any*) ethical failure.

Rebalancing Taxable Portfolios

As noted above, most of the research on the benefits of rebalancing was performed on investment portfolios that were exempt from taxes. Because the tax costs associated with rebalancing taxable accounts can be very substantial, this research is suspect in the private client world. As a result, rebalancing of family portfolios needs to be more of a qualitative than a quantitative process, although of course it should be both.

As a review, we need to keep in mind the purpose of periodic rebalancing. Let's assume that we start with a portfolio strategy that is exactly aligned with our target asset allocation. As time goes by, our portfolio will drift away from the target allocation, as various sectors of the markets rise or fall faster than other sectors. Over time, our equity allocations will tend to grow much faster than our cash and fixed income portfolios, but over the short term the opposite phenomenon could occur. In either event, the risk level of our portfolio will have changed, eventually substantially.

Suppose, for example, our target allocation has 55% in stocks, 35% in bonds, and 10% in hedge funds. In the absence of rebalancing, we may wake up some day to find that our portfolio is now invested 70% in stocks, 15% in hedge and 15% in bonds. This is a vastly more risky portfolio than we set out to own, and in a bad market environment it will be hit hard—far harder than we are likely to tolerate without flinching badly.

Or assume that the markets have been in a bear phase. In the absence of rebalancing we may wake up to find that we are invested 40% in stocks, 15% in hedge and 45% in bonds. This is far too cautious a portfolio for us. When the markets recover we will be largely left behind.

Instead of allowing our portfolio to drift with the whims of the market, we should be rebalancing periodically. But simply saying so raises a whole host of issues. Let's examine a few of the more important ones.

Setting Strategic Ranges

As with institutional investors, family investors will want to start with a target asset allocation strategy and then establish strategic ranges around these targets within which the portfolio will be allowed to move before rebalancing is considered. But a family's strategic ranges should generally be wider than an institution's. Allocation ranges that are too narrow will result in too-frequent rebalancing, and for taxable investors the cost of rebalancing will likely outweigh the benefits.

How wide should the "bands" be within which the portfolio can fluctuate? Too little attention has been given to this issue. As suggested above, most advisors use the same ranges for families that they have been using with institutions. But because the cost of rebalancing taxable portfolios is greater, the strategic bands should be wider. Even advisors who advocate wider bands for families tend simply to add and subtract 5% or 10% to or from the target allocation, resulting in silly outcomes. For example, an asset class with a target allocation of 40% might be allowed to fluctuate between 35% and 45% (12.5% either way), while an asset class with a 10% target allocation will be allowed to fluctuate between 5% and 15% (100% either way!)

A better approach would be to set the bands to describe a range of fluctuation that is consistent with the expected volatility of the asset class. For example, if an asset class has an after-tax Standard Deviation of 20%, why not start by setting the strategic ranges at plus or minus 20%? If an asset class has an after-tax S.D. of 8%, why not start with that as the strategic range? We can adjust these ranges upward or downward depending on how we feel about the tax issue, but the adjustments should be consistent with the expected volatility of the asset class, as well as its tax treatment.

Rebalance Back to What?

Let's assume that we have decided to rebalance our portfolio because our US large cap exposure, which has a target of 25% and a range of 20% to 30%, is sitting at 32%. Should we rebalance back to the target allocation (25%) or merely back to the top of the range (30%)? There is no purely quantitative answer to this question. If rebalancing can be done inexpensively, the better answer is to rebalance back to the target. But if rebalancing is going to be expensive, the better answer (assuming we are going to rebalance at all) is to rebalance only back to the top of the range. We need to keep in mind, however, that if we rebalance only back to the top of the range, a strongly rising market will require us to rebalance frequently.

A second issue to consider is whether valuations in the US large cap sector are high or low by historical standards. If we are at a 32% position in the sector but valuations remain low, we should be less eager to pay taxes and rebalance. But if valuations are high, rebalancing will be a more compelling idea.

How Often to Rebalance?

The issue here is highly qualitative, almost intuitive. My view is that taxable investors should set quantitative targets, not calendar targets. If an asset class has a 25% target exposure and a strategic range of 20% to 30%, we should *consider* rebalancing when the range is exceeded on either side. The default position should be to rebalance, but that default can be overcome if the cost of rebalancing is very high. We should not rebalance automatically on a quarterly basis, as many institutional investors do.

The default position can also be overcome for valuation reasons, as noted above. If we are out-of-balance on the upside, and if valuations for the asset class remain low or reasonable,[374] we might postpone rebalancing, being reasonably confident that a price collapse is unlikely. (If we are out-of-balance on the downside, there will be no tax consequence associated with buying into the asset class. The question will be where we get the cash to make the buys and what the tax consequences, and valuation conditions, are in the cash source market class.)

We should also have in place an over- or under-exposure level that *requires* rebalancing, regardless of the cost and regardless of what we think of market valuations. That level might be set at double the normal range, or at whatever seems reasonable (but probably not more than double). When we are out of balance by that amount we *must* rebalance. Otherwise, our enthusiasm or pessimism will seriously compromise our investment results.

Thus, the targets, strategic ranges and maximum and minimum ranges for two hypothetical asset classes (the first with a 20% S.D. and the second with a 10% S.D.) might look something like this:

Target Exposure	*Normal Range (Rebalancing Recommended)*	*Maximum Range (Rebalancing Required)*
25%	20%–30%	15%–35%
15%	13.5%–16.5%	12%–18%

We would create the same targets, normal ranges and maximum ranges for each asset class.

Summary

Monitoring the performance of investment portfolios, and rebalancing them in a disciplined fashion, are not exactly the most exciting aspects of wealth management, but they are crucial to successful outcomes. We can do

374 That is, if valuations are low or reasonable by *historical* standards. Convincing ourselves that, although P/E ratios of 40 are high by historical standards, they are reasonable because we are in a "new paradigm," is a recipe for investment disaster.

everything else right, fail here, and find that we have discharged our stewardship responsibilities poorly.

The phrase "in a disciplined fashion" was not an accident. There are two reasons why families fail to monitor portfolios appropriately and to rebalance them properly. The first is the boredom factor, and the answer to that is the same answer we would give to any boring-but-important job: discipline. It's simply part of the job we have to do, and we have to take the good with the bad. Otherwise, we are not intelligent investors carrying out serious stewardship responsibilities, we are simply dilettantes.

The second obstacle is over-enthusiasm or over-pessimism. If the markets are in a bull phase, we will be sorely tempted to let our gains run. Some of that is acceptable—markets do tend to be characterized by momentum. But there are limits. We originally set those limits (I hope) in calm moments, before we were faced with temptation. Then, no matter how strong the markets appear to be, and no matter how certain we are that they will continue to rise, once our maximum exposure has been reached we must—must—rebalance. Taking money off the table during strong markets is the way wealth is preserved.

Similarly, over-pessimism can also be the enemy of wealth preservation. In a bear market our lower ranges will be frequently tested and often exceeded, and it can be very tempting to ignore the absolute minimum exposures we set for ourselves—or, worse, to abandon those market sectors altogether. All this will do is put us on the sidelines when the recovery occurs. We will have taken our lumps during the bear phase of the market, but we won't get the benefit of the bull phase. This is no way to run a portfolio.[375]

375 Investors sometimes point out that disciplined rebalancing sometimes causes harm to a portfolio. For example, during much of the 1980s and 1990s, rebalancing in international and emerging markets equities generally took money out of better-performing domestic stocks and put it in underperforming foreign stocks, retarding the growth of the portfolio. True enough—but only true in retrospect, which is the case with every aspect of wealth management. If we had known that foreign stocks would underperform we certainly would have avoided them, but that outcome was unknowable. People who claim they know in advance which assets will outperform—i.e., market timers—have the worst of all investment track records. Disciplined rebalancing will, on occasion, slightly hurt our performance, rather than help it. But overall it will help far more than it will hurt, and we want those odds on our side.

PERFECT CAPITAL, LLC

XYZ Trust Portfolio B

Manager Guidelines: MANAGER A

Adopted [DATE]

Purpose of the Portfolio

[INSERT]

Specific Guidelines

In managing the portfolio assets, MANAGER A will adhere to the following guidelines:

The assets will be managed in accordance with the Investment Policy Statement adopted by the family. A copy of this Policy Statement has been delivered to MANAGER A.

MANAGER A will be expected to outperform the benchmarks set forth in the Policy Statement on a net-of-fee basis. MANAGER A will also be expected to outperform the universe of managers specified in the Policy Statement on a net of fee basis. Performance will be measured over a three-to-five year market cycle.

MANAGER A acknowledges its understanding of the derivatives policy set forth in the Investment Policy Statement.

MANAGER A will submit, on a quarterly basis, a report on the status of assets and accounts under management. Each quarterly report will contain the following:

- A statement listing the assets held in the portfolio, the percentage represented by each security and the percentage represented by each asset class.
- A comparison of MANAGER A's performance against the indices set forth in the Policy Statement for (a) the current quarter and year-to-date, (b) 1, 3 and 5-year results, and (c) results since inception.
- A statement that MANAGER A is in compliance with the investment policies and guidelines set forth in the Policy Statement and in these Manager Guidelines.

Agenda for Meetings

Unless otherwise notified of additional agenda items, it is expected that meetings with MANAGER A will adhere to the following procedures:

- Meetings will be held on a semi-annual basis, scheduled promptly after results are available for the prior quarter.
- The quarterly reports referred to above will be submitted at least ten days prior to the scheduled meeting date.
- Each meeting will follow this agenda:
  - MANAGER A will report on any significant changes in its (a) professional staff, (b) organizational structure or (c) ownership.
  - MANAGER A will review the performance of the assets since the last meeting, including net-of-fee results for the current quarter and year-to-date, results for 1, 3 and 5-years, and results since inception. These results will be compared and contrasted with the performance of the benchmarks set forth in the Policy Statement and with a peer group universe of similar managers.
  - MANAGER A will briefly (3-to-5 minutes) discuss its economic and capital markets expectations for the next six to eighteen months, and the implications of those views for MANAGER A's investment policies and strategies.
  - MANAGER A will compare and contrast its recommended asset allocation strategy with the policy allocation contained in the Policy Statement.
  - MANAGER A will describe any "worry points"—developments which might cause MANAGER A to review and possibly revise its internal policies and strategies.
  - MANAGER A will discuss with the family any family-imposed restrictions which MANAGER A believes constrain its ability to implement its current preferred strategies.
  - The family will discuss with MANAGER A any areas of concern to them.

Three

Chapter 17

Miscellaneous Challenges for Private Investors

The purpose of this chapter is to touch on a variety of topics that, for one reason or another, don't seem to require a full or half chapter. Some if these issues are large and complex, but apply very rarely or only to a small group of private investors. Others are important but relatively straightforward. As an assist in navigating this long chapter, here is an outline of the topics covered:

Asset custody

Concentrated stock positions

Family investment partnerships

Spending

Trusts and trustees

Asset protection planning

Soft dollars

Portable alpha

Asset Custody

Price is what you pay.
Value is what you get.
—Warren Buffett

What Does a Custodian Actually Do?

For almost all private investors, asset custody will form the base on which all else is built. A custodian—typically a very large bank—safeguards our assets by holding them in a segregated account owned by us.[376] The fact that the account is "segregated" is important. By "segregated" we mean that our assets are formally segregated from the assets of the bank that is serving as our custodian. In the unlikely event that the bank should go bankrupt,[377] our assets will not be subject to the claims of the bank's creditors. Hence, while there might be some delay in retrieving our assets, and some cost and annoyance, we will in fact get our assets back.

This is not the case, it is important to note, with brokerage firms that are acting as a custodian of our assets. If the broker goes under, our assets go with it. For this reason, all brokerage firms carry vast amounts of insurance, designed to protect investors against just this possibility. Unfortunately, one has to wonder whether the insurance firms themselves could survive the bankruptcy of a major brokerage house. Moreover, most significant insurance firms that were in the business of writing coverage for brokers announced, in mid-2003, that they were exiting the business. Families should therefore consider brokerage custody very carefully, at least if the family assets are considerable.

Surprising numbers of investors don't bother to have their assets held safely in a custody arrangement, but simply place the assets at the disposal of whoever is managing the money.[378] In such a case we are placing ourselves entirely

---

[376] Custodians are often referred to as "master custodians" because, in order for them to hold and report on the many types of financial assets investors own, a custodial institution will typically require the services of several (or many) sub-custodians. For example, it is not practical—and is sometimes not possible, due to local laws and regulations—for a US banking institution to have a custody operation in every country in the world. Instead, the "master" custodian will enter into agreements with local institutions to act as sub-custodians for the master.

[377] Unlikely, but hardly unheard-of. Most of the large banks in Houston, Texas collapsed in the 1980s, for example, as did Continental Illinois in Chicago and numerous other banks that proved not to be "too big to fail." Incidentally, the word "bankrupt" doesn't refer specifically to banks, despite their propensity to fail at inopportune times. It comes instead from the Italian, "banca rotta," rotten bench or table. On the other hand, the word "bank" also comes from "banca," via the French "banque." A "banca" was a moneylender's table.

[378] This is almost always done in the case of hedge fund investing, where investors have no choice in the matter. It should never be done under other circumstances.

at the mercy of the honesty of the money management firm and all its employees. A few years ago a money manager named John Gardner Black set up his own "custodian," pointing out to investors that if they used his custody operation there would be no charge, whereas if they kept their money in custody with banks, the banks would charge several basis points (a basis point is 1/100 of 1%). A good many of Black's clients took him up on the offer, whereupon Black proceeded to spend their money on himself and his lifestyle. Black is now in jail, but his clients' money is gone.

In essence, a custodian holds and reports on all our investment assets, including cash and securities. Money managers engaged by us will be given a limited power of attorney to direct the investment of the funds assigned to that manager (the custodian will set up separate accounts for each manager), but those managers will not have access to the cash or securities in the account. In other words if a rogue manager attempts to misappropriate assets entrusted to him, he will not be able to gain access to our assets because no one, other than us and those we designate, can withdraw assets from the bank's custody or transfer them to other accounts.

Note that certain types of accounts are inherently not subject to actual custody, and are reported by the custodian only as line-item entries. Typical examples include mutual funds (each mutual fund has its own custodian), hedge funds (which are "custodied," in a very limited sense, by a prime broker—see Chapter 12), private equity funds (which are not custodied at all), and so on.

What Services Does a Custodian Offer?

A master custodian will typically provide all the following services:

- Provide for safekeeping of our investment assets domestically and internationally
- Maintain accurate and timely records of our investments
- Consolidate assets as necessary for reporting purposes
- Clear and settle trades made at the direction of our money managers
- Transfer assets as directed only by us
- Pay bills for various services (e.g., money manager fees)
- Provide multi-currency reporting for international assets

At the request of the client, custodians can also provide more specialized services:

- Prepare reports on a cash or accrual basis

- Report transactions on a trade or settlement date basis
- Maintain records and processing trades on a tax lot basis
- Maintain tax characteristics (interest, dividends, cost basis, etc.)
- Provide unitized accounting and interim valuations
- Prepare tax returns
- Maintain accounting for family investment partnerships[379]

Finally, most institutions that offer custodial services also offer many other financial services, including banking, trust services, asset management, etc. In rare cases it may make financial sense to allow a custodian bank also to manage certain assets for us. When our custodian has a best-in-class product in a particular asset class and is willing to discount its management fee because of the custody relationship (or to discount its custody fee because of the management relationship), we may be better off allowing the custodian to manage those assets. But a custodian's asset management products must always be evaluated entirely separately from its custodial skills.

Evaluating Custodians

It is easy to identify the few financial institutions that aspire to excellence in the custody business. This is because asset custody is an extremely capital-intensive business, requiring massive and ongoing investments in technology and personnel merely to stay even with the competition. At the same time, custody is largely a commodity business with low profit margins. This unhappy combination of massive investment and low returns means that, globally, there are only a relative handful of institutions that have chosen to compete in this business.

However, once the small group of best-in-class custodians has been identified, it is more difficult to select the most appropriate custodian for our particular needs. At bottom, the decision comes down to extensive day-by-day experience with the performance of individual custodians handling different kinds of clients and assets. In making recommendations to clients about appropriate custodian candidates, the better advisors proceed as follows:

- Based on the advisor's knowledge of our needs and the skill set of the various best-in-class custodial institutions, the list of attractive candidates should be winnowed down to two or three.

---

[379] Only a limited group of top custodian banks will offer partnership accounting.

- Each finalist institution should be sent an RFP (request for proposal) seeking answers to a large number of questions about the institution's custodial abilities, overall institutional strength, how they will meet our needs as investors, and so on. Responses to those RFPs can then be consolidated into a custodian comparison matrix for easy comparison by us and our advisor.
- The primary contacts for each institution should be individually interviewed, focusing on areas of particular importance to our account.
- Fee bids should be sought from the institutions most likely to be appropriate to our needs.

Custody Pricing

While asset custody is one of the true bargains in the investment business, it is easy to mis-price custody services. Custodian pricing can be maddeningly complex, especially for taxable investors. Typically, a custodian will charge an overall fee that is asset-based. This is simple enough and can easily be compared across vendors. Unfortunately, the asset-based fee is only the beginning. Depending on the custodian, additional fees will apply for each managed account, for each line-item entry (e.g., mutual funds or hedge funds), for each transaction that is posted (dividends and income, for example) and so on. International separate accounts are typically more expensive because of the army of sub-custodians required and the problem of dealing with multiple currencies. Since no two custodians will submit exactly comparable bids across the board, it is easy to select a custodian that appears to offer the best price, only to find out that we are being nickled-and-dimed to death with other fees. Whenever possible, therefore, we should put in our RFP a reasonably exact picture of what our portfolio will look like. This won't make comparing custody bids easy, but it will help ensure that we don't make a decision that turns out, inadvertently, to be pennywise and pound-foolish.

We will also want to be sure that we aren't paying for services we don't want or need. For example, most custodians will carry mutual funds as a line-item entry, updating the value of the fund and the number of shares held once a month. Another option is to have the custodian report the mutual fund in a way that allows us to view the underlying shares. Finally, we can hold the mutual fund completely outside the custody arrangement, receiving statements directly from the fund company and following pricing via the fund company's Web site.

The cost of the first option is typically something like $500/year—in many cases there is no cost at all. The cost of the last option is typically nothing (other than out time). The cost of the middle option is typically whatever basis point fee we negotiated. (For a ten million dollar account in the Vanguard Index 500 Fund, we might be paying 5 basis points for custody in addition to the 12 basis points we are paying for the Vanguard fund—a gigantic 42% increase in cost.) Few families will find a crucial need to drill down into the actual mutual fund holdings, and for those few who do, the best source is probably the Vanguard Web site.

On the other hand, families have a recurring tendency to obsess about custody pricing, perhaps because it is so transparent. It is not at all unusual to find a family agonizing over a 1 basis point (1/100 of 1%) reduction in their custody costs, spending months negotiating with the custodian. Even on a $100 million account, this will save only $10,000/year. Meanwhile, the same family will have engaged an active US large cap manager managing $10 million, to whom they are paying 85 basis points, and who has underperformed the Vanguard 500 Index Fund by 30 basis points/year over time. This arrangement is costing the family more than $100,000/year, but nothing is done about it, perhaps because the manager isn't sending the family a bill for the cost every month. While no one should overpay for custody, it is obviously better to spend our time on the $100,000/year problems rather than the $10,000/year problems.

Custody for Taxable Accounts

Until recently, custodians largely ignored the needs of taxable investors. Most large families tended to be captive clients of a local or national trust company anyway. But in recent years custodians have realized that taxable custody is by far the most rapidly growing part of the business, and they have made up for lost time by dramatically improving the quality of their services for taxable investors. Today, almost any bank that would be a serious candidate to custody a large institutional account will also be a serious candidate to custody a large taxable account.

Services provided to taxable investors will include those offered to non-taxable accounts, but will also include careful tending to tax issues, especially tracking the tax cost basis of securities across all the family's accounts. Without this family-wide cost basis tracking, it will be extremely difficult to tax-manage the portfolio. For example, one manager may be sitting on nothing but unrealized gains, while another may be sitting on nothing but unrealized losses. If the first manager realizes its gains and the second doesn't realize its losses, the family will be stuck with a high—and completely unnecessary—tax bill.

In addition, most, though not all, custodians can provide accounting services for family investment partnerships (see the discussion below).

Securities Lending

In an effort to reduce or even eliminate the costs of custody, some families engage in securities lending transactions. A well-structured securities lending operation can not only offset the costs of custody, but can even be a small profit center. Unfortunately, securities lending is also a dicey business, and only the largest and most sophisticated families should even consider engaging in it.

Securities lending exists to meet the needs of investors who wish to sell securities short—typically, hedge fund managers, but also including other investors. In a short sale transaction, the manager borrows a security from another investor and sells it. Since the manager doesn't own the security it has sold, it will have to replace that security eventually, by buying it back in the open market. The manager hopes the price of the security will decline, in which case the security can be repurchased at a lower price, locking in a profit. But even if the price of the security rises, the manager will have to purchase it and return it to the investor who has lent it in the first place.

Since custodian banks hold millions of securities, they are obvious sources for brokers who want to locate securities their clients can sell short. Custodians will therefore establish securities lending businesses and may ask custody clients to make their securities available for lending. The technicalities of this business are too intricate to go into in depth, but in essence the borrower of a security pays for the privilege by paying an interest rate somewhat above the Treasury bill rate. Thus, for the lender of the securities, the transaction appears to be ideal: the lender is receiving interest for doing essentially nothing.[380] The realities, however, are more complex and troublesome.

In the first place, there are so many potential lenders of the most heavily traded securities (US large cap stocks)[381] that profit margins on the lending of such securities have disappeared. Most of the action therefore involves foreign securities and smaller securities, many of which are difficult to short. For most

---

380 To make matters even more complex, there are firms that specialize in investing securities lending proceeds. In other words, these firms take the modest interest we receive for lending our securities and invest it to produce slightly more interest. A very large scandal involved one of these firms, First Capital Strategies, in the mid-1990s.

381 For example, the gigantic public and corporate pension funds.

families, these sectors won't be large enough for the additional income to be meaningful. A worse problem is counterparty risk—the risk that the security we have lent won't be returned, perhaps because the borrower or broker has gone bankrupt. While such events are rare, they are not unheard-of, and one default can wipe out years and years of securities lending profits.

The reality is, therefore, that most families should avoid securities lending. It's a difficult business to understand, and the risks aren't, for the most part, worth the candle.

Brokers as Custodians

Unlike banks, brokers don't typically impose a separate charge for holding securities in "custody." This is true both for traditional full service brokers like Merrill Lynch and for discount houses like Charles Schwab. Instead, brokerage firms that hold our securities require that all or most trades take place through their own brokerage operations. As a result, it is important for us to compare the "hidden" cost of this directed trading against the fully transparent cost of bank custody. For smaller accounts and those invested mainly in mutual funds, broker custody may be less expensive. For larger accounts invested in separate account products, however, bank custody is likely to be more cost-effective.[382]

In addition, as note above, brokerage firms don't hold our assets in accounts that are segregated from the brokers' own assets. In the event of a bankruptcy, creditors of the brokerage house can seize our assets right along with the broker's own.

Smaller Banks as Custodians

By the time they have become wealthy, many families have already established long relationships with local banking houses. These may be smaller, regional banks or even larger banks that, nonetheless, don't specialize in providing custody for taxable investors. It is natural for the family to want to maintain a relationship with an institution that has served it well over the years. But the line must be drawn at the point where maintaining the relationship begins to compromise the family's wealth.

---

[382] Note that the requirement to obtain "best execution" doesn't apply when we have ourselves directed that all trades be placed through our broker. Thus, we are not only paying higher commissions, but we are also likely to be getting very poor execution, especially on more complex trades.

For example, if the local bank does not specialize in asset custody, its limited capabilities will constrain the family's ability to design and manage its portfolio in optimal ways. An obvious example is custody of foreign securities. Many smaller banks and others that don't specialize in custody are unable to hold non-US securities. This means that the family will have to invest in foreign securities through mutual funds or ADRs, rather than through separately managed accounts. Tax reporting may also be lacking, the bank may be unable to deal with complex securities, and online account access may be absent or rudimentary.

On the other hand, if the family's portfolio is relatively simple and is unlikely to become more complex over time, many smaller banks can do a perfectly acceptable job of custodying accounts. The main drawback is that most smaller banks will only accept custody of accounts they are managing themselves—a completely unacceptable trade-off for all but the smallest investors.

Concentrated Security Positions

Put all your eggs in one basket—
and watch that basket!
—Warren Buffett

Memo to investors: follow this strategy only if
the person watching the basket is Warren Buffett.

In point of fact, Mr. Buffett wouldn't think of putting all his eggs in one basket. Last I looked, Berkshire Hathaway owned many stocks, representing a well-diversified portfolio of companies ranging from huge multinationals like General Re, to mid-sized firms like FlightSafety International, to local retailers like Nebraska Furniture Mart. If we (or even Warren Buffett) found ourselves sitting on the odd pile of cash—say, $100 million—what are the odds that we would invest it all in one stock? The odds aren't just low, they are zero. Only a lunatic would even think about it.

Yet, when we end up, one way or another, owning only one stock, how many of us immediately diversify the position away? Sure, the situations are different, but they are different mainly in that when we own one concentrated position, rather than cash, we are likely to have a tax issue (and an emotional issue). But, given the low level of capital gains taxes these days, that can hardly be an excuse. Besides, it is a mistake in the first place to think of ourselves as being worth $100 million if we have an imbedded $15 million tax liability. Our real net worth is $85 million. The tax authorities are making an interest-free loan to us, and there are many ways we can leverage that opportunity. But the tax is owed and will eventually have to be paid in one way or another.

Another, related, excuse goes something like this: if I sell my $100 million position in Tyco, where will I find another group of investments that will outperform Tyco net of the tax cost I'll have to pay? Merely to ask this question is solid evidence of the fact that we have missed the point. Diversifying a concentrated position isn't a matter of improving future returns, though that could easily happen. It's a matter of dodging the guided missile that is aimed precisely at our net worth.

Although a concentrated low cost basis position can arise in many ways, the most common circumstance occurs something like this. A family has built up a successful company over the years, and the time has come to consider selling out. The family is approached by a firm that is offering a stock-for-stock deal—in other words, the family would sell out not for cash, but for stock in the acquiring company. (There can be important tax reasons to structure the deal in this way.) The family looks at the recent performance of the acquiring company's stock and it looks quite good. The deal gets done. After the sale closes, the acquiring company's stock continues to rise, and all is well.

What's wrong with this picture? What's wrong with it is that the family is living in an unrealistic and temporary world in which their wealth seems to grow every day with no effort on their part. In fact, this is an incredibly rare (and, as noted, temporary) circumstance, and it has happened that way because it *had* to happen that way. If the acquiring company's stock had been a dog for years, the family would never have considered accepting a stock-for-stock deal. Companies are only able to make stock acquisitions during those temporary periods when their stock price is on a tear—during all other periods they have to pay cash or forego making acquisitions. Thus, it isn't the case that the selling family has had the good fortune to sell to a company whose stock price seems extremely attractive—it always happens that way, and a family that reifies the phenomenon is making a serious mistake.

I don't mean to minimize the emotional complexity of a decision to sell all or a substantial part of a concentrated securities position. But the only way to avoid disaster is to decide in advance, in the calm before the storm, that we will not allow greed to overcome prudence. Sure, the terrific thing about holding a concentrated securities position is that it is a good way to build wealth. But the bad thing about holding a concentrated position is that it is a good way to go broke. Even if these were reciprocal outcomes for us—the pleasure of getting even richer being exactly equivalent to the pain of going broke—the tradeoff would hardly be worth the candle. But notice that these are *not* perfectly equivalent outcomes: the downside is far worse than the upside is good.

Imagine that we have sold our family company to Microsoft (this is some years ago) and we are now sitting on $100 million in Microsoft stock. We don't know what is likely to happen to Microsoft as a company or to the price of Microsoft stock. We do know that Microsoft stock has performed terrifically, but we nonetheless decide, in the name of prudence, to diversify our position. Big mistake. If we had held onto Microsoft, our $100 million would now be worth $500 million. On the other hand, our original $100 million has now grown to $200 million, so we probably won't throw ourselves off a bridge.

Now imagine the same situation except that the buyer was Enron. Again, we can't know the future of the company or the price of its stock, but we do know that Enron stock has performed extremely well. We decide to keep our $100 million in Enron. Huge mistake. Enron goes bankrupt and our $100 million is now worth nothing. We need to avoid bridges for awhile.

In other words, the decision to diversify in the Microsoft case was wrong, but not terminal. The decision *not* to diversify in the Enron case was wrong, and it was terminally wrong. These are the best and worst cases, and they aren't equivalent at all—the worst case is far worse than the best case is good. Since we can't know the future when we sell our company for stock, the best we can do is think through the possible outcomes in a disciplined way. If we do, we will never—not ever—come to the conclusion that we should keep all our wealth in one stock, anymore than we would think about betting all our wealth on Black 28.

Strategies for Diversifying Concentrated Positions

Strategies for diversifying concentrated stock positions come and go, as investors and the IRS play a never-ending game of catch-as-catch-can. Hence, it isn't worth going into extravagant detail about specific hedging and sales strategies, since any strategy could quickly become obsolete via action of the Service or a court. Nonetheless, the following are examples of strategies investors are using as this is being written.

Outright sale of all or part of the position. The simplest strategy is often also the best, and this is particularly the case now that the long-term capital gains rate has been reduced to 15% for most wealthy investors. For investors who are hopelessly conflicted about whether to diversify completely away from a concentrated position or not, selling half the position will often be the best course. In the Microsoft/Enron example given above, and assuming that we had a zero cost basis in the stock, we could sell half our $100 million concentrated position and net $42,500,000, giving us an overall net worth of $92,500,000. If the price of the concentrated stock fell 10%, we would be better off having sold and paid our taxes. In addition, while it's better to be worth $100 million than to be worth $92.5 million, the difference is unlikely to affect our lifestyle. More important, we are now fully in control of $42.5 million of our net worth. No matter what bonehead strategies the executives in the acquiring company might pursue, no matter what accounting scandals might strike, no matter what the capital markets think about the acquiring company, we are to a considerable extent masters of our own fate. If we don't sell at least a substantial portion of our concentrated position, however, our fate will remain in the hands of people who don't much care what happens to us, especially by comparison with what happens to them.

Exchange funds. An exchange fund is a partnership created by a third party (typically a financial firm) in which each limited partner contributes its own concentrated low cost security and receives in return a partnership interest in all the securities contributed by all the partners. Since the contribution of assets to a partnership is not typically a taxable event, the partners in the exchange fund have managed to convert very narrow (and therefore risky) positions into much more broadly diversified positions at no tax cost. The IRS isn't happy about this, and has imposed many restrictions on how exchange funds can operate. For example, when we contribute our stock to an exchange fund it must remain in the fund for seven years. When we take out our limited partnership interest it will come out in the form of the diversified positions, but we will still have our original low tax cost basis in them. We have managed to diversify our risk—an important objective—but it has taken us a very long time and we still have our tax problem.[383]

Puts and calls and collars. A traditional hedging strategy involves the use of puts and calls. Suppose we decide, probably inadvisably, not to diversify our $100 million concentrated stock position in, say, Tycoon Industries (ticker symbol TRBL). Nonetheless, we know that if Tycoon loses more than 25% of its value we will be very, very sorry. Such a loss will begin to impact our lifestyle and our philanthropic programs. We therefore buy protection by arranging for a "put" on TRBL. If TRBL is selling at $50/share, we will arrange to have the right to put the stock at $38 (25% below the current price). If TRBL hits the $38 strike price, we will be taken out of Tycoon. The trouble with this strategy is that it can be expensive protection. If TRBL drops to $39/share, our put will

383 There are other issues associated with exchange funds, including the "behavioral" issue: families tend to put lousy low basis securities in exchange funds, not low basis securities they expect to outperform dramatically. As a result, unless the firm organizing the fund is very careful, there will be a broad "dumbing down" of our investment position as well as a diversification of it.

expire worthless. We will have paid dearly for protection that wasn't used, and now we will have to pay for it all over again by buying another put at some price. Eventually, our entire net worth could disappear in unused puts.

To deal with this problem, investors will sometimes deploy puts and calls simultaneously, creating an equity "collar" around TRBL. By structuring this collar carefully, we can create a so-called "costless collar," that is, the cost of the put is exactly offset by the value we receive for selling the call. The cost of puts and calls varies with many factors, including the relationship between the current and strike prices, the duration of the transaction, the volatility of the stock, and so on. But let's say, for the sake of argument, that we can buy a put on TRBL at $38 and use the proceeds to sell a call at $63.[384] We have now "collared" our stock at no "cost." So long as the price of TRBL stays between $38 and $63, nothing happens and our collar will eventually expire. If TRBL touches $38, we will be taken out at that price. If TRBL touches $63, we will be taken out at that price.

Of course, there is no such thing as a "costless" derivative transaction. We are paying a financial services firm to execute these transactions (and we should get several bids), and the friction of those costs will come out of our hide. More fundamentally, we are paying for the ability to avoid some of the downside risk in TRBL by giving up some of the upside risk. Many investors will find this tradeoff unappealing.

But the main trouble with collars is probably emotional. When the price of Tycoon stock begins to plunge, we all too often begin to panic. TRBL is clearly on its way to $25, we think, so why wait to get out until $38? Let's unwind the collar—at great expense—and sell out at $42. No sooner do we do so then TRBL, after dropping to $39, rises to $62. The same phenomenon occurs on the upside. No sooner do we establish our $38 to $63 collar than TRBL begins to skyrocket. Clearly, we think, the stock is on its way to $100, and we're damned if we're going to get taken out at $63. When the stock reaches $60 we unwind the collar—at great expense—only to watch as the price touches $62, then begins a sickening plunge to $35.

A collar may or may not be a great idea—it's almost certainly a worse idea than selling all or part of the concentrated position—but once we've entered into a collar we should live with the results. Constantly unwinding collars, like

---

[384] Equity collars can be structured in almost any way we wish. We can buy a put on TRBL at $48 and sell a call at $75. We can buy a put at $25 and sell a call at $55. An equity collar with a strike price of the put very close to the current price will resemble a variable prepaid forward arrangement. See the discussion below.

constantly watching our puts expire worthless, is a good way to destroy our wealth even if the stock performs well.

Variable prepaid forwards. If we are willing to sell all or part of our concentrated position, but wish to defer the tax consequences of the sale, we might consider a variable prepaid forward, or VPF. A VPF is similar to an equity collar, except that it is designed both to hedge a concentrated position and to provide us with cash we can use to reinvest, pay down margin debt, or whatever. To enter into a VPF transaction, we determine the floor price for our stock (our downside protection, net of the cost of the transaction), the ceiling price (how much of the upside we will participate in), the size of the cash advance we will receive (which we will have to repay at maturity), and the maturity of the transaction (i.e., how long we will be deferring the tax consequences of the arrangement—say three years from now). At maturity, we will have the option of settling the transaction by delivering cash or our stock. Because a VPF transaction is not considered to be a sale for tax purposes[385] until the transaction matures, there is no immediate tax consequence to our VPF.

The possible outcomes of our VPF are complex and depend on whether we settle the transaction in cash or in kind ("physical settlement"). Cash settlements will incur tax consequences that depend on whether the final price of our stock is below the floor, above the ceiling, or between the floor and the ceiling, but in any event we will not have sold our stock and will continue to own it. In a physical settlement, the number of shares of our stock we will have to tender will again depend on the final price of the stock and where that price falls relative to the floor and ceiling prices. If the final price is below the floor price, we will have to deliver all our shares, of course. If the final price is between the floor and ceiling prices, or above the ceiling price, we will have to deliver some, but not all, of our shares.[386]

Making price volatility our friend. One of the many problems with having most of our wealth tied up in one security is that the price volatility of individual stocks tends to be dramatically higher than the price volatility of a diversified portfolio. If we think back to our old pal, variance drain (see Chapter 3),

---

[385] For regulatory purposes, however, the sale is construed to occur when the VPF is executed. Thus, for insider trading and restricted stock (Rule 144) purposes, it is much easier to manage short-swing and volume issues using VPFs.

[386] Examples of VPF settlement outcomes via cash or physical settlement are given by Scott Welch in his excellent article on VPFs, "Analyzing Alternative Hedging Strategies," *The Journal of Wealth Management* (Summer 2003), pp. 13-16.

we will remember that the more volatile an investment's price is, the higher its return must be to compound our wealth. Hence, even if our concentrated stock position manages to beat the return of the broader group of stocks of which it is a part (the S&P 500, for example), it might still compound our wealth more slowly than the diversified position would have done.

But price volatility can also be thought of as an ally, as well as a foe. By sensibly managing that price volatility, we can add return to our concentrated position and perhaps make up for some or all of the variance drain. The most common volatility-managing strategies are "overlay" programs, in which covered[387] call options are written on the concentrated position. Conservative overlay strategies are designed to add yield to the portfolio (typically in the range of 200 to 400 basis points/year) and to ensure that the stock will not be called away. More aggressive strategies can add considerably more return—say, up to 600 basis points/year—but they risk having all or part of the stock called away.

Equity options overlay strategies are complicated in the extreme to execute—the phrase "don't try this at home" resonates especially in this area. Fortunately, there are firms that specialize in designing and executing these strategies, and investors interested in overlay programs should interview several such firms before proceeding.

Family Investment Partnerships

It's not that he's mercenary.
It's just that he loves the stuff.[388]

Most substantial families are probably familiar with family partnerships that are designed to reduce estate taxes.[389] But family partnerships can also serve investment purposes.

In a typical case, the senior living generation of a family will control most of the wealth. This generation is able to access the best managers (most of whom impose high minimum account sizes), can take advantage of fee break points, and

---

387 The options are "covered" because we own the stock we are writing calls on. If we didn't own the stock, our options would be "naked."

388 P. G. Wodehouse, *How Right You Are, Jeeves* (1960).

389 The notion is that since the family members now own much of their wealth in an illiquid partnership, the IRS should accept a lower (discounted) value on those assets for estate tax purposes—in effect, a discount for lack of liquidity. This notion, by the way, drives the IRS crazy, and it tends to attack family partnerships on sight. The courts have, to date, issued decisions on family limited partnerships that are difficult to reconcile.

they will also have available to themselves sophisticated investment strategies that require investors to be "accredited," that is, to have a certain minimum income and/or net worth. Younger generations may be stuck with inferior managers or mutual fund products. But by creating family investment partnerships (or limited liability companies—LLCs) to "pool" the family's investment assets, the senior generation can significantly expand the investment opportunities available to the younger generations while simultaneously reducing investment costs.

From the point of view of money managers, the client is not the individual family units but the partnership itself. Hence, the partnership is able to meet the high minimum account sizes demanded by many of the best managers. The middle and younger generations of the family might not otherwise have access to these managers. In addition, of course, the family partnership is able to take advantage of fee break points, giving all members of the family the advantage of lower investment costs. Finally, by investing through separate account managers, rather than mutual funds, younger family members can tax-manage their portfolios, significantly enhancing their net returns. The family can leverage these advantages by involving the middle and younger generations in meetings with money managers and other advisors, helping educate them about investment issues.

Family investment partnerships are sometimes established in a vertical fashion and sometimes in a horizontal fashion. In a horizontal partnership (by far the less common these days), the family creates an entire, diversified investment portfolio in which all members of the family participate (via the partnership). Horizontal partnerships provide maximum leverage, because all the family's assets are pooled into one partnership, but they can be clumsy investment vehicles. If there are three or four living generations, for example, what possible investment strategy would be appropriate for all the family members? When families organize horizontal partnerships, many of the more astute members of the family will put the core of their wealth in the partnership, but will keep other assets out in order to customize their own strategy.

Vertical partnerships are typically established for each asset class in which the family plans to invest. Thus, there might be separate partnerships for US large cap, US small cap, international, emerging markets, fixed income, hedge,[390] private

---

390 We will need to remember that, technically, an unaccredited investor doesn't become an accredited investor merely by participating in a large family partnership—the family member must meet the accreditation standards on his or her own. This rule is often winked at by families and alternative investment funds, however.

equity, and so on. Individual family members[391] can put whatever percentage of their own assets they wish into each category, allowing for significant customization.

The main problem with vertical partnerships is complexity. Partnership accounting is always complex, and having to deal with ten partnerships, rather than one, can ratchet up the paperwork burden substantially. Fortunately, excellent software exists for managing these issues, and many of the better accounting firms and custodian banks can be engaged to handle the accounting, preparing Form 1065s, K-1s, and so on.

Finally, families can take the route of forming a single master partnership that has unitized funds corresponding to each asset class. The advantage is that only one Form 1065 and K-1 needs to be prepared. The disadvantage is that the 1065 cannot be completed until each asset class is finalized. Thus, a family member invested only in fixed income must wait until the 1065 is complete—which can't occur until the private equity K-1s have come in—in order to file his tax returns.

Note that there is no reason why a traditional family limited partnership designed for estate tax-discounting purposes cannot also serve as a family investment partnership. Indeed, there can be special advantages to doing so. When the IRS challenges family limited partnerships it will typically argue that there was no reason for the formation of the partnership other than avoiding taxes. If one reason for forming the partnership was to pool family investment assets, that can be a compelling business reason for a partnership that also claims discounted values for gift and estate tax purposes. On the other hand, the cohort of family units that is appropriate to participate in a family limited partnership formed for discounting purposes may be quite different from the cohort of family units that would be appropriate for a family investment partnership. Each family will have to work these issues out for themselves.

Spending

I spent most of my money on boats, booze, and broads.
The rest I wasted.
—Tycoon

---

[391] Most families include their foundations in the partnerships, though this can be controversial. If, for example, the foundation's assets are significant in relation to the family's assets, self-dealing issues might arise. In addition, the IRS will scrutinize these partnerships carefully to ensure that cost basis is allocated properly among taxable and tax-exempt partners.

I have touched on the issue of spending in earlier chapters—see, especially, Chapter 3—but I want to emphasize here the importance of attempting to control spending from taxable investment portfolios. Perhaps because Congress has established a rule that charitable foundations must "spend," that is, give away, 5% of its endowment each year, many families and institutions seem to believe that spending 5% of their asset base is somehow appropriate. Nothing could be further from the truth. The reality is that spending much more than 3% is likely to prove problematic over time, given the many headwinds that family investors face in trying to invest successfully.

Aside from simple profligacy (which, while hardly unheard-of, is actually quite rare), families tend to overspend in two circumstances. The first arises when family members are simply unaware of the impact of high spending on the preservation of their wealth. These family members can go on over-spending for an entire lifetime, leaving the consequences to be borne by their children and grandchildren. The second occurs when the number of family members drawing on the asset base multiplies faster than the asset base: families can be far more fertile than investment assets.

At the 40,000-foot level, a quick-and-dirty analysis of the impact of portfolio withdrawals on portfolio growth would look something like this:

Inflation	3%
Spending	5%
Return required to stay even	8%
Impact of fees, costs & taxes on an 8% return	2.5%
Net likely return	5.5%
Net necessary return	8%
Annual wealth decline	2.5%

Sure, we could shoot for a much higher rate of return, but the risk tolerance of most families for gross returns much above 10% is extremely low. Families stretching for such returns will likely abandon their portfolios at precisely the wrong time, resulting in permanent damage to the portfolio. We could also pray that inflation won't be as high as 3% (dream on). We could pay close attention to controlling investment costs and taxes.

But the best way to have any hope of preserving wealth—much less growing it—is to spend it more rationally. A family that begins spending at 3% will have no difficulty remaining at that level. But a family whose lifestyle, including charitable giving, is built around a 5% or 6% spending rate will suffer the pangs of hell trying to squeeze down to a sustainable withdrawal rate.

The best way to understand the impact of high spending is to realize that in the truest way possible high spending means that we are spending down our principal. In the old days, people thought of principal preservation as simply keeping the absolute level of the capital intact. If a family had $50 million and spent only the dividends and interest, they were "preserving their capital." This attitude has long since been discredited, and for good reason: $50 million twenty years ago is worth about $25 million today—some preservation of capital!

Instead, we need to think of our capital in total return terms. If we can realistically get an 8% gross return on our entire portfolio, and if that means 5.5% net of taxes and fees, and if inflation is 3%, we can only spend 2.5% of the portfolio value each year. If we can realistically get 9% per year gross, then we can spend 3.5%, and so on. It doesn't matter whether that 2.5% or 3.5% is coming from what used to be called "principal" or what used to be called "income." In fact, spending from the proceeds of long term capital gains will usually be more tax-efficient than relying on high-taxed dividends and interest,[392] and will also enable us to achieve higher returns.

Trusts and Trustees

It is better to have a permanent income
than to be fascinating.
—Oscar Wilde

Private Trust Companies

For very large families—those with liquid assets at least over $100 million—the private trust company (PTC) can make a great deal of sense. Such families are already likely to have significant infrastructure in terms of a family office, and hence the incremental cost of setting up a PTC can be minimal. And since a PTC vastly simplifies many of the jobs the family needs to do—including complex accounting and reporting and providing ongoing trusteeship and administration of family trusts—the true net cost can easily be negative.

Trusts have been around for a very long time. They were an invention of Anglo Saxon common law, and they are largely unknown in Code jurisdictions (most of Europe, for example).[393] Until the late 1980s, when the Rockefeller

---

392 The recent reduction in the dividend tax will change this calculus, but only slightly.

393 Some jurisdictions have created the trust concept legislatively—Liechtenstein, for example.

family established a PTC, virtually all substantial families used the services of a commercial trust company or the trust department of a commercial bank. That option was never particularly desirable (aside from the poor quality of the investment performance, leaving sensitive family decisions to the trust committee of a corporate entity unrelated to the family was especially problematic), but with the massive consolidation of banks, leaving most American communities with no true local trust company, it has become unacceptable for any family that can afford another option.

The main advantage of the PTC is that it can provide fiduciary services directly to a family. Other forms of family office organization can support individual trustees or work with commercial trust companies, but they lack trust powers. A family that forms a PTC can thus avoid having to deal with an unaffiliated fiduciary and can, if desired, avoid ever having to burden any family member or friend with the risks of serving as an individual trustee. In addition, of course, a PTC is by its nature a far more private operation than a commercial trust company.

Until recently, PTCs were problematic for many families as the result of legal barriers in most states. For example, for centuries trust companies had been required to serve the needs of a broad public in order to obtain a charter. Only a few US jurisdictions permitted the formation of a trust company designed to serve only one family, and those jurisdictions tended to be remote from population centers. These geographic and legal barriers boosted costs to a point where most PTCs formed before 1995 had to work with other families in an attempt to spread the costs of the operation. (Even the Rockefeller PTC became a multi-family office.)

Beginning in the mid-1990s, however, states began to understand the need for PTCs. By 1997, the Conference of State Bank Supervisors had promulgated the model Trust Modernization Act, which authorized PTCs on a reciprocal basis.[394] As of this writing, according to John P. C. Duncan (probably the leading legal expert on PTCs), thirty states had adopted the model Act or versions of it, including Connecticut, Illinois, New Jersey, New York, Ohio, Pennsylvania, Virginia, and Texas. Notably missing are California (California is always notably missing), Florida, Maryland and Massachusetts.[395] With so many states jumping on the bandwagon, many families will find it possible to

---

394 In other words, the Act allows a PTC chartered in one jurisdiction to maintain a full-service trust office in any other jurisdiction that has adopted the model Act or a similar measure.

395 "The Private Trust Company: It's Come of Age," *Trusts & Estates* (August 2003), p. 49ff.

charter a PTC in a favorable jurisdiction (for example, one with a low minimum capital requirement) but to have the main office in their own town. On the other hand, if most of the family's existing trusts are in one state, it may be prudent to establish the PTC in that state. Courts will look more favorably on a petition to replace a trustee if the new trustee is domiciled in the same state.

Total Return Trusts

Most trusts are designed to pay "income" (mainly interest and dividends) to one set of beneficiaries, while the "principal" (the original corpus of the trust plus any undistributed appreciation) accrues to the benefit of another set of beneficiaries. From the time the concept of the trust was first developed until about the 1950s, trust assets tended to produce far more income than capital appreciation. The long-term result was typically that early income beneficiaries fared well, while later income and principal beneficiaries fared poorly. (The decline of the English aristocracy was prominently fueled by this quiet phenomenon.) All that began to change half a century ago, and by the end of the 20th century many sensibly invested trusts were yielding well under 2%. Today, therefore, the problem has reversed itself. Sensibly invested trusts—that is, those with predominantly equity-oriented portfolios—tend to appreciate handsomely over time, but they produce little in the way of current yield in our low-dividend, low-interest-rate environment.

Properly drafted trusts can easily deal with this problem by providing both a floor and a ceiling for payouts to current income beneficiaries. But what about the hundreds of thousands of trusts that were drafted years ago? State legislatures, under pressure from the legal and financial community and from income beneficiaries, have grappled with this issue, and roughly half the states now address it in one of two ways.

The Uniform Principal and Income Act. The UPIA, adopted in 1997, allows trustees to adjust distributable income by transferring principal to income or income to principal as required to achieve fairness as between income and principal beneficiaries. The UPIA applies only to trusts that calculate the payout to beneficiaries by reference to "net income." The UPIA, or a version of it, has been adopted in twenty-four states and another three or four have the Act under current review.

Under the UPIA approach, a trustee can invest the trust assets in any manner that is prudent, without regard to how much "net income" the trust will generate. Then, if the income is so low as to be unfair to the income beneficiaries, the trustee can make an adjustment by transferring principal to income and making a larger income distribution. If the income is so high as to be unfair to the ultimate principal beneficiaries (an unlikely situation these days), the trustee can transfer income to principal and make a smaller distribution. A provision added to the UPIA in 2000 limits trustee liability for making good faith adjustments.

Unitrust legislation. Another approach, adopted by four states and under consideration by another eight, permits trustees of net income trusts to convert those trusts to unitrusts. In a unitrust, distributable income is specified as a percentage of the trust assets as those assets appreciate or depreciate annually. Hence, a trustee can invest the trust assets in any manner that is prudent, then pay out a specified percentage of the trust value without regard to whether the payout includes income, principal, or both.

Note that a few states, notably New York, have adopted both approaches, giving trustees the choice of which to pursue.

The IRS view. The Internal Revenue Service has issued proposed regulations that endorse both the unitrust and UPIA models. Hence, the IRS will honor total return approaches to all trusts, including such trusts as marital trusts and generation-skipping trusts, in states that have adopted total return legislation. Importantly, the IRS provides a safe harbor only for total return payouts between 3% and 5%.

Total return trusts in states without total return legislation. Newly drafted trusts can adopt total return approaches regardless of state laws. But what about older trusts domiciled in states that have not adopted total return legislation of any kind? There are two possible solutions for these trusts:

- *Resorting to discretionary principal distributions.* Many net income trusts authorize the trustee, in its discretion, to make principal distributions to income beneficiaries. Some trustees, particularly if they feel that they may otherwise lose the business, will use their discretionary power to distribute principal to augment low income distributions. If a trustee is recalcitrant, many trusts permit the trustee to be removed and replaced by an institution with a more modern outlook.
- *Moving the domicile.* If necessary, the domicile of a trust can be moved to a jurisdiction that permits a total return approach. Court approval may be required.

The desire to have a trust managed on a total return basis is, of course, only one of many considerations in judging a trustee's performance. However, my experience has been that trustees who refuse point blank to explore approaches that make simple common sense are likely also to be undesirable from many other points of view.

Open Architecture Trusts

Most newer *private* trust companies (PTCs) operate on open architecture principles, selecting portfolio management services by engaging the best managers available. More recently, some old-line trust companies with public charters have begun to offer open architecture, or (more commonly) semi-open architecture approaches. In other words, these firms are willing to accept fiduciary responsibility without bundling it with asset management (although most bundle it with custody services). These offerings vary widely and need to be examined with care—the skill set and experience required to operate successfully in an open architecture format are not easily acquired. But for families who need trust services, want open architecture, and cannot form their own private trust companies, open architecture trust companies may be worth looking at.

Semi-Open Architecture Trusts

An option that is growing very rapidly is for families to convince their trust banks to allow them to operate in a semi-open architecture manner. Under this arrangement, the family's trust bank continues to serve as trustee and custodian, manages some portion of the trust, and allows the balance of the asset base to be managed by best-in-class managers selected by the client (and approved by the bank). Given the consolidation that has taken place in the banking industry, and especially on the trust side of the bank business, many families will find that their trusts have ended up at an institution that actually has something approaching a best-in-class investment product. Often this will be bonds, since fixed income is an asset class that thrives in a large, institutional environment.

Even if the family bank appears to have no products remotely approaching best-in-class quality (a distressingly common occurrence), a family can often structure a fixed income portfolio that the bank will manage to strict guidelines, resulting in a bond portfolio that, while it will be unlikely to outperform, will at least rarely underperform dramatically. A final option when there is no place else to hide is to allow the family bank to manage equities on the condition that all equity exposure managed by the bank be in index products. These will likely be very expensive index products, when they exist at all, but what the family will give up in fees will be more than made up for in avoided underperformance.

Asset Protection Planning

A sweater is something you wear
when your mother is cold.
—Folk saying

Asset protection planning is a crucially important topic, but because it involves far more than investment issues—specifically, insurance issues, personal security, and so on—it is largely beyond the scope of this book. With regard to the non-investment issues, suffice it to say that every substantial family should engage a specialist in asset protection planning (firms such as Marsh Private Client Services, Aon, Chubb, etc.) and have a complete audit performed. This audit will identify areas where family assets may not be properly protected, will identify areas where the family is paying too much (many risks should probably be self-insured), and will identify areas where bundling risks together can significantly reduce insurance costs. Some intermediary organizations offer risk bundling for health insurance and similar issues. If the family is high profile enough, personal risks, such as kidnapping and personal security, should also be evaluated.

From an investment point of view, the main issue associated with asset protection is the use and misuse of asset protection trusts, or APTs. In this connection, it should also be kept firmly in mind that asset protection trusts are designed to protect assets from *creditors*, not from the tax man. Recent publicity about the Pritzker family's attempts to avoid taxes through the use of offshore trusts notwithstanding, APTs have no particular tax advantages—that is, none that any other trust would not also have. Readers who see APTs as potential tax shelters need read no further.[396]

Traditionally, APTs have been formed offshore, but as interest in asset protection has gone down-scale, domestic APTs have made an appearance. These days, for example, the typical investor interested in asset protection is probably a physician. Malpractice litigation is completely out of control in many jurisdictions, and malpractice insurance is consequently expensive. An unlucky (or

---

[396] APTs are considered to be "grantor" trusts for income tax purposes. I.e., the trust itself files informational tax returns, but the taxes will be paid by the settlor—the family member who establishes the trust. In addition, beneficiaries of the trust must file Form 3520 with the IRS, disclosing their interest in a foreign trust. Offshore trusts can be used for tax avoidance purposes only in cases where family members are not US citizens and are not domesticated in the US.

less-than-competent) physician will find that it is unavailable at any cost. As a result, quite a few physicians have decided, reluctantly, to "go naked," that is, to practice medicine without malpractice insurance coverage.[397] To protect some portion of their assets from large legal judgments, many of these doctors have established asset protection structures.

While this discussion may be helpful to such doctors, its main intended audience is substantial families. Like physicians, large families live in a litigious world and are particular targets of litigation and litigation attorneys. To paraphrase the famous bank robber, Willy Sutton, wealthy individuals are sued "because that's where the money is." If someone falls on the sidewalk in front of a working class home, they are just badly out of luck. They will have to pick themselves up, dust themselves off, and take more care in the future. But people who fall outside the home of a wealthy family have won the lottery. In addition, of course, many prominent families are actively involved in leading roles in commercial and public service activities, and those roles are inherently more likely to subject them to litigation by disgruntled parties.

Having said all this, the occasional gigantic liability damage awards assessed by lunatic juries (usually in places like Texas, Mississippi and The Bronx) significantly overstate the likelihood that a private family will ever be hit with a truly crippling judgment. Anecdotal evidence notwithstanding, most jury verdicts are more realistic, and the courts, especially at the Federal level, have grown increasingly hostile to boxcar judgments.

Still, the likelihood that our homes will burn down is also remote, but most of us protect ourselves against the possibility nonetheless, and therefore it is not out of the question for some families to consider APTs. For those families, let's take a look at how APTs work and what they involve. This discussion, it should be emphasized, is intended for a lay audience. The actual rules and practices in this area change constantly, and our best source of guidance is an attorney who practices regularly, but not exclusively,[398] in this area of the law.

---

397 In an attempt to respond to this problem, many health care organizations have established their own offshore insurance companies (usually in the Cayman Islands) to provide malpractice insurance to their associated physicians.

398 There is a cottage industry consisting of lawyers and bankers who sell APTs to people who may or may not need them. It is useful to avoid an attorney whose livelihood depends on convincing people to establish APTs.

What Are Asset Protection Trusts?

When a US-based litigant obtains a judgment against a family, the next step is for the successful litigant to enforce that judgment by levying against the family's property. An APT is a legal structure, typically[399] in the form of a trust, which has been so designed and sited as to make the enforcement of US judgments difficult or impossible. APTs must be established in a jurisdiction that has created special legislation authorizing such trusts, as well as special laws that make the enforcement of judgments against the assets of such trusts difficult. Historically, these jurisdictions were small, offshore islands—the Bahamas, Bermuda, the Caymans, the Cook Islands, Gibraltar, Guernsey, Jersey, Nevis, St. Kitts, the Turks & Caicos Islands, etc.[400]—but more recently several US states have adopted asset protection legislation.[401]

To take advantage of these plaintiff-unfriendly laws, a family establishes an irrevocable trust in one of the jurisdictions. A local bank will serve as trustee, that bank or a bank in another offshore jurisdiction will serve as custodian of the assets, and a non-US person may be designated as a "protector." (Often, the trust will establish a limited liability company into which it will place the assets.) Funds in the trust will be invested and income will be sent to the family at the discretion of the trustee.

Now let's imagine the worst case—a US litigant has obtained a judgment against the family that wipes out its US assets. Having foreclosed on all the US-based assets, the litigant now investigates the possibility that assets may have been stashed offshore. During discovery proceedings, the family, not wishing to commit perjury, admits that an offshore asset protection trust exists in, say, the Cook Islands.

The litigant quickly engages counsel in the Cook Islands and begins the expensive and time-consuming process of trying to levy on the family's offshore trust. Ultimately it turns out that, under local law, judgments can only be

---

399 Other asset protection structures exist. Liechtenstein, for example, recognizes a legal entity known as an "anstalt," in effect a revocable corporation owned by whoever happens to have physical possession of the corporate stock certificates. The American IRS considers this and similar vehicles to be nothing more than revocable trusts, which can be "looked through" to the beneficial owner.

400 No international law compels a sovereign nation to accept the laws or judgments of a foreign government. Many countries, of course, have entered into treaties that obligate them to recognize each other's laws and judgments, but those countries don't include the island nations listed above.

401 E.g., Alaska, Delaware, Nevada, Rhode Island, Utah.

enforced against APTs if those judgments are filed within two years of the creation of the APT. (Fortunately the APT was established twelve years ago.) In addition, Cook Island laws allow foreign litigants to prevail only if they can prove actual fraud, not simply civil liability. This means that the litigant, despite the fact that he has been successful in the US courts, will have to try his case all over again in the plaintiff-unfriendly Cook Island courts. Finally, it turns out that discovery procedures in the Cook Islands are extremely limited, so the litigant cannot even determine whether the offshore trust is large enough to justify all the effort and cost.[402]

Discarding this approach, the litigant convinces a US court to take jurisdiction of the "person" of the family patriarch and force him to instruct the Cook Islands trustee to repatriate the funds, or if that is impossible, to begin paying the income from the trust to the litigant. To avoid landing in the Hoosegow for contempt of court, the patriarch duly writes to the trustee, giving the demanded instructions. However, the trustee, suspecting that the family is proceeding under duress, turns to the "protector" for guidance. The protector looks into the situation, finds that, indeed, the family is proceeding under duress, and instructs the trustee to ignore instructions from the family until further notice.

The litigant is now at a dead end, and the offshore trust has served its purpose. Indeed, most litigants will not push matters anywhere near this far, given the enormous cost in time and expense, and the highly uncertain outcome.

US-Based APTs

In essence, the difference between an offshore asset protection trust and a garden-variety spendthrift trust is that the latter is established by one person for the benefit of another person, i.e., to protect the other person from his or her self-destructive tendencies. APTs are really "self-settled" spendthrift trusts, established by one person to protect himself or herself from the consequences of his or her actions. This idea was considered an impossibility under the Common Law, and for many years was considered contemptible by all US jurisdictions. But this smug attitude changed quickly when the US jurisdictions realized just how much money was involved.

---

402 Many offshore trusts also contain a "flight clause," causing the trust to exit the Cook Islands (for example) and reestablish itself in another friendly offshore jurisdiction the instant a creditor appears on the scene. These clauses tend to sound better than they are, however. In my experience it is harder to flee an offshore jurisdiction than a family might wish to be the case. See, for example, the case of *Walker v. Reese*, 286 Bankr. 294 (MD 2002).

Alaska, in 1997, was the first US jurisdiction to modify its trust laws to permit spendthrift clauses in self-settled trusts. As money began to flow into Alaska, other states took notice and promptly modified their own disdain for these trusts. Delaware quickly followed Alaska's lead, and, as this is written, Nevada, Rhode Island, and Utah have also acted to permit APTs.[403]

The attractions of US-based APTs are that they are far less expensive to establish, less expensive to operate and maintain, utilize legal systems that are familiar and that rely on long-settled precedents for most points of law, and (except possibly for Alaska) exist in places that are easy to get to. The fundamental problem with US-based APTs—and it is a significant problem, indeed—is that, on their face, most US APT laws appear to fly in the face of the US Constitutional requirement that each state give "full faith and credit" to judgments obtained in other states. While no US APT has, to my knowledge, been tested, it would seem that any prudent family that is serious about asset protection will want to avoid US APTs until this key legal issue has been settled.

Cautions about APTs

The main caution about APTs is that the time to set them up is long before a potential liability has arisen. Once litigants or other creditors begin to circle around the family, it is probably too late to engage in this or any other asset protection strategy.[404] The reason is that US courts, already hostile to APTs, will almost certainly consider any transfer of assets to such a trust to be a "fraudulent conveyance."[405] This will enable the court to toss a family member in jail for contempt until the assets are repatriated or the litigant's judgment is otherwise paid off.[406]

---

403 Most of these states have also eliminated the Rule Against Perpetuities, a Common Law principle that limits the duration of trusts to "lives in being plus 21 years." As a result, APTs established in those states can, theoretically, persist forever.

404 Note that many APTs contain a so-called "Jones" clause (don't ask me where the name comes from) allowing the trust to pay creditors who were in existence when the trust was established.

405 Fraudulent conveyances are technically a part of the law of bankruptcy. The concept originated with the English Statute of Elizabeth in 1571. Virtually every US jurisdiction has enacted similar legislation, mainly modeled on the Uniform Fraudulent Transfer Act of 1984.

406 On the other hand, some families, faced with a known potential liability and having no APT in existence, might well feel that there is little to lose by setting one up. Perhaps the courts will find it valid. Even if the US courts toss the APT out, the family has lost only the expense of setting it up.

Other issues to keep in mind have to do with costs and investment returns. In addition to the legal costs associated with establishing APTs, most of the ongoing costs—trustee fees, custody fees, investment management fees—will dwarf similar asset management costs incurred in the US. Worse, unless the settlor of an APT is extremely careful, investment returns are likely to be seriously under par—the investment management skills of most offshore institutions are far, far below minimally acceptable levels of competence by onshore standards.

A Note about Swiss Bank Accounts

Not so long ago almost anyone could walk into a Swiss bank and open a numbered account, secure in the knowledge that (except for a few senior bank officials) no one would know whose account it was, no taxes need ever be paid on the earnings in the account, and no private litigant or obnoxious government bureaucrat could ever find—much less seize—the account. This happy state of affairs existed for most of the twentieth century because, for most of that century most people, and certainly most rich people, considered that it was none of anyone's business what they did with their wealth.

But the wheels began to come off the system after World War II, when news of Swiss complicity with the Nazis, and of Swiss insensitivity to the plight of the Jews, brought Swiss banks in particular and Switzerland in general into an unwonted state of disrepute. Never mind that Switzerland was a tiny country sharing a very long border with a powerful and aggressive Germany, and that Swiss support for Germany never approached the level it reached in, say, Sweden.[407] Moral standards changed after the war and the Swiss were the scapegoats. The problem got worse as it became clear that every two-bit dictator in the world seemed to be using Switzerland as a safe haven for the treasures they had stolen from their countries, and that every other rich American criminal seemed to manage to slip off to Switzerland to live in high style, rather than be dragged off to the pokey like ordinary criminals.[408]

But the real nail in the numbered account coffin was the desire of the big Swiss banks (and other large Swiss companies) to do business far beyond the borders of little Switzerland. Firms like CSFB (Credit Suisse First Boston) and UBS (Union de Banques Suisse) became global powerhouses, earning far more

---

[407] Swedish public opinion was solidly behind the Nazis until it became clear that Germany would lose the war.

[408] Except possibly for the Monica Lewinsky affair, President Clinton's pardon of Marc Rich was probably his single most wrong-headed act as President.

of their revenues and profits outside Switzerland than inside. Even Swiss private banks like Pictet & Cie and Lombard Odier & Cie ventured far beyond their historic habitat of Zurich and Geneva. These firms weren't about to protect the needs of wealthy families who wished to remain anonymous if the cost of that protection was the inability to compete on a level playing field around the world. As a result, the likelihood that American courts would seize Swiss bank assets in the US to pressure the banks (or the Swiss government) into disclosing the details of numbered accounts meant that no numbered account would ever again be secure.

Today, Switzerland maintains that it is happy to cooperate with American investigators when the alleged crime in the US is also a crime in Switzerland, but that beyond that their hands are tied. Thus, if an American citizen is accused of securities fraud, the Swiss are happy to cooperate. But if the crime is tax fraud—which apparently, though inexplicably, is not a crime in Switzerland—the banks are helpless. This is unmitigated nonsense. Anyone who has supposedly committed tax fraud in the US has almost certainly committed many other crimes as well, the list of which is limited only by the imagination of the prosecutors. Consider various conspiracies, mail fraud, Common Law theft, and so on. One of these crimes is almost certain to be a crime in Switzerland, freeing the Swiss banks to offer their eager assistance.

The long and short of it is that families who want to hold assets in Switzerland are free to do so. However, these families must be willing to bear the breathtaking costs and lousy investment returns associated with Swiss banking practices, and must be willing either to pay taxes currently on the accounts or to risk seeing their photos and stories on the front page of the New York *Times* as unpatriotic tax cheats. For everyone else, the lure of Switzerland has dimmed mightily.

Soft Dollars

There is no arguing with unreasoning imbecility.
—Samuel Johnson

Soft dollar practices are a sleazy backwater of the investment business and one that should be abolished by the regulatory authorities forthwith. The phrase "soft dollars" describes a series of practices that are conducted out of sight of investors and that very directly and seriously harm our interests. Soft dollar arrangements can take many forms, but the essence of it goes something like this. A money management firm could hire its own analysts, conduct its own securities research (or buy research for cash), buy its own Bloomberg machines, etc. In that case the costs associated with those activities would be reflected in its ongoing operating costs and would affect its profitability.

But there is a dirtier way to pay for these things, namely, to overpay for trade execution. In other words, our manager agrees to pay a brokerage commission of, say, 6 cents a share instead of paying the 1-2 cents per share the broker would otherwise charge. The nice thing about this squalid alternative is that *we* pay the commission, not the money manager. In fact, if the manager is a mutual fund, the soft dollar commission payment isn't included in the fund's annual expense ratio, giving investors a very false sense of what the fund's actual expenses are.[409] For the soft dollar payment the manager receives in return a bundle of services, typically including (a) the trade itself, (b) a "kickback" from the broker (euphemistically referred to in the industry as "payment for order flow"), (c) research generated by the brokerage firm, (d) a capital commitment from the broker,[410] (e) IPO allocations, and (f) computer equipment and services.[411]

Soft dollar practices originated in the pre-1972 days of fixed brokerage commissions, when brokers could not compete on price. Though they are "legal,"[412] they have effectively placed a limit on how low commission rates can go, namely, about five cents per share. The industry estimates that the services bundled around soft dollar trading constitute about 60% of the total value

---

409 According to the New York Times, the RS Mid Cap Opportunities Fund incurred estimated commissions and over-the-counter spreads of 1.8% in 2001, more than doubling the fund's published 1.5% expense ratio. Richard Teitelbaum, "Know a Fund's Cost? Look Deeper," *New York Times*, February 9, 2003, p. B11.

410 When a manager sends a large order to a broker (typically >$5 million), the broker may commit to a price and then work the order, in effect putting his own capital at risk in the transaction.

411 Until recently, managers often received more outrageous services, including free vacations, for directing soft dollar orders to brokers. The SEC has cracked down on this practice, but the Commission estimates that 30% of money managers continue to employ soft dollars for non-research products and services. See "Inspection Report on the Soft Dollar Practices of Broker-Dealers, Investment Advisors and Mutual Funds," Securities and Exchange Commission (September 1998).

412 Section 28(e) of the Securities Exchange Act of 1934 was amended in 1975 to permit soft dollar agreements where "the commissions paid are reasonable in relation to the value of the brokerage and research services provided." SEC regulations have expanded on this "safe harbor" somewhat, but the area remains murky. The 1975 amendment should be repealed forthwith.

of the commission payment, or $0.03–$0.035 per share. Roughly one-half of all commissions in the U.S. are paid in soft dollars, as part of an explicit agreement between the manager and the broker.[413]

What's Wrong with Soft Dollar Payments?

A lot. Here are the main concerns:

- As noted above, the existence of soft dollar arrangements effectively places a floor under the commission rates brokers charge, artificially inflating investment costs for everyone.
- More broadly, soft dollars corrupt the efficiency of the capital markets. A manager who trades in soft dollars is paying far more for its trades than it would pay if the soft dollar services were unbundled. True, he is receiving other services, but because these services and the commissions are bundled together, he has no idea how much he is paying for each service. This lack of transparency of important costs represents perhaps the most anachronistic and inefficient aspect of American capital markets practices. (Well, with the possible exception of the New York Stock Exchange's inexplicable persistence in the use of specialists.)
- The value of soft services varies materially from manager to manager. All institutional managers pay about the same commission, but the value of the "soft" services varies dramatically from manager to manager. IPO allocations, for example, may be highly prized by a small cap growth manager, but they will be of no interest to a large cap value manager.
- The overall quality of execution is impaired. Because the broker isn't competing for the orders (the fund has already committed to direct them to him), the quality of execution of soft dollar trades is materially worse than the quality of execution of non-directed trades.
- In case anyone had any doubts, the brokerage industry doesn't actually use most soft dollar payments to produce research. A recent study from TowerGroup projected that technology spending among brokers would likely decline nearly 12% between 2004 and 2008. If soft dollars were banned, TowerGroup projected a 36% decline![414] Hmm.

---

413 *The Economist* (July 7, 2001).

414 Will Leitch, "A Soft-Dollar Ban Would Hurt Technology Spending," *Wealth Management Letter* (July 14, 2004). The full report is available from TowerGroup at www.towergroup.com.

- The value of soft dollars belongs to the client, not the money manager. Money managers are allocating trades on behalf of assets owned by their clients. By accepting financial kickbacks and goods and services, and in return paying higher commissions and accepting poorer execution, the manager is effectively increasing its own fee and decreasing the client's return. Managers get away with this practice only because most clients don't understand what is happening with their commission dollars.

What's to be Done?

A recent study estimated the explicit costs of soft dollar trades to be four times the costs of trades channeled through non-intermediated electronic systems and the implicit costs to be three times greater.[415] That study also found that 51% of chief investment officers at major money management firms felt it would be "desirable" or "highly desirable" for commissions to be unbundled. (Only 8% felt it would be "undesirable" or "highly undesirable.") A survey of sophisticated clients would surely find that a far larger majority would want to see the practice abolished. For example, David Swensen, who manages the Yale University endowment, refers to soft dollar practices as "odious." According to Swensen, "Soft dollar activity flies in the face of reasonable governance. * * * Soft dollars and directed brokerage, the slimy underbelly of the brokerage world, ought to be banned."[416]

Yet nothing happens. The reasons nothing happens are (i) money managers and brokers are locked into cozy arrangements that benefit both at the expense of investors, (ii) managers that refuse to enter into soft dollar arrangements will not pay less, and hence it is difficult for any individual manager to refuse to play the game, (iii) clients don't understand the obscure practice and how much it works to their disadvantage, and (iv) the SEC, supposedly the investors' watchdog, is asleep at the switch.

Probably the best that individual investors can do is to make pests of ourselves over soft dollar practices, making managers and brokers as uncomfortable as possible. Beyond that—write your Congressional representatives!

---

415 Robert Schwartz and Benn Steil, "Controlling Institutional Trading Costs: We Have Met the Enemy and They Are Us," *Journal of Portfolio Management* (Spring 2002).

416 David F. Swensen, *Pioneering Portfolio Management* (The Free Press, 2000), pp. 272, 277.

Portable Alpha

Alpha, you see, is like girls and roses;
it lasts while it lasts.[417]

Those of us who are regular readers of the investment journals—and who, no doubt, need to get a life—have been hearing about portable alpha strategies for several years.[418] But it has only been in the last twelve months that these strategies have moved out of the realm of academia and into more mainstream discussion.[419] So what exactly is portable alpha all about, and what relevance does it have for the management of real investment portfolios?

Sources of Outperformance

To answer this question, it is necessary to review briefly the chief—and, in most cases, the only—sources of investment outperformance: market return and manager alpha.[420] Outperformance in this context refers to investment return beyond that obtainable on "risk-free" securities—United States Treasury bills for a US investor. T-bills generally return something very much like the consensus estimate of short-term inflation. There is a bit of a lag in both directions, but over time tax-exempt buyers of T-bills who have no spending needs will roughly maintain the real purchasing power of their assets but will not grow those assets net of inflation. For taxable investors it's another story altogether: net of taxes, taxable investors in T-bills will get a little poorer every year. Of course, it's a rare taxable or tax-exempt investor that has no spending needs. In practical terms, therefore, virtually all investors in risk-free assets will get poorer over time—hardly a "risk-free" proposition!

---

417 Paraphrase of a remark attributed to Charles de Gaulle: "Treaties, you see, are like girls and roses; they last while they last."

418 Most recently, for example, see Dorsey D. Farr, "The Long and Short of Tax Efficiency," *The Journal of Wealth Management* (Spring 2004), p. 74.

419 Goldman Sachs has been in the forefront of the attempt to introduce portable alpha strategies to investors. See, especially, the series of three Open Letters to Investors entitled "Active Alpha Investing," by Bob Litterman, the head of Goldman's quantitative group. These letters are available from Goldman Sachs.

420 Particularly thoughtful investors can also add value through tactical asset allocation strategies. These strategies tend to work best, however, when they are limited to very compelling opportunities.

Since few investors are satisfied watching their wealth slowly disappear, most of us are looking for investment outperformance: the ability to earn an increment or premium over the risk-free return.

Market return. No sensible person would invest in an asset riskier than a Treasury bill unless the investor had a reasonable expectation of receiving a greater return on that investment. Hence the theoretical case for the existence of stocks, bonds, and every other investment asset. Beyond the theoretical case for the existence of the risk premium, we have powerful historical evidence as well. Over long periods of time, for example, US equities have returned a substantial-but-inconsistent premium over T-bills. That premium was substantial, indeed, in the 1980s and (especially) the 1990s, but has actually been negative during the first few years of the 21st century. Predicting future equity premia is fraught with difficulty, but many observers believe that something like 4% is reasonable over the intermediate term. If we add that 4% to the return we expect on T-bills—and if we are right both about the size of the risk premium and the return on T-bills—we will get the future return on stocks.

Note that this premium is completely independent of manager or investor talent. We can obtain the equity risk premium cheaply by simply investing in an index fund, buying an exchange-traded fund, or by using derivative strategies such as index futures.

Manager alpha. I have elsewhere addressed the complex topic of manager outperformance,[421] but for purposes of this discussion let's assume that it exists (as it almost surely does) and that it can be accessed by intelligent, very diligent investors (as it probably can be). Alpha, incidentally, is a measure of risk-adjusted outperformance, risk in this case being compared to the risk of the broader market. After all, since we can get the risk premium on the broader market by investing passively, any manager who subjects our assets to greater risk than that will not survive[422] unless he or she can justify the increased risk by obtaining increased returns. The principle is exactly the same as the one stated above: no one would invest in stocks unless they outperformed T-bills, and no one would (or should) invest with a manager unless the manager either outperforms the market or takes less risk.

---

421 See Chapter 13.

422 Perhaps we should say, "*should* not survive." It's astonishing how many managers incur greater-than-market risk while generating lower-than-market returns and still manage to attract investors. Roughly two-thirds of all the mutual funds in the Morningstar universe fit this description.

Assuming, however, that we can identify managers who can outperform on a risk-adjusted basis, we now have access to both sources of investment outperformance: market return and manager alpha. So what does "portable" alpha have to do with all this?

Portable Alpha Strategies

Porting alpha within an asset class. Let's take a very simple example. Assume an investor, Betty, whose entire $100 million portfolio will be invested in US large cap stocks. (Yes, Betty needs to find a better investment advisor.) Betty very much needs to get the market return on large caps, but she would like to do somewhat better if possible. She decides to allocate her large cap exposure between market return and manager alpha on a 70%/30% basis. In other words, Betty has some degree of confidence in her ability to identify outperforming managers, but she is not so confident that she wants to bet the farm on it—or even half the farm.

The traditional method of implementing this strategy would be for Betty to invest $70 million in an index fund (or exchange-traded fund) and to invest the $30 million balance with the potentially outperforming managers she has identified. What's wrong with this picture?

Portable alpha strategies begin with the insight that it is not necessary for Betty to tie up $70 million of her capital in order to expose 70% of her large cap portfolio to the market return. Betty could obtain that return derivatively—by, for example, holding S&P 500 index futures[423] and using the capital she has saved to invest with the alpha manager. Since futures are a leveraged bet on the S&P 500 Index, she can obtain $70 million worth of market exposure for far less than $70 million.[424] With the capital she has saved, Betty can invest more money with the high alpha managers she has identified.

Note that Betty has thus maintained her $100 million allocation to US large cap stocks, and she has also maintained her 70% allocation to the market return. But she has greatly *increased* her exposure to manager alpha by "porting"[425] capital from a sector of the portfolio that cannot outperform the market (although it can outperform T-bills) to a sector of the portfolio that can

423 Portable alpha strategies require the existence of an index future, an exchange-traded fund, or a swap contract on the market portfolio. Managing portable alpha strategies using ETFs and swaps will be considerably more expensive.

424 $50,000 of margin debt will buy $1 million of S&P 500 index futures, for example.

425 "Port," orig., to carry. *Webster's New World Dictionary* (1998).

outperform the market. Capital is moving in one direction, but alpha is moving in the other direction, to her market return portfolio. In addition, Betty could (and should) short the market to the extent she believes her high-alpha managers are carrying deadweight[426] in their portfolios, and she could also structure her fee arrangements with the high alpha managers so that she pays little or nothing for market performance but much more for risk-adjusted outperformance.

If Betty is right about her ability to identify outperforming managers, her "portable alpha" portfolio will significantly outperform the more traditionally structured portfolio, simply because the traditional portfolio tied up far too much of her capital in a strategy that cannot outperform.

Porting alpha between asset classes. Let's look at another simple example. Assume that an investor, the Widget Pension Plan, is very focused on matching its assets (the pension fund investment portfolio) and its liabilities (the value of the retirement benefits it has promised to its employees). Widget therefore owns a $100 million portfolio invested entirely in bonds.[427] Widget isn't much interested in porting capital from the Lehman Aggregate Index to active bond managers because Widget believes that the alpha an active bond manager can produce is likely to be very small. On the other hand, Widget would very much like to enjoy the alpha it believes hedge funds can produce. The trouble is that Widget has no allocation to hedge funds and doesn't want to have one. What to do?

Now that we are experts on portable alpha, the answer is child's play. Widget will hold futures on the bond index and will use the proceeds to invest with the outperforming hedge funds it has identified. (It will also, of course, hedge out any market return exposure these managers have by shorting those benchmarks.)

---

426 Deadweight is that portion of a manager's portfolio that clones the manager's benchmark, but on which active management fees are being charged.

427 Although this strategy of "liability matching" has its proponents (they surface just after every bear market), it has some shortcomings. The first is that the plan's liabilities aren't really known, but can only be estimated, so the bond portfolio may be matching something other than the plan's liabilities. The second is that interest rate changes affect both the value of the bond portfolio and also the size of the liabilities, but not necessarily in the same increments. In other words, a 1% change in rates can have a far more profound impact on assets than on liabilities, or vice versa. Finally, the liability matching strategy condemns the Widget Company to higher (though, presumably, less uncertain) plan contributions.

Widget has thus transported capital from the bond portfolio to the hedge fund managers and has transported the hedge fund managers' alpha back to the bond portfolio. If Widget is right about the outperforming managers it has identified, it will get the benchmark bond return it needs plus the alpha its hedge managers have produced. The Widget Company may never have to make another contribution to its pension plan!

Challenges Associated with Portable Alpha Strategies

Recall that we began by saying we were using simple examples. True portable alpha strategies are designed to leverage investment capital across many different asset classes and market return strategies—few investors are going to have single-asset-class asset allocation strategies. Investors employing portable alpha will likely be using market neutral strategies, active overlay strategies, currency trading and global tactical asset allocation. But whether our portable alpha strategies are simple or complex, we will face several significant challenges.

The challenge presented by negative alpha. While it is straightforward to identify managers who have outperformed in the past, it is enormously difficult to identify in advance managers who will outperform in the future. (See Chapter 13.) Thus, there is a very real chance that our high alpha managers will turn out to be low alpha managers or even negative alpha managers. Using traditional strategies, unhappy surprises associated with manager underperformance tend to have relatively little impact on our wealth. In the case of Betty (above), for example, if her high alpha managers underperform the market by ½ of 1% per year, the actual harm to her US large cap portfolio would be only 30% of ½ of 1%—that is, 15 basis points—because she has only allocated 30% of her large cap exposure to these managers. And if (in a more sensible case) only 30% of Betty's capital had been exposed to the US large cap asset class, rather than 100%, then the damage to her overall portfolio would have been only 30% of 15 basis points, or 4.5 basis points per year. Betty might not be happy, but she would still be alive.

But with portable alpha strategies, we are making a much bigger bet on our ability to identify outperforming managers. If we are wrong, the leveraged underperformance of the active managers could overwhelm the risk premium provided by the indexed portfolio, leaving us with a very risky and expensive T-bill portfolio—or worse.

The challenge presented by trying to manage portable alpha portfolios. Except for the very largest investors using the most sophisticated risk-control technology and employing the most experienced investment professionals, investors will tend to find that portable alpha sounds better in theory than it does in practice. How many investors have significant experience buying index futures or owning short positions in a benchmark? How many have in place risk controls designed to monitor leveraged market exposure daily? How many investors using traditional strategies even bother to calculate and manage market and active risk on an ongoing basis? How many investors have created "risk budgets" designed to eliminate sources of unintended risk, to identify sources of outperformance, and to quantify marginal contributions to risk and return? How many investors are prepared to abandon the traditional view of portfolio design as one focused on asset classes and instead refocus on sources of alpha and beta, regardless of asset class?

Moreover, given that the most efficient portable alpha strategies will focus on high-risk products with low correlations that are not capacity-constrained—i.e., strategies that are very difficult to access—most investors will find that they are relegated to less efficient strategies. The risk-return tradeoff in these strategies is likely to be less compelling.

The challenge presented by tax drag. For tax-exempt investors—such as the Widget Pension Plan—the taxability of different investment strategies is irrelevant. But for taxable investors, taxes are likely to be the single largest drag on investment returns. And for these investors, portable alpha strategies, because they rely on the use of complex derivative instruments, will often have the effect of converting long term capital gain into short term gain. Yes, the recent tax bill has reduced tax rates, but we need to keep in mind that the difference between ordinary income taxes and capital gains taxes has actually increased, from 1900 basis points to 2000 basis points. Thus, taxable investors will want to approach portable alpha strategies with very considerable caution.

Summary

Theoretically, portable alpha strategies make a great deal of sense, mainly because they deploy investor capital far more efficiently than do traditional strategies. But this efficiency comes with costs, and investors who wish to use portable alpha strategies will want to consider those costs very carefully. My guess is that most investors who use portable alpha strategies in the future will rely on outside firms to help them design, implement and (especially) monitor those strategies.

AFTERWORD

On Happiness

Afterword

On Happiness

Happiness, Madame, happiness.
—Charles de Gaulle[428]

Tolstoy was right: all happy families *are* alike, and that is true whether the families are rich, poor or middle class. The characteristics that tend to lead to happiness are simply not wealth-dependent. Indeed, science is telling us (we already knew this) that human beings have a genetic predisposition toward being happy or unhappy. We all know people who seem to have every reason to be happy, but who in fact are chronically morose and unpleasant to be around. On the other hand, we all know people who face a mountain of miseries but who are always cheerful and upbeat.

Thus, nothing in this book is intended to suggest that merely being wealthy will inevitably lead to happiness. It won't, any more than merely being poor or merely being middle class will inevitably lead to happiness. Happiness, to the extent that it goes beyond genetically-wired predispositions, is almost always earned.[429] We earn it by being productive, by overcoming obstacles that challenge

428 Late in their lives, Charles de Gaulle and his wife were being interviewed by an American television journalist. Although the interviewer had done his best to include Madame de Gaulle in the conversation, *Le Grand Charles* utterly dominated the proceedings. Finally, as the interview neared its end, the determined journalist turned directly to Madame de Gaulle and asked, "What is the most important thing in life?" Madame de Gaulle's command of the English language had never been robust, and her accent was usually impenetrable, but in this case she had understood the question perfectly. She settled back comfortably in her chair and replied, "A penis." A stunned silence followed. But General de Gaulle merely leaned toward his wife and said, "*Hap*piness, Madame, *hap*piness."

429 A recent study at Emory University measured brain activity in the striatum, the portion of the brain associated with pleasure. One group in the study had

us (but that aren't so daunting that they are impossible to conquer), by living in and helping to create a close and loving family environment, by making and keeping friends and acquaintances. None of this happens without effort, and hence the challenge of being happy is at its essence the same for all socioeconomic levels.

Of course, the specific form each of the challenges takes can be powerfully affected by our level of material wellbeing and by the social and cultural circumstances[430] of our lives. A welfare mother, possibly barely more than a child herself, living in an urban ghetto or a bleak rural township with her three children, faces a certain set of challenges to her own happiness and that of her family, and those challenges are different than the challenges faced by a suburban soccer mom. The welfare mother's challenges can be so Herculean that they will defeat her, leading to misery for herself and her fragile family. But they are not different in kind from those of the soccer mom. The path to happiness for both women is the path we articulated above—work, family, friends.

And the same is true for wealthy families. For this small but crucial group of Americans, the pathway to happiness is the same as it is for everyone else. And, unsurprisingly, the outcomes are about the same as well. The canard about the rich living lives of opulent emptiness is as bigoted—and hopelessly wrong—as the notion that all inner city Americans are drugged-up gang members or that all suburban families are conformist boors. Happiness among the rich is about as evenly distributed as it is among just about any other group of Americans.

Hollywood Stereotypes of the Rich

Many of the stereotypes about wealthy families are generated, or at least perpetuated, by silly Hollywood versions of the rich, where all the children are spoiled trust fund babies, all the parents are emotionally stunted, all the lives are lived in dreary splendor. But, after all, we can't really blame Hollywood for this. Most of us are pretty boring, normal families, while dysfunctional families, like

---

to work to receive money while the other group was paid without having to earn it. The brains of those who had to work for their money were more stimulated, that is, they experienced more pleasure. "Are Lottery Winners Really Less Happy? People Get More Satisfaction Earning Their Cash, Study Finds," *The Associated Press* (May 13, 2004).

430 The so-called "Whitehall Studies," conducted in Britain since 1967, have demonstrated that social status alone is a far better predictor of health even when other issues (smoking, eating habits, exercise) have been controlled for. See Patricia Cohen, "Forget Lonely. Life Is Healthy at the Top," New York *Times* (May 15, 2004), p. A17.

it or not, make for far more interesting viewing. If Tolstoy were alive today he might have written, "All happy families are bad sitcom material."

But even among the wealthy themselves, who should know better, there is a sense that their families face higher odds of being happy and productive. To be sure, the challenges facing wealthy families who aspire to happiness—that is, all wealthy families—are different from those of other families, in the same way that the challenges facing welfare families are different from those facing middle class families. But the actual outcomes, as noted above, are about the same.

The Rich and the "Faux Rich"

Another issue that tends to cause confusion in this regard is the confounding of two kinds of prominent families: the truly rich, that is, those who control very significant amounts of private capital, and the "faux rich," those who merely enjoy extremely high incomes. The latter might eventually control significant capital, but the dynamic that drives their lives and their characteristic neuroses is the relatively sudden thrust from a middle income (or worse) past to a very, very high income present. Such people are more analogous to lottery winners than to the truly rich, and their typical patterns of behavior are similar to the dysfunctional practices of lottery winners.

There are very few ways in the US or any other democratic society for anyone to legally earn a huge income, and in virtually every one of those sectors of the economy the jobs come with enormously high risk. Is the CEO of a Fortune 500 corporation really worth being paid hundreds of times as much as a factory worker? Maybe so, but many people will be skeptical, including many CEOs themselves. Worse, the job of any CEO can suddenly disappear, its occupant summarily fired, often for reasons wholly beyond the CEO's control.[431] And along with the job, out the window go the high income and all the perks and the CEO's reputation.[432] Private capital, on the other hand, if it is wisely managed (see Chapters 3 through 17, above), never goes away.

Let's look at a sector of the economy where enormously high incomes can be earned—the entertainment industry.[433] In the entertainment business, the

---

431 According to a study by one insurance company (Mass Mutual), the average tenure of a CEO of a nonfamily business is four years.

432 In the "Whitehall Studies," cited above, high-status individuals who occupied insecure positions actually had the *worst* health outcomes. Patricia Cohen, op. cit., note 429, p. A19.

433 We could also have looked at the investment banking business, where a similar phenomenon of high-income-at-high-risk predominates. Investment bankers are paid mainly according to the size of the deal they are working on.

incomes earned by the most successful people reflect not some extraordinary level of talent, but simply the *local value* of whatever talent exists.[434] To illustrate this point, let's begin by considering a woman—we'll call her Helen—who is not in the entertainment business at all, but who is an exceptionally able administrative assistant to corporate executives (a person we would not long ago have called a secretary). Helen is organized, pleasant, diplomatic, reliable, and so on, and the executives to whom she reports during her career are very lucky to have her. Very few Americans are as good at their jobs as Helen is at hers. Unfortunately for Helen, there is only so much that her talents are worth—the local value of her talents as an executive assistant might allow her to lead a nice, comfortable lifestyle, but she will never become rich. In other words, Helen is a lot like most talented people—she will be successful and will enjoy her work, but her annual income will never make the front page of the Wall Street *Journal.*

Now we'll contrast Helen with another, roughly equally talented person. Imagine a television industry executive—we'll call him Larry—who has a specific talent, namely, the ability to anticipate what television shows Americans are going to like and watch. In the general scheme of things, this is a modest enough talent, roughly equivalent to Helen's. But Larry is lucky—the local value of his talent is enormous. The network pays Larry millions of dollars a year simply because the shows he has picked for the network tend to draw slightly more viewers than the shows other people have picked for other networks. This slight advantage means hundreds of millions of dollars in advertising revenue to Larry's network, so allocating a small percentage of that to keeping Larry happy seems like a bargain.

Meanwhile, Larry, a middle class kid from Queens, has never seen so much money in his life. He spends it lavishly, so that everyone will know how important he is. Tiny slights—Larry was recently assigned a seat in the rear rows for a bonzo Hollywood opening, and not two weeks ago his regular table at Spago was occupied by a media mogul—wound Larry deeply, sending him into a rage. Larry routinely works 100-hour weeks, has been divorced twice and is currently dating a gorgeous but brain-dead starlet. He would barely recognize his own children if they wandered into his office. What little spare time Larry has is spent with his personal trainer, trying desperately to remain buff in the face of advancing middle age.

---

434 I exclude individuals who are truly preeminent in their fields, as opposed to those whose talent levels are similar to the talent levels of people in other industries.

But for all this, Larry is not the superficial twit he seems to be.[435] He is simply a relatively ordinary guy who has suddenly been thrust into the position of earning a huge income and whose job, reputation and salary are constantly in danger of suddenly going away. The grinding insecurity this engenders manifests itself in Larry's nauseating insistence on proving how important he is. But Larry is right to feel insecure. Sure enough, Larry's infatuation with modestly sexy sitcoms—his claim to fame in the industry—has overstayed its welcome. The public is tired of watching self-absorbed nincompoops exposing their neuroses at 9 p.m., and has turned its attention to "reality" shows. Caught completely off-guard, his network's ratings plummet and Larry is summarily—and very publicly—fired. There went his high income, his power to "greenlight" shows, his table at Spago, essentially everything that dominated Larry's life has disappeared in an instant. Helen, meanwhile, continues to climb the corporate ladder, getting herself assigned to ever-more-senior executives. And the truly rich, meanwhile, continue to be rich.

The Real Way the Rich Are Different

The need to control the world around us is an instinct deeply embedded in the human soul. And a good thing it is, too: else we would all be naked and living in caves. If something is irritating us, we change it. Even if something is OK, but could be better, we change it. Wealthy families are no different than anyone else in this regard, with the singular distinction that it is far easier for the rich to buy control of their lives than it is for anyone else. And there lies the rub.

Most attempts to buy control of our world are harmless enough. A working class family, rather than swelter through a hot, humid summer, will put a window air conditioning unit in the parents' bedroom. A middle class family will air condition most of the rooms that adults spend time in. An upper middle class family will install whole-house air conditioning. But a wealthy family, having just purchased that charming old mansion put up in the 19th century,

---

435 Speaking of superficial twits, we are reminded of most of what passes for on-screen talent in Hollywood. Ben Affleck, Jennifer Lopez and their ilk may be modestly talented, indeed, but their appeal to the viewing public is worth millions and millions of dollars to their studios and record labels. But while some talent is in fact serious and permanent—Sinatra's career spanned half a century, and Johnny Carson's late night show lasted thirty years—most on-screen "talent" is illusory and very, very short-lived. The insecurity this phenomenon generates, and the bizarre behavior associated with it, are too well-known to be detailed.

will install enough HVAC to keep all twenty-two rooms at a perfect 70 degrees all year around—and hang the (ridiculous) cost.

So what? The trouble comes when the habit of buying our way out of the normal irritations of life extends to buying our way out of irritations that are inextricably entwined with our happiness. Consider the three arenas of life that will largely determine whether or not we will be happy: raising children, preserving a happy marriage, engaging in a productive work life. All three activities are fraught with a large variety of day-to-day irritations. Infants can be colicky, making our lives a living hell until they grow out of it. Toddlers learning the joys of independence make the phrase "the terrible twos" a gargantuan understatement. Pre-adolescents become involved in so many activities that we have to put our lives on hold just to drive them from place to place and attend their many (and often crushingly boring) events. Teenagers—well, no need to dwell on that subject. Then, suddenly, our children are grown and out of the house forever, and we spend the rest of our lives missing them.

As for marriage, never was a more bizarre arrangement invented. The idea that two adult human beings can share the same space, eat at the same table, supervise the same children, sleep in the same bed, *everyday of their lives*, is preposterous. This is a good working definition of hell, if nothing else. And yet most of us not only get married, we usually get married more than once (the triumph, as the saying goes, of hope over experience). The day-to-day irritations imposed on us by the institution of marriage are so numerous and so troublesome that long books are written about how to manage and minimize them. Nonetheless, like democracy, marriage is the worst of all possible outcomes—except for all the others.

Or consider work. No one who has ever held a job can possibly harbor any romantic illusions about the "joy of work." On a day-to-day basis, working is a pain in the neck. We have to get up earlier than we want to. We have to put on uncomfortable clothes. We have to commute through maddening traffic. We have to work with some colleagues we don't like and would never spend time with if we had any choice in the matter. Our bosses are invariably hopeless jerks. And, in the end, we are infuriatingly under-appreciated and underpaid. When we meet some idiot who claims to "love his work," who "would do it for free if necessary," we know we have encountered a dangerous lunatic. Yet, virtually all of us do in fact work, including most of us who have no financial need to do so.

For most human beings, the irritations associated with raising children, staying happily married, and working productively are assumed to be nothing less than a part of the human condition. Unless we don't wish to pass our genes along, unless we wish to be alone and lonely, unless we're happy to starve to death in a gutter, we put up with these irritations and get on with our lives. And the ultimate result is happiness.

But suppose we didn't have to put up with them? Suppose we could, in fact, buy our way out of all or most of them? Wouldn't we be tempted to do it? Of course we would. And there lies the danger for the wealthy. In an attempt to control obvious irritations, we manage to buy our way out of happiness.

Children and the Wealthy

If, for example, children are an irritation—as they certainly are—well, that is why God invented nurses, nannies, day care, tutors, boarding schools, etc., etc. If we are wealthy enough, we can move our children from birth through college without ever laying eyes on the little creeps. But this, of course, would be a serious mistake. As noted above, the irritations associated with raising children are inseparably bound up with the joys associated with raising children. We can't experience the latter without experiencing the former. Moreover, the way we deal with those irritations teaches our children volumes about what it means to be an adult, about maturity and patience, about what Moms and Dads are all about (including the fact that Moms and Dads sometimes lose it altogether).

Yes, it's annoying in the extreme that little Freddie's soccer tournament is being held at a rural backwater three hour's drive away, and on a weekend when our office work is piled to the ceiling. And, yes, it's more than mildly provoking that little Susie's middle school play happens to be scheduled on the same night as our favorite annual black tie affair. But slipping Freddie fifty bucks as we head off to the office, or sending a dozen roses to Susie in lieu of our presence, are just more ways of buying our way out of happiness. No, we don't have to attend every single soccer tournament, and, no, we're not monsters if we sometimes favor black tie affairs over middle school plays. But we can't let those choices become habits.

The fact that we *can* buy our way out of these irritations, and thousands more like them, doesn't mean that we *should* buy our way out of them. The easier it is for parents to buy their way out of the irritating aspects of childrearing, the more likely we are to do it. It is extremely easy for the rich to do it, and hence not doing it—avoiding the temptation as often as possible—is one of the great challenges the wealthy face in pursuing happiness.

Marriage and the Wealthy

Sociologists tell us that more than half of all first marriages end in divorce, and that even higher percentages of subsequent marriages end in divorce.[436] But even these statistics understate the true rate of marriage failure, since many couples stay together for religious or financial reasons, or simply out of inertia. The simple truth is that long-term happy marriages are quite rare. And, given the challenges posed by living together with another human being, this should come as no surprise to us. The only way to eliminate divorce is to prohibit it, and the only way to eliminate unhappy marriages is to abolish marriage itself.[437]

The rich face all the same challenges to staying happily married as anyone else. But, in addition, we face the temptation to buy our way out of the irritations that inevitably accompany our marriages. The classic example of this is the spouse who routinely treats the other spouse badly, then "makes up for it" with an ISB (I'm Sorry Bauble), carefully sized to the scale of the offense. The message the offending spouse sends with the ISB is this one: "I can treat you any way I wish, as long as my offensive conduct is followed by an appropriate ISB." The message the offended spouse is sending is this one: "You can treat me any way you like, as long as you pay for it with an ISB."

There is nothing wrong with ISBs—even a poor spouse can afford a small bouquet of flowers or a fifth of Johnny Walker. The trouble comes about when the ISB is not a token of our remorse and our love, but a substitute for it. If we have done something that hurt our spouse, even inadvertently, the way to "make up for it" is to apologize sincerely, to let our spouse know that we are remorseful, to assure our spouse that we will do our best not to let it happen again. Skipping this extremely difficult step, and proceeding straight to the ISB, is simply a way of buying our way out of happiness, and it's a road that is especially easy for wealthy spouses to take.

Marriage is a difficult business, and most marriages will fail in one way or another. But being one half of a happy marriage is perhaps the most certain

---

436 Actually, the 50% figure appears to be a guess, not a statistic. And affluent families actually have significantly lower divorce rates than poor families. See Sue Shellenbarger, "No Comfort in Numbers: Divorce Rate Varies Widely from Group to Group," Wall Street Journal (April 22, 2004), p. D1.

437 Incidentally, by using the term "marriage" I am engaging in a bit of shorthand for any long-term, loving relationship. I realize that many people are offended by use of this term for couples who are simply "domestic partners." But these relationships are subject to the same challenges as more traditional marriages, and to the same satisfactions and joys.

route to happiness for rich, middle class and poor alike. Simply being aware of the temptations that bedevil wealthy spouses can go a long way toward avoiding the pain that results from a failed marriage, or from being alone in life.

Work and the Wealthy

Among all the misconceptions about the wealthy that are harbored by people in general is the notion that the rich don't work. This odd idea seems to have gained currency in the same way as so many unsound notions about the rich—from Hollywood and from the rare, spectacular examples of international playboys and their ilk. What is, in fact, far more interesting and salient about the rich is how hard they tend to work despite not having any financial need to do so.

This issue of working hard, of being productive and of generating happiness out of that productivity, is perhaps best examined by looking at another example of the phenomenon, namely, the wives[438] of extremely successful men. Talented men, men who are destined for great success in life (and in this case we include financial success), tend to marry women who are a lot like themselves: talented women who can also look forward to great success in traditional terms. But what often happens is something else altogether. The couple wants to have children. Only the wife can have them, and she is probably (though not certainly) more maternally inclined. Society frowns on men who stay home while their wives work. All these and many other factors dictate that in most cases the wife will stay home with the kids.

Eventually, the last child toddles off to school and now the wife is faced with a question about what to do with her life. Her choices are so wide that it is difficult to know where to begin. And the world is a very different place for her than it was when she was first married. She could launch herself into a traditional career now, when she is probably in her late thirties, but she would be competing against and associating with colleagues who are far younger—not an attractive proposition.

Moreover, although the children are in school during the day, they get out at 3:00 p.m. What's to happen to them then? Who will pick them up, take them to their (increasingly numerous) activities and play dates? Someone could be

---

438 Wives of successful men are a far better example than husbands of successful women partly because there are far more of them, and partly because the social pressure on men to work is so powerful that husbands of successful women tend overwhelmingly to engage in traditional work whether they really wish to or not.

hired to handle that chore, to be sure—money is no object for these successful families—but is that really the best way to handle it? Already the husband frequently arrives home after the kids are in bed—should the wife really emulate that work schedule?

And what about the wife's social life? That life has been built around a series of friends and activities that aren't constrained by the usual ten-hour professional workday. Should she give up these friends and these activities and start all over again?

Finally, there is the question of financial need. None of the above would matter a whit if the wife's income were crucial to the financial survival of the family.[439] But we have already postulated that the husband can provide all the financial needs. Thus, these women have no financial need to work.

What becomes of this group of women, the talented wives of very successful men? Well, we know what becomes of them, because we all know so many of them. Some launch themselves into demanding careers, becoming every bit as successful, financially and otherwise, as their husbands. A few do little or nothing—the proverbial "ladies who lunch."[440]

But most of them, by far the great majority, carve out busy and productive lives that don't look like "traditional" successful careers, but that are crucially important to American society and richly rewarding to the women. These lives typically include elements of after-school childcare, part-time work or work that pays far less than the women could ordinarily have commanded, and active volunteer or public service activities. The children of very successful men grow up to be well-adjusted and happy in considerable part because of the career "sacrifices" made by their talented wives. Non-profit organizations and social service agencies are able to hire astonishingly talented women, despite the low salaries and benefits they offer. And at the core of most successful schools, churches, and organizations devoted to helping the less fortunate are strong cores of talented and energetic women who, in another life, might have been at the very top of some profession or corporation.

No one looks down on such women. If anything, we wonder what motivates them to keep so busy, to accomplish so much, despite having no financial

---

439 "Survival" is a relative word in this sense, of course. But many middle class families find, for example, that they cannot afford to buy a home in a good school district unless both spouses work. See Elizabeth Warren and Amelia Warren Tyagi, *The Two-Income Trap: Why Middle-Class Mothers and Fathers Are Going Broke* (Basic Books, 2003).

440 As noted above, societal pressure on men to work, or to seem to work, is so strong that we rarely encounter "the gentlemen who lunch."

incentive to do so. And the same is true of wealthy families. Members of those families typically have no financial need to work, but the outcomes for them are exactly analogous to the outcomes of the wives-of-successful-husbands. Some work fifteen-hour days, six-and-a-half days a week, as frantically driven as though the wolf were at their very door. A few do little or nothing. But the vast, overwhelming majority carve out busy and productive lives that may or may not look a great deal like "traditional" careers. But these lives are crucial to American society and richly rewarding to those who lead them. They are lives lived in devotion to family and society, and they enrich all our lives.

Given the enormous productivity of the wealthy, I am always puzzled by wealthy people—almost always the first generation, the ones who made the money—who say they plan to leave nothing, or very little, to their children, on the ground that inheriting a large pile of money will inevitably ruin them. For the most part, this is simple nonsense. Having money will ruin children if they lack character and otherwise it will not. If children lack character, they are already ruined, whether they have money or not. Therefore, the job of wealthy parents is not to disinherit their children, but to build character in those children and then to pass the stewardship of the family assets on to them in their turn. It is, in fact, remarkable how often the stewardship of wealth is better handled by second, third, and fourth generations than by the first.

A Note About the Uses and Abuses of Trusts

A thorough examination of the issue of common law trusts would require ten or twelve volumes of small text.[441] For our purposes here, the only point I wish to make is that, while we are pondering (and dazzled by) the tax savings associated with the clever use of trusts, we need also pause to consider how those trusts are likely to affect our children, grandchildren, and more remote descendants. Because of the bizarre nature of our tax laws and regulations, the failure to employ trusts can result in the loss to taxes of a very substantial portion of a family's capital. But the failure to consider the effect of trusts on their beneficiaries can result in the loss of a very substantial portion of a family's happiness, primarily via the infantilization of those beneficiaries. Like so many aspects of life that are crucial to our eventual happiness, taxes are an irritant. But removing that irritant must be done carefully if we wish to avoid dire consequences for our descendants.

---

441 In case you think I am exaggerating, take a look at the classic work on this subject, *Scott on Trusts*, by Austin Wakeman Scott, Mark L. Ascher, and William Franklin Fratcher, Volumes I-XII (Aspen Publishers, Inc., 4th ed., 1998), pages 1-6,837(!)

To consider how this works, let's examine a different, but analogous circumstance. Not so many years ago our bizarre tax laws provided that the full estate tax would be applied against a family's assets upon the death of the first spouse—typically the husband. This was, in one sense, simply a trap for the unwary, since part of the tax could be avoided by taking advantage of the "marital deduction." This involved setting up a "marital deduction trust" under the terms of which the marital deduction amount would be placed in a trust for the benefit of the surviving spouse—typically the wife.

But consider the terms that had to be incorporated in the trust to satisfy the greed of the IRS. The trust had to provide that the surviving wife would be entitled to the income from the trust, but that the trust principal could be invaded only under special circumstances, typically constituting some sort of emergency. If these terms were adhered to, this portion of the family's assets would not be taxed until the wife died.

Note that I said that this arrangement was "in one sense" simply a trap for the unwary. In fact, it was much more. Consider the position of the surviving wife. Before her husband died, the assets were theirs to spend as they wished. If she wanted new curtains, they could raid their savings and buy them. But now, suddenly, the husband has died and an important portion of the family assets are now held in trust. If the wife wants to buy new curtains, she has to suffer the indignity of writing a letter to the bank, requesting permission to use principal from the trust to buy new curtains. The bank's "trust committee" will likely look askance at such a request, fearing potential liability since the bank is a trustee and fiduciary. Moreover, the bank handles all the investment decisionmaking, simply sending periodic account statements to the wife so that she can see, after the fact, what they have been doing with her money. The wife, who was a few months ago a full and free human being, has been reduced to the status of a ward of the bank. This is probably not what the husband had in mind when he considered all the taxes he would save by establishing a marital deduction trust.[442]

---

442 It is interesting to observe how social changes impact laws. Back in the old days, when marital deduction trusts were common, it is true that many wives were already infantilized, at least financially, as the husbands made all the financial decisions and, when the husband was gone, it was probably just as well that the bank was placed in charge. But all that changed dramatically in the second half of the twentieth century, and at that point the infantilization of wives after their husbands' deaths became, quite suddenly, completely unacceptable. Also quite suddenly, Congress changed the laws so that estate taxes are now levied only at the death of the second spouse.

And it is also probably not what wealthy families have in mind when they set up clever trust arrangements that avoid significant taxes. And yet, infantilization is a very real possibility unless the settlors of trusts consider the effects those trusts will have on their descendants. In some cases, the tax savings will not begin to outweigh the likely damage to the dignity of the descendants, and the trusts should not be established. In other cases, the tax savings will be so significant that a compromise will have to be made. But that compromise should leave in the hands of the beneficiaries every possible right, duty and obligation that the law will allow, including the right to replace the trustee, the right to control (within the principles of prudence) the investment strategies and managers employed by the trusts, and the (qualified) right to invade principal.

Failed Stewardship and Family Unhappiness

From the point of view of the poor and of levelers everywhere, it might seem to be only simple justice for the rich to be wretchedly unhappy. Alas, this is not the case—the rich are as happy as anyone else, although the particular challenges to happiness that the wealthy face tend to be somewhat different. But there *is* one certain route to unhappiness for the rich: if stewardship of the family's capital is so poor that it disappears, disappears to the point where the family is no longer wealthy and can no longer deploy its capital in creative ways, unhappiness will descend like a dark curtain on the family, perhaps for generations.

It is always a wrenching experience for any family to slip down the socioeconomic ladder, and it almost always leads to misery in one form or another. When a working class family, clinging precariously to its hard-won respectability, slips back into poverty, an infinitely sad event has occurred. And in every high school, the most unhappy children are those whose parents are high achievers and whose expectations for their children are correspondingly—and all-too-often unreasonably—high. The fact that Daddy chairs the symphony board shouldn't have implications one way or the other for whether little Billy becomes a truck driver, but in fact the implications are huge. Even when the socioeconomic slippage occurs primarily as the result of broad economic dislocation—as in the Great Depression, when many families fell one or even two rungs down the ladder—the pain of the experience often persists for generations.

How much worse it is, then, for a family that is rich to cease to be rich solely because some generation of the family has failed in its stewardship of the capital. The sense of failure and the shame associated with that failure, the pressing weight of abused privilege, always results in unhappiness, and frequently it results in multigenerational neuroses that settle like a miasmal haze on subsequent generations. These are the families with dark secrets, the families with rigid and brittle personalities, the families with a perpetually negative outlook on life and its possibilities, the families pathologically concerned with appearances, with social slights, with the need to associate with the right people.

If we wanted to prioritize them, then, the challenges for the wealthy come down to these:

> First, we need to stay rich. Failing this, the other priorities will rot and die.
>
> Second, we need to do everything we can to ensure that younger family members will lead productive lives. This is a challenge for all families, of course.
>
> Third, we need to improve the world we were born into, through the creative use of the capital we deploy.
>
> Finally, if possible, we will want to grow our wealth in real terms. Important as this goal is, it is also important to note where it ranks among life's priorities.

* * *

The first duty of a family in the possession of private capital, then, is to manage that capital competently. This is a serious and honorable business, it is hard and demanding work, and success in that enterprise is the only sure platform from which the family can pursue its own happiness. In addition, as I have noted at great length (see Part One), its implications for the continued preeminence of America and for the continued economic and social progress of the rest of the world can hardly be overstated. The failure of stewardship is a momentous defeat for a family, and it is a momentous defeat for the society that depends so heavily on wealth as the engine of its competitiveness.

The goal of life is not wealth but happiness. But happiness cannot be pursued directly. It is the result of a process, and for wealthy families that process begins with the successful stewardship of their capital. Like everything else on which happiness ultimately depends, the stewardship of wealth is a process that is filled with day-to-day irritations and that requires effort and persistence. But it is neither impossible nor beyond the capability of any family that takes the issue of stewardship seriously. See Chapters 3 through 17.

About the Author

Gregory Curtis is the Chairman and founder of Greycourt & Co., Inc., an open architecture firm providing investment advisory services to substantial families and select endowments. Prior to founding Greycourt, Curtis served for many years as president of a family office for the Mellon family and as President of the Laurel Foundation, a private charitable foundation. Before that he was an attorney with the law firm of Reed Smith. He has also worked on the staffs of John V. Lindsay, then Mayor of New York City, and Richard G. Lugar, then Mayor of Indianapolis. Curtis is a Vietnam Era veteran, an attorney and a registered investment advisor.

Curtis has more than thirty years' experience advising wealthy families on broad wealth management issues, including portfolio design, implementation of best investment practices, design and oversight of family offices and family investment partnerships, philanthropy, family dynamics, estate, tax and insurance planning, and issues associated with closely held businesses. Curtis also has extensive experience working with foundations and endowments, both as an in-house executive and an outside advisor.

Curtis is a past Director and past Chair of the Board of The Investment Fund for Foundations, a non-profit firm that provides investment management services to non-profit organizations, and a past Chair of the Board of Visitors and Governors of St. John's College (Annapolis and Santa Fe). He has been a founder or co-founder of numerous non-profit and civic organizations, including Grantmakers of Western Pennsylvania, The Emerging International City and the Contemporary Arts Stabilization Trust. He is currently a Trustee of The Pittsburgh Foundation and of St. John's College. Curtis is a winner of the Academy of American Poets Prize.

Curtis holds an AB degree from Dartmouth College, cum laude with high distinction in English literature, a JD degree from Harvard Law School, cum laude, and he is a graduate of The Endowment Institute at Harvard Business School. Curtis also holds an honorary BA degree from St. John's College in Santa Fe.

INDEX

0-595-33200-5

Printed in the United States
23903LVS00002B/97-195

9 780595 332007